3⁵¹

DEACCESSIONED

THE INDOMITABLE JOHN SCOTT

THE INDOMITABLE
JOHN SCOTT:

CITIZEN OF LONG ISLAND

1632-1704

By

LILIAN T. MOWRER

PREFACE BY
HAROLD HULME
Professor of History, New York University

FARRAR, STRAUS AND CUDAHY

NEW YORK

"TIME WILL DO HIM GREAT RIGHT"

Lady Vane

TABLE OF CONTENTS

Preface: DR. HAROLD HULME, *New York University*   xi
Author's Note   xiii

PART I

I. CIVIL WAR	3
II. JOHN IS DEPORTED	12
III. THE SCOTTS OF SCOT'S HALL	16
IV. SALEM	23
V. JOHN'S EDUCATION	32
VI. DIFFICULT YEARS	38
VII. WESTWARD HO!	43
VIII. LONG ISLAND	48
IX. LANDED PROPRIETOR	56
X. JOHN'S EARLY SUCCESSES	60
XI. RESTORATION ENGLAND	69
XII. MASSACHUSETTS' SECRET AGENT?	82
XIII. THE SECOND HOMECOMING	95
XIV. THE PEOPLE'S CHOICE—PRESIDENT SCOTT	103
XV. JOHN URGES THE DUTCH TO REVOLT	109
XVI. GOVERNOR WINTHROP STRIKES	124
XVII. CONDEMNED—AND VINDICATED	128
XVIII. ENGLAND ACQUIRES NEW NETHERLAND	140
XIX. JOHN STANDS BY THE PEOPLE	145
XX. JOHN'S SACRIFICE FOR FREEDOM	150

vii

PART II

XXI. GET-AWAY   165

XXII. EXPLORER OF THE SPANISH MAIN   171

XXIII. MAJOR-GENERAL SCOTT ON ACTIVE
SERVICE   181

XXIV. THE BATTLE FOR ST. CHRISTOPHER   186

XXV. ROYAL GEOGRAPHER   192

XXVI. COLONEL SCOTT IN HOLLAND   196

XXVII. DEBORAH EGMONT AND THE RECRUITING
OFFICER   205

XXVIII. DISPONTEJN GOES TO JAIL   213

XXIX. JOHN IN THE THIRD DUTCH WAR   219

XXX. THE SECRET DOINGS OF JOHN SCOTT   227

XXXI. BRITISH AGENT   236

XXXII. FRANCE LOSES AN ALLY AND JOHN
LOSES A JOB   244

PART III

XXXIII. A BOURBON AS PATRON   253

XXXIV. A CURIOUS EXPERIMENT   259

XXXV. YEARS OF MYSTERY   268

XXXVI. PEPYS APPROACHES JOHN   274

XXXVII. THE POPISH PLOT   278

XXXVIII. "BUCKINGHAM'S JOHN"   284

XXXIX. THE PLOT THICKENS   292

XL. JOHN WARNS KING LOUIS; AND
RECEIVES A STRANGE CONFESSION   297

XLI. JOHN ACCUSES PEPYS   306

XLII. COUNTER ATTACK   315

XLIII. THE AFFIDAVITS   325

XLIV. JOYNE'S JOURNAL   334

XLV. THE LEGEND OF JOHN SCOTT   344

XLVI. MURDER IN THE DARK   357

XLVII. LAST DAYS   370

EPILOGUE   382

APPENDICES   391

BIBLIOGRAPHY AND ABBREVIATIONS   411

INDEX   429

PREFACE

To THOSE versed in England's colonial and domestic history during the second half of the seventeenth century John Scott, a minor figure in that colorful time, is remembered as a notorious but picturesque and piquant rascal. Loved by many in America, despised by a few in England, Scott's evil repute has rested largely on depositions which Samuel Pepys obtained but never used to blacken John, a leading and most damaging witness in the parliamentary investigation of that admiralty secretary. Wilbur Cortez Abbott, among others, in his writings of twenty-five to forty years ago on Scott, basing his work largely on the Pepysian papers, is chiefly responsible for giving this seventeenth century character such a disreputable name among students of history.

Now after a careful examination of these same documents Lilian Mowrer has found that the depositions against Scott were made by malevolently inventive witnesses whose evidence would have had little chance of acceptance even in the notorious English Restoration courts. Becoming deeply interested in John Scott she followed him back and forth across Long Island Sound, the Atlantic Ocean, the English Channel, the North Sea, and into the Caribbean. With the help of hundreds of papers and documents she has reconstructed his life from birth in 1632 to his death in 1704.

This gifted, artful man with his widespread interests and far-flung activities—Long Island landowner, West Indies buccaneer, Dutch Colonel, Royal Geographer, English officer and agent in the Low Countries, French gun caster, a coachman's murderer, and Speaker of the Assembly at Montserrat in the Leeward Islands—Mrs. Mowrer has vividly brought back to life in a style the envy of most stolid historians. At the same time she has made excellent use of the historian's tools: records, papers, and documents in New England, New York, and Long Island communities, in England's British Museum, Public Record Office, and Bodleian Library, in France's record repositories, and in Holland's archives. She has made John Scott a respectable, loyal subject of Charles II. She has shown him to be a man of many and varied abilities. She has disclosed a rough, at times crude, but charming personality in a man whose character was as straightforward and honest as that of most men of his day. She has followed his career with all the fascinating details at her disposal. All this Lilian Mowrer has done with imagination and insight and has soundly based her work on the finest materials the most meticulous historian could desire. This is a brilliant historical biography. I believe that it will rehabilitate John Scott in the eyes of students of English and American history and will instruct and delight the reader seeking knowledge and adventure.

HAROLD HULME
Professor of History
New York University

AUTHOR'S NOTE

ABOUT 1950 I became interested in John Scott of Long Island, a colorful seventeenth century adventurer whom Mrs. Mary Van Rensselaer in her own two-volume *History of Seventeenth Century New York* considered long since well worth a full-length biography.

I had read history at Liverpool University, at the Sorbonne in Paris, and at the old *Sapienza* in Rome. The bold speculative *Seicento* always interested me most, so my prospective hero fitted right into the period I knew best.

From Wilbur C. Abbott's standard monograph on "Colonel" John Scott, I knew that Scott's testimony, at the time of the Popish Plot, had sent Samuel Pepys to the Tower of London for treason, and that the famous diarist (who was at that period Secretary of the British Admiralty) had, to save his head, collected a number of sworn statements, all designed to discredit his accuser and prove that he, Scott, was the traitor.

Though biographers have leaned heavily on this material (or on others' work about it) none of the papers themselves have ever been published. They remain in the Bodleian Library among the Rawlinson Collection. So to get firsthand the full Scott story I went to Oxford to examine just what Pepys' informers had charged.

The massive brown leather folio volumes are a veritable treasure-trove of the alleged doings of "that arch scoundrel, that most unscrupulous and plotting adventurer" (as one writer, G. D. Scull, calls him), a series of charges culminating in the accusation of Scott's dismissal from the Dutch forces for embezzling seven thousand pounds sterling, and court-martial by the British Admiralty for cowardice in action!

For weeks and weeks I pored over this rich mine, laboriously copying out essential passages. But as I continued I was gradually struck by the similarity of the various affidavits and by the fact that few who testified to Scott's infamy had known him personally or possessed firsthand knowledge of the incidents they were writing about—indeed, one sworn statement came from a patient in a London hospital whose barber had related what a friend of his knew of Scott's doings in Holland!

I come from a long line of lawyers; talk of legal procedure was commonplace in our house. The credibility of witnesses was something we children learned immediately to ask about. And as I continued reading Pepys' affidavits I kept wondering about the people who had written them, and if it were not possible to check the charges against other testimony or proven fact. All the witnesses spoke of Scott as an inveterate traveller, in New England, Holland, France, the Caribbean. Such a notorious figure would surely have left traces behind him.

My quest led me first to The Hague and to seventeenth century Dutch military files and army yearbooks. That John Scott served in the United Provinces forces was correct, his promotion to colonel a matter of official record. But neither desertion nor dismissal marred his career. The Civil Courts did, indeed, record an embezzlement case, but it was Scott who prosecuted another man for swindling army funds, and the sum was seven *hundred guilders,* not seven *thousand pounds!* Moreover, to my amazement, I found in Dr. H. Hardenberg, director of the *Algemeen Rijksarchief* (state archives) an enthusiastic admirer of my subject. This distinguished scholar did everything he could to further my work, for he himself had once considered writing the "definitive" life of John Scott, a personage highly regarded throughout the Netherlands.

But if Scott had not been "dismissed" by the Dutch and had never embezzled anything, what about the alleged court-martial? I hurried to the Public Record Office in London, as I had been advised that the Admiralty Papers there would give the full record of action in the Caribbean, site of the supposed trial. Failing to find any mention of it, I first concluded I must have simply overlooked the item in all this voluminous material. So I engaged a professional archivist and had it further searched. Moreover, Mr. Kenneth Timings, Keeper of the famous Round Room and expert in naval matters, courteously checked the results for me and also found nothing.

Since it now appeared certain that my subject had no more been court-martialled by the British than dismissed by the Dutch, I began to doubt if he were really the rogue I had chosen to portray.

Investigation went on for several years, for despite his "notoriety" most of John's life was virgin soil.

The trail led next to Paris. Like all my predecessors I had accepted the version that Scott's story before the House of Commons, of British naval papers treasonably delivered to the French, was a lie invented to damn Samuel Pepys; and that Scott's own gun-casting fiasco at Nevers, in France, had been carried out with the connivance of certain "unfathomable scoundrels," as Arthur Bryant describes them.

But *Quai d'Orsay* diplomatic archives, manuscripts in the *Bibliothèque Nationale* and, above all, the very hard to obtain Marine Documents in the *Archives Nationales* place Scott in a completely different setting from the "nest of thieves" he allegedly frequented. They show him working with some of the highest officials in the land, and with the permission of France's First Minister. Far from being an obscure penniless cheat, he was the English officer, invited, as

foreign military expert, to observe the French troops at Besançon, where Louis XIV achieved a brilliant victory. Another setback for the affidavits.

Three times I went back to Europe to learn more of this
unknown John Scott I had discovered. Then in the Record
Office one day, leafing through the Flanders state papers, I
suddenly recognized John's handwriting—no less than forty
military-intelligence reports—which he had sent to the English
Secretary of State during the Third Dutch War. No previous
biographer seems ever to have made use of them although
they are packed with information. Also overlooked has been
Scott's long letter to Charles II in 1664, which, even allowing
for some *post-hoc* self-justification, reveals a totally new aspect
of Scott's New England feud with governors John Winthrop
and Richard Nicolls. Still other manuscripts by Scott, in the
British Museum, not only give a vivid picture of the man
himself but reveal a very specialized knowledge of early
colonial settlement.

And finally, among other Record Office papers is a document from Montserrat, in the West Indies, over Scott's unmistakable signature, which shows that instead of fading
away, a shady fugitive from British justice lurking on the
Continent, Scott spent his declining years in dignified public
service, was Speaker of the Leeward Isles Assembly, in short,
a man "of good sense, honesty and repute," as is calendared
in a colonial series of state papers.

By this time the evidence pointed to one conclusion: John
Scott was not the devious character Pepys' informants had
made him out to be. Pepys himself must have arrived at a
similar conclusion, for he made no use of the assembled
material, seemed indeed, even at the time, to have doubted
its authenticity. He thrust it all away among his private
papers, no more dreaming that it would ever come to light
than that millions would one day be poring over his own
diary. Only in the nineteenth century, when Lord Braybrooke first published excerpts from the diary, were the

affidavits discovered and the "legend of Colonel John Scott" became current.

Whether the legend can resist the impact of new material remains to be seen. According to fuller information John Scott emerges as both a colorful individual and a typical representative of a yeasty historical epoch—one of those picaresque figures who embodied the concept of the Renaissance "universal man." Soldier, explorer, pioneer, something of a scientist and poet, his roving life certainly did not lack boisterous, violent incident, but it brought him in close touch, too, with William Penn, and with John Locke; he was friend of an English Duke and a prince of the blood in France, yet moved easily through the shadowy political half-world, a British agent among other secret agents, in the plotting-est age of all time. I have tried to present him as he was, not as interested persons—with an axe to grind—said he was. But how well I realize what Samuel Eliot Morison meant when, after much sage advice, he warned me that I was "about to deprive America of one of its best-loved rascals." And added that the task would not be easy!

For the feel and color of my story I have faithfully followed Scott's traces in Holland, France, and New England; have visited the house he built at North Sea in 1661, sailed in and out of Scott's Cove, near Scott's Landing on Long Island Sound—names which keep his memory fresh to this day.

Much of Scott's English background is topographically very familiar. I grew up in London and spent two of my school years at Kent College not too far from Ashford, the ancient market town for which he named his Setauket estate. I know the (modern) Scot's Hall and the villages of Smeeth and Brabourne.

The dialogue in this book is all from existing documents, most of it verbatim, occasionally from the subject's written words, or from published statements of what was said.

Over the years devoted to research and writing I have received valuable help which I most gratefully acknowledge.

To my friends in the Library of Congress I am indebted for much patient assistance and the continued use of a study room, with unlimited access to rare material and transcriptions of town records.

Thanks to Governor Abraham Ribicoff, my work in the Hartford State Library was beautifully expedited. There I found some crucially illuminating manuscripts concerning John's early land deals, all of which seem to have been carried out with impeccable legality.

Through the kindness of the Reverend Dr. Arthur Adams, Director of the New England Historic Genealogical Society, I was permitted (in 1957) to examine at length the personal papers of Henry Edward Scott (no relation), historian and one time editor-emeritus of the aforesaid distinguished organization's publications. Many of his extensive notes on the Scotts' genealogy confirmed my own conclusions, particularly on the subject of John's land holdings.

Bernard Bailyn, Associate Professor of History at Harvard, read the first half of my typescript and gave me the great benefit of his specialized criticism. I want to thank Colonel Myron Scott, who read my entire manuscript, and was always ready to talk Scott shop with me and share his findings of a life-long study of the Scott genealogy. I am also particularly indebted to Ruth Anna Fisher, late of the Congressional Library's Manuscripts Division, for patiently helping me to decipher the photostats I brought back from London of all the manifold (and much damaged) membranes of the Mitford Chancery Proceedings.

Above all my thanks go to Edgar Mowrer, who not only forbore with good-humored equanimity my eight years' preoccupation with another man, but who steadfastly encouraged my work with constructive and unstinting critical comment.

PART ONE

PART ONE

CHAPTER I

CIVIL WAR

The preachers thundered in their pulpits . . . and cried
out against all that were for moderate proceedings: Thine
eye shall not pity and thou shalt not spare . . .
—Bishop Burnet, *Hist. of His Own Times*, I, 8.

"A King Ought To Be Instructed How To Rule Well."
—John Scott, S.P. 29/419, f 50.

SIXTEEN FORTY-TWO was an ominous year for the English. It
marked the crucial turning point in the Great Rebellion, that
heroic conflict between King and Parliament, which cost
Charles I his head and turned England into a Puritan republic under Cromwell.

It was also the year which brought the subject of this book
onto the fringe of history for the first time, and fate could not
have chosen a more appropriate occasion. Though all unaware of the great issue of the day—the individual's fight
against arbitrary power—our youthful hero was nevertheless
to find himself thereafter continually caught up in this determined struggle. His brief initial appearance during the
stirring historic events which overshadowed, and well-nigh
overwhelmed him, set the theme for his later career and
shaped much of his destiny.

For eleven mortal years—practically this young man's life
span when the story opens—King Charles I had ruled without
parliament, while his subjects muttered and cursed as their
constitutional liberties were whittled away. Rioting broke out

with increasing vehemence in the London City and angry crowds surged through the narrow streets leading to White-hall, protesting the royal religious orders and arbitrary courts, the hateful ship-money and monopolies; young apprentices elbowed their way into Westminster shouting that grievances be redressed before supplies be voted.

Unwillingly Charles met many of their demands, but on one point he would not yield. He would not give up control of his army, but chose rather to resort to arms.

Breaking with parliament, he abandoned disloyal London to seek recruits elsewhere, and on August 22nd, 1642, at Nottingham, he raised his royal standard—ancient symbol of feudal duty. Then both sides knew that there could be no turning back and that Englishmen must fight Englishmen before they could decide if monarchy was to remain absolute, or if subjects might preserve and increase their freedom under law.

Yet these same Englishmen were far from ready to join the ranks. The extremist demands of the more fanatical Puritans struck many as unreasonable in the face of all that the King had conceded. So the great issues from which the whole Western world was ultimately to benefit were decided in a war waged by two small minorities. Only a handful of followers rallied to Charles, and the parliamentary forces at first were equally meager. England possessed no standing army; only a limited militia whose members were divided in their loyalties. Charles' strength lay in his Cavalier officers and hard-riding squires, trained by his nephew, Prince Rupert, who had learned war on the Continent in the tradition of storm and plunder. Against these were pitted the Puritan lords, the yeomen and merchants, Welsh pikemen, and Irish camp followers, these last ready to match Rupert's infantry in ruthlessness.

Neither side knew the art of war; the first pitched battle at Edgehill was indecisive, despite the initial advantage of Rupert's shock tactics. Both sides retired, the Roundheads to

London, the King to Oxford. Suddenly in early November, 1642, Charles decided to stake all on a single *coup de main* in an effort to retake his capital. With banners flying and all the troops he could muster, he rode southwards, while London feverishly prepared to withstand the royal invader.

Not since the Wars of the Roses had an English sovereign been awaited with such terror. Grimly citizens organized defenses, their fears inflamed by news sheets and highly polemical Sunday sermons. Wildest rumors flew about the fierce fighting *en route*—"hundreds killed each side," said gossips.

But worse than stories of battles were persistent whispers and published reports of plundered towns, and civilians killed for resisting hungry soldiers. Charles Stuart, gentle, cultured, chaste, obdurate, was no man to hold his soldiery in check; the cities he occupied received short shrift, despite his good intentions.

Not that the Puritans were any milder. Before Cromwell imposed iron discipline, they too looted and murdered, stripped and flogged women, burned churches, fired on crucifixes, pawned organ pipes for pots of ale.

Sober citizens were appalled at such desperate happenings. When reports spread that the King intended to cross the Thames at Kingston and march on Kent, many, regardless of political sympathy, flocked to London as the safest place to live.

Among the Kentish gentry who fled were a young war widow and her eldest son John Scott.

To a ten-year-old country boy, London at such a moment must have stirred the wildest feelings and one can imagine John's excitement as he explored the crowded streets and gaped at all the military doings that were fast transforming a bustling medieval city into an armed camp commanded by a new breed of Englishmen—the somber self-righteous Puritans—who were suddenly there in its midst, taking over the government, reversing its oldest traditions.

Under English administration, troops were always mustered by the gentry, but it was precisely this class that had suffered most from Charles' arbitrary rule. Squires had been so harried by petty restrictions and regulations, by knighthood fines and the like, that they, who traditionally should all have been King's men, were now slow to support him, and some were showing interest in the other side. This lack of enthusiasm of the many was offset by the fanatical loyalty of the few.

John's father, Colonel John Scott, a Kentish squire of passionate conviction, had been one of the very first to declare himself. He had sold his estate worth twenty-two hundred pounds a year to put fourteen thousand three hundred pounds at the King's disposal.[1] He had already sacrificed his life in a preliminary skirmish at Alford, in Hampshire.[2] Now his widow awaited the outcome of a struggle which, whoever won, seemed to promise nothing but the bleakest future. But for John, only the exciting present must have filled his mind.

What boy worth his salt would not have thrilled at the steady beat of drums all day? London squares rang with the commands of officers drilling their homespun recruits; town criers hourly proclaimed the urgent necessity of furnishing men, money, and above all horses. The royal cavalry was considered the decisive arm and Roundheads knew they must be prepared to meet Charles' professional officers in a mounted charge. The House of Commons gave this top priority. "Horses!" "Saddles!" "Horses!" recur as a never-ending *leit-motif* in Proceedings and Orders of the Day.

John saw private coaches left standing in mews and courtyards as their animals were seized for army use; carters and farmers coming into London were stopped and forced to hand over their steeds. Sometimes the Lord Mayor in velvet robes and silver lace would go in stately procession on foot to a Company dinner; and the little boy caught a glimpse of municipal magnificence almost regal in its pomp and color. Every day brought some stirring scene with actors to play their parts; it was like a continuous historical pageant, infinitely more entertaining than Holinshed's long-winded chronicles they had read to him at home.

By pushing his way into the Guildhall one day, John could have listened to that man of tragic destiny, Sir Harry Vane, Puritan son of the King's own Secretary of State. This young firebrand whose solemnity belied his extremist views on God and politics, had been Governor of Massachusetts when only twenty-four, and was now pursuing a reckless policy of constitutional revolution. His Guildhall speech, if John really listened to it, would surely have placed him, in the boy's eyes, as "the enemy," for how was it possible to accuse one's sovereign of wrongdoing? As Harry Vane put it, Charles had done a very wicked thing to take up arms against his people. Were not the people themselves questioning King Charles' "divine right"; indicting him with their Grand Remonstrance, in terms such as never before in history had been addressed to an English monarch?

Everything became much clearer when action cut this discussion and the Roundhead Earl of Essex galloped up with the breath-stopping announcement that an attack on London could be expected any moment and 4,000 horses must be procured instantly!

A tremendous hubbub swept the City, all officers and soldiers were ordered to report at Parliament Yard in Westminster. John saw guns mounted on Tower Hill and Temple Bar, posts and chains set up in Covent Garden and in St. Martins-in-the-Fields, watch-houses and barricades from suburban Hyde Park Corner to St. James. Women and even little children dug ditches in Piccadilly and piled up earthworks at Lambeth and around Constitution Hill.[3]

What could a country lad, brought up with the simple teaching, *Fear God, Honor the King*, have thought of this spectacle of his monarch's proud capital thus engaged in flouting royal authority and preparing to oppose it with armed force? Something within him may have stirred, some instinct of loyalty, unfelt before but linked to him by a thousand mysterious associations with the remote past, transmitted from father to son through countless generations in the King's service.

But while love of King and Country was a family tradition, John's immediate reaction was purely personal. For him the issue demanded participation. All his life he showed this same readiness to be "involved," to respond to any challenge. The sight of those children toiling for the enemy provoked his own instant resolve to serve the King. Or at least, so we may legitimately suppose.

For when he returned to his mother that night his plans must have been laid. He had been to Branford![4] (Brentford.) He had seen the royal army on its outskirts and the Parliamentarians waiting to oppose it. He had apparently reached his great decision to declare himself for the King. Soldiering was out of the question—he was too young. But the daily Roundhead proclamations concerning dire need of horses and saddles prompted his own form of service. "For a small expression of his loyalty," as he later wrote King Charles, he decided to put enemy cavalry out of action, "by cutting the bridles and girts of the then parliament's horses."[5]

London next day awakened to the boom of distant guns. The Royalists, having stormed and occupied Brentford, were attempting to march on Hammersmith where the parliamentary ordnance lay, and take London by assault. At this new development, the Earl of Essex rode posthaste to report the situation at Westminster, but even as he spoke in the House, the artillery roar grew louder and drowned his words. Leaving the frightened Members he dashed out and galloped back across the parks in the direction of the guns. For Prince Rupert, taking advantage of a dense fog, had fallen unexpectedly on the Roundhead troops, who had a hard time holding the position and waiting desperately for replacements.

All that night London poured out men. Every hour they

marched forth, lords and gentlemen and apprentices of the Trained Bands, 24,000 strong—the biggest and best equipped force yet assembled. And in the dense fog it was easy for a young boy to keep up with the soldiers as they trudged westwards along the Old Bath Road, yellow flares from smoking torches streaking their path towards the hamlet of Turnham Green.

It was almost noon when John reached the destination. The fog was lifting, its acrid smell still filled the air, and to the boy's eyes all must have seemed disorder and confusion. There were acres and acres of soldiers spread over the common; some already in battle rank, others still seeking position, like the column he had accompanied. Hazily, far off in the distance, was a glow of red. Those were the Royalists, his people; that was where *his* King must be.

All around him he could distinguish Puritan coats and stiff black hats; parliamentary officers were moving among their men, talking in simple encouraging words. "Come, my honest brave lads, pray heartily and fight heartily and God will bless us."

The boy's fingers tightened around a knife. One can imagine him stealthily moving towards a group of army mounts tethered at a picket rail. There were no soldiers near him now, nobody would be watching the tall pale lad; they were listening to their officers, and some of them were on their knees praying.

John was a country lad, used to horses. He surely knew how to nuzzle an animal, breathing a reassuring sound, gently taking its bridle. With deft movements of the knife he could hack at a saddle girth, damp with sweat and the soaking mist. He severed the strap, easing the saddle weight a little, then slit the bridle. Under his knowing hands the horse moved tranquilly unalarmed; John could go to work on another saddle. Soon, it too was out of action; he ruined a third. Normal fear would warn him to keep the horses between himself and the tents as he cautiously crept down the line, intent on his furtive sabotage. Suddenly figures appeared as from nowhere, soldiers closed in on him; rough hands pushed and pulled at him, blocking escape. He was passed from one group to another, shoved into an improvised guard-house, his hands and feet securely shackled, but there was no time to deal with him. Bugles were calling, shouted orders rang out, the entire camp was seized with movement with troops wheeling into line.

The fog had finally lifted and a pale sun shone faintly over the two armies drawn up in battle array. On that icy morning of November 13th they stood opposite each other, eyeing their chances, measuring their strength. But no bugle sounded the advance; no standard bearer proudly waved his men to charge.

The King knew that his small forces and light field artillery were hopelessly outmatched by the overwhelming numbers before him. All that bleak winter day they stood without action, each fearing to risk a decisive move, until at nightfall, the King sounded the retreat. The battle of Turnham Green was never fought.

Yet the City won a bloodless victory over the Crown—and little John Scott's fate was sealed. If King Charles could not take his own capital, the royal cause was ultimately lost, and John with it, for the triumphant Roundheads would show scant shrift to a camp follower caught destroying army saddles. In an age when every man, woman, or child was hanged for wilful damage involving as little as five shillings' worth of property, John's prank could well have cost him his life.

He was brought before a parliamentary Committee to answer for his crime. Three separate times he faced his judges as they considered what to do.

A kinsman of his, Sir Edward Scott, was at this time a member of Kent's *Committee of Safety*,[6] a locally important position due probably to his county standing rather than to Party affiliation, for he was no Puritan. There is no evidence, however, that he ever intervened in John's favor. Yet someone in the family must have helped. For it is on record that five hundred pounds was paid to the Committee "to prevent," as John phrased it later in his petition to Charles II, "further mischief."[7]

This was an immense sum in those days, an amount Mrs. Scott could not possibly have raised herself, with her estate already pledged by her late husband to Charles I.

Whether this five hundred pounds was a fine, a bribe, or a recognizance demanded as security for her son's appearance before the Committee during sessions, is not clear. John called it a "gift."

Followed several months of agonizing uncertainty, then sentence was finally passed. Banishment!

Ten-year-old John was ordered to be sent to New England "under the tuition of one Downing."[8]

BIBLIOGRAPHICAL NOTES

1. *Hutch. Pap.*, II, 104.
2. Ll. *Lives*, p. 668.
3. *Jours. of H. of C.*, V, 419; *CSP Ven.*, XXVI, 93.
4. *Hutch. Pap.*, II, 104.
5. *Ibid.*
6. *Arch. Cant.*, XXI, 228-29.
7. *Hutch. Pap.*, II, 104.
8. *Ibid.*

CHAPTER II

JOHN IS DEPORTED

Maine . . . "a countrie rather to affright, than delight one"!

". . . We had a blowing and dangerous passage of it . . . and to tell you the very truth of it, for somedays upon land, after so long and tossing a passage, I was so giddy that I could hardly tread an even step; so that all things, both above and below, . . . appeared to me like the Kentish Britons to William the Conqueror—in a moving posture."
—George Alsop (1638-?), *A Character of the Provinces* . . . , p. 93.

ALL THROUGH the blustery mid-spring of 1643, the little ship *Seabridge* battled her way across the Atlantic, her high decks awash as mountainous green waves swept her along a southwest course till she reached the Azores. There, her long-suffering passengers, battened down under hatches for safety, had a merciful respite from the cramped discomfort of their improvised quarters and the mortal danger of being struck by their "unfixed goods" hurled from place to place by the giant seas. For a few blessed days they basked in sunshine, stretched their aching limbs till the dread moment came for returning to the dark hold. Then on and on they sailed again, into the wonder and peril of an empty sea, all sense of certitude once more left behind, till calmer water finally brought them staggering out on deck. There on the far horizon, their land-hungry eyes glimpsed the faint outline of the Maine

coast, and they thanked God, on their knees, that the New
World was actually in sight.

The *Seabridge,* bound for Boston, was a sturdy little two-
master, no bigger than a modern harbor trawler. She rode
well, was all shape like a wineglass, and among her few score
passengers there was one at least to whom ocean travel was
no new experience.

Emmanuel Downing, a wealthy London lawyer, was making his third Atlantic crossing. His interest in New England
was almost proprietary for he was one of the principal financial backers of that grave Puritan, John Winthrop, Boston's
founder.

But though willing to adventure his money Downing had
felt little inclination, at first, to forsake his elegant London
house and liveried servants for a pioneer's existence in a deso-
late wilderness. His heart, however, followed his fortune, and
in 1638 he finally dared the Great Migration, taking up his
residence in Salem. Three years later when pressing colonial
business necessitated someone's return to England he was the
logical choice. Now, his mission accomplished, he was going
back to Salem again in 1643, a seasoned traveller very well
able to make himself comfortable on the ten weeks' voyage.
With his private cabin on the poop deck, with his mattresses
and bedding, his books and supplies of wine and beer, he
could close his ears to the creaking timbers, the piercing protests of frightened cattle in the hold, the groans and agonized
retching of the seasick scurvy-wracked emigrants, who, devoured by lice and tormented by dysentery, were stowed away
in the limited space between the towering stern and fore-
castle. Above all he could ignore the presence of some twenty
children, temporarily under his charge.

As former Attorney in the Court of Wards—that special
division for legislation involving minors—Mr. Downing had
been persuaded to look after these urchins who were being
shipped to the colonies under circumstances about which
official history has always been reticent.

Traffic in children was the ugly by-product of an intrepid age when individual religious fervor did not exclude a startling lack of compassion. With ruthless logic, settlers noted that they lacked workhands and servants while English slums teemed with humanity living in filth and squalor unchanged since the Middle Ages. For centuries this unwanted population had been kept down by the Black Death which periodically swept through Europe carrying off most of its victims from pestholes among the cities' destitute. But with the passage of time the plague's virulence waned; it could no longer be counted on to maintain an equable balance between rich and needy; the Poor Rates rose alarmingly, and deportation of paupers was conceived as a means of relieving overcrowded parishes.

Doubtless it all began innocently enough, with church collections taken up for poor little orphans, and bishops blessing the practice. But the whole system fell into such disrepute, children were kidnapped or stolen, their parents inveigled or bullied into selling them into what practically amounted to slavery that by 1645 legislation had to be devised concerning illegal traffic in human lives.[1] All of which New England merchants hotly contested under their national rights and "libertie to transport."

The twenty children Emmanuel Downing was bringing over with him on this particular trip were, however, "allowed by Parliament," as John Winthrop noted in his diary; and one, he added, a scurvy victim "was withal very noisome and ill-disposed."[2]

But not all Downing's charges were in such a state. There was another whose condition and fortunes were wildly at odds with those of the cowed, ignorant ragamuffins among whom he found himself. His future, he was stoutly convinced, would be wholly different from theirs. The voyage, which held them quaking captives in their bunks, was, for him, high adventure. If we can judge from his subsequent known behavior, there was certainly not an inch of the ship's surface he did not explore, no sail nor bit of rigging he did not learn to name and handle. Sailors might curse him for being always underfoot, but his unquenchable curiosity and ready smile wrung from them answers as well as oaths. Orders to remain below he simply ignored; authority irked him and to flaunt it was his custom. At the first opportunity he was on the poop, or high in the crow's nest watching for French or Dutch pirates who had been known to attack emigrant ships, and whose appearance he doubtless longed for, his lively vanity aflame with half a dozen versions of his own daring in dealing with them.

A sailor's life, in most boys' daydreams then, was the chosen vehicle for self-glorification, and John Scott, on the *Seabridge* at the age of eleven, was surely no exception to his kind. His first encounter with tilting decks and heaving seas doubtless fulfilled that pricking urge to play the hero which was to plague him all his life. It may have even proved a decisive part in determining his character and contributed to his restless need for change and excitement, desires that drove him to continuous travel.

With the wind whistling round his ears, dreams of glory might well have kept up his courage, stopped any fearful wondering about life in the New World. But nights were different. Crouched in his narrow hammock in the suffocating darkness there must have been many a dreadful moment when John realized that he was exiled and alone.

BIBLIOGRAPHICAL NOTES

1. *CSP. Col.*, 23, *Acts of Pr. Council*, Ser. I, 92, 93; *Pro. Debates of Parl.*, I, 185-86.
2. John Winthrop, *Hist. of N. E.*, II, 184.

CHAPTER III

THE SCOTTS OF SCOT'S HALL

"Scot's Hall shall have a fall;
Ostenhangre was built in angre (pride);
Somerfield will have to yielde;
and Mersham Hatch shall win the match."
—Old Kentish Proverb.

OF ALL THE DOCUMENTS that tell the story of John Scott there is one of particular interest among the time-blackened parchment scrolls of the Public Record Office in London.

Officially indexed as *Colonel Scott's Pardon*,[1] it is written in court Latin, and is one of those Patent Rolls, in which, during the opening years of each monarch's reign, magnanimous incoming Majesty reviewed past misdemeanors and punishments and quite frequently ceded to the intervention of interested friends powerful enough to elicit kingly benevolence.

The royal pardon when it finally passed the seals, specifically refers to him as "John Scott Esq., lately of Scot's Hall, in our county of Kent." It thereby refutes one of the most persistent slanders in John's wayward existence. For he had always maintained his kinship with the Kentish Scotts of Scot's Hall, despite others' ill-intentioned denials. And although as son of a younger branch he certainly never lived in that stately pile, indeed, as a boy, may never have set foot in it, yet he drew unshakable reassurance from this firm knowledge of deep roots in English soil, and connection with a family

16

whose service to king and country extended over centuries. Much of his defiant conduct among the Puritans of the New World, and his unquenchable energy on returning to the Old, becomes comprehensible in the light of his background and tradition.

For these Scotts were of an unusual historical vitality. Knights, not nobles, they furnished uninterruptedly warriors and statesmen to their country's service. There was Sir William Scott, Lord Chief Justice of England under Edward II and III, Sir Edward Scott K.B. called to sit in judgment upon Charles I . . . their very name is rooted in antiquity. Saxon in origin, a scot was the silver coin (*sceattas*) levied for draining land; its use and meaning are as durable as taxes themselves; lucky people still talk of going "scot-free."

Today of course the Scotts are legion, but not all are of the Saxon breed. Scot's Hall Scotts claim such a strain, although the family as it concerns us here belongs to Kent—at that, most Saxon of all the English counties. Fifteen hundred square miles of rolling country between the Thames Estuary and the English Channel, Kent is the gateway to Britain, the path of foreign invasion. Here came the Romans, the Normans, the Spaniards, and men of Kent stood alert on their chalk cliffs ready for the invader. Here were the five ancient coastal defenses, the Cinque Ports; furnishing, at one time, most of the ships and men for the King's navy. Two Scotts, in different centuries, were Lord Wardens of the Cinque Ports, no less than five Scotts were Knights of the Shire, acting as Royal Land Surveyors and Sheriffs, rallying men and arms to fight their country's enemies.

Uncounted Scott manors dotted the Weald—a dense forest when the Romans landed and found Kent ruled by four separate Kings! North of the Weald stands Canterbury, with ancient Watling Street leading to London and the North. Chaucer's pilgrims passed this way to pray at the holy shrine, and many a traveller found hospitality at Scot's Hall, "a goodly mansion set in a vast park," as Evelyn wrote in his Diary.

How much of his family's history was known to our John Scott banished from his native land and on his way to an unknown destiny in 1643? Probably not very much. He was only eleven when the good ship *Seabridge* took him to the New World. He might have heard about his namesake, John Le Scot, the Palatinate Earl of Chester, for to this premier peer of the realm fell the honor of carrying the sword of state—the Curtana—at royal coronations, and small boys remember stories about splendid swords. John Le Scot proudly bore it when Henry III was crowned, but was the last Chester ever to do so. As Saxon noble, whose pre-Conquest status gave him very special privileges, he aroused the envy of his ambitious King, and when he died in 1244, Henry III seized his lands and title, bestowing both upon his own son, the Prince of Wales, who holds them to this day. There were other Scots whose fate was not dissimilar, whose possessions were taken by jealous overlords.

Most famous of them all was John Baliol, King of Scotland. According to both Kentish historians, Hasted and Philipott,[2] the Scotts of Scot's Hall at Brabourne and Smeeth are lineal descendants of the now extinct family of Baliol, and through it of the Scottish kings (of the Malcolm-Cranmore line). The Baliol family merged with Scot through William Baliol Le Scot, last surviving close relative* of that tragic John, chosen by England's Edward I to rule over Scotland.

John Baliol was the second Scott to lose everything in a historic clash with a mightier power. For in the Wars of the Scottish Succession—that bloody feud involving Baliol and Bruce—Edward I vanquished all claimants and seized the throne himself, triumphantly carrying off to Westminster the symbol of victory, the sacred Stone of Fate, the Scone Seat itself!

---

* Brother or cousin? hotly disputed by historians.

Proscribed Baliols changed their surname and disappeared; and after the fourteenth century no Scott rose above the status of landed gentry. Scotts might marry daughters of an Earl or Duke, but each earned his knighthood for himself.

On board the *Seabridge,* during that interminable crossing, our John might possibly have recalled these tales and remembered those knightly marble figures on the family vaults which he had certainly seen in Brabourne parish church, or in the Scot Chapel at Smeeth, that little village in East Kent he later listed as his home.

On many a Sunday as the sermons droned on, John could gaze at Scott effigies and read the family details.

"To perpetuate the memory of Monseigneur William Baliol Le Scot," runs a wall memorial tablet—you can see it still today. That was an early one, England was still under French influence, for William Baliol Le Scot died in 1313.

The memorial brass of another Sir William decorates a polished black marble slab in the chancel floor—a brass such as any small boy would prize, for it shows a knight in full armor with "guarded" spurs, for this Sir William had been sword-bearer to Henry V and fought at Agincourt. Another Sir John Scott is buried in the Chancel—a man of many professions. He toiled over the daily accounts of King Edward IV, whose Household Comptroller he was; he was Marshall of Calais, England's beachhead on the Continent when war threatened with France—a war he helped to avert by negotiating a truce with Louis XI.

Over his once sumptuous tomb still hangs a crested trophy-helmet, flanked by sword and banner. These belonged to Sir Thomas Scott, one of the most illustrious of his name. His properties stretched into three counties—in his day a Scott could ride from Smeeth to London and never leave his own land; he was deputy-lord-lieutenant of the county and planned its coastal defenses under constant threat of Spanish invasion. At the time of the Great Armada, he commanded the Kentish forces, serving under the Earl of Leicester, who, for such staunch service, suggested to Queen Elizabeth that he be raised to the peerage.

But tradition has it that Elizabeth petulantly remarked Sir Thomas already possessed more influence in Kent than Majesty herself. And withheld the title.

An earlier Thomas Scott found no burial in Brabourne but achieved a kind of immortality all his own. For he was that Cardinal Archbishop of York[3] in Shakespeare's *Richard III* (Act II, Sc. 4) who twice befriended Edward IV's hapless Queen Elizabeth, and, standing alone between her and the London mob, persuaded her to take sanctuary in Westminster Abbey, depositing with her, as guarantee of his protection, the Great Seal of England—an act of daring championship for which Richard later imprisoned him in the Tower.

Like their men, the Scott women were a hardy breed, well favored and full of vitality, but loss and disaster did not spare their beauty. Nowhere, as on the distaff side, did the ancient prophecy of downfall find such complete fulfillment.

Caste stamps its children indelibly in England, and our John carried his heritage in his blood. Sitting in the soft gloom of the ancient churches he was one with his ancestors; arms or the law had beckoned innumerable Scotts, the record of their lives was everywhere about him.

But slowly the family fortunes waned—as the old proverb foretold—"Scot's Hall shall have a fall." It had been muttered for a century though only one Scott gave it any attention. Reginald or Reynold, first cousin to "Armada" Scott, hardly rates a line in the Memorials, yet his life was marked by that flamboyance that streaked so many a Scott career. For he published a book whose first edition shook England to its foundations, was publicly burnt by the common hangman and years later received a rebuttal by no less a writer than King James I himself.

The work immemorially connected with Reynold's name is entitled: *The Discovery of Witchcraft,* 4-to, London, 1580, reprinted in 1651 and again in 1655.

A century in advance of his time, the writer pleaded for more humane treatment of the poor creatures burnt as witches, but whose rantings against Henry VIII's Reformation were frequently inspired by its religious opponents, afraid to speak out themselves. The verse they mouthed about Scot's Hall, did it not predict the downfall of Henry VIII's supporters? Were not all the Scotts office-holders under the King? while the owner of Mersham Hatch, destined to "win the match," was he not the only related Scott who still acknowledged papal supremacy?

Reynold's speculations showed keen political insight, but his Christian compassion offended scholars and unlettered alike. In his day the reality of witches was unquestioned, and his book was universally condemned. Even after its public burning James I continued to fulminate against its author, and the King's own book, *Demonology,* published in 1597, was written mainly to "refute the errors of that damnable heretic Scot."

The Scott doom, traced to its source as a bit of popish propaganda, gained popular belief. The downfall was slow, for the steady drain on family fortunes was concealed at first beneath splendid happenings.

No less than three Scotts accompanied Henry VIII to that memorable encounter known as the Field of Cloth of Gold, where, in unparalleled display, without precedent even in that glittering age, the faithful entourage cheerfully ruined themselves for rich adornment to do honor to their King.

The Scott income was somewhat restored during the sober management of the great Sir Thomas, but after his death, more than thirty manors in Kent alone were sold to provide for his seventeen children. The Civil War brought terrible financial losses, particularly to the King's side—and the Scotts were royalists to a man.

How many years does it take a name to die? Little John Scott had no answer to this grim question as day by day the *Seabridge* bore him nearer his American destination. Slowly and surely he sailed toward a fate he could, perhaps, have avoided, but from which, given his temperament and tradition, there was small chance of escape. And, all things considered, it was curiously like so much which had happened before.

BIBLIOGRAPHICAL NOTES

1. Patent Roll C, 66, 3384, 28.
2. *Vill. Cant.*, p. 131; *Arch. Cant.*, XXI, 222-29.
3. Accounts of presents (*exennis*) given to Archbishop of York, Thomas Scott of Rotherham, *HMC Montague-Beverley*, p. 170; *Harleian Soc. Pub.* (*Visitation of Bedford*), XIX, 49, 191.

CHAPTER IV

SALEM

"If Salem meant peace and liberty to Endicott's and Higginson's way of thinking, it meant oppression for others."
—Samuel Eliot Morison, *The Builders of the Bay Colony*, p. 40.

As THE *Seabridge* neared the end of its journey and prepared to dock, the children were given special attention.

They were ordered on deck, a barber cut their hair, and two of the most pitiable looking boys were furnished with wigs.

"Boston," wrote John Scott some years later, "arched into the sea on piles so that the ships come up to the doors,"[1] and this single sentence makes vivid the scene which probably greeted the passengers. Townsfolk crowded out to welcome the new arrivals and watch the goods unloaded, while a few men started sizing up the human cargo with knowledgeable eyes and sharp interest. They asked questions, felt muscles, estimated each child's capacity for work.

Mr. Downing hovered around, talking to a four-man committee* charged with disposing of the children, collecting the monies paid for them, procuring beds for those who found no immediate master.[2] To little John the business might have seemed somewhat strange, but soon a man leading two horses

---

* These were: Mr. Glover, Mr. Russell, Ensign Weld, and Mr. Edwd. Tynge. Mass. Records II, 45.

met them, and Boston was quickly left behind, John riding pillion with Downing's servant.

During the next two days the horses picked their way slowly over rough trails through endless forest, the trees so straight and tall that the lowest branches were high above their heads. Among clearings tall rank grass and massive bramble patches made the going difficult, while there were so many waterways to ford, or get around, that John must have grown sore and weary and longed for home, wherever that was going to be.

But fatigue was forgotten on entering Salem. This was a compact little village on a rocky promontory jutting to the northwest between two other settlements, which, the servant told him, were Marblehead and Beverley. At the time John first glimpsed it, the inhabitants numbered about a thousand. Densely forested hills dropping down to stony beaches cupped the great bay, where pinnaces and shallops rocked in safety; the many inlets were alive with Indian-type canoes. From the neck of the peninsula a causeway stretched to Winter Island; Fort Pickering, newly erected, mounted guard to the north. Crowded wharves rang with the noise of shipwrights' hammers; two thriving taverns sold wine and strong ale at a penny a quart.

The horses, knowing they were home, quickened their pace and turned into crooked Essex Street, heart of the town's activity. Downing rode ahead, greeting citizens from time to time, glancing right and left to note what houses had been built during his absence in England. There were now about four hundred in all, with gaping lots or small patches of corn and beans between them. Most of the "Common" was a sort of swamp, but further along stood a market place, and little "cent shops"—homes whose front rooms displayed goods for sale, "carsey wastkotts, pettycoats" and the like. At an intersection of Essex rose the First Church, white and bare, its nail-studded oak door chained and locked. Outside were the heavy wooden stocks, the grim whipping post, for public punishment, a pillory where "premeditated" liars stood, their tongues thrust through a cleft stick.

To John, fresh from the Old World, the place must have seemed bleak and empty, but to its inhabitants Salem was one of the most flourishing centers of the whole New England Commonwealth, a model among the tiny independent settlements clinging precariously to a strip of coast between an impenetrable forest and the pounding Atlantic.

In less than twenty years, the handful of Salem colonists had transformed a few Indian clearings into a comparatively prosperous community already subdividing into several townships. Gone were the days when the first planters had burrowed into earthen pits against the relentless rain and cold. Forgotten were the primitive sod-roofed dugouts and wigwams they had first erected, the days and nights of gnawing hunger, the scurvy and smallpox that had riddled their ranks. Now their saw-pits were busy all day turning out solid oak beams and planks for sturdy buildings; their timbered, white plastered homes with beautiful doorways and many gables recalled some of the elegance of their native Tudor style.

By 1643 Salem could boast a roaring shipping trade; it had weathered its religious dissensions and little political controversies and had become a pleasant place to live in. Like other towns in the Commonwealth it was beginning to loosen ties with England: by the time John Scott arrived, Massachusetts had already abolished the oath of allegiance to the Crown, and had established the political framework for practical independence.

* * * * *

After a good night's sleep and a breakfast of roast pigeons John was ready to explore the comfortable farm where Downing lived. Life in the colonies might have its compensations. His tutor, he learned, was a man of privilege, married to Lucy Winthrop, the governor's sister. He was a great sportsman and had laid out a private game preserve with two ponds for the decoy ducks he had just introduced.

Alas, John's enjoyment of this pleasant estate was short-lived. Almost immediately Downing went to visit his old neighbor, Lawrence Southwick, taking his small charge with him. The two men talked long in low tones, eyeing John all the time with such intensity that the boy felt he was up for sale. As indeed he was.

For a given sum, Lawrence Southwick agreed to take over from Emmanuel Downing one John Scott, deportee, until the latter attained his majority, to teach him to read and write; and to make him master of a trade.

Shortly thereafter, the General Court at Boston invited Downing to give the customary accounting of what children he had taken into the ship with him, and get a receipt for what had been paid into the Treasury.[3] This turned out to be a considerable sum, and conceivably, John's five hundred pounds were part of it. The Records show that a Goodman Turner was allowed one hundred pounds of the Children's Money; that the sergeants should have twelve pounds out of the same fund; and that Mr. Dunster, President of Harvard, should have a hundred and fifty pounds for his college—*out of the money due the children sent out of England.*[4]

In the case of foundlings or paupers such procedure might have seemed natural. But for a Scott to be sold as a bonded servant must have been a shock.

This then was the way Downing fulfilled his trust! Rage filled the boy's heart and resentment at his treatment never left him. Nearly twenty years afterwards the memory of it still made him furious, and in a petition to the King of England he charged that Downing "had dealt with him most perfidiously."[5]

Now, powerless to resist, friendless, alone, he had no other course but to do as he was ordered. With his hair cropped close to his skull to mark his lowly status, he entered the Southwick household, a menial in a society that was still harshly class-conscious.

The Southwicks were North Country people from Lancaster, originally a county family, with a coat of arms dating from 1275. But hard times had driven Lawrence to America in 1627. He returned to England later to fetch his wife, Cassandra, and their two small children. They probably took the *Mayflower* on its second or third trip in 1628-29, traveling with William Bradford, the historian, and John Endicott, who were bringing more colonists to join Salem's pioneers.

Colonial records show that Southwick applied for freemanship in 1630, but it was not until September, 1639, that he and his wife were admitted to Salem's First Church and became eligible to vote. The Southwicks accepted the franchise with no great grace; like many other "old planters" they were hostile to the Governor's religious autocracy, and were soon to declare themselves Quakers.

A few years before John's arrival, Lawrence had built a house on Main Street and had begun manufacturing glass— on the famous Glass Fields—but he did not have sufficient capital to ride out the prevailing depression, and soon abandoned the works.

He was then appointed to the distinguished office of Cowkeep. This was a full-time most necessary task and the cowherd was a town functionary under bond. The work was no sinecure: wolves prowled and there were Indians around, friendly enough but always ready to steal. Constant disputes and lawsuits over property damage enlivened the job but Southwick must have been a likable fellow for he figures frequently in local wills, receiving small legacies of money, an animal or a "spott" of meadow.

The Town Records speak of a Joseph Scott as cowherd, too; there is no mention of a John. Yet, if a rankling memory is evidence, our John had to assist his master with the cattle. Years later, while being entertained by members of the Boston General Court, he was accosted by one Thomas Joy, himself of humble birth, who asked him loudly if he had not once "kept cows." For this impertinence, John boxed his ears twice and lodged a formal complaint with the Commissioners, who, judging the insult provocative, fined the fellow "200 lb (sic) and bound him over for good behavior."[6]

Even without the hated cow shift, John's life would not have been very happy. There was too little fun in the Southwick household for a boy's taste, and he was not old enough to appreciate the family's solid worth. Of the five children, when John Scott came to join them, the eldest, John, was twenty-three and they ranged down to little Daniel, and daughter, Provided. Large and well built as their house was, according to the times, with its projecting second story and steep roof sloping almost to the ground behind, it must have seemed pretty bare to a Kentish Scott.

The upper rooms held one or two beds of imposing size for the seven inhabitants (John probably had a straw sack in a niche near the narrow stairway), but the heart of the place was the "Great Room" downstairs, filled with all the ceaseless activity of pioneer life.

From the blackened rafters hung smoked hams, strings of dried peppers, herbs, apple rings and such; at the end, a huge fireplace with seats each side, equipped with every kind of pothook, trammel, or hanger, with swinging crane and heavy spit, which small boys had to turn when meats were roasting. Handwrought andirons held the immense logs, and woe betide the lad who let the fire go out in winter.

In the *Greate Room* no one was ever idle, as John immediately discovered. Cassandra and her eldest daughter spun flax, wove it into coarse cloth, bleached and dyed it, then made it into clothes for the whole family. Even the smallest children helped in the seasonal candle-dipping and soap making, fetched water for the vast periodic washdays, stirred great bubbling pots of fat. Making and baking bread, salting meat and fish in the "powder-tubs" as well as the daily cooking, naturally fell to the women, but the men brewed and bottled birch beer, helped scour the heavy wooden trenchers, the leather milkpails and pewter vats.

Round the walls ran shelves and cupboards; there was a

large dresser, a capacious chair for Lawrence and stools for
the rest of the family. All else was luxury, and the Southwicks did not believe in luxury. What furniture there was,
Lawrence and his sons fashioned, as well as all the implements
for working their clearing. One had to be carpenter, mason,
blacksmith—to toil as farmer, tanner, and rude mechanic.
John's training was thorough, if rough. He became a seasoned
settler, competent to deal with any emergency; exalted perhaps by the thought of all that was being accomplished in a
new land, or rebellious amid employments which never
ceased.

At the far end of the room was a refectory table where
grownups sat on a bench while hungry children waited their
turn for a bite. How insipid were the Indian dishes of *sup-
pawn* and *samp*—thick cornmeal porridge, or unparched corn,
beaten and boiled to a mush—young people's daily fare! But
Salem air was sharper than anything John had known at home
and doubtless his longhandled hornspoon dipped into the
common platter as heartily as the rest. Sometimes there were
stews—hotch-potch—and on holidays a bit of spitted meat.

After supper Lawrence read the Bible and the others
gathered around, making brooms, weaving baskets, whittling
loom-spools, sap-buckets, latches, all the things they made of
wood. Night after night the ritual never varied. Almost
against his will John absorbed something of the Southwicks'
religious fervor. Whatever his thoughts in those first years of
interminable family worship the habit of prayer and medita-
tion became his for life, no matter how belied by occasional
wild behavior. His letters and writings reveal the serious bent
of his nature—the "creature of celestial extract" as he put it,
who should "ever be looking upwards from whence he came."
Such an attitude came only slowly, there was too much rebellion in his heart at first for the Southwicks' piety to prevail.

Sunday brought a respite from never-ending chores and
seemed the longest day of all. Morning and afternoon there

were services at the meetinghouse, with heavy fines for non-attendance and sermons lasting hours. Inside all was bare and white-washed. No memorial brasses or monuments here to stir the imagination; no vestments or rich hangings, not a gleam of color to delight the eye; Puritans were only too glad to forget the "pope-tainted" effigies. Instead of stately prayers and the elaborate singing of choral music, John heard the preacher's high nasal whine and the congregation's drone, "lining-out" the psalms. Poetry and parish churches were among the loveliest products of his seventeenth century England: a young boy might not know these things and still feel pretty homesick those Salem Sundays in the bleak meeting-house.

Even legitimate excuses for jollity, the annual Fairs, provided little fun. Villagers from far and near came to sell their farm goods, occasions which in England would have been celebrated with lusty drinking, dancing, and, for the older boys, a bit of sport with a willing wench.

In Salem the atmosphere never relaxed. All dancing was strictly forbidden in John's day, and servants were punished for daring to approach any of the opposite sex. To a fun-loving boy like John bigotry could go no further.

Yet what twelve-year-old could possibly have grasped the passionate convictions of these Puritans who set out to create a Bible Commonwealth and whose dauntless courage conquered a wilderness and carried the seed of political liberty into a new continent?

The recent translation of the Bible into the English vernacular had revolutionized their minds, setting them aglow with the loftiest ideals and a strange self-importance,* filling their everyday speech with a wealth of apt phrases and pithy proverbs. To those literal-minded Englishmen the Old Testament was a divine statute book in which they sought not only principles but mandates, and found a Godlike approval for

---

* Puritans believed that God had selected New England as their chosen land. "This place is appointed me of God." Win. Pap. *Journal* I, p. 7.

everything they did. And if the Hebrew scripture's harsh spirit led them into excesses, they humbled their pride and were ready to admit their errors. Not, however, before they had done irreparable harm to others, and John was to see the whole Southwick family suffer bitterly from Puritan decrees and ultimately be banished from the colony under pain of death.

BIBLIOGRAPHICAL NOTES

1. *Col. Pap. Gen. Ser.*, XXI, 345-47 (notes relating to Massachusetts).
2. *Mass. Rec.*, II, 45.
3. *Ibid.*, 89.
4. *Ibid.*, 83, 84 (Nov. 13th, 1644).
5. *Hutch. Pap.*, II, 104.
6. *N.Y. Hist. Soc. Coll.* (Vol. 1869), II, 47 (*Clarendon Papers*).

CHAPTER V

JOHN'S EDUCATION

"How harde wyll it be for one browghte yp amonge
boockes and learned to lyve in a barbarous place where is
no learnynge and less cyvillytie."
—A letter to John Winthrop before he sailed
for New England.

As JOHN GREW OLDER life became more irksome; petty restrictions and duties permitted no real outlet for his restless vitality. He was far too intelligent not to be aware of the real opportunities for advancement and prosperity the New World offered, and the ready initiative he had displayed even as a little boy must have suggested a dozen likely projects. But for him there was no bright horizon. Work as he might with other men clearing the stubborn soil of rock and roots, the acres he planted would never be his; not a single possession rewarded his wearisome toil. And of all the harsh circumstances about him, none could have been more hateful to his awakening manhood than the inability ever to exercise his own free choice. From morning to night he was told what to do.

No love or warmth of affection softened the difficult years from boyhood to adolescence; the New England conscience precluded all show of feeling and his eager outgoing nature met no response. This forbidding atmosphere was something he could not penetrate for it effectively quenched that spark of insight through which he might have achieved a more sympathetic understanding of his surroundings. Days were always too busy for boyish daydreaming or all the little unimportant things that make up a happy childhood; and in the midst of a large family his solitude was almost complete.

At odds with himself, young Scott in Salem was also at odds with the world he lived in, for it was impossible for him to forget he was among the enemy. At heart he remained a Royalist, while around him were Roundheads who had fought his King, killed his father and sold him into bondage. They had deliberately sought this life and made it to their liking; to him it was exile.

Escape was, however, impossible. Beyond the Southwick home was a wasteland—a geological "divide," its barren hills gashed with rock and glacial remains that are visible still. In other directions Indian trails led into endless forests. Boston was two days away, and who had time or money for such a trip?

A welcome break in the dreary round was the eight days with the militia that claimed even servants every year. From the age of ten, boys were trained to handle half pikes, bows and arrows, guns.[1] The rough camp and rougher usage were a far cry from the glamorous role John had assigned himself at Brabourne, but he learned his lesson well, and laid the foundation for a useful profession.

And always there was the sea! Like a magnet it drew him, to watch the tide surge with a roar into the Neck at Marblehead, where it seethed and boiled and threw up waves fifty feet high. Or from some bold cliff to gaze out on the ocean, his mind afire with thoughts of its immensity and danger and the chance for adventure. He slipped off to the wharves to pick up gossip from new arrivals. Salem's outer bay was always full of foreign ships; salty sailors from Virginia, merchants from Europe, all brought news of the great world.

Once in a while sun-blackened buccaneers swaggered through the town, gold earrings dangling, their wide short breeches belted with a strip of hide, knives, or cutlass and powder horn thrust through the leash. To a boy who all his life was to crave excitement, their lure was irresistible. These men John followed with frantic interest. He would edge nearer as they swigged buttered rum in taverns, bragging of their latest adventures. Fearsome oaths sprinkled their talk of Spanish merchantmen overpowered by their long low swift-sailing sloops, looted and abandoned; of ways to beat the trading laws; of English colonial governors who winked at their exploits, gave them privateering commissions, let them sell their spoils in Jamaica, Porto Rico, Trinidad. There was always the excuse that if they did not, then the Dutch in Curaçao would profit by the plunder. Did not the rich prizes attract traders to the islands? And was not the outfitting of freebooters itself a great industry? John's eyes widened at the revelations; boldly he questioned them further, drinking in their talk.

Even in pious Salem such characters went uncensured. No beadle ever stopped them as they puffed their pipes, though ordinary mortals were fined a shilling for daring to "drink tobacco" in public; even their most audacious deeds abroad found no condemnation in port.

Spanish colonial policy had acquired such a reputation for murderous cruelty and oppression that anyone who assailed it seemed to be an avenger of innocent victims. To Puritans, Spain was the arch enemy who burned Protestants at the stake, so even churchmen could argue that these daredevils, however questionable their calling, were still striking a blow at antichrist. A bit of casuistry not without influence on an impressionable lad, who was later to follow in their footsteps and then to reflect in his writings upon the Spirit of Adventure for Profit!

To drag himself from such colorful creatures and walk Salem's streets and market place was to return to another, drabber world. Yet even here an occasional Indian, like some gaudy bird of paradise would flit by, his savage finery offsetting his sharp glance and gliding gait. Skins of bear or beaver flowed from one shoulder, bright hummingbirds made ear pendants, elaborate tattooing decorated faces of inscrutable gravity. These were the great landowners, these were the true aristocrats whose estates covered a continent. To John they could never be just savages! No one who held that much land could fail to impress a Scott.

* * * * *

Not all his formative years were at the mercy of casual contacts. Much as John's untapped energies drove him to seek outside interests, one consolation he could always find at home. Lawrence Southwick may have been a hard taskmaster, but he was a man of his word, and he had agreed to teach John to read. Actually this was not necessary, for a boy of John's condition had certainly had a year or so at grammar school, and some knowledge of Latin. But the promise stood, and presumed a certain amount of time for reading. Formal education was, of course, out of the question. But the Southwicks were gentlefolk; they were intelligent, their talk enlightening. Recorded testimony in local lawsuits shows that even Cassandra was highly literate with an alert mind ready for precise argument, though her tongue was somewhat sharp. John learned to hold his own in conversation no matter with whom he came in contact. Books were always within reach; there were not many, for ship space was far too precious for settlers to bring over their libraries, they had to make a drastic choice. But their selection, judged from old inventories, was sound, and as years passed they sent to Europe for more.

Everyone had a Bible, of course. John heard this read aloud each evening; its rhythm and construction ring through his own prose. Histories and classics were the greatest favorites: Plutarch's *Lives,* Ovid's *Metamorphoses;* Machiavelli's *Principe* and *The Advancement of Learning* by Bacon, were all available in Salem in John's time. *The General Hystery of the Netherlands; Turkish Histery; Commentarys of ye Warrs in France; England's Heroicall Epistles,*—a boy could learn a lot about the world from such volumes. Hakluyt's *Voyages* —found in so many homes—he must have read again and again, for his own "Relaçon on the Battle of St. Christophers," written in 1667[2] recalls that other writer's trenchant geographical observations laced with personal tidbits which make a country and an epoch live.

A book which may have had some effect upon his thinking was the *Swedish Intelligencer,* included in one of the Salem libraries of the period. It could have opened up a vision of government agent work in foreign countries, for John was to prove himself a born reporter. In the Preface of his own *Histories*[3] now preserved in the British Museum, and the Bodleian Library, he wrote:

"I made it my business likewise to purchase or borrow all the histories and journals that I could hear of whether Latin, Italian, Spanish, or Portuguese, French, Dutch or in any language. . . ."

He admits he was not master of most of these languages, but to learn them got assistance from natives of the different countries he met on his travels, or from Englishmen who spoke them and who could help him. Books appealed to him primarily for the light they threw on experience. Always he related what he had read to his own ardent observations; his interest and curiosity about life in general never left him. In one of his writings he tells of questioning for days two prisoners he held on a Caribbean voyage, pumping them about places they had visited and getting out of them everything they knew.

"About the Eighteenth year of my age," he wrote (i.e. while still a Salem apprentice)—"I took up a resolution to make America the scene of the greatest actions of my life. Thereto I set myself a work, if possible, to find out the Latitudes and the Longitudes of all places" (the latter were not only then unknown but considered, by some scholars, unknowable) "both on the continent and in the Islands . . . as also the names of what Persons and of what Nations . . . who possessed them . . . and how these Colonies have prospered or declined in Trade . . ."

This was a very important decision. For the first time John saw no contradiction between his American sojourn, however enforced, and becoming "both of some reputation to myself, and a General advantage to the English nation."

Some time during these early years he must have had leisure to practice the elaborate handwriting of the period, laboriously tracing between ruled lines decorative capitals and elegant lettering, with all the patience and application of a professional scribe. For even in an age of exquisite writing, one of his royal petitions bears a note by the endorser: "the original from which this was copied is a most beautiful piece of penmanship."[4]

It is possible also that about this time he first began making rough sketches of the maps which were to accompany his proposed great work. This he never finished. But his description of the items he had particularly in mind, "the rocks, landshelves and soundings about every island, and in the entrance of all ports and havens," show a scientific interest in such matters.

An interest which well nigh ruined his historical reputation.

BIBLIOGRAPHICAL NOTES

1. *Mass. Rec.,* II, 99; III, 268.
2. *CSP Col. Ser. Am. and W. I.,* 1661-68, No. 1524.
3. Sl. MS., 3662, Plut. C. II, G, ff 786-761. (The folio numbers run backwards since Scott's MS was, by an unfortunate accident bound upside-down with Byam's Extract Narrative of the State of Guiana. That the MS is Scott's cannot be doubted by any careful student. Not only does he clearly identify himself in the text, but the long personal Preface is signed with his name in full. That his authorship could ever have been doubted or overlooked is due to the circumstance of binding.)
4. *Mass. Hist. Soc. Pro. (1867-69),* 1st ser., X, 391.

CHAPTER VI

DIFFICULT YEARS

"The Quakers died not because of their other crimes—how
capital whatsoever, but upon the super-added presump-
tuous and incorrigible contempt of authority."
—Governor Endicott to Charles II, *CSP Col.
Ser. Am. and W. I.*, 1661-68, No. 26.

IT WAS JOHN'S FATE to be living with a family outspoken in
its disapproval of Winthrop's highhanded influence on the
Administration. Overlooking the Governor's exceptional gifts
of leadership and organization, the Southwicks carped continually on the inequalities which existed in Salem, the abuse
of power by persons in high places, and, above all, the absence
of real religious liberty. Freedom of conscience was, of course,
the last thing Puritans were ready to grant. Freedom was
only for those who thought as they, and the Southwicks were
not in this category.

From the moment of its foundation in London, the Society
of Friends had caught the imagination of the Southwick
family. To the austerity of Puritan living they soon added the
Quakers' belief in personal guidance by an "inward light,"
in vehement appeals to conscience, as well as in the sublime
necessity of speaking out at all times to testify to their faith.
One can only guess John's reactions to this new religion
which must have seemed strangely confusing: he now found
himself member of a family in almost perpetual defiance of
the law. With all the zeal of the newly converted, the South-

38

DIFFICULT YEARS † 39

wicks refused to abide by man-made decrees, paid no taxes, abstained from churchgoing, and claimed a special mission from heaven to rebuke their neighbors for bigotry and intolerance. Their outward meekness and irreproachable lives masked an independence regarded by Puritans as rank heresy.

Such fanaticism spread rapidly through New England and the Southwick household became a Quaker center. Punitive legislation directed against Sectarians appeared as early as 1646, but from the outset Quakers were hard to handle. To their very real piety they joined an emotional extravagance, part product of the century's intellectual ferment, but doubtless due, as well, to years of Puritan suppression. How could the law deal with (and what indeed must John have thought of) a woman like Deborah Wilson, who cast off all her clothes and in broad daylight ran stark naked through proper Salem —to symbolize, so she said, mankind's miserable condition? What of other Quakers who stalked the town smeared with ashes and human filth, calling loudly upon all men to repent? Nor was that all. Quakers so persistently defied Court rulings that they became suspected of sinister designs against the government itself.

Theirs was a shattering example for a lad already tormented by thwarted ambition and resentful to the point of rebellion. Yet whatever John thought of their strange views and excesses, he could not but respond to the irresistible appeal Quakers exerted on all the disenfranchised, voteless citizens and indentured servants alike. The unfaltering courage of these "rebels of God" won his respect, opened his eyes to their spiritual quality and an independence undeterred by personal loss and bitter hardship. Theirs was an example that powerfully influenced his later life and was to determine the course of his most memorable decision.

John never became a Quaker, his religion—like his politics —always had a middle-of-the-road quality. But the Southwicks left their stamp upon him. Quakers everywhere recognized it and befriended him; they remembered the noble family he had lived with and the merciless treatment accorded it.

Lawrence and Cassandra were subjected to ruinous fines, ferocious whippings and repeated imprisonment. Their children, Provided and young Daniel, inspired by their example, deliberately stayed away from church, and, unable to pay the subsequent fines, were ordered to be shipped to the West Indies to be sold as slaves to raise the money! To Salem's honor not a captain would transport them,* and many townsfolk were ashamed of the brutal sentence.

Evidently relations worsened, or the Southwicks were ruined, for in December 1647 Lawrence petitioned the General Court for permission to dispose of John "as per covenant with Emmanuel Downing." And the Court ordered Lawrence to "put forth said Scott for three years to any honest man."[1]

That he should again be disposed of, till maturity, like a chattel, aroused afresh John's resentment against the perfidious Downing. Though transfer of bond servants was not unusual, he saw it as intolerable insult. Such treatment he would not endure, and he ran away to sea.

But Lawrence Southwick had no intention of relinquishing so valuable a piece of property; he had acquired the right to dispose of John for profit, and heavy penalties were exacted from runaway servants. The lad was picked up in port the following May (1648) and taken to Boston to answer for his escapade. His term of apprenticeship was extended to make up the period of his absence, and he was ordered to "satisfy his master to the amount of 35 shillings";[2] this sum apparently being the costs for the suit.

Present that day at the General Court of Election was Mr. Emmanuel Downing himself. He and John faced each other, possibly for the first time since Downing had brought him over from England. John was now sixteen, a tall slender

---

* John Greenleaf Whittier's poem "Cassandra" recalls this moving incident, though with a poet's license, he uses the mother's beautiful name rather than the daughter's.

youth with powerful shoulders and a shock of cropped brown hair. His eyes smoldered under bushy eyebrows, there was a hot glare in their gray depths as he stood defiantly in the dock, ready to pour out his grievances the moment he got a chance to speak, something the judge showed no intention of permitting. Downing liked his ease, and the sight of the boy may possibly have aroused a twinge of conscience. His own sons he had been reluctant to bring to America, fearing their education would suffer, yet he had not hesitated to condemn this well-born lad to long years of service. Such disturbing thoughts he promptly banished by pushing on to the next bit of business—the disposal of the defeated Pequot Indians' territories, with all their consoling opportunities for profitable real estate development.

The Southwick case was quickly disposed of and the Court adjourned after voting to John Winthrop, Junior, three thousand acres of Pequot land "near to the Narragansett country."

It was an odd coincidence that this grant should have been made on May 10th, 1648, the very day John was in the dock. For on the bench, among the magistrates and assistants, were Richard Bellingham, Simon Bradstreet, and Major Humphrey Atherton, the great Indian fighter, who had just defeated the troublesome warlike Narragansetts, whose country offered speculators even *greater* rewards and profits.

John returned to Salem with the Southwicks. He knew now he was powerless before the law; serve his time he must, and on the contract's humiliating terms. One good thing came of the incident: at least he did not have to change households. And when John himself came to write a contract for his own apprentice, Hallelujah Fisher, in 1665, he stated specifically that there should be one master only.[3] Not that this was much comfort to him in 1648.

The treatment rankled and he would not remain silent. Before long he was hauled into court again, this time to be "admonished for profane cursing."[4]

All his subsequent life he vented his feelings in violent swearing. "Prodigious oaths" and blasphemies studded his conversation, and the exuberant force of his temperament led him into wild exaggeration, and "lavish extravagant expressions," as one contemporary wrote. Years of silence were erupting as his leashed vitality burst its bonds.

The verbal explosion possibly cleared the atmosphere, for his pent-up energy led him into none of the offenses so common among other indentured men. New England records are full of the punishments meted out to those who served their masters badly; who stole, lied, malingered, brawled or even attempted murder. No such charges mar John's reputation.

But his choice of profession, once free, and the speed with which he hurled himself into a life so totally different from his bonded existence, give some indication of what went on in his mind and point to a spirited determination to wipe out hateful memories as violently as possible.

BIBLIOGRAPHICAL NOTES

1. *Rec. of Quarterly Courts,* Essex County, Mass. I, 130.
2. *Mass. Rec.,* II, 245; III, 131.
3. *Oy. Bay. TR.,* I, 17.
4. *Rec. of Quarterly Courts,* Essex County, Mass. I, 180.

CHAPTER VII

WESTWARD HO!

"A bolder race of men, both as to personal valor and conduct, certainly never yet appeared on the liquid element or dry land."
—Alexandre Exquemeling, *History of the Buccaneers of America* (Preface).

JOHN'S YEARS OF SERVITUDE came to an end at long last, but he received none of the land, cattle or money which most decent masters settled on their apprentices when their terms expired. By 1652 Lawrence Southwick was ruined and John had to shift for himself.

Not for an instant did he hesitate in choosing a profession. There was one bold way to tempt quick fortune and slake his thirst for adventure; he went to sea. He set sail just as he had done before when he ran away, but this time there was no one to haul him back, and current conditions made the getaway easier.

The Puritans, he knew, had not only settled New England but had planted colonies in the Caribbean where their godly principles were somewhat modified by the prevailing lawlessness.

Charles I had already given tacit consent to a little licensed freebooting by the Providence Company settlers in the Bahamas. Cromwell went even further. He issued letters of marque and reprisal to daring spirits finding their way into the Caribbean basin. So it was no trouble at all for John to get himself transported to the very heart of adventure. He had only to hang around Salem Harbor till a ship was sailing in the right direction, talk himself aboard, and take the short-term service which was common usage in those days.

From all the evidence available, he turned up in Tortuga —the "Turtle" island at the head of the Windward Passage, an hour's easy sail from the main sprawl of Hispaniola (Haiti and San Domingo), a name etched on his mind since those chance encounters with buccaneers in the old Salem days. Here lived the freest of all free creatures—completely their own masters, and brothers all—royal Navy men who had jumped ship, Cavaliers fleeing Cromwell's persecution, Highland Scots from debtors' prisons, Hollanders, with stark memories of the Inquisition. The bond between these "Brethren of the Coast," as they called themselves, was hatred of oppression, their common enemy was Spain. Such social outcasts suited John's mood, life in this male paradise was entirely communal. John spent long days hunting the wild-running sharp-horned cattle, bringing down his quarry with deft use of dirk and knife, or with deadly musket aim. He learned to stretch the carcasses on greenwood hurdles— *boucans** (as the original French hunters named them)—to smoke and cure the meat for the Haitian markets.

In and out the myriad islands, John began to maneuver the little single-decked vessels or lean swift lateen-rigged craft; took to raiding the sea lanes with other buccaneers, shooting at Spaniards as well as wild boar. At nights or during the noon-haze heat, he shared the rigorous lookout, for thought of possible Spanish invasion sobered even the most reckless.

From the shy friendly natives, the Arawaks, he picked up his first knowledge of an Indian language. He found their conversation "full of mirth and good humour," (as he wrote in his History of the Indians[1]) and on closer acquaintance he came to relish their "witty jealous conduct."

---

* These early Frenchmen on Tortuga who brought home the wild stock, called themselves *Boucaniers* from their principal occupation. The name stuck and swept round the world, bringing recruits.

Tortuga, in its heyday, was certainly a unique experience and John, it seems, took to the life with gusto. Here was a society where a man proved his worth by sheer capacity and where those with a rancorous personal score to pay—all the "Lutheran dogs and heretics" as Spain called them—had a chance to discharge their long-stored hate. Here John's boundless energy, initiative, and dash of braggadoccio found a natural outlet among men quick to recognize a leader. Here for the first time he was "happy and successful" (as he later wrote to his King),[2] gaining experience as mariner and, inevitably, as fighter, for no one could have attained any prominence unless he became expert in such matters.

John's abilities speedily asserted themselves. Already familiar with the use of arms, he learned the handy strokes of cutlass, pike and broad-axe; how to prime a pistol. He took part in the swift isolated raids on coastal towns and even Spanish ports, harried and burned Spanish ships. He crossed the Caribbean without benefit of chart or beacon, sailing unerringly and closer to the wind than could the big square-rigged Spanish ships. He learned to set up a mast; became familiar with the sudden violence of hurricanes, when the awful yellow darkness warned it was better to seek no haven but to ride out the storm at sea. Rain like steel rods blinded the navigators, screeching winds tore at the sails and cordage. Along with the other men, John pitted his puny strength against the elements' fury as swirling branches, torn from island forests, flailed the air, and sheets of spray raked from the crests of forty-foot waves almost swamped the ship.

Such toughened sailors, like the one John became, were a continual challenge to the Spaniards who for more than a hundred years had decreed that no ship should navigate from the Bahamas to the South American mainland except under Spanish license.

In a way he was serving a national purpose, for buccaneers contributed to their country's safety by keeping prowling warships from home waters.

They certainly weakened Spain with their "war-and-no-war" tactics and could be counted upon as auxiliaries once hostilities were openly proclaimed. In John's day their fighting companies served with the regular forces of contending states. The notorious Henry Morgan, John's Caribbean contemporary, fought under Colonel Venables in two of Cromwell's expeditions to seize West Indian territory.

The English dictator, in a shrewd effort to distract domestic discontent by foreign conquest, worked long on a grandiose scheme—his Western Design—to conquer Hispaniola, an enterprise doomed to end in humiliating failure though he did succeed in capturing Jamaica.

It was during this "Hispaniola Affair," as John called it, that Cromwell's attention lit upon Scott, whose deportation to New England had been brought to his notice. The Lord Protector rescinded the banishment order. John's exploits on the high seas had gained him his most precious reward; he was once more a free man in every respect.

"He (Cromwell) offered me great employment,"[3] John's letter to the King continued. "But I preferred to gain my bread among strangers, even among the Indians of America, beyond the reach of all temptation."

For in this tropical world fringed by the great green arc of little islands, political passions still raged, and Roundheads and Cavaliers regarded each other with cold enmity. John, ever a staunch Royalist, would not join Cromwell's ranks no matter what the refusal cost. "Everywhere I went I saw those whose loyalty was the cause of their poverty, as is so with many of Your Majesty's gentlemen."[4]

When the First Dutch War broke out, John accepted a captain's commission from a colonial governor and, with a "letter of reprisal," fought in his country's service.

But he did not continue this existence for long. Much as it seemed to attract him at first, it did not fit into his resolution "to make America the scene of the greatest actions of my life."[5]

So he sailed back to New England, richer in experience, if not in pocket, and within a short time, as he informed the King, he was "employing himself in and about an island called Long Island."[6]

BIBLIOGRAPHICAL NOTES

1. Sl. MS., 3662, f 785.
2. SP. Dom. Car., II, 29, No. 419.
3. *Ibid.*
4. *Ibid.*
5. Sl. MS., 3662, f 786.
6. *Hutch. Pap.,* II, 104.

CHAPTER VIII

LONG ISLAND

> In an economy lacking both coin and a reliable and unfluctuating system of paper property, real estate was the best form of investment . . . and it is an unmistakable fact that the merchants were extraordinarily involved in the buying and selling of land.
>
> —Bernard Bailyn, *The New England Merchants in the 17th Century,* p. 101.

Now BEGINS THE ODYSSEY of John's rapid rise to recognition in the place which historically is always linked with his name. "John Scott of Long Island" is how he became known both to contemporaries and posterity, and his move to this lush well-populated region established a lifelong pattern of always being in a trouble center at a period of dramatic upheaval.

Long Island was the scene of one of the earliest colonial controversies, for it had been planted by both English and Dutch settlers constantly in feud over their boundaries. The scattered English settlements on the eastern end of the island were loosely administered by the New England Commissioners, and enjoyed a greater freedom from Puritan severity than any other part of the country. This strongly appealed to John, whose friends in Southampton and Southold (former Salem people, irked by repression there), now found themselves living in what practically amounted to little independent republics, to the infinite envy of the rigidly governed Dutch colonists occupying the western end of the island.

In 1654, the date of John's arrival, war between England

and Holland was still going on, and the local situation was tense. To prevent the mainland Indians from crossing Long Island Sound to exploit this white man's quarrel, John Youngs, son of Southold's Pastor Youngs, and a man already of some repute, was commissioned as privateer to patrol these waters.

Was it the bond of the sea which brought Youngs and Scott together? Theirs became a deep and lasting friendship and the two were side by side when "they appeared before Van Tienhoven, a Dutch Sheriff at Fort Amsterdam, and were heard and examined"[1] as early records show. Whether this was on account of Youngs' scouting the Dutch-held coast or for reasons connected with the island's disorders is not stated. Apparently the two young men's explanation was satisfactory since they were immediately released. But the incident pointed up the tinder-box situation.

Anglo-Dutch rivalry in the New World was at its height. Both countries claimed large portions of American territory for reasons each considered irrefutable. Dutch traders had planted posts along the Hudson at the very moment the English were settling Massachusetts Bay; the Dutch had made their way into the interior as far as Hartford, Connecticut, and spread thinly onto Long Island up to Hempstead—shared with the English.

Just before John's arrival, New Netherland had successfully absorbed the Swedish Delaware settlement and was ready to tackle New England. But the English settlers were proving formidable obstacles to Holland's expansion, and soon found in John Scott a sturdy champion.

As so often in the seventeenth century, events in the Old World largely determined those in the New.

So long as Catholic Spain threatened Europe, England and Holland remained allies, and their respective subjects on the North American continent preserved an uneasy truce. But the moment His Catholic Majesty's power was checked, English and Dutch sailors flew at each other's throats contesting supremacy everywhere on the high seas; while English and Dutch colonists clashed over possession of the towns that dotted both sides of the Sound.

The mounting tension in this hotly disputed area was heightened by the intransigence of the two top men concerned, whose careers crossed John's and brought him onto the stage of world history.

Governor of New Netherland since 1647 was Peter Stuyvesant, a likable, despotic, peg-legged old soldier, obstinately determined to allow his countrymen no voice in the conduct of their own affairs. His attitude conflicted not only with his enlightened home government, but with the policy of the Dutch West India Company under which the colony operated, and which was pleading with its agent in America to liberalize the medieval restrictions that hampered individual initiative. In John's time Dutchmen on Long Island openly made unfavorable comparisons between Stuyvesant's tyrannical administration and the greater freedom allowed English settlers, even those living in Dutch towns.

Strategically placed for intrigue in this quarrel of the century, was Britain's Envoy to the Hague, George Downing (later Sir George), none other than the son of that Emmanuel Downing who had brought John to America. A bold imperious man, keen, subtle, not too scrupulous, he preferred to bully rather than persuade, and continually outran his country's orders. He disliked and distrusted Holland's Republican rulers and was reckless of the risks he incurred in his fierce determination to drive the Dutch from commercial and colonial fields.

As a youth in Salem and Boston, George Downing had taken to the policy of "pious aggression" with a zest that launched England on a brilliant colonial career, which made his own fortune, and bequeathed his name to one of London's most famous streets. Such a character at the helm puffing on smouldering fires, and an opposite number like Peter Stuyvesant, set the scene for the explosion which ultimately blasted John from America.

In this political struggle Scott was still no more than a pawn. He was literally spying out the land, shuttling back and forth across the Sound. Writing of these early days in his first petition to the King Charles II (1661), he said he "was forced to court any employment to acquire a livelihood,"[2] and a document of this period gives his occupation as smith. Strong, willing, accustomed to danger and hardship, he was prepared to try anything.

At one time, in total disregard for the scandal it caused among other colonists, he even went to live among, and work for, Indians. Life in Tortuga may have given him a taste for their companionship, and a seasoned pioneer, like himself, would certainly have been invaluable to them.

With his interest in language he picked up their dialects, learned their ways, won their confidence. He found the Long Island tribes less attractive than the fun-loving Arawaks: "North American Indians," he wrote, comparing the two, were "more morose, dull, shrinking, and infinitely worse-humored, with a great sense of the injuries they sustained from the Europeans. They are strict computers of wrongs . . ." a matter with which John would readily sympathize ". . . but such people as have purchased their lands fairly have lived with them in peace and enjoyed a quiet neighborhood."[3]

His lonely boyhood was a good preparation for this sojourn among the "savages," as New Englanders always called them. John clearly did not regard them as such. He wrote with great sympathy of their tribal and personal customs, defended their reaction to foreign "invasion" since it was "the Christians who ever first injured them . . . wresting away their country by force, where God and nature had given them a propriety." And he cited several instances of historical massacres and wars precipitated by European greed and ignorance of Indian tradition. He constantly praised those who "with fair and gentle means" sought to convert the natives to Christianity. On this subject he waxed voluble, for John had, at one time, considered writing a study of Indian religions, but found, as he said, it already "done to my hand by several pens."

With characteristic thoroughness he devoured all six volumes of José d'Acosta's work on the subject* and in the Preface to his own Histories makes a fascinating reference to this author's opinion, namely that the affinity of certain Indian words to Hebrew led to the conclusion that the aboriginal Americans were one of the lost tribes of Israel!

Like this same Spanish author who blamed his countrymen's cruelty in pursuing ruthless personal ends under the mask of religion, John too, felt that conversion by fire and sword was no way to bring Indians to the love of God. And he commended most highly the English pastors, John Elliot and Abraham Pierson, for their "indefatigable preaching of the Glorious Gospel to the poor heathens."

John's writings about Indians completely dispel the suggestion that this interlude in his life was, in any sense, a cynical calculation intended to lead to a fortune in real estate. They not only reveal a very genuine compassion for simple souls cheated and dispossessed, but his Preface goes beyond, to implications of a deeper nature. Evidently John recognized that these natives, like other human beings, possessed definite "natural rights." For "truly it is not unworthy to notice," wrote John, "what was once said by an Indian Prince in the northern parts of America. A Gentleman showed him a patent he had for his country from the King of England. Said the Indian, 'Your master may give you a commission to govern his people in any place where you may settle, but *my* territories he cannot give you, for by the same rule,' quoth he, 'might I send my people into England to settle there.' "⁴

Indians instinctively trusted John, particularly Wyandanch, powerful chief of the Montauk tribe, and an unwavering

---

* *Historia naturale e morale delle Indie,* par José d'Acosta, Venice, 1596.

friend of Englishmen. These Montauks were the "royal tribe," and Wyandanch, from whom all the whites on the island bought their land, was the Grand Sachem of all the neighboring tribes, with sole right to dispose of their holdings.

Now clearly John was at a moment in history when daring determined men could do very well for themselves, and from his apprentice days in Salem, he had watched, and heard tales about those who seized opportunity boldly and profited greatly thereby.

To chart the Americas, as he stated in his Histories, had been a youthful ambition, and John's earliest writings indicate that he had pondered deeply concerning the transfer of property from natives to whites, and the fundamental problem of just who owned America!

Since his personal fortune hung on this question, the reader, at the risk of tedium, must now give it some attention.

English claims to the new continent (disputed by Dutch, French and Spanish), were based on its discovery by the Cabots in 1497-98, and the formal "taking possession, under Letters Patent," a century later by Sir Humphrey Gilbert. Title to it was thus vested in the Crown and only the King of England, or his grantees, could buy (or conquer) land from the Indians.[5] King James I conveyed Long Island to one of his favorites, the Earl of Stirling, so the earl, and his heirs, theoretically had the right to exact payment for any land there. Quit-rents were indeed established for Southampton and other early townships, but with the passage of time individual settlers ignored this formality—distance bred indifference on both sides.

Sometimes the Crown chartered trading companies to colonize parts of the New World, but here again, original intentions were drastically altered by the new and unfamiliar conditions. When John Winthrop emigrated to New England in 1630 taking with him the precious parchment of the Massachusetts Bay Trading Company, he and his officers were supposed to serve as president and board of directors of a joint-stock corporation. But they became, instead, governor and executive council of a colony which assumed powers completely unforeseen in the charter. Gradually they transformed themselves into a quasi-independent self-governing community, partitioning out the land both to towns and private individuals.

Even before the Pilgrims sailed for the New World, there had been acrid discussions about future land ownership. The adventurers, who put up the money, wanted it all held in common for seven years, to safeguard capital. But the planters wanted homes that could not be taken from them. They remembered with bitterness England's ancient copy-holding system under which the tenant could always be foreclosed by his landlord. They were determined to be freeholders, registering their property in law. And this was the system which came to prevail in North America and under which John Scott operated.

The elder Winthrop, just before departure, had summed up his own conclusions about the Indians and their continent. "That which lies common and hath never been replenished or subdued, is free to any that possess or improve it . . . So if we leave them sufficient for their use we may lawfully take the rest . . ."[6]

And take it he did. Convinced of his divine mission to rule, he gathered the reins very tightly into his hands and restricted membership in his colony to Church members only* so that it was an exceedingly small group who claimed exclusive rights to create townships, apportion land, and exclude strangers, not only French or Dutch, but Englishmen as well! Within a year he had decreed at the Boston Court: "No person whatsoever shall buy any land of any Indian without leave of the Court."[7] Nevertheless the majority of settlers continued to do so, and purchase from natives, with

---

* ". . . a deprivation of civil privileges which, had it occurred in England by act of parliament might well have been the first in a roll of grievances." Hutch., *Hist. of Mass.*, I, 26.

"Three fourths of the people remain out of the Church." Lechford. *Plaine Dealing*, p. 73.

or without Boston's sanction, was upheld by local magistrates.

Diaries of the period give a most revealing picture of how the early white men acquired their lots, and town records as late as the 1670's include Indian deeds turning over to most honorable citizens vast areas for no more than a few household goods or an old musket. And historians have applauded these same men for their valuable, if primitive, surveying.[8] Not until the mid-eighteenth century, with its greedy land barons and alarming increase of conflicting land claims, was Winthrop's 1631 act reinforced, and all title-deeds negotiated without a state license were declared null and void.

From the very beginning Governor Winthrop established a pattern of behavior which was to have far-reaching consequences of the greatest national importance. Reprimanded by the home government for exceeding his authority (appendix A), he argued haughtily: "Our allegiance binds us not to the laws of England . . . nor do the King's writs . . . go any further than the English shores."[9]

This was a daring precedent to set. For if Massachusetts could defy England why should not other American dependencies cut loose from Massachusetts? or from any other New England colony? Observant and thoughtful New Englanders remarked the policy with varying reactions, and its influence was certainly not lost upon John Scott. For, confronted with a situation involving such an opportunity, he did not hesitate to act decisively, and in accordance with prevailing local laws.

BIBLIOGRAPHICAL NOTES

1. *Rec. of N. Amst.*, I, 174 (Court Minutes). There is no record of John Scott being in jail at this time, as Abbott avers. Scott and Youngs could even have requested this hearing.
2. *Hutch. Pap.*, II, 104.
3. Sl. MS., 3662, f 772.
4. *Ibid.*, f 771.
5. *Kent. Comm.*, p. 379.
6. Winthrop, *Life and Letters,* I, 311, 312.
7. *Mass. Rec.*, I, 112.
8. Thompson, *Hist. of L.I.*, I, 398.
9. *N.Y. Col. Docs.*, III, 136; Winthrop, *Journal,* II, 301.

CHAPTER IX

LANDED PROPRIETOR

". . . our Hartford friends, having opened the back door
to the frontier, and invited all and sundry to that 'most
fatt and pleasant country' must not take it amiss if the
head of the Bay house endeavour to keep his family together, and prevent the lad who took the coat from getting
the cook too."

Governor Winthrop's letter (defending himself) when
relations between "River" and "Bay" became strained and
Hooker accused him of maligning the new (John Winthrop, Jr.'s) colony.

—J. Winthrop, *Life and Letters,* II, 421.

ONLY WITH FULL CONSENT of the Indians did John Scott feel
he could legitimately acquire their property and, true child
of his century, he was reasonable enough to suppose that by
fair dealing and a friendly attempt to understand the native
viewpoint, he could attain his ends.

It was during the late 1650's that he began trading for
land. His knowledge of geography stood him in good stead:
he had travelled over Long Island, had sailed round it, studied
its topography, and he was, moreover, the trusted friend of
the tribe with sole right to sell it.

"He purchased a great tract of land from them,"[1] runs the
record, in reference to the transfer of the island's middle
section lying between the English and Dutch settlements.
". . . near one third of Long Island," wrote John in his
petition to Charles II in 1661.[2] And Governor Stuyvesant,

reporting to Their High Mightinesses, in Holland, mentions this same amount as having been bought by John Scott.

Numerous legal documents of the period give an idea of his holdings and when his estates were assessed by Governor Francis Lovelace, in 1669, even a cursory estimate revealed very considerable properties, with houses and land in Huntington, Setauket, Hempstead; also lands at Madans Neck, and "a great quantity of land lying betwixt Wading River and the Ould Mans."[3] He was obviously a recognized landowner, for the saintly Minister Hooker,* writing to John Davenport in Boston, March 1663, says: "I spent the forenoon with Winthrop, Thomson, (John) Scott of Long Island, in debating the business of the colony. . . ."[4]

In ten years he had come a very long way.

Wyandanch, John's friend, died in 1659, but this loss did not at first affect the latter's influence with the Montauks, for Quashawam, the late chief's widow, known as the "Sunk Squa," became inheritee and showed our young colonial a touching fidelity.

In a document of February 11th, 1663, signed with her mark and with the names of two English witnesses, the Sunk Squa called John Scott her "ancient and great friend" and gave him her power of attorney "irrevocably to examine and demand and sue" for all lands on Long Island and islands adjacent, bought and not paid for, belonging either to English or Dutch, and "sell all lands not already sold."[5] This deed was registered February 17th, 1663, with Henry Pierson, Southampton's Recorder, and was duly recognized. Within a short time, on February 27th, 1663, the town of Jamaica voted that their notaries, Nathaniel and Daniel Denton, "agree with Captain Scott to confirm our deeds of purchase from ye indeans."[6]

---

* Hooker came from Marfield, Leicester (B. 1586), and was a graduate of Emanuel College, Cambridge. It is said his influence in his Chelmsford (Essex) ministry "shone through the whole country." His teachings were known in Holland as well as England. He settled in Hartford, Connecticut, in 1636.

Not all towns, however, welcomed such examination and confirmation. Huntington, for instance, knowing that its purchase deed of 1653 had been signed only by a local chief, and did not bear the great Wyandanch's mark, refused to submit to the Sunk Squa's order. And at a Town Meeting the members voted that should Captain Scott demand to examine their title, he should not be allowed to do so unless he produced a commission from King Charles II; and that further, if he ordered the constable to call a Town Meeting for this purpose, the constable should disobey him.[7]

Huntington was claiming a little peninsula, Horse or Lloyd's Neck, believed to have been included in the original purchase, but which had subsequently been sold (1654) to a Samuel Mayo. Since Mayo obtained Wyandanch's confirmation (May 14th, 1658) and registered his title-deed in Massachusetts, September 1st, 1658,[8] Huntington feared its own claim to this section would not be recognized.

This was the dispute that John, acting for the Sunk Squa, went to adjust. As a matter of fact, litigation over these acres was to drag on for two hundred and twenty-five years; it became one of the most fully reported land-suits in New England. John's brief part in it hardly deserves the scorn of certain nineteenth century regional historians, particularly as the final verdict established the original Wyandanch boundary as *line of title* for *private* ownership.[9] (Appendix B.)

The Sunk Squa's agreement with Scott stood, however, until it was voided by Governor Richard Nicoll's new land rulings in May 1668.[10] But the old legal document shows the degree of friendship and trust between John and the Indians and explains in a measure the reason for the title by which he is generally known.

BIBLIOGRAPHICAL NOTES

1. Rawl. MSS., A 175, f 147. Dorothea Gotherson's letter to Samuel Pepys answering 13 specific questions.
2. *Hutch. Pap.*, II, 104.

3. Rawl. MSS., A 175, f 125.
4. *CSP. Col. Ser. Am. and W. I.*, 1661-68, No. 422.
5. S-ampton. *T.R.*, II, 37-38.
6. *Rec. of Jamaica*, LI., p. 28.
7. Hunt. *T.R.*, I, 58 (copied from original records, p. 43 in Court records).
8. *Hunt. T.R.*, I, 15.
9. *Ibid.*, 57.
10. *Early Col. Docs.* LI., p. 606.

CHAPTER X

JOHN'S EARLY SUCCESSES

"Not that I seek glory . . . to myself, for I am not so vain
as not to know my abilities are too low and do merit
rather your indulgence . . . but accept me if in order to
be of service I am willing to erect this pillar for the bearing
of my name, and I pray your forgiveness for this one point
of my ambition because it comes attended with all the
affection and duties which I owe my native country. . . ."

—John Scott, Preface to his *Histories*

JOHN SCOTT'S INTERESTS were not all in American real estate,
however profitable this turned out to be, and we must now
recapitulate the previous ten years to catch up on his personal
life and follow his steadily rising star. For he was making his
mark in other ways. His diversified talents found so much
fulfillment that his life falls into almost sharply separated
phases, each differing from the other, each presenting a new
facet of his restless sporadic brilliance, but given cohesion by
his consciousness of destiny and an abiding love for England.

Those early days of freedom in Long Island saw a succession of experiments. He hunted whales, traded in furs and his
irrepressible energy soon brought him in conflict with the
law. In the spring of 1654 he was involved in a prominent
slander action with Nathaniel Sylvester.

This wealthy Quaker shipping merchant had arrived in
grand style from England and had purchased a large estate on
Shelter Island, in Peconic Bay, bringing Negro slaves and the
finest building materials to create a show-place which he gen-

erously offered as an asylum for Quaker refugees. Here, in 1659, came Lawrence and Cassandra Southwick, broken and banished, to make their wills and to die almost immediately within three days of each other.

Quakers at this time were no more popular on Long Island than they were in Massachusetts, and it irked Sylvester that he was considered "subversive" and censured for entertaining "the cursèd sect." Being an outspoken hot-head he declared that the government acted tyrannically and if anyone meddled with him he would "pistoll them."[1] Scott must have been feeling very solid with the town authorities at this moment, for both he and John Youngs offended the pompous gentleman by commenting unfavorably on his statements and behavior, whereupon he brought a libel suit against them. They were not impressed. Youngs responded with a counter suit in which John may have proved a formidable witness. Sylvester apologized to the magistrates for his hasty words, dropped his action, and the men settled matters amicably among themselves, agreeing to drown all rancor "in ye lake of oblivion."[2]

The incident is revealing as far as John is concerned; lawsuits became his meat. He never thereafter overlooked an opportunity to prosecute, and in an age excessively prone to litigation, the number of his cases is notable, to the great good fortune of his biographers. But once he had won a judgment (and he was invariably successful), or his adversary had ackowledged his error and expressed regret, no one could be more sweetly reasonable than John. In consequence his legal battles did not detract from his local reputation.

In 1657, he was made a freeman of Southampton,[3] a sure indication that he was in good standing both with the Church and his fellow citizens, and "of peaceable and honest conversation" as the certificate reads. That same year he was appointed tax commissioner for Southampton, and, together with Henry Pierson, the Howells, and three others, chosen to establish the town rates and to register and tax cattle in

Northsea, Southampton's port on Peconic Bay in Long Island Sound. Here in 1658, he bought land and later built himself a handsome house.*[4]

People were beginning to notice this vivid young man, whose buccaneer swagger must have set him apart from the stolid farmers. And there was one who watched him more closely perhaps than all the others. Her name was Deborah, only daughter of Thurston Raynor, a prominent man of means (originally from Ipswich, England)[5] who had been magistrate in New Haven and Stamford, Connecticut, before coming to Southampton, where he enjoyed the prestige of those highly regarded positions, the first in the land.

As a very young girl, Deborah had been the victim of an unhappy experience. Wooed in 1650 by John Kelly, a young craftsman from the West Indies, she had discovered, after promising to marry him, that his former wife, whom he had declared dead and buried, was very much alive, merely "dead in sin," as Kelly airily explained, trying to excuse his unbecoming conduct. He assured Deborah that he would get a divorce, but she broke off the engagement, and he was unchivalrous enough (or so madly in love) as to pursue her with threats and warrants. When these failed, he tried to compel her to marry him by disparaging her fair name. Deborah's parents had no other recourse but to take the matter to court —the first breach of promise suit in New England. Kelly, after expressing his deepest regret for having distressed the maid, was fined £10 and, we must suppose, invited to leave town, since immediately afterwards his home lot came up for sale.[6]

It was a shattering ordeal for a young girl and for several

---

* Scott's Landing and Scott's (so-called) Cottage are still standing (1957). The house was moved from its original position on Scott's Road in the old whaling town to form the guest wing of Peter Salm's Northsea estate, *The Port of Missing Men*. The massive interior hand-hewn beams still show the original adze marks under the delicate eggshell blue paint; the six gabled second-floor windows looking east and west, the steeply sloping roof and heavy wrought-iron weathervane all belong to the date carved on the lintel, 1661.

years Deborah moped miserably at home. Then she met John, and he was like no other young man she had seen. There was allure in the set of his fine body; his "hot eyes" (as a contemporary recalls) were an exciting contrast to the colorless Kelly; and surely she had never listened to such a torrent of talk about so many different subjects.

Was it a love match on his part? From the distance of three centuries it is difficult to guess. She was undoubtedly a very good catch for John then, and, as far as any woman occupied a lasting role in that wanderer's life, Deborah held this position. Unquestionably it was she who inspired the poem he wrote, "To A Wife," whose opening verse somewhat wistfully foreshadows something of their future relationship, and maybe, reflected his own ideals and desires.[7]

> "Prudent and chaste, gentle, easy, kind,
> Much in his sight and ever in his mind;
> At home he leaves, at home he finds a wife,
> Sharer of all that's good, or bad, in life."

She would certainly have had to be very kind to overlook his many long absences from home. Indeed, but for that first unfortunate engagement, her father might never have consented to his daughter's marriage with a man probably younger than herself and only at the very beginning of his career. But married they were, in 1658, and almost immediately John bought the estate and horses of one Mark Meggs,[8] and was soon afterwards granted eight acres—not too far from his father-in-law's lot—on condition of living there three years and promising to build.

Father Raynor need have had little apprehension about John's ability to succeed. Within two years he was an attorney, conducting the town's affairs; and his legal debut was a typical example of his business aplomb.

Southampton's established lawyer was Josiah Stanborough, one of the town's founders. His name is on the first Southampton document for "setting forward" the plantation and undertaking to lay out its boundaries.

It was Stanborough who handled the Raynor case; and his name appears as one of the "perfect" freemen who had, in 1649, the authority to "give or let" any land that year.

And it was precisely Mr. Stanborough whom John Scott had the temerity to sue for trespass in September 1658.[9]

On a second occasion John appeared in court against Stanborough, this time with his own partners, brother-in-law Joseph Raynor, and young Richard Howell, son of that Edward Howell who was Stanborough's old colleague and one of the town's original planters.[10]

These legal proceedings ended, as did so many of John's suits, with everyone agreeing that all differences, "from the beginning of the world till this day" were to be forgotten.

What was Stanborough to think of this brash young man who so hotly rushed into law, and defended himself so volubly in court? The first impact of John's personality was invariably favorable. People liked him immediately, as many great men were to prove, and Stanborough seems to have succumbed to the Scott charm. Did he urge him to take up law and become his partner? It looks as if he did.

Josiah Stanborough came from Stanstead, in Kent, and he must have known something about the Scott background. Then he himself was a man of very vigorous action. In his early days the Court had censured him for resisting a constable, and a legal opponent had once offered to fight it out with his bare fists.[11] Perhaps he recognized a kindred spirit.

Or it is just possible that the trespass suits were prearranged. One certain way of determining ownership of land was to force a court decision about the precise extent of its boundaries. The remarkable number of John's suits for trespass suggests that that is exactly what he was doing—in this particular case perhaps with Stanborough's consent and approval.

By April 30th, 1660, John was listed as attorney handling

a suit for a whaling company, which he, true to form, consented to arbitrate.[12] The following month he and Stanborough together, for Southampton, sued Easthampton in a boundary quarrel, delivering their warrant and agreeing to appear at the General Court at Hartford, Connecticut,[13] where a preliminary agreement was reached, in a case destined to last for decades.

It was the age of land disputes. Not only Southampton and Easthampton were at law, but Southampton and Southold were in controversy over meadowlands which each claimed;[14] there were legal differences between Flatlands and Flatbush;[15] a lawsuit between Gravesend and Flatbush;[16] the list is unending.

More than half the entries of all the Court and Town Records in practically every Long Island town are concerned with the registration of land lots and legal proceedings over their boundaries. It was a golden age for attorneys, and judging from the record, John seems to have been in great demand: his rapid grasp of a situation, his ability to pack information into clear terse phrases, had people turning to him wherever legal troubles threatened. Not that this took all his time: he was "on with an old love" again, the sea.

He had become part owner of a sixty-ton ketch called the *Hopewell,* stoutly built in Salem and furnished with everything necessary, including guns, for a trip John intended making to Newfoundland. The price was one hundred and twenty-five pounds sterling, a goodly amount, but John made a down payment of £75, and went to Boston to pick up his treasure and sail it back to Southampton.[17]

To a former privateer the possibilities of coastal trading were endlessly rewarding, especially with people who "had neither license nor ability to launch out at sea," as the Connecticut archives reveal.[18] Back and forth across the Sound among the English, Dutch, and Indians John drove a thriving business, carrying biscuits, beef, pipe-staves, livestock; within a few months (March 1659/60) he paid two Dutchmen outright for their sloop, the *Fleur de Luce* which he kept riding at port in Northsea.[19] A frigate belonging to him was reported in New Haven in 1660. Doubtless it was during these sailing days that he began making mental notes for the great New England map which is now among early colonial treasures in the British Museum.[20]

With a wife, land and houses, ships, legal status, John might feel justly established and well on the way to solid success. There was a little John Scott, too, born during those first years of marriage. There is no birth registration, of course, but the grant of a parcel of land to him, recorded in 1679, indicates that he was over eighteen at that date, and could legally take up his share of "the great division of land, formerly belonging to his father."[21]

Everything pointed to a distinguished honorable career for the Salem former bound boy. His friends were among the town's leading men; he was associated in community work with Henry Pierson, son of the Very Reverend Pastor Pierson;[22] and with the old planters, Edward and Richard Howell, Southampton's founders.[23] He was Josiah Stanborough's law partner; a co-magistrate with Richard Woodhull—one of the most esteemed surveyors of the period and a valuable real estate dealer.[24] And from his early days as privateer he had kept a military rank, for in many legal documents he is referred to as Captain John Scott, Esq.[25] There was a compelling something in him which made men listen to him, and his awareness of this characteristic did not detract from its effectiveness. Speaking impersonally of himself he once remarked that it was his good fortune to "prevail upon men." He never came into a coffee house if there were a hundred in the room but "that they all flocked about him to hear him discourse; he could impose anything upon them."[26]

Others were quick to recognize and try to profit by this quality. For when the news reached New England of King Charles' glorious Restoration with its promise of settled government after years of civil disturbance, each colony looked about for a representative to send to England to promote its interests and enlarge its charter.

From Massachusetts went Samuel Maverick; from Rhode Island, Mr. Clarke and George Baxter; from Connecticut went Governor John Winthrop; and, unofficially, from Long Island, went Captain John Scott. Not quite unofficially, either. Before he left, he was entrusted with a mission by the Atherton Land Company, an ambitious project of a group of Massachusetts and Connecticut merchants for establishing a new colony on territory acquired from the Narragansett Indians.[27]

When John sailed for London on the *Oak Tree* in October 1660, he had behind him men of the caliber of Simon Bradstreet, John Winthrop, Jr., Edward Hutchinson, Emmanuel Downing—all Atherton Company members.[28] And their hopes in him must have been equally high, for John Winthrop subsequently wrote to Connecticut's Deputy-Governor, John Mason: "The proprietors about Narragansett have taken a good way, by empowering Captain Scott to petition His Majesty for continuance within your patent . . ."[29]

BIBLIOGRAPHICAL NOTES

1. Hoadley, *Rec. N. Hav.*, pp. 92-93.
2. *Ibid.*, pp. 78, 89, 94, 364.
3. Howell, *Hist. of S-ampton*, p. 384.
4. S-ampton *T. R.*, I, 118, 36 (or 49 in original records at S-ampton).
5. *Ibid.*, 136.
6. *Ibid.*, 61-63; 79, 138.
7. Rawl. MSS., A 176, f 79.
8. S-ampton *T.R.*, I, 120.
9. *Ibid.*, 121, 148.
10. *Ibid.*, 121.
11. *Ibid.*, 40.
12. *Ibid.*, II, 2.
13. *Ibid.*, 3.
14. *Early Col. Docs.*, L. I., p. 599.
15. *Ibid.*, p. 586.
16. *Ibid.*, p. 588.

17. S-hold *T.R.*, I, 214-15.
18. Conn. Arch. For. Corr., No. 21.
19. S-hold *T.R.*, p. 472; *NY. Col. Docs.*, XIV, 459.
20. Add MSS., 5414, f 21.
21. S-ampton *T.R.*, II, 73.
22. *Ibid.*, I, 118; II, 37-38.
23. *Ibid.*, I, 121.
24. Br-haven *T.R.* (1880 ed.), I, 8 (1924 ed), I, 75; Thompson *Long Island*, I, 398.
25. Br-haven *T.R.* (1880 ed.), I, 8.
26. Morn. MS., Joyne's Journal I, ff 315-16.
27. O'Callaghan, *Hist. of N.Y.*, p. 49; Leonard, *Hist. of N.Y.*, p. 90.
28. Conn. Arch. MS., I, f 326.
29. *Mass. Hist. Soc. Coll.*, 5th ser., VIII, 77 (*Winthrop Papers*).

CHAPTER XI

RESTORATION ENGLAND

"I have not so much money in my purse as when I came to you . . . nor have I been able to give my brother one shilling since I came into England, nor to keep any Table in My House, but what I eat myself; and that which troubles me most is to see many of you come to Me at Whitehall and to think that you must go somewhere else to seek your Dinner."

—His Majestie's Gracious Speech to Both Houses of Parliament Aug. 29, 1660.

Captain John Scott was just twenty-eight when he sailed from America, "a proper handsome person" as a contemporary wrote, full of lusty life and ambition. And what more likely opportunity for new success than Restoration London, where the citizens were madly elated at the return of Charles II?

With the King back on his throne, his good subjects were not only revelling again in the pageantry and glitter dear to their hearts. They fondly imagined that, in the King's person, they would recapture Merry England's happier days so that the luxury trades, dead these twenty years, and the stagnating shipping and national industries would revive, and haul them out of the economic depression the Puritans left behind them.

To these native optimists were added all the returning Cavaliers who by every boat and along every highway came flocking to the capital, eager for compensation, convinced that their Monarch would honor his obligations, and delighted by the pomp and royal trappings to which Charles submitted in the time-consuming business of holding open court. For John, whose London memories were surely quenched by colonial austerity, the scene must have ravished the eye.

The old palace of Whitehall was practically a town in itself. Sprawling for nearly half a mile along the Thames banks, its timbered walls rose in a medley of architectural styles enclosing suites of formal chambers and apartments, halls, courtyards, terraces, linked by winding corridors and overlooking well-spaced gardens, bowling greens and tennis courts. Great gateways led down to the water and commanded the entrance to the chief banqueting hall. For this was not only the royal dwelling place. It housed the King's Ministers of State, his courtiers, chaplains, ladies, and musicians, all his footmen and personal servants.

Center of the court diversion was the long stone gallery running the length of the Privy Garden. Soft lights illuminated its painted ceiling, and the damasked walls hung with priceless pictures Charles I had loved to collect and which his son had piously reassembled. Dancing flames from the massive fireplaces drew glowing color from the assembled throng. Above the stir and gossip was the music of the King's fiddlers, brought back by their royal master from his travels abroad.

Every day the velvet curtains before the Private Apartments were flung wide and His Majesty came striding through the gallery, followed by his Ministers, and suppliants from the Royal Bedchamber or Council Room. This was the great moment to attract the royal eye and gain access to the royal ear, and those who sought favors became regular attendants at these gatherings.

John found the stately routine made to his requirements. As agent for the Atherton Company he procured the right introductions, bought himself elegant clothes, and for the first time fitted a great light-colored curling wig over his own brown locks. Then, confident and splendid, he made himself a frequent Whitehall visitor. His appraising eye immediately grasped the possibilities of rewarding encounter. In this court of youth he noted that a certain young man was invariably at the King's side. This was Thomas Chiffinch, Keeper of the Royal Jewels, and one of the pages of the King's Bedchamber.

From all the English squires of good family, Thomas Chiffinch had been chosen and brought to Court by Brian Duppa, Bishop of Salisbury, the Prince of Wales' tutor, a man zealously careful of the character of those serving the Prince. Thomas had followed his young master into exile, shared the hardships and humiliations of those bitter years on the continent, and returned to enjoy the Restoration triumph. He was a man of absolute integrity, enjoying the highest regard at Court, and so beloved by Charles II that the King would visit the youthful Chiffinch ménage in St. James's Park and dine with them alone.

It was natural that John should gravitate to Thomas. The Chiffinch family place was at Staplehurst, not twenty miles from Smeeth and Ashford; it was a manor ancient as those of the Scotts;* the name of Staplehurst, and its inhabitants, figure in the household accounts which Sir John Scotte kept for King Edward IV in 1464.[1] No Scott of Scot's Hall could be a stranger to a Chiffinch.

Then, too, as reward for his devotion, Thomas had been given a position in the Excise—the Customs Office—and was to become the Receiver-General of all the revenues from Foreign Plantations.[2] So what more likely than that he should be interested in colonies and this attractive young colonial?

For the confusion of historians there were two Chiffinches —brothers. When Thomas died tragically in 1666, literally from one hour to the next, surely a Plague victim, the whole Court mourned his loss, and the King was inconsolable. Then Thomas' brother William was appointed to fill his place. William was a man of a very different stripe. A libertine,

---

* Staplehurst was in the Hundred of Twyford and was fief of Pympe and Nettlested, both Scott properties. (*Vill. Cant.*, p. 304)

pimp, and obsequious time-server, delighting in dubious intrigue, he brought to his vicious back-stairs influence an almost scientific perfection.

John Scott never had any dealings with this unsavory character; indeed, William Chiffinch had no influence to peddle
until 1667, when John had left London. But he surely knew
about him. And John's oft-quoted letter to Secretary Williamson,
written in 1663 from New England, probably meant
exactly what it said, and was neither polite turn of phrase,
nor cynical flattery when it included his services to "noble
Mr. Chiffinch."[3] Contemporary readers were in no doubt as
to which Chiffinch he meant.*

John could have had no better entrée to Court than
Thomas. It could have been the latter who passed him on to
Joseph Williamson (secretary, then, to Sir Henry Bennet, who
subsequently became Lord Arlington, Secretary of State).
Williamson was an important figure on the newly created
Council of Foreign Plantations, a fact-finding board expressly
designed to deal with overseas possessions. A first-hand report
on the colonies—even the brash, uninhibited details that John
first furnished—was of immense value to a man like Williamson,
whose meticulously compiled notebooks reveal how
much he came to learn about affairs across the seas.

Williamson took to John from the first, and presented him
to Bennet, who never forgot him, and on numerous occasions
was very helpful to him. John maintained this important connection all his life, and on a footing of singular intimacy. For
some of his longer dispatches (1671-72)—there are about forty
of these in the Public Record Office—are addressed to Sir
Joseph, when he had finally become Secretary of State himself, and are signed "yours most affectionately" or "yours
fondly" in John's unmistakable handwriting.[4]

With Chiffinch and Williamson as his patrons at Court,

---

* This letter is calendared among the Colonial Office Papers as "services
to Thomas Chiffinch." *Col. pap.,* XVII, 102.

John felt emboldened to put in a petition on his own account. With due formality, he presented his plea to the King, asking that in recognition of his father's services to Charles I, and of his own efforts as a child in the royal cause, there be bestowed upon him the governorship of Long Island, where he owned considerable land.[5] Or, at least (for John was always reasonable, and, in his own peculiar manner, modest), that the inhabitants of this Island be allowed to choose their governor and assistants annually. Not for nothing had John lived within sight and knowledge of those who clung too long in office, to the detriment of other likely candidates.

No answer to the petition was immediately forthcoming; Whitehall was besieged with supplicants. All requests had to be sifted and probed, the worthless eliminated, the authentic encouraged, the lucky rewarded. Clearly, it was impossible for Charles to satisfy everybody. He had inherited a staggering burden of debt, and the national coffers, when he had finally come into his long delayed inheritance, were hopelessly inadequate to provide for his country's needs.

Of this, John had little inkling in 1660. He was elated at the thought of a possible governorship, and may have dreamed of being founding father of the fourteenth original North American colony. Besides, fortune was smiling upon him in a very special manner in the person of a beautiful, remarkable woman, Dorothea Scott, great-granddaughter of Sir Reginald Scott, and heiress of Scot's Hall.

Dorothea, after a lively Royalist girlhood, had become a dedicated Quaker, marrying one of Oliver Cromwell's stern-faced officers, Major Daniel Gotherson. With typical Scott aplomb, she preached regularly in a hermitage between two Kentish breweries, where "Scott's Congregation," as it was called, listened to her religious improvisations with awed delight. She had published a book of spiritual experience, *A Call to Repentance,* and this she presented to the King when she went to Court to congratulate him on his Restoration. Charles never overlooked a beauty, no matter what her religion.* And amused perhaps by the book's dedication which bade him, in round Quaker terms, "O King, take heed to it as to a light shining in a dark place," he detained her in conversation, and witnessed an encounter that she herself described afterwards in a letter to Governor Lovelace: "Being at Whitehall with the King, in whose presence was John Scott, who told me his name was Scott and that he was of the family of the Scotts of Scot's Hall, which I was ready to believe because some of our ancestor's pictures were very like him."[6]

John indeed carried his heritage in his face and figure— the handsome lines, the lithe upright carriage, maintained to the last, for the Scotts were a well-favored family. His features were clear-cut, the eyes deep-set "having large hair on the eyebrows" as one admirer wrote. "He hath a very hot look," said another. The pupil of one eye was slightly larger than the other with a golden fleck in its liquid depths giving him an almost insolent stare. Women apparently found this irresistible, although on one occasion he had real cause to regret it for he was mistaken for a "wanted" man known to be marked by a squint!

Now began one of the happiest periods in John's life. Openly acknowledging the kinship, the Gothersons took him to live with them at Hunsden House, in London, and at their Godmersham place in Egerton, Kent, for "greate part a year" as Dorothea wrote,[7] giving John the advantage of a good background from which to conduct the various affairs that had brought him to England. The warmth of his high spirits, plus an innate seriousness, seem to have beguiled them, and

---

* As it is highly improbable that there should have been *two* pretty Quakers at the same time at Court, we can assume that Dorothea was the one mentioned by Pepys in his Diary (January 11th, 1664), to whom the King teasingly remarked that her quaking religion would be admirably suited to his old courtier, Sir John Mennes, as his beard was the stiffest thing about him, and that if her desires were as long as the petition she carried, she might well lose them.

for the first time, after so long, he must have had the sensation of "belonging" again.

The "thees" and "thous" fell trippingly from his tongue. The Quaker jargon of his lonely boyhood was paying magical dividends; and Dorothea's probing interest in the good of his soul seemed all only too familiar, though with what sweet difference from the bleak austerities of the Southwick household.

Gotherson's interest in "his loving kinsman," as he called John, had its practical side, for the old man was a Long Island landowner himself. He had bought two townships in Oyster Bay in August 1633 through the agency of John Richbell, who disposed of land there and was one of the island's foremost merchants, handling property and produce for New Englanders and Englishmen alike.[8]

Gotherson never profited by this investment, and his lots were later seized and sold for debts he had incurred with his bailiff, Mathew Prior.[9] But listening to John's glowing accounts of New World prosperity, he seems to have forgotten the ill luck which had hounded all his business ventures.

Daniel Gotherson was an unsuccessful merchant (even heiresses during the Civil War had little choice of husbands). He had made an unfortunate loan at one time to Thomas Scott the Regicide (no relation), £300 of which, if he ever got it back, was earmarked for agent Richbell to settle some of his Long Island obligations. Gotherson had been declared a bankrupt in 1650, and even when John appeared on the scene could not have been very prosperous, for he was borrowing small sums of money[10] and had just taken a little government job, furnishing secret information about Kentish Quakers and other suspicious dissenters; i.e., he was reduced to spying upon his co-religionists. He was also keeping a wench on the sly in Kent—a widow Rogers—but Dorothea packed her off to Oyster Bay, together with the illegitimate child.[11] All of which did not prevent his publishing a book of pious epistles (printed in London by James Cottrel, 1662) in which he exhorted his readers to "see their durty Dregs, and repent their abominations."

Sustained by self-righteousness, in due time he felt ready to risk another speculation and buy land through John. Being a declared bankrupt he had to be wary about acknowledging any extensive purchase, lest he be suspected of disposing of hidden assets. The deed drawn up between the two reflects a nice sense of legal caution. For this much-discussed document reads:

> "I, John Scott, of Ashford, on Long Island . . . do author-ize Daniel Gotherson . . . my true and lawful attorney for me . . . and in my name and for my use to treat for (i.e., acquire the English title) 20,000 acres . . . on the south side of Long Island and between . . . etc. etc. and there-upon to conclude for such sum of money as he in his prudence shall think a fit consideration for ye whole or any part of the said 20,000 acres so sold.*
>
> Signed, John Scott"[12]

But the fate of this, and another sales agreement, is bound up with John's career in a way we must now consider. For calendared among the state papers of 1665, is Dorothea's peti-tion to the English courts which shows Gotherson's ill-luck pursued him to the end:

> "Dorothea Scott, widow of Daniel Gotherson, heir to the younger house of Scot's Hall, Kent; For an order to Francis Lovelace, deputy-governor of Long Island, to consider whether she has any claim to certain land there for which her husband disbursed £2,000 to John Scott, but *thereby dying*

---

* According to the exhaustive findings of the historian, Henry Edward Scott, editor emeritus of the N.E. Historical Genealogical Society, Boston, he considers this power of attorney is to *sell* land, not to *buy* it, Pepys' endorse-ment notwithstanding. The document is printed incorrectly by G. D. Scull (in his *Dorothea Scott-Gotherson-Hogben*, p. 58), and it is *not*, as Scull asserts, in John's handwriting. Scull also confuses the seal—the Scott arms on the sinister half of the shield, empaling Gotherson and Scott—not Scott and Tuke, as Scull says. H. E. Scott's papers, N.E. His. Gen. Library, Boston. Package 4.

in debt his lands are taken, and though she brought him an estate of £500 a year, she and her six children are reduced to work for their bread."[13] (Italics added.)

John was in the West Indies when this happened. He did not learn about it till much later when he renewed an affectionate correspondence from Holland. The two were not to see each other again till they met in London in 1678, and the old friendship was resumed. Whether John ever got that two thousand pounds for the land is problematic. Gotherson, his wife said, died six thousand pounds in debt, so that it seems improbable that he could have raised any large sum in cash so shortly before his death. Governor Lovelace testified that Scott was paid *"in money and jewels"*[14] and that the latter, according to Dorothea, whose trinkets they were, were worth £200. If he received anything more is doubtful. (Italics added.)

Lovelace also located some of the land involved. "But Colonel (Governor) Nicolls interposed and said the case could not, in his time, be examined," wrote Dorothea in her formal plea for assistance.[15] Lovelace advised her to petition the King. It was some years before she got around to doing this, and then it was the Duke of York, not Charles II, who accorded her a hearing. He turned the matter over to the Admiralty, where it eventually came to Samuel Pepys' notice. And by that time Pepys had a case to prove!

Thomas Lovelace (brother of Francis), now governor, handled the investigation not too willingly, and reported to Pepys in 1680. "In all Long Island there is no such town as Ashford, notwithstanding the mention made thereof by Scott," he wrote, quick to impute fraud.* What he failed to mention, or did not know, was that all John's land had been confiscated, and that moreover, there had been a major crisis

---

* Ashford, originally called Cromwell's Bay, was successively thereafter named Setauket and Brookhaven. It was mentioned as Ashford in the first meeting of the eight magistrates.

in the island's land tenure in 1666. At that date the new Duke's Laws were enforced and property owners were required to repurchase their title-deeds, or lose their estates by default. Many a man lost his home-lot and the courts were filled with angry claimants.

But what most harmed Dorothea's chances of recovering her property was the fact that Thomas Lovelace was himself petitioning the King for the return of his own land on Staten Island, also seized for debt.[16] And it is understandable that he would not jeopardize his own chances by pushing very vigorously a similar case.

But all this only came out much later. At the time of John's first visit to England, private land deals were not his chief interest. He had far greater irons in the fire. He was officially negotiating for recognition of the Narragansett territories whose ownership was being disputed by Connecticut, Massachusetts, and the Rhode Island colony. And foremost, of course, was his own petition to be Long Island's governor.

Acquaintance with Williamson had opened his eyes to the vast colonial organization going on under Clarendon's Foreign Plantations Council and encouraged his hopes of profiting by this redistribution of titles and property. With a prospective governship pending, he did his best to promote interest in Long Island (Appendix C), a place about which the Court seemed to know very little. Indeed, nothing was more paradoxical in this budding imperial age than its almost complete ignorance of geography. Maps were rarities studied by few, and even the informed public did not know where overseas possessions lay or cared much about that great European population, mostly English, which existed outside of Europe.

But while John was talking up Long Island to his friends, he himself was acquiring a new viewpoint. He was too astute not to be affected by Whitehall's attitude, and, English royalist at heart, he may well have sympathized with much that he heard discussed. From words and hints dropped by Chiffinch and others as they paced the Long Gallery together, he began to understand how the Foreign Plantations Committee would affect New England. Its advice and decisions would tighten bonds with the mother country and formalize relations which had been previously handled somewhat casually, and which Massachusetts already had been increasingly slighting.

Cromwell had interfered little in colonial civil affairs, but he looked upon New Englanders as constituting the Puritan garrison in America. Balked at home in his desire to maintain a standing army, he turned overseas to those men of "proven metal." To the colonies he sold his Scottish prisoners,[17] and at one time was ready to remove all the Irish—en bloc—to his newly acquired Jamaica and repopulate Ireland with staunch Massachusetts Protestants![18]

Charles II had a far greater understanding of men and their needs. He handled colonial affairs with a warmth of heart and prodigality which astonished New England agents when they came to London on charter business. Full of misgivings and suspicion, they had been well received, accorded several hearings before the Privy Council and finally granted very liberal charters. Only later did they experience the sterner Stuart policy.

The British colonial system, as John was to learn in his early days at court, involved more than just trade and commerce—namely, politics!

And although after the Restoration these functioned mainly through the Navigation Acts, English officials and Colonial Boards were beginning to provide the machinery through which colonial control was to be both maintained and tightened.

In America John could hardly have been aware of this. Colonists were too close to their own affairs to realize they were members of an empire and involved with the rest of the world despite themselves.

When the men of Massachusetts issued writs in their own

name, coined their own money, exercised arbitrary power and forbade appeals to the Crown, they were overlooking a far-reaching consequence. For once France or Holland became convinced that England would not intervene to protect an independent area, French and Dutch settlers might easily be tempted to invade it.

This much John, in London, could realize. And his viewpoint about Long Island local friction must have certainly undergone change as well. The constant boundary disputes between Dutch and English towns at its Western end would now be clearly recognized as an extension of general Anglo-Dutch rivalry. Desperate as these incidents seemed over there, they were but a small part of a much graver international situation, to be remedied only by international action.

His stories at Court, therefore, of Dutch encroachments and depredations took on political overtones lacking at home. His racy accounts of the West India Company's vast profits from smuggling, its contraband tobacco trade with Virginia and Maryland—all at England's expense—went beyond travellers' tales of picturesque and far-off happenings, and must have impressed certain authorities with his knowledge of what was really going on.

For the Foreign Plantations Council sent him back to America, on an official assignment to warn the Dutch they should live quietly and not injure the English. His mission was duly noted in Sir George Downing's correspondence,[19] and was the subject of a report Governor Stuyvesant sent Their High Mightinesses in Holland.[20] Rumor already had it that John had been made Long Island governor, and Stuyvesant was loud in his lamentations about English designs on New Netherland.[21]

BIBLIOGRAPHICAL NOTES

1. *Arch. Cant.,* I, 250-58.
2. Egerton MS., 2395, f 370.
3. *N.Y. Col. Docs.,* III, 48.

4. S.P. Fl. 77/41, f 65; ff 151-52; *passim*.
5. *Hutch. Pap.*, II, 104.
6. Rawl. MSS., A 175, f 147.
7. *Ibid*.
8. *Oy. Bay T.R.*, I (appendix), 684-85; Book A, 42.
9. *Ibid*.
10. G. D. Scull, *Dorothea Scott otherwise Gotherson-Hogben*, p. 56.
11. Rawl. MSS., A 175, f 123.
12. *Ibid.*, ff 128, 129, 131-35, 136-37.
13. *CSP. Dom.*, 1664-65, No. 98.
14. Rawl. MSS., A 175, f 119.
15. *Ibid.*, f 144.
16. *Ibid.*, f 120; Rawl. MSS., A 173, f 185.
17. *Mass. Hist. Soc. Pro.*, LXI, 4, 29.
18. Harlow, *Barbados*, pp. 106-7, 112, 116.
19. *N.Y. Col. Docs.*, II, 334.
20. *Ibid.*, XIV, 506.
21. O'Callaghan, *Cal. Hist. MSS.*, I, 296.

CHAPTER XII

MASSACHUSETTS' SECRET AGENT?

> ". . . in the same year that the Bay lost her charter John
> Winthrop gained one for Connecticut, giving her self-
> government on the Massachusetts model, gobbling up
> New Haven, and extending her boundaries west to Lake
> Erie and the Mississippi. Probably the £500 that Con-
> necticut appropriated for the 'expenses' of the Winthrop
> mission were also of some assistance."
>
> —S. E. Morison, *Builders of the Bay Colony*,
> p. 284.

JOHN'S RETURN TO THE NEW WORLD in his quasi-official role
was something of a triumph. He was made much of in Boston
and was entertained by Council members, to whom he
boasted of his favor at Court. Wearing his fine new clothes
and with a gold medallion of the King on a golden chain
round his neck, he regaled his listeners with tales of his adventures, of what My Lord Chancellor had said, and what
intimate matters concerning New England had been discussed
in his presence.

Long Islanders had heard the rumors of his promotion to
governor, and not a few were irked by all this sudden recognition, and wrote spiteful letters about his self-important airs.
Power, it is true, lent an additional swagger to his self-confidence, and he was quick to assert the King's authority bestowed on him. Writing to the Southampton magistrates
(Captain Youngs and John Ogden, November 27th, 1662) he
declared: "Whereas His Honored Majesty Charles II our

dreade sovereign hath invested me with power to command both affairs and others, for any affairs that I have occasion to transact: by virtue of which power and in His Majesty's name, I demand the procuring of the body of John Cooper . . ."[1] Cooper, apparently, had uttered derogatory expressions about Charles I "of blessed memory" and also about Charles II "in whose name, I, John Scott, do promise to prosecute said John Cooper on a charge of high treason . . ."[2]

In England, words spoken against the Throne were, in sober truth, treason punishable by death. It would have been hard to make such an accusation stick in easy-going Long Island, but, inflamed with his new ardor, John Scott seemed trying to do just this.

He did not have much time to ruffle around and exercise authority, however, since he was recalled to London: "having strick Command from the Kinge to return with all speede," as one of the correspondents recounted.[3]

It is just possible that John returned to England with a secret understanding to keep Boston informed about matters under discussion in English administrative circles. According to the historian Chalmers, the General Court had frequently "approached" the King's ministers and subsidized certain Privy Council clerks in order to learn state secrets or to obtain, surreptitiously, documents before they were made public.*[4]

John certainly carried back with him very explicit instructions on kindred matters, and was, probably on this occasion, Massachusetts' agent. So altogether it was a very different man who appeared at Whitehall on his second visit. His confidence was also bolstered by Chiffinch's whispered information that his petition had been accepted. For within a few

---

* A committee for this very purpose had been appointed and empowered to employ "some friend" in England "for the improvement of our information" and "to give us the best advice how our affairs stand there . . . the charges for such a service to be paid out of the public Treasury." *Mass. Rec.*, IV, prt. 2, 101.

months he was notified officially by State Secretary Henry Bennet, that "His Majesty had received good testimony of his loyalty and great sufferings . . . and was fully satisfied of his particular abilities to serve him and was most graciously inclined to encourage his desires."[5]

His suit, however, was to be referred to the Foreign Plantations Committee which would examine what other claims or grants (if any) existed, that the King might take the right course both in "gratifying the petitioner and respecting the good of his other subjects."

This was a distinct blow, for another claimant to Long Island did exist. This was none other than Connecticut's governor John Winthrop, who was in London again when John returned and who had just obtained a charter for Connecticut, a charter whose extensive boundaries he himself had somewhat artfully defined, for they included "the islands thereunto adjoining." Did this mean the numerous little offshore islands in the Sound, or did it refer to densely populated Long Island itself, lying the whole length of his southern shore? If John's petition were to be granted, more particularly if Long Island's inhabitants were to be permitted to elect their governor annually, it could prove a sad day for John Winthrop, who had held continuous office in Massachusetts for eighteen years before becoming Connecticut's governor in 1659, a post he clung to uninterruptedly until 1676 (brushing aside rules against successive gubernatorial terms).[6] One can imagine what he had to say when John's petition became known!

Winthrop's warnings to the King were hardly necessary, however. Between a mature administrator of proven experience, and a flamboyant young man with a golden tongue, there could be only one choice. Little as Charles II loved Puritans, his inherent good statesmanship counselled against creating another small state; his policy was to consolidate, not diffuse, power. So John's petition to govern Long Island was refused.

Since the ambitions of John Scott were destined to clash with those of John Winthrop, a glance at this "Puritan of Puritans," as he was called, is not without interest. His portrait* shows a man of unusual nobility of countenance, with the long Winthrop nose accentuating a long face and neck framed in dark hair cut harshly across the forehead and falling uncurled to his shoulders. His almond-shaped eyes under heavy brows show warmth; a drooping mustache almost hides the upper lip; the lower is unexpectedly full and somewhat peevish. There is great intelligence and hypersensitivity in his expression. There is vanity as well, an aspect that the exaggerated flourishes of his signature seem to confirm.

He had a great deal to be vain about; his life was one long calm assumption of power.

Born at Groton, Suffolk, in 1605, he was educated at Trinity College in Dublin, where he lived a while with his uncle, Emmanuel Downing. He was an experienced traveller before he joined his father in the New World, where he was elected Assistant to the General Court, and founded the town of Ipswich.

From his early boyhood his father had entrusted him with the heaviest responsibilities, giving him an assurance and authority which amounted almost to a sense of infallibility.

On one of his return trips to London, old family friends, Lord Saye and Sele, and Lord Brooke, undertook to furnish men, money and supplies for a plantation along the Connecticut River. Young Winthrop, following the pioneer settlers in 1639, was appointed governor for one year. From a wilderness of rocks and stunted trees, he helped settle the towns of New London and Groton, planting his own orchard and building himself a fine stone house, but spending much of his time commuting between the two states. It was not until 1658 that he relinquished his Massachusetts offices and lived permanently in Connecticut.

---

* Painted in England about this period and owned by Grenville T. Winthrop, Esq.

He was a good governor, despite complaints of "authority too long held"; his rule was milder than that in other colonies where the rigorous Mosaic law prevailed. But, like so many early colonials, Winthrop was possessed with the lust for land. He managed to acquire an unusually large assortment of estates for himself, and all his life pursued an aggressive policy to extend his state boundaries.*

His hold on Connecticut was precarious, and he knew that he did not own the land he governed.† It was this anomalous position that Winthrop had hastened to London to correct, begging the assistance of Lord Saye and Sele, to whom he wrote that "the colony had as yet not so much as the copy of a patent."[7] The word inspired the remedy, for to Charles II he told another story. He begged the King for a *"renewal* of his patent, since the original was lost in a fatal fire at Saybrook, and the duplicate was lost among the papers and cargoes beyond the sea during the late civil troubles."‡[8]

Historians agree that this was "an uncomely lie." But for the virtuous Winthrop all was condoned and forgotten in the enthusiasm over the eventual success of his mission. His

---

* "The story of Connecticut's land claims is neither a simple nor an inviting subject to deal with. It begins with the extent of land mentioned in the draft of the Warwick patent . . . asking for nothing west of the Connecticut River. But in the deed granted . . . was territory running one hundred and twenty miles along the coast and west to the south sea . . . How are we to account for this extraordinary discrepancy, and who was responsible for it?" C. M. Andrews. *Col. Per. of Am. Hist.*, II, 140.

The Committee of the Privy Council said that "King Charles II was surprised in his grant to Connecticut as to the boundaries." *Acts Privy Council Col.*, III, 14.

John Winthrop Jr. was finally made to promise "not to intermeddle with any town" already established. *Mass. His. Soc. Coll.*, 3rd ser, II, 9.

† The Earl of Warwick, who had first conveyed it to Lord Saye and Sele, had never received a patent for it. The Records of the early New England Council show that it had never passed the seals, and was therefore invalid. S. F. Haven, *History of Grants*, pp. 22-24, *Conn. Pub. Rec.*, II, 403-04.

‡ Even C. M. Andrews admits that this "is a strange document to bear the signature of John Winthrop Jr. . . . it contains what Winthrop must have known was not an accurate rendering of the facts. . . ." *Col. Per. Am. Hist.*, II, 132 n. It is very significant that John Scott hoarded a copy of this Winthrop letter among his private papers. (Rawl., Mss. A 176 f 113.) We can well imagine what *he* thought of it!

charter, which he himself had drafted, was more liberal than
anyone had thought Charles would grant: it made Connecticut virtually independent. Its boundaries were extended to
the east as far as Narragansett Bay, taking in some of the
Providence Plantations of Rhode Island; its northern borders
went to the south line of Massachusetts (thereby swallowing
parts of New Netherland); on the west it reached to the
Pacific Ocean (at that time believed to be much closer than
it is); while its southern limits annexed all of New Haven
and reached a line which Winthrop interpreted as including
Long Island.

It is highly probable that the King, in enlarging and
strengthening this smaller colony, hoped to provoke a little
healthy New England rivalry and thereby curb the formidable insubordination of Massachusetts. This was quite in
line with Clarendon's policy of overlapping frontiers. In this
particular case, however, royal favor was also won in no small
measure by the Connecticut governor's astute gift of a valuable ring, the same which Charles I had once presented to
Winthrop's father. The youthful monarch's filial devotion
was a very well known fact, and Winthrop Junior showed
nice feeling (and considerable political perspicacity) in returning to Charles II the royal memento.

He lingered a year in London, resting on his laurels and
working hard to placate John Clarke (Rhode Island's agent
for the Providence Plantations), who had strenuously opposed
Winthrop's inclusion of the Narragansett Country in his new
charter. Unlike the suave governor, and lacking the latter's
powerful contacts, John Clarke ignored diplomatic manners;
and during an audience with Chancellor Clarendon vilified
Winthrop to his face for "injuriously swallowing up the one
half of our Colonie." John Scott, who was professionally interested in the Narragansett lands, had been a spectator of
this regrettable scene and reported it with gusto on that first
return trip to America, revealing that the Lord Chancellor
had publicly rebuked Clarke, asking him if he were not

ashamed of his impudence and marveling at Winthrop's patience and restraint.[9] When it came to hectoring, John himself was not to be outdone and he added his own fuel to the Narragansett controversy by "taking a very threatening tone with the governor of Rhode Island."[10]

The territory in question, stretching between the Pawcatuck River and Narragansett Bay, was actually included in the charters of both Rhode Island and Connecticut (a further example of Clarendon's tricky colonial policy), and it contained the area the Atherton Land Company planned to develop.

That old Indian campaigner, Major Atherton, had originally obtained two tracts of land adjoining the Bay for himself and John Winthrop, Jr., buying from the Sachem Scuttup in 1659 "when no English pretended any title thereunto." This grant was duly confirmed by the Massachusetts Court,[11] and John Scott was taken into the Atherton Company almost from its inception. In October of 1660, just before he sailed the first time for England, he signed an agreement with Humphrey Atherton, Thomas Stanton and eleven members, that in the event of the Narragansett land being officially recognized as theirs they would not sell nor share any part until it was first offered to the Company *as a whole* at such a price "as indifferent men shall judge." (With a note, especially added by John, that the Indians be treated courteously.)[12]

The original Atherton area was vastly extended, however, after that. In 1661 the United Colonies, to punish the Narragansett Indians for killing some Englishmen, fined them 735 fathoms of wampum (which was legal tender). John Winthrop acknowledged the receipt of a small part of this sum, covering the transfer charges,[13] but to pay the balance the native chiefs executed a mortgage deed with the Atherton Company. They agreed that unless they paid Connecticut's governor the remaining 595 fathoms within four months they would forfeit to the Company their whole country![14] This technique of fine, mortgage and foreclosure was no unusual procedure for taking land from the savages, although not often practised on such an extensive scale, nor by such high authorities. In this case the sum—paid in full to Winthrop as governor—was quite beyond the Indians' capacity to repay to the Atherton Company.

So the rich mortgaged Narragansett acres fell into the hands of the distinguished speculators.

Poor Mr. Clarke, in London, laboriously negotiating the renewal of *his* charter which covered this territory, "could not be put to rest," as was reported by Sir Thomas Temple (governor of Nova Scotia) and Captain Scott returning home together in 1662. For the Atherton patentees, to bolster their claims, had turned up in Massachusetts an old grant for the disputed land antedating Mr. Clarke's. A copy of this had been duly forwarded—as further instructions—to the "pure and unsuspecting Mr. Winthrop."

The only flaw in this scheme was that the patent was not worth the paper it was written on since it had not been officially signed and registered. Volumes have been written about this pseudo patent, and the whole Narragansett controversy became one of those bitter expensive land disputes which dragged on for more than a century. Impossible to present here even a fraction of the arguments for and against the opposing claims. From the welter of discussion, however, emerges one salient fact: the Atherton Company members, doubtless aware of the forgery, made no use of the patent but adopted other means to obtain their ends. Abandoning their pretension to charter rights and relying upon right of purchase only, they decided to appeal directly to the King, since all land titles were (ultimately) vested in the Crown.

Just whose bright idea this was is not proven. Some nineteenth century writers attribute it to the "knavery of John Scott," the Company's confidential London agent. His nimble wits may well have deduced from his Whitehall experience that more important than any right to land was knowing the right people who disposed of it. But if this conclusion was his, the subsequent plan was not the result of his "infamy" or "uncerimonious" and "sinister proceeding," as certain historians affirm. It was known to, and approved by, all the Atherton associates.

Chancery Records show he was given a "letter of agency" signed and sealed in Boston on December 26th, 1662, by Thomas Alcock, Edward Hutchinson and other Narragansett plantation owners, which empowered him to "solicit the matter, in order to obtain His Majesty's order of reference."[15] And Winthrop himself wrote what a good course the Atherton Proprietors had taken in sending Scott to the King.[16] Later when Winthrop personally attempted an amicable compromise with Clarke, he regretted that John had taken up the boundary dispute officially.[17]

To plead the Atherton case was a mission after his own heart. All John's myriad law suits at home seemed but a preparation for this supreme appearance. He was well aware, of course, that no plaintiff ever approached the Stuart court empty handed. Though possessing nothing comparable in value to the jewelled ring which Winthrop gave the King, he had the good taste to offer "a parcel of curiosities" (to the value of sixty pounds—the Company promised to pay)[18] and these went through friend Chiffinch's hands to their appropriate destination, while Chiffinch himself was gratified to see his name placed on the list of members.

"There were several hearings of the said matter before the King and his Council"[19] and undoubtedly John spoke with his customary eloquence, thundering against John Clarke and his Rhode Island associates, whom he blamed for hindering the new development and represented as "enimys to the peace and well-being of His Majesty's good subjects."[20]

The main point of his pleading was not so much to claim new territory as to transfer from Rhode Island and the Providence Plantations the *jurisdiction* over it and grant this either to Connecticut or Massachusetts. No matter what admiration later generations showered on Roger Williams' lofty experiment, those hard-headed Yankee entrepreneurs, bent on exploiting their real estate, wanted no part of Rhode Island's unorthodox liberalism. It led to unstable, unpredictable government, they declared.*

The case, reinforced by John's beautifully penned petition in the name of Winthrop, Simon Bradstreet, et al,[21] was highly successful. He secured a letter from the King, countersigned by Henry Bennet, stating that the Atherton Associates "had a just propriety in the lands," and that the King "having been given to understand that his good subjects Thomas Chiffinch, John Scott and John Winthrop," etc., were disturbed unjustly "by certain unreasonable and turbulent spirits of Providence Colony" recommended the owners to "the neighbourly kindness and protection" of the four New England Colonies—Massachusetts, Plymouth, New Haven and Connecticut.[22]

It has been often pointed out that the King, in this circular letter, included New Haven, although but a few months previously he himself had rendered this colony a political nonentity by permitting Connecticut to annex it. Moreover a few weeks after he signed the famous missive, Chancellor Clarendon passed under the Great Seal the royal charter of Rhode Island which included more or less the selfsame territory Charles had recommended to the special protection of the four colonies!

Royal ignorance of geography can hardly be held responsible for these self-contradictory frontiers. It was in all probability Clarendon's intention to weaken the New England Confederacy by providing a constant source of distraction over disputed boundaries, and thereby lighten his task

---

* Contemporary writers seemed to share this view for it is echoed in innumerable letters and documents stigmatizing the "rebel band" and "the ungoverned people," and Rhode Island, "a refuge for evil-livers, malefactors, buggerers . . . and men who work and drink on the Lord's Day." *Mass. Hist. Soc. Coll.*, 5th ser., IX, 27-30; *Ibid.*, 2nd ser., VII, 80.

of increasing the colonies' dependence on the mother country.[23]

The King's letter was, however, received with the greatest enthusiasm and for the time being was all-important. New Haven made it the foundation for renewed resistance to union with Connecticut, and acclaimed John as her champion of independence.[24] On repeated occasions the commissioners of the three orthodox sister colonies referred to it in legal disputes with all loyal respect for its authority. John, who had obtained it, was the hero of the hour.

Attention having been focused on him once again, the Foreign Plantations Committee remembered his outcry against the Dutch, and his complaints of their invasion of the New England mainland and islands, particularly of Long Island. So they ordered him to draw up a *Narrative* (with the help of Samuel Maverick and George Baxter) of "the King's title to that area," and of Dutch general behavior, local strength, and to suggest a "means to make them submit to His Majesty's Government, or to expel them."[25]

Not one of the trio had any love for New Netherlanders. Maverick's dislike was already recorded in his letters to England; George Baxter, at one time Stuyvesant's secretary, could not endure the latter's tyranny, educated as he had been in the principles of English liberty; while John's tenacious memory went all the way back to his bitter boyhood and Salem's icy winters. For was it not certain treacherous Dutch pilots who had steered the earliest Pilgrims to those bleak Cape Cod shores, reserving for themselves the temperate zones along the Hudson where the English had fondly imagined they were going to settle? Bradford, the contemporary historian, suggests that this was the reason for Scott's initial bias against Holland.[26]

It might have played a role; John rarely missed an opportunity for settling scores. But his Narrative was surely the result of something more than personal animus. His sudden plunge into public affairs seems to have awakened within him a latent grasp of wider issues, as events were soon to prove. For the document he produced hinted at a policy of the utmost importance, not only to the American colonies, but for England and the British Empire generally. Although he made only suggestions susceptible of the widest interpretations and of various courses of action, he nevertheless pointed out, and in the very strongest terms, three crucial features of strategic significance: (1) that it was impossible to enforce the Navigation Acts as long as New Netherland lay between New England and Virginia; (2) that the entire Dutch territories in the New World were very precariously held; and (3) that their conveyance to English hands *would not be impossible*.

And this counsel alone entitles him to some historical prominence. For it fitted in most marvelously with certain grandiose schemes already latent in the mind of the Merry Monarch who, for all his pleasure-loving nature, was as shrewd a King as ever ruled England and a great imperialist to boot. Buttressed by his growing Navy, he was even then considering England's alliance with France and the partition of the Dutch and Spanish Empires, transferring their extensive overseas possessions to the English Crown. Long Island must have looked like a promising little beginning and, always generous to a fault, he could make his brother's fortune by presenting him with this rich morsel.

The Narrative assignment denoted the degree of recognition John had won in official circles. Not only this. The Privy Council, when he returned to America again, put the stamp of its approval on him by commissioning him to bear the latest royal instructions concerning enforcement of the Navigation Act.[27] Here was one immediate response to his Narrative—England struck boldly at Holland through its carrying trade.

But the Act also aimed at punishing New England for evading the King's customs dues—a policy that rankled for a century. The ill-advised severity of this directive was later to prove one of the main reasons for the Colonies' break with

England. And as bearer of such ill tidings John was lucky that history merely forgot his role in this instance instead of meting out to him the punishment usually reserved for messengers bringing bad news.

BIBLIOGRAPHICAL NOTES

1. Conn. Arch. Towns and Lands, I, 40.
2. *Ibid.*, 24.
3. *N.Y. Hist. Soc. Coll.* (1869), II, 47 (*Clarendon Papers*).
4. Chalmers, *Pol. Ann.*, 412-13, 461.
5. *Hutch. Pap.*, II, 381.
6. *Conn. Pub. Rec.*, II, 346-47.
7. Van Rens., *Hist. of N.Y.*, I, 402.
8. Rawl. MSS., A 176, f 113.
9. *N.Y. Hist. Soc. Coll.* (1869), II, 47.
10. *Ibid.*
11. *Mass. Hist. Soc. Coll.*, 5th ser., IX, 31.
12. Conn. Arch. Col. Rec., I, f 326.
13. *Mass. Hist. Soc. Coll.*, 5th ser., IX, 12.
14. *Ibid.*, 25.
15. Collins, Ch. Pro., 221.
16. *Mass. Hist. Soc. Coll.*, 5th ser., VII, 77.
17. *Ibid.*, XXII, 35, 53.
18. Collins, Ch. Pro., 221.
19. *Ibid.*
20. *CSP. Col. ser. Am. and WI.*, 1661-68, No. 493.
21. *Mass. Hist. Soc. Pro.* (1867-69), 1st ser., X, 391-92.
22. Conn. Arch. For. Corr., I, 2.
23. P. L. Kaye, *Eng. Col. Admin. under Ld. Clarendon,* Johns Hopkins Press, XXIII, Nos. 5, 6.
24. Hoadley, *Rec. of N. Hav.*, pp. 500-02.
25. *N.Y. Col. Docs.*, III, 46.
26. Bradford, *Hist. of Ply. Plant.*, I, 158-60.
27. *N.Y. Col. Docs.*, III, 44.

CHAPTER XIII

THE SECOND HOMECOMING

". . . Lands! Lands! . . . one of the Gods of our New
England which the Eternal will destroy!"
— Roger Williams to John Winthrop, Jr. *Conn.
Pub. Rec.,* II, 65-67.

ARMED WITH THE PRIVY COUNCIL's instructions and the King's
letter to the four colonies, John's second homecoming was
even more triumphant than before. He had quite a retinue
with him this time. He brought back his old mother, rescued
from the hardship and poverty to which political upheavals
had reduced her, and he must have felt no small satisfaction
in setting her up in her own establishment on "one of his
principal bouweries" (as the records read), with Thomas Feis,
a trusted servant, to look after her.[1]

On shipboard with him too had been young Daniel Gotherson, Dorothea's eldest boy, and Hallelujah Fisher, a Kentish
parson's son, both of whom he took into his own household
at Ashford (Setauket). There was some excitement and much
gossip over his reappearance (judging from letters neighbors
wrote with their usual envious comments).[2]

For the first time he made much of his wife, that sweet,
patient creature who saw so little of her brilliant, erratic
husband, and who now had a second son, Jeckamiah, to welcome him home.[3] He showered her with gifts, hanging about
her neck the jewels Gotherson had given him; he dressed her
in the fine clothes he had bought in London for her and

showed her off to the townsfolk insisting, with playful devotion, that her train be carried behind her, like any English
countess. He was happy and magnanimous, seemed to be the
man of the hour in New England, with prospects of even
greater position and public service before him. Even if he
had not succeeded in becoming governor of Long Island,
there is little doubt that he had heard hints of what was in
store in that direction and what possible honors *might* be his.

In many ways he was a changed man. His two trips to
England had not only deepened his ties with his own country.
He had spent time and effort getting to know his family background, visiting Scott ancestral seats, searching documents,
wills, parish registrars, tracing, with his customary exhaustive
energy, the Scott pedigree through innumerable generations.

Surely it was on this last visit that he brought back the long
parchment scroll, twenty-six inches wide and several feet
long, with all the family names written in black ink and the
marriage lines traced in red. This pedigree, still extant in
1909* (Appendix D), bore a number of details that suggest
it might have been John's own work, or done under his supervision. It is considered, by those who have seen it, extraor-
dinarily attractive. Names of man and wife were written in
two linked circles (each the size of a quarter) these circles
leading to a shield two-and-three-eights of an inch long by
one-and-three-quarters wide, on which the arms of the husband (dexter) and those of the wife (sinister) are emblazoned
in heraldic tinctures. There were sixty-three of these shields
on the scroll, and at the foot of the pedigree there was a large
heraldic achievement, on the shield of which are eight quarter-
ings. Both color and decoration suggest some of John's own
elaborately painted maps.

The date of this manuscript-pedigree, which was not signed

---

* It was examined then, on January 9th, for some five hours, by Henry
Edward Scott, genealogist, historian, and editor-emeritus of the New England
Historic Genealogical Society. My description is taken from the notes among
his papers, which I was permitted to see May 14th, 1956.

nor attested, seems pretty closely fixed, for it mentions Thomas Scott, John's younger brother, known to be living in 1663; and it referred to the 1663 betrothal of the child heiress, Lady Ann Scott, Countess of Buccleuch, to the Duke of Monmouth. So what more likely than that he produced the work in London, or had it drawn for him there?

All his adult life John was deeply conscious of his English background, perhaps exaggeratedly so. This is understandable. One cannot take a high-spirited, well-born boy and subject him to long years of bonded servitude without some influence on his personality. John's craving to be recognized as belonging to the "squirearchy" must have been considerably enhanced after he learned that this class in England owned most of the land and ran all of the local government. Such facts gave food for thought. John himself owned quite a bit of land, and he was definitely part of the New England government. He was tax commissioner of Southampton, and Long Island's chief magistrate. He had, in fact, in the land of his exile, reconquered by his own efforts much the same position to which he was born at home.

This knowledge gave him new confidence. His orders took on a peremptory tone.

On this second return he was regarded, too, as something of an authority on public affairs, people turned to him for assistance, he became a most sought-after attorney, whose talents (and whose favor at Court) were well recognized. The town of Southampton, disputing Connecticut's taxation claims, asked his advice on the matter, which he gave in no uncertain terms. He told them to suspend all payments—which they did. He substantiated this judgment later by declaring that he:

"fully and absolutely affirmed that the land (Southampton) was not within the line of Connecticut; it had another lord, viz. the Duke of York, to whom the soil was given by the King, after its surrender by Lord Stirling. . . .

"Moreover from the moment of the granting of its charter, Southampton had no reason to pay taxes, indeed, it were more fitting that Connecticut should pay Southampton back monies"![4]

To Easthampton he gave similar advice, charging money for it too, although this was normal. Since 1660 he had handled (with his law partner, Stanborough) Southampton's boundary dispute with Easthampton, and he was not likely to forego legal fees when dealing with the old adversary. He assured the Easthampton magistrates that under the *Combination* which they themselves had made with Connecticut, 1649,[5] but which Winthrop was now trying to void, they owed the Hartford Court nothing. Easthampton, however, bewildered by changing events and unsure about results of such a decision, appealed to Hartford for further clarification.[6]

John's bold assertions defining the limits of Connecticut's rule must have enraged Winthrop. Since obtaining his charter, the governor had overlooked no opportunity of insisting that the whole of Long Island was his. Acting on this assumption he had been extending his sphere of influence, selecting for himself choice lots of Long Island property. Now came along this troublemaker with his unsettling news of royal intentions, and, to add insult to injury, backed by some show of royal favor. Could anything be more provoking?

And there was another reason for Winthrop's displeasure. The famous letter John brought back from the King, concerning the Narragansett land: why was it addressed to the governors of all *four* colonies instead of giving Connecticut sole right of settlement? Had Winthrop negotiated the matter privately with Rhode Island's Mr. Clarke, could he not have done very much better?*

---

* Both Connecticut and Rhode Island continued to petition Charles II concerning their claims to the Narragansett lands, both as to ownership of the soil and jurisdiction over it. When Charles sent his four commissioners to New England in 1664, they decided that the territory should be taken from the two colonies and rechristened King's Province, till a final settlement could

But John had come home, not only with the blessings of the Privy Council, but with the reputation of having made his mark with the Committee of Foreign Plantations as well. It was the head of that august assembly, Chancellor Clarendon, who had bought out the Earl of Stirling's Long Island patent, to present to his son-in-law, the Duke of York. In the interim, before the English armed intervention on the island, Clarendon felt he was running the place, and it was doubtless he who ordered Winthrop to give John some local office.[7] Reluctantly, we may be sure, Winthrop appointed John commissioner of Ashford, giving him magisterial powers throughout the whole island.[8]

The other colonists, impressed by his ability to get things done, welcomed John with marked cordiality. New Haven, mindful of his championship of its rights, reimbursed him for all his English expenses. Its General Court gratefully recorded the friendship he had shown the colony, and the respect in England that he had won;[9] it set up a special committee to "treat with him for the purpose of obtaining a patent for Delaware," and, against all eventualities, placed troops at his disposal.[10]

The clamor for his assistance grew. Men on the west end of Long Island petitioned him to come and "settle their condition," claiming the Dutch were abusing them.[11] Another appeal concerning a quarrel with the Dutch reached him from three men who, "recognising your understanding and

---

be reached. Governor Richard Nicolls, the chief commissioner, however, reversed this ruling, declaring it null and void, so the struggle continued, with each colony sending its agents to London to present its claims.

In 1683 the King appointed Edward Cranfield, Esq., to go to the disputed area, examine all claims and report. Cranfield assembled the greatest number of Indian Sachems ever brought together, and after full and ample testimony by them and by English witnesses, reported (December 4th, 1684) that property of the soil was vested in the heirs of John Winthrop, Major Atherton and their associates. And that jurisdiction over it belonged to Connecticut. *CSP Col. Ser. Am. and W. I.,* 1681-85, p. 743.

However, like so many decisions concerning land, this one did not stick, and later the territory was included in Rhode Island's boundary where it remains to this day.

expert knowledge" begged his counsel for settling lands on the Raritan River.[12] He was retained by Hempstead to handle all boundary disputes and other town matters.[13]

When news reached him from England that Sir Edward Scott had died at Scot's Hall, John and his servants put on long mourning out of respect, and he declared he would surely inherit a fortune since Thomas, the deceased's only boy, was generally known to be Prince Rupert's son. John was unaware that the parents had been ultimately reconciled, and that just before his death, Sir Edward acknowledged his bastard and made him his heir. Not that John would have inherited anyway. Younger sons, in England, get only poor pickings. But he was feeling his oats, and dreams of wealth were an indication of his exalted condition.

He was dealing in Long Island land again. He had begun the development of a large territory, some thirty-two miles square, east of Nanemosett Brook, which Mahmasutee (or Massitewse) had long since sold him.[14] (Appendix E.) Here, on a tract that reached across the island from sea to sea, were Daniel Gotherson's acres and the houses he had had built, sending over from England workmen and building materials. Gotherson's bailiff, Mathew Prior, owned property on this new development and lived with his family at Ould Mans. There were numerous settled groups at the nearby attractive Mount Sinai, and Deborah, even while John was in England, had, with the devoted assistance of Captain Youngs, moved all her belongings and servants from Southampton and Northsea, and had taken up her residence on this new estate, called Scot's Hall.*

In England, John had visited the Kentish ancestral place and seen the stately red-brick Jacobean mansion with its great banqueting hall and adjoining picture gallery full of family portraits.[15] Its formal flower gardens, handsome stretches of

---

* Youngs describes this big move to John in a long letter which he signed "your faithfull friend till death." Rawl. MSS., A 175, f 116.

water, the Ladies Walk and extensive rookeries may have impressed him but could have meant little to him—he had gone there but once—and as a stranger.

His own Scot's Hall* was a long one-story building with a wing or two, situated on Scott's Cove. Besides the main building it comprised kitchens and stables. He must have intended extensive ornamental additions for when it all came up for sale a quantity of glass and iron was found on the premises. It also contained a considerable amount of tea, so John apparently lived there in some style, for this was just then becoming the fashionable drink in America and cost as much as sixty shillings a pound. The beautiful colored map he drew of New England, gives some idea of this whole section. The original coastal settlement of Cromwell Bay he had re-christened Ashford, in memory of the old market town at home; and other place-names recalling his English forebears are sketched in, such as the villages of Smeeth and Brabourne.

John had not undertaken this extensive planting alone; he went into it with a number of partners. Their agreement of December 5th, 1663 (as attested in the original documents in the State Library in Hartford), shows that some of the most distinguished Long Islanders were in with him, particularly Richard Woodhull, Daniel Lane, Joseph Hand, Zacherious Hawkins, whose seals appear on the parchment.[16]

His real estate ventures by no means absorbed all his energies. He found time to prosecute a neighbor—he was standing no impertinence now, and sued a Charles Barnes for slander—won the case and forgave the offense, with costs assessed to the defendant.[17]

And mindful of all the historic happenings about to take

---

* Scot's Hall was sold, 1666, and added to the local minister's house to provide space for public purposes, religious and secular. It was later used as a tavern, on the lonely forest track between Setauket and Southold. It is thought by some to exist still, as portion of the present-day Crystal Brook Club House. N. Y. *Historical Magazine,* XVI, 445.

place, he wrote a long letter to friend Williamson in London preparing him for drastic changes and begging him to see the Dutch Ambassador to make sure that no diplomatic steps be taken until New England—and by this he meant, possibly, himself—could "make itself heard."

For the English settlers on the west end of Long Island, he announced (somewhat prematurely, it must be admitted), "long enslaved by the Dutch, had, *at Connecticut's instigation*, rebelled."[18] (Italics added.)

BIBLIOGRAPHICAL NOTES

1. Fernow, *Rec. of New Amst.*, V, 172-74.
2. *N.Y. Hist. Soc. Coll.* (1869), II, 47.
3. *N.Y. Gen. and Bio. Rec.*, XLVI, 23.
4. Conn. Arch. Towns and Lands, I, f 29.
5. *Ibid.*, ff 8, 9.
6. *Ibid.*, ff 32, 37.
7. S.P. Dom. Car., II, 29, No. 419.
8. O'Callaghan, *Hist. of N. Neth.*, II, 499.
9. Hoadley, *Rec. of N. Hav.*, pp. 549-50.
10. *Ibid*, p. 515.
11. *Conn. Hist. Soc. Coll.*, XXI, 146.
12. *Mass. Hist. Soc. Coll.*, 5th ser., I, 397-99.
13. *Rec. of N. and S. Hempstead* (1654-1880), I, 156.
14. Thompson, *Hist. of L.I.*, I, 32.
15. Add. MSS., 5414, f 21.
16. Conn. Arch., MS. I, ff 312-13.
17. S-ampton *T.R.*, II, 31.
18. *N.Y. Col. Docs.*, III, 48.

CHAPTER XIV

--⋅◦⫸❘❙◦⋅--

THE PEOPLE'S CHOICE—
PRESIDENT SCOTT

"... they that dare not say what they are (*affairs being ripened*) and strive not to be what they ought to be, it may be feared will submit to anything, and consequently may expect, in the end, to come to nothing." (Italics added.)

—John Scott to Sir Francis Rolle, M.P., 1676.
Rawl. MSS., A 175, f 182.

WHEN JOHN SCOTT RETURNED to New England from London in November 1663, it did not take him long to sum up the political situation in Long Island. The many appeals for help reaching him from inhabitants there made him realize how very unsettled conditions had become. Isolated towns on the western—the Dutch—end were threatened by Indians on the warpath, and were angrily complaining about the scant protection their government afforded them. Other towns—in the English section—were strenuously resisting Connecticut's attempts to exert authority over them.

"Exalted" (as Dutch Stuyvesant complained) by the possession of his new charter, Governor John Winthrop, early in 1663, had declared Ostdorp (Westchester) on the mainland and certain English towns on Long Island, annexed to Connecticut. And he sent Captain Talcott with armed troops "to reduce them."[1] John heard tales of the wild disorders which ended that raid. Stuyvesant, infuriated, went personally to Boston to protest to the United Commissioners against these "unlawful obstinate and unwarranted proceedings." But he obtained no satisfaction.

As the island situation worsened, and even his Dutchmen grew restive, Stuyvesant appointed three deputies to go to Hartford to persuade Governor Winthrop to re-organize the boundary line long since established (1650) between the respective English and Dutch possessions.

For four weary days his men travelled over land and water to reach Connecticut's capital, only to be kept cooling their heels on arrival.

The English governor was cold and uncommunicative, obviously temporizing until all the towns had revolted and he could take over. His charter, he maintained, included not only Long Island, but extended to the Pacific. "Where then lies New Netherland?" he demanded. For him New Netherland did not exist. The Dutch patent was for purposes of trade only; it conferred no right to the soil.

Negotiations dragged on for days. Connecticut's General Court refused to abide by the 1650 boundary agreement and insisted on full rights to "accept the surrender of the English towns," arguing that it was impossible to restrain them since they had already rebelled against the Dutch. (But omitting to mention, of course, that Connecticut itself had deliberately provoked this revolt.)[2]

The baffled Dutch agents found themselves confronted by an ultimatum confirming Winthrop's annexation of Westchester. All Stuyvesant could do was to withdraw them and report to Holland, begging once anew that the States-General take up the whole dispute with England.

But by attempting to raise the quarrel to an international level, Stuyvesant was unwittingly running into even greater dangers. Colonial and commercial rivalry between the two mother countries was at such an explosive point that it was about to burst into the Second Dutch War. At The Hague, Sir George Downing was busily intriguing against him; while John Scott, having contributed his own part to New Netherland's downfall, by his *Narrative's* drastic suggestions of an English invasion, had just reached America officially bearing the royal Navigation Acts instructions which were salt in Holland's wounded self-esteem, and a deadly blow at her carrying trade.

For nearly a year the old Dutch Director-General had been plagued by the "flying rumors" that Scott's petition to be made Long Island's governor had been granted. He thanked God when this proved untrue, but his peace of mind was short-lived as a succession of raiders attempted to wrest western Long Island from him. Young "hot-heads with a pretended commission from Hartford" had appeared shouting to Dutch settlers to renounce their citizenship, rioters had taken up arms at Gravesend, while "eight mounted and well-armed mutineers" entered Jamaica, urging with loud seditious talk that Hollanders pay neither tithes nor taxes.

True, nothing came of it all. Raids petered out in personal squabbles and the riots merely led to the paying off of old private scores. But to add to the general unrest, Indian massacres spread, forcing him into an expensive war; and even Nature seemed against the old Dutchman, for floods and an unwonted earthquake wrought terrible havoc. Heartsick and discouraged, he sent a few soldiers to quell the riots and made up his mind to accept Winthrop's Westchester ultimatum.

John Scott's return to New England had quickened the tempo of revolt on Long Island.

His boldly confident answers to all appeals heartened English subjects living in Dutch towns and longing to throw off bureaucratic tyranny; while inhabitants of English towns, threatened by Connecticut, saw in him their possible savior. The Dutch authorities, aware of increasing tension, redoubled contacts with their home government; there was a flood of Remonstrances, Resolutions; Letters of Advice, Orders in Council.

Winthrop now judged the moment propitious for another armed assault, formally to incorporate the whole of Long

Island with his colony. To command the expedition he picked none other than John Scott, and the Connecticut governor himself administered the oath of office.[3]

But it was already too late for union. Unknown to Winthrop a situation had arisen on the island which Captain Talcott, who had commanded the first Long Island invasion, should surely have reported to his superior.

The inhabitants of the English towns—Hempstead, Gravesend, Flushing, Newtown, Oyster Bay and Jamaica—refused to be annexed to Connecticut! They were no more anxious to pass under its Puritan rule than they relished being counted among Dutch colonials. There were Quakers, Baptists and other "subversive" sects, all anathema to Connecticut's religious ruling. These righteous islanders foresaw future punishment and coercion for their beliefs, and were determined to avoid such dire consequences. Moreover their recent petition to be protected from the Indians had brought only evasive double-talk from Hartford. And with the prospect of savage death and property destruction or confiscation, they considered their plight desperate.

A short time before John's homecoming, they had entered into an agreement among themselves, a Combination, as they termed it, to manage their own affairs, irrespective of the River colony.

Neither the word nor action was without precedent. Easthampton's inhabitants had long since made a similar decision *vis-a-vis* Connecticut, declaring they would pay no taxes to Hartford, and would maintain their own administrative officers.[4]

With the sturdy assurance of settlers long familiar with Town-meeting government, these English townsmen resolved to draw up rules, elect deputies and choose their own magistrates. As a last resort they had written John Scott begging him to give "his expert consideration" to their problems. By this act they not only recognized the influence he had won in London, but showed that his conduct on Long Island inspired them with confidence. Therefore, after receiving Winthrop's commission in Hartford, John went directly to Hempstead to confer with the delegates of the Combination which had invoked his aid.

"There was a full debate on January 4th, 1663/4,"[5] covering the matter of Connecticut's annexation orders. The delegates first explained their dread of Puritan rule and their determination to avoid it and preserve freedom of worship. Then John told them what he had heard at the Restoration Court and of Charles II's plans for taking Long Island and presenting it to his brother, the Duke of York. They "therefore did further, fully empower Captain John Scott to act as president until His Royal Highness the Duke of York, or His Majesty could establish a government among them."[6]

This is the first recorded use of the presidential title in America.

Their decision placed John before a terrible dilemma. On the one hand he had just accepted a commission forcibly to incorporate Long Island with Connecticut. On the other, as a Long Islander himself, he obviously shared the desires of the delegates from those autonomous towns to preserve their virtual independence. Moreover, although John's contacts with Winthrop in the Atherton Land Company had presumably been cordial he could hardly (as Episcopalian committed to freedom of conscience) have had much sympathy with the "Puritan of Puritans"; while as a royalist and a protegé of the Earl of Clarendon,[7] he felt very much the "King's servant."

Winthrop had appointed him to high office in the colony, and John liked to be important. Yet the temptation to save Long Island both from the Dutch and from Connecticut and place it at his monarch's disposal must have been prodigious.

John was never one to flinch from a challenge. Whatever his reasons, all we actually know is that "affairs being ripened" he made his choice.

In the name of the delegates of the English towns, "he

proclaimed the majesty of our dreade sovereign Charles II"[8] over the disputed territories, and resigned Winthrop's commission.[9]

It was as President Scott, not as Hartford's emissary, that he wrote forthwith to Stuyvesant to clarify matters. Then away he rode to rouse the Englishmen and reduce the Dutch towns.

BIBLIOGRAPHICAL NOTES

1. *Early Col. Docs., L.I.,* p. 517.
2. Andrews, *Col. Per. Am. Hist.,* III, 62n.
3. Hoadley, *Rec. of N. Hav.,* p. 541.
4. Conn. Arch. Towns and Lands, I, Doc. 7, ff 8, 9.
5. *Ibid.,* f 25.
6. *Ibid.*
7. SP. Dom. Car., II, 29, No. 419.
8. Conn. Arch. Towns and Lands, I, Doc. 7, ff 8, 9.
9. *Ibid.,* f 31; O'Callaghan, *Hist. of N. Neth. Reg.,* II, 512.

CHAPTER XV

JOHN URGES THE DUTCH
TO REVOLT

". . . great affairs are not compassed by being afraid to attempt them; in doing them by half we betray our fear and stop in the midway as if we resolved to go back at the appearance of the first oppositions."

—John Scott, Rawl. MSS., A 175, f 182.

WITH FLAGS FLYING, trumpets sounding, and the insistent beat of drums, President Scott, at the head of a company of one hundred and fifty armed men, horse and foot, clattered into Breukelen on the western—the Dutch—end of Long Island. It was January 11th, 1664, a brisk, cold morning with a bright sun shining over the sparkling East River and highlighting the tall grass prairies which stretched in endless miles beyond the town limits. A morning for audacious, vigorous action to set the blood a-tingle. John halted his men before Sheriff Hegemann's house, and the uproar and confusion of their arrival attracted a group of settlers who began crowding round the newcomers, curious and somewhat fearful of all this military display.

John dismounted and, accompanied by a few of his men, greeted the Sheriff affably, talking to him in the easy, complimentary fashion he had learned at Court. But the Dutchman responded with little grace. He was surprised by this sudden invasion and suspicious of the foreigner. Relations between Dutch and English on the island, he knew, had gone from bad to worse over the years. But he was unprepared for a force of such formidable proportions—all New Netherland had no greater. He demanded to know what they wanted.

"Our business is with Peter Stuyvesant," answered John smoothly. "We came here hoping to see him. Though we understand from one of our messengers that the letter we recently sent him has given some offence. . . ."

In a flowery epistle[1] John had written the Director-General announcing his own arrival and assuring him that it boded no hostile intent. But he pointed out certain "hostile acts committed by the Dutch" and made a significant reference to his own sovereign Lord and King, who was a "strict avenger of his people's wrongs." It concluded with the hope that a meeting between the writer and the Governor would be speedily effected, and ended by saying that all proof of the aforesaid details would be reserved "until I have the good fortune to kiss your hand, which will be tomorrow morning, about twelve of the clock at Flatbush (Breukelen) if it please you to come and meet me there, which shall be considered a favor by him who is His Majesty's faithful servant. . . ." etc., etc.

The letter, though a trifle high-handed, was not lacking in the customary courtesies. But on the envelope was written simply Petrus Stuyvesant. The stiff-necked Governor had, quite naturally, felt slighted at the informality of the address, and did not go personally to Brooklyn, but sent his commissioners.

"The Lords of the States-General and the Honorable West India Company must be so acknowledged," observed the Sheriff, who had heard about the incident. "Failure to do so is not only a slight upon the persons in question but tends to disparage Their High Mightinesses in Holland as well."

John murmured appropriate excuses. He had no intention of explaining to the Sheriff that he had deliberately omitted the official title of Director-General of New Netherland since it was precisely to deprive Stuyvesant of that title that he was undertaking this present mission.

His eyes wandered to the growing numbers who crowded round his men, and lit up with satisfaction.

"Do you hold any commission?" went on the Sheriff, mindful of his duties. "Have you some proposition to address to the Governor who has his abode now in Manhattan?"

John brushed him aside. He had a commission, but more important to him, he had an audience. "I have a few words to say to these people," he answered, and ordering his troops to approach, he began to make a speech.

He spoke in English, but with ringing, authoritative tones and a popular appeal that made his phrases intelligible to Dutchmen in the crowd.

"This country you inhabit is unjustly occupied by your leaders," he told them. "It belongs to the King of England and not to the Dutch. If you acknowledge His Britannic Majesty's sovereignty you will be permitted to remain in your homes. Otherwise you will be forced to leave."[2] He repeated his words slowly, forcefully, extolling the benefits of English rule, impressing some of his listeners, angering others. The Sheriff, shocked, had meanwhile fetched the commissioners who had been sent to meet with John—Cornelius Van Ryven, Secretary and Receiver-General of New Netherland; Stevens V. Cortlandt, New Amsterdam's Burgomaster; and John Lawrence, an Englishman who held various important positions under the Dutch.

These had been waiting for John's arrival and had heard the concluding portion of his declaration. The worried Secretary went over to where the speaker stood. Nobody, he maintained, had the right to utter such words, nor to suggest that anyone other than the Lords States-General and the Incorporated West India Company had any rights there. The country had been discovered by the Dutch, purchased by them from the Indians, and parts of it peaceably possessed for thirty and forty years. He recited all the well-known arguments, and

undertook to prove them all to Captain Scott's complete satisfaction, if only he would be so good as to accompany him to
New Amsterdam (Manhattan).

But John had noted the effect of his words on his listeners
and had no intention of letting the initiative slip from his
hands. He was not now inclined, he answered, to go over.
But after some deliberation, he agreed to ride to the Ferry
(leading to Manhattan) where he would await Mr. Stuyvesant's visit.

He was once again asked to show his commission but
answered that his questioners should first produce theirs. The
matter was allowed to drop.

John left his foot soldiers with orders to march to Gravesend. Then leaping on his horse, and followed by his mounted
troops, he rode with the Secretary to the Ferry where once
again he harangued the crowd concerning the King of
England's rights, and the freedoms Dutch would enjoy under
his rule.

This angered Van Ryven, who remonstrated that only the
Lords States-General could be proclaimed here. John, catching fire, retorted that if anyone were to speak for the States
he could cut the feet from under them. Van Ryven professed
not to understand such belligerent words. Whereupon Captain Scott retorted in Dutch; "I will stick my rapier in the
guts of any man who proclaims the States here or who says
this is not the King's land."[3] Murmurs of approval and ap-
plause ran through the crowd behind him, and Secretary Van
Ryven changed his tone.

The whole boundary dispute could not be settled in such
a manner, he murmured. It was a question to be taken up by
their respective heads of government. His tactful words
mollified John who readily admitted it would be no credit
for armed troops to kill an unarmed man.

"Though we come with but a hundred soldiers," he continued, "we are prepared to wait. If my Company are ready

to follow me, I do not fear to proceed to Manhattan and to proclaim the King there.

"I do not have to remind you, I suppose, that your people have broken the peace between England and Holland. Your General dispatched a frigate of armed soldiers against certain Englishmen at Gravesend. I have the names of two who were so roughly handled that one died in consequence."[4] The ferryboat, meanwhile, was being readied for the trip to the mainland. Van Ryven and his fellow commissioners said they would cross over and report to the Director-General and the Council. Once again they asked Captain Scott for his commission, or for some writing they could show the Council.

John drew from his pocket a memorandum in the form of instructions from the Hartford commissioners for himself and for Captain Youngs who was accompanying him. He began to read it aloud then, changing his mind, thrust it back in his pocket again.

"Let Mr. Stuyvesant come over and I shall speak to him of weightier matters. I shall wait one hour for an answer."

His manner was so uncompromising that the Dutchmen felt there was little chance to do anything further. Leaving John Lawrence with him, they took the ferryboat to go and confer with Stuyvesant. Scott, however, did not wait for the Governor. News reached him that difficulties had broken out between the Dutch population and his soldiers and that the latter, excited and rather drunk, were running from house to house with drawn swords and daggers threatening the people and demanding the surrender of one of John's men who had been attacked with an axe.

John rode back at once; he would brook no insubordination among his troops. There had been enough lawlessness on Long Island. It would defeat his purpose to lose his initial advantage. Only too well he knew that in just such a manner a decade previously two serious English attempts to unseat Stuyvesant and repudiate Dutch rule had failed. He had no intention of adding his name to those unsuccessful standard-bearers, one of whom—Captain Underhill—was serving under him now.

True, the Director-General had been angered by his informal letter, and had been all for returning it unopened. But he finally permitted the messenger to read it aloud. And when his commissioners reported the details of that first Brooklyn meeting, Stuyvesant sent a note and acknowledged, not only John's letter, he recognized John's title as well! Archives in Holland refer *to the presidency of Captain John Scott* and mention the different magisterial appointments he made under it.[5]

Stuyvesant sent John a long official communication (addressing him as Honorable, Prudent and Most Worthy Sir) in which he rehearsed the whole boundary quarrel, refuting the English charges and defending the Dutch position, point by point. He agreed to submit all differences either to the respective sovereigns in Europe; or to discuss it further with John at a future meeting.[6] The latter course was chosen and it was agreed to meet at Hempstead.

It is this correspondence and Stuyvesant's readiness to treat with John that differentiate his intervention on Long Island from that of all the other agents and agitators. These made their appeals to the "silly common people without any address to us," as Stuyvesant put it;[7] whereas John, with a *sangfroid* born of past experience, had tackled matters in a different spirit and immediately at top level. Moreover his troops were not local recruits influenced by personal quarrels, but men assigned him by New Haven.[8]

Encouraged by these preliminaries and with the solid support of his confederated English towns, John set out to win over the Dutch towns along the East River—Midout, Amersfort, New Utrecht, Boswyck, and of course Breukelen. He stormed in with his men, stirring up the Dutch inhabitants, delighting the few English; shouting to the assembled crowds: "Are you King's men or State's men?" He made inflammatory speeches exploiting old grievances, appealing to his listeners' sneaking desire for a share in local government. He threatened dire reprisals on those who resisted. But his personality and eloquence may well have impressed them; he introduced something of the English style and ceremony he had witnessed in London, and had the wit to dramatize it.

At New Utrecht he took possession of the blockhouse, where he made a great symbolic act of having his men overthrow the cannon from the porthole it occupied. At his orders, the cannon was then set up in another, which he called the King's port. And he fired a salute to the King in commemoration of the event. He called upon all citizens to doff their hats to the English flag. When the son of Burgomaster Martin Krieger refused to do so, John struck him with a cane.*9 He summoned the local magistrate and insisted he submit to the King's authority. The trembling man assured John that the King was already his friend since Holland was not at war with England, but that he himself was a subject of the Dutch to whom he had taken an oath of allegiance. John informed the inhabitants they must all change their allegiance.

At Midout John had the British ensign hoisted in front of the Sheriff's house. Then, standing by it with uncovered head, his plumed hat held reverently over his heart, he addressed the people at considerable length. Proud memories of all the majesty and sanctity of English law must have come flooding back to him, carrying him away with his own eloquence. In his letter to Stuyvesant, John had written that the liberty of His Majesty's good subjects was "more dear to me than my life." Now he dilated on the subject: greater freedom than ever would be theirs, he told his audience, since the land belonged to His Majesty King Charles II, right and lawful lord of all America from Virginia to Boston. They

---

* There are two eye-witness accounts in different towns of young Krieger being caned "by the English." Either these erroneously attributed this incident to more than one place, or else Krieger was a brat who went around deliberately defying the English in order to provoke trouble.

would have their own Assembly, they would elect their own Governor, choose their own officers, vote taxes—it was the liberty and independence granted to all Englishmen at home and established in the colonies by the Founding Fathers. Henceforth they would pay no tithes to the West India Company, nor need they continue to obey Peter Stuyvesant. He was no longer their governor, not even a general, just a private citizen, like themselves.[10] He reiterated his phrases as forcefully as he could, pressing his points home with vivid example, gesticulating energetically to make his meaning clear.

"He jabbered away like a mountebank," read the Dutch archives, which put John's "seditious acts," his "unblushing shamelessness," his "attendant mob," in as unfavorable a light as possible. What other line was feasible, for the record? How else could they obliterate the memory of those winged words? Though the Dutchmen, crowding around him, did not grasp every fact, his intention and purpose were only too plain. There was explosive contagion in the force of his ideas. For nearly thirty years these good burghers on Long Island had meekly accepted conditions imposed by Stuyvesant in the name of the Trading Company, although Dutchmen in Holland enjoyed far greater independence, and the English example at their side was a daily reminder of their own curtailed liberties. Now a fiery eloquence reminded them of their plight, lit their imagination; their desires became suddenly articulate.

But coupled with prospects of freedom was the possibility of having to fight for it—if they were to attain it and remain Dutch. Thrilled as many might be at John's words, they were also afraid. They were afraid of losing the fat farms which they had wrung from the wilderness by years of unremitting toil; they feared for their fine houses, so solidly built of Dutch brick and tile, laboriously imported and exactly like buildings at home. And they were furious with Stuyvesant for leaving them in the lurch, for giving them no defense against the invader; while all the help the States-General offered were formal communications appealing to past loyalties, and tactless reminders that many of them, instead of opposing these usurpers, were already seeking office from them.

Yet the glimpse of citizen participation which John's speeches conjured before them seem to have run like wildfire through their ranks. New Amsterdam's Burgomaster addressed a rousing Remonstrance to Stuyvesant, complaining bitterly not only of Long Island's situation, but of the precarious defenses of all New Netherland! Fortifications should be increased, he recommended, and a stepped-up recruiting plan put in action. "With two hundred men in separate vessels we could sack and destroy all the English settlements to Cape Cod," he concluded with unexpected vigor, while the magistrates roundly supported him. "All the English towns are open and entirely defenseless."

Such bold measures apparently never occurred to the complacent Director-General.[11] He pleaded that his funds were exhausted. But they would not let him off with so easy an excuse.

Thirty thousand guilders were immediately subscribed to underwrite a new war. The national mood seemed suddenly to stiffen.[12] And as though John were aware of the change, he too became more insistent. The Dutch were convinced that he was receiving secret orders, or had some intelligence and encouragement from England.[13] Which, to a certain extent, his instructions certainly gave him.

What Stuyvesant most dreaded was that John's troops would provoke an act of violence or bloodshed and that he would then use this as a pretext to make himself master of the North River, plunder the towns and drive the Dutch out in utter ruin.[14]

As the Dutch towns began to waver and John's success seemed likely, he adopted a new strategy, playing for time to land his fish. When Stuyvesant sent his commissioners, a second time, with an official memorandum of terms to be discussed, John was hard to locate. The Dutchmen rode eighteen hours to meet him in Rustdorp (January 15th) only to be told that he was still in Flushing. They sent a messenger there to inform him of their arrival, begging his presence. But when he galloped into town around four in the afternoon, he was still not ready to comply with their request. He put them off again, excusing himself by saying he was hungry, having not yet broken his fast; he would snatch a mouthful at the Minister's house. He dined with the Reverend Zacheriah Walker and it was almost evening before he was available for the commissioners at a meeting, where, despite their protests, his troops accompanied him.

To the usual request for his commission he pulled out an unsigned document* and boasted, in an excess of enthusiasm, that the whole of Long Island had been granted to him. But his good sense immediately reasserted itself and he admitted that it had been granted to the Duke of York, whose agent he was. He reminded the crowds that not only had he been sent by Hartford to "assist His Majesty's subjects in their just cause," but that he had been invited to come by many of these self-same subjects, and was negotiating for them in his capacity as President. Would they acknowledge him as such? The crowd roared approval of President Scott. And instead of producing his commission, he read them a collection "from diverse histories" which showed that the English explorer Henry Hudson had discovered the North River in 1603, which made it indubitably an English possession. He did not,

---

* This could well have been a copy of the instructions given him by the Committee of Foreign Plantations to devise means to "make the Dutch acknowledge and submit to His Majesty's government, or, by force, to compel them thereunto, or expulse them." N.Y. *Col. Docs.*, III, 57-61; CSP *Col. Ser. Am. and W. I.*, 1661-68, No. 713. Stuyvesant, reporting home, refers to "a certain letter in form of a commission written in favor of the aforesaid Scott to those of Long Island, copy whereof being handed to us I have thought necessary to annex it to the appendix No. 5. Dated Fort Amsterdam in N.N. last Feb. 1664." (N.Y. *Col. Docs.*, II, 234.)

This appendix however no longer exists. It was among the early West India Company papers, at The Hague, which were sold as waste paper in 1821. Brodhead's Final Report.

of course, mention that Hudson, at the time, was in the service of the Dutch East India Company, which would have meant that it belonged to Holland.[15]

"I shall return," he pronounced in prophetic tones, putting his documents away. "I shall come back again in April of this year with my published commission."[16] And this time he was publicly admitting that he knew of the Duke's plans for that spring expeditionary force.

Curiously enough, and despite the recommendations of his own Narrative, he did not seem to believe that the campaign would extend beyond Long Island.

The Dutch commissioners meantime had produced their Memorandum, which he examined, and there was much discussion of mutual terms. They all had supper amicably together and then, "it being midnight, and fine weather," they resolved to return to Fort Amsterdam. It was John who had the final word.

"There is only one way or means to put a stop to English claims to Long Island," he told them. "That is to see and agree as soon as possible with the Duke of York. I know for certain that the King has granted him the island, and he has been creditably informed it will furnish him revenues of thirty thousand pounds annually. The Duke is resolved if he cannot obtain it voluntarily, he will seize it by force and for that purpose will send two or more frigates to take not only the aforesaid Island, but the whole of New Netherland as well."[17] That last was a bold threat John inserted himself, for his later statements and behavior prove that he did not believe the moment was ripe then for the taking of all New Netherland.

This was the situation Stuyvesant so anxiously had to ponder as his commissioners returned, and the time approached for the showdown with his opponent at Hempstead.

Mindful of the budding independence fanned by John's oratory, the perplexed Director-General turned to his subjects for consultation and advice. The City fathers listened in amazement as Stuyvesant, for the first time during his long tenure of autocratic rule, assured them "he deemed it his duty" to ask them whether they would advise forcible measures, and, if so, on what scale?

That, of course, was the crux of the predicament. He was outnumbered, he told them, "as six to one." This was a gross exaggeration, though he afterwards explained that he could not be certain that President Scott's hundred and fifty men might not, at any moment, be considerably reinforced from Connecticut, and he was in no position to oppose Connecticut.

It was insufferable, his listeners admitted, that such a mob should not only spark English revolt but seek to impose rebellion on peace-loving Dutch subjects.

The militant spirit showed signs of flagging, the freedom-fighters seemed losing their zest. Instead of devising strategies, the meeting began to seek scapegoats. The Lords-Director in Holland, they grumbled wrathfully, were really to blame. Protection was up to them. Why should solid burghers be expected to do anything more than look after their own cities? As for the forthcoming encounter with President Scott, they left that entirely up to their Director.

And Stuyvesant, in reporting to the Amsterdam Chamber his final decision, signed himself your "faithful, forsaken, and almost hopeless servant and subject."[18]

He decided to make a truce with John. Delegates from the several English towns assembled with their President at Hempstead that February morning, 1664, "for the purpose of concluding a treaty."[19] Director Stuyvesant, escorted by a guard of ten soldiers, proceeded to meet them and draw up the terms of the agreement.

"For the preservation of the good people and for the prevention of the effusion of blood," so it ran, all the English towns on the western end of Long Island were to remain unmolested under the King of England for the term of twelve months, and until His Majesty and the States-General settled all difference . . . during which period they were to have free access to the Manhattans, and the other places possessed by the Dutch, who, on their side, were to have like liberty to visit the English towns for trade or justice *"according to the laws of England."* The Dutch towns and bouweries were to abide without molestation during the same time under the States-General. (Italics added.)

John signed this with his usual flourishes, Captain Underhill witnessing the signature, two others signing as representatives of the Long Island towns. Van Cortland and John Lawrence were witnesses for Stuyvesant.[20]

The long dispute was over. John had won—for England if not for himself. The Dutch had abandoned every point their enemies had assailed. Westchester was given up, the Connecticut River gone, and with this last documuent, Newton, Flushing, Jamaica, Hempstead and Gravesend passed out of their hands. This was the preliminary act which led to the outright surrender of all New Netherland.

The armistice agreement made specific reference to Connecticut's concurrence. Captain Youngs testified that "it was with the consent of Connecticut;"[21] so Governor Winthrop should have felt no great surprise at the turn of events. However, he sent his Secretary of State, John Allyn, to Hempstead to seek out those obstreperous deputies who had dared to elect John President. John Scott did not hesitate to meet with him. He had resigned Connecticut's commission, he acknowledged, when he was elected the people's leader. Since he knew Long Island was not in Connecticut's charter, he probably considered that he—as its chief magistrate—had as much right to operate there as had Winthrop . . . perhaps more!* It could

---

* Thomas Thomson of Easthampton testified that he had heard John Scott declare that Connecticut had acted rebelliously . . . and that for his part, he was the King's sworn servant . . . *Conn. His. Soc. Coll.,* XXIV (*Hoadley Memorial*), 10-11.

have occurred to him that he was exceeding the King's authority. But John had grown to manhood in the shadow of individuals who exceeded authority with the greatest impunity.

Allyn reserved judgment and returned to report the situation, while Winthrop fumed over the outcome. Most historians now agree that he had been personally involved in the intrigues to oust the Dutch from Long Island.[22] Those who had stirred the troubled waters in which he hoped to fish had been his own agents. Yet here was someone else who in the space of a few weeks had brought to a successful conclusion a twenty-year-old dispute; whose plans to capture the place had not been unlike his own, but who, instead of adding to Connecticut's territory, had acted "in the name of the King and for the people's good."

One can guess at the Governor's reactions. But John went tranquilly ahead swearing in his magistrates, confirming his appointments made according to the truce and his agreement with the Combination of English towns, administering oaths to men "to execute power under the King of England and without relation to Connecticut or any other colony,"[23] issuing passes for sojourn in New Amsterdam;[24] putting everything on record in a maddeningly legal manner. Not so tranquilly he also began asserting his "magistractical" powers, seeking out those who dissented, imprisoning a luckless Walter Salter of Flushing for disrespect to his Majesty, threatening to hang the same for such offense.[25]

Winthrop's patience boiled over. He summoned his General Assembly, and at his bidding it acted with unusual promptitude. It issued a proclamation—a hue and cry—for the arrest of John Scott. And it threatened to take action against anyone who interfered with the course of justice, or did not immediately give aid to those officers of the law "proceeding against a notorious malefactor."

BIBLIOGRAPHICAL NOTES

The conversation in this chapter is taken, verbatim, from existing documents.

1. *N.Y. Col. Docs.*, II, 393.
2. *Ibid.*, 394.
3. *Ibid.*
4. *Ibid.*
5. O'Callaghan, *N.N. Reg.*, pp. XX, 87, 146.
6. *N.Y. Col. Docs.*, II, 396-98.
7. *Early Col. Docs. L.I.*, p. 518.
8. *N.Y. Col. Docs.*, II, 515, 550.
9. *Ibid.*, 404, 405.
10. *Ibid.*
11. O'Callaghan, *Hist. of N.N.*, pp. 502, 503.
12. *Ibid.*
13. *N.Y. Col. Docs.*, II, 406
14. *Ibid.*, 231, 406.
15. *Ibid.*, III, 399-400.
16. *Ibid.*, 402; *Conn. Hist. Soc. Coll.*, XXI, 146.
17. *N.Y. Col. Docs.*, II, 234, 400.
18. *Ibid.*, 232.
19. O'Callaghan, *N.N. Reg.* (1626-74), p. 146.
20. Conn. Arch., MSS. Coll., I, No. 6 (Papers of Robert Winthrop).
21. *Ibid.*
22. *N.Y. Col. Docs.*, III, 381; Conn. Arch., Col. Boundaries, II, f 10.
23. Conn. Arch., Towns and Lands, I, f 23c.
24. *Call. of N.Y. Hist. MSS.*, prt. 1, X, 13.
25. Conn. Arch., Towns and Lands, I, f 37.

CHAPTER XVI

GOVERNOR WINTHROP STRIKES

"... when Connecticut's imperialistic ambitions were gratified and she obtained a charter which gave her all her
neighbour's territory, a very large proportion of New
Haven's inhabitants indicated that they preferred the
'Christless rule' of Connecticut ... to that of New
Haven's churches. Throughout the whole process of absorption of the smaller colony by its aggrandized neighbour,
both the action and the manner of Connecticut are difficult to defend."

—James Truslow Adams. *The Founding of
New England,* p. 319.

ONE GREY MARCH MORNING, in 1664, a small detachment of
Connecticut troops, reinforced by some tough-looking Indians, stealthily crept along the sandy shore towards the extreme west end of Setauket Harbor, known then—and now—
as Scott's Cove. They had come over from the mainland under
the command of Nathan Seeley, a Hartford marshal, who had
received orders to proceed as unobtrusively as possible. Their
movements, however, did not escape the sharp eyes of John
Scott, who was in residence at Scott's Hall, his new estate,
where he had retired after signing the truce with Stuyvesant.
His wife and children, several servants and twelve of his New
Haven followers were with him, and when Winthrop's armed
men entered the grounds and were within twenty or thirty
rods, he called out, and in the King's name commanded them
to stand off at their peril.[1]

Surprised that he had seized the initiative, they halted in

124

indecision and John immediately ordered them off his land. This time they did not move.

"In the King's name I demand your business!" he shouted. Seeley, noting the presence of the New Haven veterans, requested a parley, and John, never one to refuse a reasonable offer, granted it. Each approached the other accompanied by two musketeers. John and Nathan Seeley faced each other belligerently, and the marshal said he had come with orders for his arrest.

"On what grounds?" demanded John.

Seeley read him the commission he held from Connecticut, charging Scott with "sundry heinous crimes touching His Majesty," and asked John if he would surrender quietly.

"I would sacrifice my life's blood on the ground before I ever yield to you or to any of Connecticut's jurisdiction with that of New Haven," was John's answer. And his men behind him applauded and shouted "So will we."

Seeley shuffled uneasily, baffled and perplexed.

"Stay a moment," went on Scott, quick to follow up an advantage. "I will fetch you a letter under Governor Winthrop's own hand. I do not doubt but that it will satisfy you fully."

He went into the house and brought back a letter, reading it to the officer, declaring it was dated March 25th (afterwards corrected to March 14th old style). It was about the Governor's wish to meet John and talk over the Narragansett proposition.

"If you will go back to your company," declared John, "I will procure a commission under His Majesty's seal, which will put me in command of you all."

He made a dramatic flourish, producing a document and declaring he would go down to Seeley's company and read this same commission. And he would see if the proudest among them dared touch him!

Young Daniel Gotherson, who had followed John out of the house, watched the proceeding with widening eyes. The array of soldiers seemed frightening enough, but it was the Indians, their faces dark and impassive as they fingered their white man's weapons, who most appalled him.

John strode alone to the head of the group. He read his paper, which, he said, had the "seal manual" on it.

"Take me if you dare," he shouted. "I will see if the proudest among you will dare lay hands on me."

There was a long pause. Then, at a signal from the marshal, the Indians fell on him, and Seeley shouted: "I arrest you in the King's name and charge you to follow me."[2]

The New Haveners protested angrily as John struggled with his captors, but Seeley's troops held them at bay. The marshal then demanded that John turn over certain men who had accompanied him on his recent campaign. These were Captain Woodall and two other magistrates who had been commissioned by Winthrop to go along with Scott to help reduce the Long Island towns to Connecticut. John ignored the command, nor did Seeley's threats intimidate him, helpless as he was. He ordered his own men to look after them and take them back to New Haven. Seeley, feeling no doubt that he had his hands full enough with this obstreperous prisoner, let the matter drop. He gave summary orders to the Indians and his troops, and John was overpowered and dragged away, struggling wildly, cursing, and threatening his captors with the gallows.

Daniel followed the disorderly procession, horrified at the sight but unable to help. After some time Seeley, who had received orders to avoid public places, turned into a narrow footpath through the woods and young Gotherson grew afraid as the dark trees closed about them. He turned to run.

"Stay with me, stay with me," implored John, fearful of what might happen to himself or to the boy, and needing him, perhaps, as a witness to the violent scene. But Daniel continued his flight.

Arriving at a lonely wayside inn, John insisted that the boy be taken in and looked after, which was done. And then the Indians hurried their captive away.*

Bound, and like a criminal, he was dragged through isolated ways, then thrust into a waiting ship. Seeley had been expressly commanded, *by no means to proceed through New Haven.* Realizing John's great popularity there, Winthrop, it would seem, feared some reaction in that quarter with a possible rescue of the prisoner. The orders effectively prevented this, and John, despite his wild imprecations, was ultimately delivered at Hartford.

By this time the General Assembly had blown up the original charge into a formidable case.[3] But John, disregarding his deplorable condition after the terrible journey, had lost neither his courage nor his legal sense. He protested formally that Connecticut Colony Courts were prejudiced, and offered to stand trial before any court in New Haven, Boston, Plymouth or Virginia.[4] He then lodged an official complaint against the marshal who had arrested him and against his accusers.[5] All this Winthrop brushed off as mere impertinence and had John thrown into jail, chained to iron stocks, to await trial.

BIBLIOGRAPHICAL NOTES

1. Conn. Arch. Towns and Lands, I, f 31.
2. *Ibid.,* ff 31-33.
3. *Rec. of Part. Crt. (Probate-Rec.* Conn.), III, 16.
4. *Conn. Hist. Soc. Coll.,* III, 154-55 *(Wyllys Papers).*
5. *Mass. Hist. Soc. Coll.,* 4th ser., VI, 525.

---

* Daniel's mother, Dorothea Gotherson, gives this account of her son's disappearance from John's custody, though her letter has always been studiously ignored and John accused of "barbarously selling him into slavery." The boy was later found at a New Haven inn, where he was performing quite menial tasks, and was subsequently redeemed by his family for £7. Rawl. MSS., A 175, ff 149, 98.

CHAPTER XVII

CONDEMNED—AND VINDICATED

Sense: Wilt thou all the glory have
Which war or peace commends?
Half the world shall be thy slaves
The other half thy friends

Soul: What friends? if to myself untrue?
What slaves unless I conquer you?
—John Scott, *Combat between
Soul and Senses.*
Rawl. MSS., A 176.

THE NEWS OF JOHN'S ARREST caused an immediate reaction throughout all New England, for thoughtful and influential people at the time all regarded this as a shocking event.

One of the first to appeal to Governor Winthrop was Captain Underhill,* who wrote his "honored Unkell" how much he was "trobbled by your unexpected burden from the west of Long Island." He marvelled how people could offend God by "torning and torning again. Greate was the people's cri for Captain Scott, he *sought not them, but they him.* They cried him up, Hosanna today, and down with him tomorrow."[1]

This statement, coming from one who was with John throughout his whole campaign, is highly revealing, although

---

* Underhill's second wife was the daughter of "the Winthrop woman"— widow of one of Winthrop's sons. Underhill always addressed Winthrop as uncle, and was used by the latter as chief "trouble shooter" on Long Island.

Underhill himself "had his mind changed" later by his "diere and louing onckel."*

Protests began pouring into Hartford, many from the highest in the land. The Reverend John Davenport put in an immediate plea. Davenport was the most celebrated nonconformist preacher in the New World and the founder of New Haven. When he had quit England during the great Puritan Migration his acknowledged eminence then had attracted Archbishop Laud's attention, who mentioned him by name to Charles I.

It was, Davenport assured Winthrop, the love he bore the governor that constrained him to protest John's arrest.

"The acting of your General Assembly doth seem very strange, if not irrational to unbiassed observers and hearers thereof," he wrote. And he outlined four serious infractions of the law involved in the action; (1) that they take accusations against such a man as Captain Scott from such witnesses as his accusers (against whom he has protested officially) would be enough to discredit their testimony in any court in England; (2) Winthrop's marshal was sent to New Haven, Branford, Milford, Stratford and Fairfield to apprehend Captain Scott just as though these places were already under Connecticut's jurisdiction, and this at the General Court's orders!† (3) The marshal's commission stated that if any officers were to resist or delay delivery of what was demanded, they were to be charged with "abetting and concealing a notorious malefactor.[2] Which accusation the marshal made twice, most absurdly. . . ." (It is evident that Winthrop expected opposition to the arrest, or the warrant would not have been so worded.) (4) "The law of England does not

---

* Stuyvesant reported to Holland that the people of Long Island, who had first elected John Scott as President, afterwards *had their minds changed by those of Hartford.* N.Y. Col. Docs., II, 407.

† Davenport had strenuously opposed New Haven's union with Connecticut, above all Winthrop's highhanded manner of obtaining it. *Mass. Hist. Soc. Coll.,* 4th Ser., VII, 523-24.

allow any man to be proclaimed a malefactor until convicted."

Davenport wrote more in sorrow than in anger and his letter is phrased in most respectful terms. It was customary at
this period for churchmen to transact public affairs, so his
intervention was entirely within his province. But his indignation took on political and personal overtones as he declared
Winthrop's action was abundant cause to refuse any union
with a colony which "multiplied injuries against us. For
yourself, Honored Sir," he added, "I fear you will not do
yourself right unless you protest against these irregular, illegal, I had almost said, unchristian actings, and enter it
upon record."[3]

Another formal protest reached Winthrop from Richard
Bellingham, a Patentee of the original Massachusetts Charter,
Boston magistrate and onetime Governor of Massachusetts.
It is plainly indicative of John's good standing that charac-
ters like this sprang to his aid.

Bellingham dwells on the disgraceful details of John's
arrest, reminding Winthrop that "this gentleman is one for
whom his Majesty hath respect and that, during his late residence at Court, he approved himself faithful to the interest
of His Majesty and of his subjects in these United Colonies."

Governor Bellingham assures Winthrop that he has no
desire to "intermeddle in others' affairs," but writes as a
faithful friend trying to be helpful in sending an account of
the circumstances which have made "an awful impression in
some parts, the consequences of which" (if Winthrop, in his
prudence, does not prevent) "may be truly dreadful."[4]

Much more indignant was William Leete's letter to Winthrop on March 31st, 1664. Leete, a noted Puritan and staunch
republican, had been Cromwell's agent in the New World.
He was one of the original signers of the New Haven Plantation Covenant and its governor from 1661 until its union
with Connecticut in 1665. In spite of this long association,
however, he had never opposed Winthrop's annexation of

that colony (an attitude his fellow-colonists did not share.) Indeed, we may suppose that he sympathised with the latter's expansionist aims, for in a previous letter addressed to Winthrop in London (April 12, 1661), he had written:

> "I wish that you and we could procure a patent to reach beyond Delaware, . . . If war should arise between Holland and England *it might suit the King's interest; a little resistance might so reduce all to England.*"⁵ (Italics added.)

What Leete had only hinted at, John had been bold enough to accomplish. And when one of his servants arrived post haste to inform the governor of his arrest, Leete went immediately to New Haven to take "large and ample testimony," as he assured Winthrop, concerning the "violent surprisal of Captain Scott," and of the "unusual warrant and the hostile seizure in time of parley . . . by a kind of Army, part English, part Indian"; dragged from his own land, "which he held by Patten under the Broad Seal, then and there shown unto his surprisers, *as also was the commission under the King's sign manual* for his conduct and assistance. And this too, in addition to the well known fact that he held the King's letter addressed to the four colonies under which he is daily expected to act in pursuit of His Majesty's pleasure." (Italics added.)

Leete's indignation boils over remembering how all this "was slighted" and of Scott, he wrote:

> "His Majesty's domestic and public servant, one of considerable interest and expectation at Court, also a known friend of this country, and enemy to the New England enemies . . . and yet he must be ignominiously handled and interrupted. And that, *after,* if not *because,* he *asserts the King's prerogative and the Duke's interest upon Long Island, opposite to Connecticut's claims by the Charter.*" (Italics added.)

(Leete did not flinch from accusing Winthrop to his face and putting his finger on the crux of the matter. "This seems strange to me, as (I believe) it will to yourself. . . . how he hath been branded with the infamy of a notorious malefactor and so dealt with thus far."

The writer goes on to express a hope that Winthrop "interpose in the matter." In these lines, however, Leete can only be suspected of irony, for he must have known that the warrant for John's arrest came, after all, from Connecticut's General Assembly, and that its terms—*read aloud in court*—[6] sanctioned such unprecedented action. "Assuredly this action and the manner of it is like to be so universally evilly resented in New England and Old, that it gain some to *prosecute for vindication,* in a high degree," he warned.[7] (Italics added.)

From Plymouth Colony came a letter from the Governor and his Assistants in John's defense, "having never," as it stated, "heard anything but that Captain Scott was a gentleman well deserving of the country, one that his Majesty was pleased to employ in his service."[8]

It is evident from the intervention of all these distinguished men that they not only felt that Winthrop was acting injudiciously, but that the case was sensational enough to have repercussions in England. Leete was particularly afraid that Scott's *person* was endangered, "and that, fatally." Therefore he offered to send some of his officials to Hartford to testify in the prisoner's favor,[9] calling attention to the *"extremity of danger* he is now in" and urging the magistrates to do their best to prevent Scott's "ruin."[10] (Italics added.)

The Massachusetts Council also sent official representatives to Hartford—Major-General John Leverett and Captain William Davis—to intervene personally before the trial and support the prisoner's plea that his case be tried elsewhere in an unprejudiced court.

Other commissioners to intercede were Captain William Bradford and Thomas Southworth from Plymouth, and Captain Prince from New Haven.[11] Their concern was urgent and sincere. They were also aware, and probably remembered with some misgiving, that John was privy to all their recent political deals with the King's ministers at Whitehall, and they certainly would not have wished to have such matters made public should John decide to defend himself by implicating them—a tactic he never adopted.

Nor did John lack for supporters among the rank and file either. The freedom-loving people of the English Towns, for whom he had deserted Winthrop, loyally sprang to his defense. A document, signed by one hundred and forty-four citizens of Hempstead, Newark (Jamaica), Folestone and Hastings, declared they were "fully satisfied with the new arrangement and the magistrates elected and sworn in under its provisions," and praised Captain Scott, "our chosen President, without whose assistance our towns would have been in a confusion by reason of the divisions among us." While it expressed the most courteous reference to Connecticut's General Assembly, it stated nevertheless that "if you should intermeddle we might declare to the world . . . your design to destroy us."[12]

From Flushing came a Remonstrance, signed by thirty-nine inhabitants, many of them Quakers, reciting the "miseries and indecisions under Dutch rule" and stating in the most emphatic terms that "the worthy Captain Scott had acted in accordance with the will of the people" only *after "our very strong*est solicitations did prevail upon him," and that his "unparalleled industry" on their behalf—"maligned by a few malevolent spirits"—had brought to an end a "labyrinth of confusion and trouble. If we should, at such a time as this, be silent we should be showing the greatest ingratitude in the world and the very stones, in our silence, might rise to proclaim his innocence."[13] (Italics added.)

How the sensitive Winthrop must have writhed under such universal condemnation! Only a year before he had borne the brunt of New Haven's bitter criticism of his Charter maneuvers, and now again he was being censured. Rarely has a Governor been so rebuked, and the subject of such concerted disapproval. How he must have wished that the whole matter could be quietly disposed of without a public trial!

From the records it looks as if someone pushed such an idea to almost fatal lengths. Suddenly, John became deathly ill. Governor Leete informed his Council that "Mr. Scott's trial is said to be on the 8th of May next, *if he be not dead before*, as was like to have been the other day, *by poison*."[14] (Italics added.)

The same terrible suspicion that someone was trying to do away with him was repeated by Deborah Scott in her appeal to Governor Winthrop, surely one of the most touching letters of the century.

The original, preserved in the archives of the Massachusetts Historical Society in Boston, proves what an exceptional character she was. In an age when most women could neither read nor write—even the outstandingly competent and doughty Lady Moody could only trace her name in large block letters—Deborah wrote four pages of neat script with well-spaced lines and margins. Lacking all elegant flourishes, it is true, but most legible, the text and signature are in the same round hand, and the letter's only blemishes are the faint, circular stains blurring some of the words—her tears, falling on the paper as she wrote.

"For the Worshipful Governor Winthrop at Connecticut. Having an opportunity, I could not omit but present to your consideration my sad and disconsolate state, being exceedingly afflicted and disturbed in my spirit, in respect of the injurious charges of some of our Colony against my dear husband who hath not meritted any such thing at their hands.

"So I doubt not but yourself can testify; but if they had any just occasion of difference he has tendered them a legal hearing anywhere but among them that are his professed enemies, as you have been fully certified by some of our friends.

"Therefore, I shall not trouble you with much at this time,

only concerning myself, who am not well and with child, and with the daily rumors which I hear do so aggravate my sorrow that I fear it will bring me to an untimely end; *for I think it is his life they are at.* [Italics added.]

"Sir, I think as you are Chief, it does behoove you to show yourself active in this thing, lest the last end of it be worse than the beginning; for it is not enough for one in your place to stand as a neuter; for Pilate washing his hands did not excuse him, and the wise man saith, if thou forbear to deliver them that are drawn unto death, and those that are ready to be slain, if thou sayest behold, we knew it not; doth not he that pondereth the heart consider it, and he that keepeth the souls of all men doth he not know and shall he not render to every man according to his works! But if you forbear to speak, I hope God will rend out some other way both for his and my safety and deliverance. Thus with my humble services to you and Madame Winthrop I subscribe myself,

> Your servant,
> Deborah Scott"

But Winthrop remained obdurate. John had thwarted his ambition of grasping captivating Long Island; that little jewel on the Sound he had wanted for over twenty years.* Beside this loss, his annexation of Westchester seemed tame and unimportant. He was not touched by the appeals—indeed he seemed angered by the widespread intervention, treating his prisoner yet more harshly, and keeping him in heavy chains even when brought to court to be arraigned at the bar.

At the beginning of May Connecticut's General Assembly declared all John's property within the limits of the Colony sequestered, and commissioners were appointed to take an exact invoice of his estates.[15]

---

* As early as 1636 Winthrop had tried to buy a large tract of Long Island land from the Sachem of the Western Niantics but the United Colonies commissioners would not permit his verbal arrangements with the Indians. *Mass. Hist. Soc. Coll.,* IV, Vol. 7, 57 n.

Convinced of the rightness of his cause, John was no submissive prisoner. He was violent, abusive, heaping threats on his jailer and all who came near him. For this conduct he was placed in even heavier shackles and the jailer ordered to treat him with greater severity. One can imagine how all the old sense of injustice and fury must have revived under such ignominious treatment.

But anger did not blind his reason, and his innate good sense ultimately prompted an apology to rid himself of the shameful irons.

With tongue-in-cheek abasement, he addressed "an humbell petition" to the Hartford Court, stating that he had

"Run himself into a labyrinth of misery by the evil advice of bad instruments as well as his corrupt nature . . . and knowing that you sit in God's stead, who delights in shewing mercie, do, for His sake, beseech your favorable report, which shall be deemed by your poor suppliant a signal kindness never to be forgot, . . ."[16] etc., etc.

He knew how to pour it on. And that touch about sitting in God's stead was a calculated tribute to the august magistrates who really exercised a police power practically absolute and wholly supported by the church.

The irons were removed. It was the least that Winthrop could do, for John, after all, had not originally opposed the latter's claim to Long Island. This he had made clear at that historic Hempstead meeting.

Indeed, he had written Secretary Williamson in London, praising Winthrop's prompt action in stepping in to oppose the "cruel and rapacious Dutch on Long Island."[17] And his own truce with Stuyvesant, with the exception of one small detail, was not unlike Winthrop's ultimatum to the Dutch Commissioners. By the latter's terms, Westchester on the mainland was to be English, and the disputed Long Island towns were to remain autonomous *"untill there be a deter-*

mination of the case."[18] (Italics added.) In John's truce, Westchester went to the English, while the other towns "should remain under the King of England . . . until *His Majesty and the States-General do fully determine the whole difference. . . ."* (Italics added.)

Therein lay the crux. John had put an end to Long Island's turmoil, but its ownership was still not settled, for he had not established the Duke of York's jurisdiction.

It was not only Winthrop's sounder political judgment that kept him silent about the English King's designs, whereas John had openly boasted of this knowledge. Discretion served Winthrop's own purpose, for doubtless he himself intended making the "determination" about those island towns (or at least influencing it). His proprietorship of Long Island would thus never be questioned.

John aroused his ire, "and the jealousy of the General Court," says Riker,[19] not only by bringing an age-old quarrel to a swift conclusion, but by leaving the island's ultimate fate open to discussion, and thus thwarting Governor Winthrop's attempt at a quick snatch.

For that he had to pay. His trial was set for May 24th. John was well aware of the peculiarities of contemporary law courts, where presentment of a case before a panel of jurors was practically tantamount to conviction.[20] So he waived his right to trial by jury and was brought before the Court of Magistrates, Connecticut's Particular Court.

There were ten charges against him,[21] of which the first, and most serious, was speaking words tending to defame the King's Majesty. He was also charged with gross profanation of God's Holy Day and calumniating a Commission officer! There was no word of the real cause of Winthrop's wrath. (Appendix F)

The Court found him guilty of all ten charges, of course (Leete wrote "Scott was sentenced before he was heard.")[22] and ordered him to pay a fine of two hundred and fifty pounds; to continue in prison during the Court's pleasure; and to find security for his good behaviour in the sum of five hundred pounds. It also degraded him from his Long Island magistracy and disenfranchised him. Captain Youngs was ordered to sell his property to pay the fines (exorbitantly high, for not one person in ten had any cash income). It is interesting to note, too, that the order for the sale preceded the verdict by some thirteen days![23] No wonder John considered Connecticut's courts prejudiced. And it certainly looks as though someone were in a very great hurry to get hold of his land.

John did not "pleasure the Court" however, by remaining long in prison. He had other plans in defiance of the Governor. He had managed to survive attempted murder and was not to be deterred by iron bars. With the imminent prospect of injustice triumphant, he could only resort to native wit, and the active assistance of the patient Deborah. He petitioned the Court for a meeting with his wife and brother-in-law Joseph, a visit apparently allowed him. Gossip records that Deborah was later observed approaching the prison precincts "being then big with child." Gossip, for once was right. And she was considerably bigger, no doubt, from the coil of rope she carried under her skirts. John's garret cell was "three stories high," too lofty even for his cool nerve and long legs to negotiate without some pretty stout assistance.

Before summer was over he made his getaway. Sustained by the knowledge of his own innocence, and with or without Joseph's help, and that of his Quaker friends in Flushing, he went right back to Long Island where, significantly enough, Winthrop did not dare arrest him again.

John's erstwhile jailer, Dan Garrad, complained to the Court (in July) that John's escape left him in debt for "diet and time attending him for the space of twelve weeks."

The court allowed the man ten pounds (out of John's money) "if he can come by it."[24]

BIBLIOGRAPHICAL NOTES

1. *Mass. Hist. Soc. Coll.,* 4th ser., VII, 525.
2. *Conn. Pub. Rec.,* I, 421.
3. *Mass. Hist. Soc. Coll.,* 4th ser., VII, 525-26.
4. *Ibid.,* 596-97.
5. *Ibid.,* 549.
6. *Conn. Pub. Rec.,* I, 418.
7. *Mass. Hist. Soc. Coll.,* 4th ser., VII, 553-55.
8. Conn. Arch. Towns and Lands, I, f 34 A.
9. *Mass. Hist. Soc. Coll.,* 4th ser., VII, 553-55
10. Hoadley, *Rec. of N. Hav.,* p. 540.
11. *Ibid.,* p. 541.
12. Conn. Arch. Towns and Lands, I, f 26a.
13. *Ibid.,* f 32, b, c.
14. Hoadley, *Rec. of N. Hav.,* p. 540.
15. *Conn. Pub. Rec.,* I, 430.
16. Conn. Arch. Towns and Lands, I, f 38.
17. *N.Y. Col. Docs.,* III, 47; *Conn. Pub. Rec.,* XV, 537.
18. *Mass. Hist. Soc. Coll.,* 4th ser., VII, 189.
19. Riker, *Annals of Newtown,* pp. 60-61.
20. *Columbia Law Review,* XXI (1931), 416-48.
21. *Rec. of Part. Crt.,* III, 16.
22. *Mass. Hist. Soc. Coll.,* 4th ser., VII, 554.
23. *Conn. Pub. Rec.,* II, 16.
24. *Ibid.,* I, 436; II, 37.

CHAPTER XVIII

ENGLAND ACQUIRES
NEW NETHERLAND

"Courage, Courage my soul now learn to wield
The weight of thy immortal shield."
—John Scott.

WHILE JOHN LANGUISHED IN PRISON history was in the making.
The suggestion, outlined in his Narrative, that the Dutch
were less firmly entrenched at New Amsterdam than was
formerly believed sparked a plot which had been a-brewing
in London more than a year. The energetic Duke of York,
England's Lord High Admiral, with men close to the King
like Lord Berkeley and Carteret, as well as prominent merchants, aided and abetted by the implacable Downing, had
all had predatory eyes fixed on the Manhattans, center and
heart of the Dutch trading area.

John's Narrative, complaining of Dutch encroachments
and recommending action, had the advantage of stressing
local conditions and pointing out how cheap such conquest
would be—a telling point with the impecunious Charles. It
was included in a report submitted January 29th, 1664, and
proved, as C. M. Andrews points out, to be "more directly
influential" than others in the general preparations for England's first armed invasion of the North American continent.
Whatever the ethics of the case, the logic of the situation
was irresistible.

In March 1664, Charles II formally granted to his brother

James all the territory between the Connecticut River and Delaware Bay—New Netherland's exact boundaries. The grant specifically included Long Island, for which thirty-five hundred pounds was to be paid to the fourth Earl of Stirling, heir of the original grantee.* The entire transaction was naturally a top secret, even after the expeditionary force, under the command of Colonel Richard Nicolls, was already on the high seas.

Three others, Sir Robert Carr, Sir George Cartwright and Samuel Maverick were nominated with Colonel Nicolls as royal commissioners to take possession of the country and settle the boundaries. As a secondary objective they were instructed to investigate the "arrogant theocratic government of Massachusetts," whose growing independence angered the Privy Council.

Nicolls sailed from Portsmouth on May 15th. His ships lost each other in the fog, but about July 20th the Commander and Sir Robert Carr touched Cape Cod, and a week later all reached Boston. The commissioners had been authorized to raise additional troops in New England, and for a full month they haggled with Massachusett's sharp-witted Puritan magistrates, who showed little inclination to comply and participate in the attack on New Netherland. Connecticut proved more amenable. Governor Winthrop, tactfully complying with a decision he could not prevent, turned it to his own advantage. He met the ships and obtained from Nicolls a promise that all that Connecticut had established on Long Island should be recognized by the incoming governor. Assuring himself by this agreement that his own recent land rulings would be upheld, Winthrop placed himself and some

---

* The Duke of York expected to borrow this sum from his father-in-law, the Earl of Clarendon. But he never paid it, but promised Stirling instead £300 annually, from the profits of the province. As there were no net profits, Stirling received nothing; and in 1687 petitioned the Treasury for payment. (*Cal. Tr. Books,* VIII, part III, 1174-75; *ibid,* IX, 237.) By 1760 a second petition put the amount due at £7,000. After this date, however, all recognition of the claim fades from public records.

troops at Nicolls' disposal to join the march on the Manhattans.

A rendezvous was fixed for the west end of Long Island
and the ships, after some delay, sailed for the Narrows.

Rumors that a hostile squadron was on its way from England had preceded its arrival, and Stuyvesant began, in late
spring, to fortify New Amsterdam, and make other provisions
for defense. But at this critical juncture, when every hour
was precious and his success depended upon untiring energy
and vigilance, a belated dispatch arrived from Holland stating
that no danger from England need be feared! King Charles
was merely desirous of enforcing uniformity of Church and
State and had dispatched frigates for the purpose of introducing Episcopacy into his colonies! This report seemed to be
confirmed by the English squadron's month-long stay in
Boston.

All suspicion of invasion was dispelled and Stuyvesant,
convinced that all was well, left his capital for Rennslaerwyck
to direct a campaign against the Esopus Indians.

On August 19th the English ships were sighted. The Dutch
Director-General, alerted by a furiously riding courier, hurried back down the river. The day after his arrival in Manhattan, four stately black frigates flying the red ensign of
England at their mastheads, sailed up the Lower Bay, an-
chored just below the Narrows, blockaded the North River,
and sent ashore a company of soldiers who occupied the
Blockhaus on Staten Island.

Frenzied activity now seized the Dutch. Every third man
was ordered to work on the city defenses; guards were placed
at New Amsterdam's gates, military rationing hastily introduced, and all brewers were forbidden malt to brew beer.

For a moment it looked as though the defender might offer
serious resistance, for Stuyvesant was putting a very brave
face on the situation. Nicolls also feared that turbulent, popu-
lous Long Island would rise and give his troops trouble, and
he sent an appeal for reinforcements.

John Scott, but shortly out of prison, had found his way home. His reputation seems to have survived most triumphantly Connecticut's ill treatment, for when he heard Nicolls' summons he had no difficulty in recruiting some Long Islanders and mounting them with his own horses.

Nicolls now began negotiations for surrender; but Stuyvesant, despite his people's waning ardor, was adamant. He had only one hundred and fifty trained soldiers, his capital was open along the banks of both rivers, its only defense a hastily erected wood fence. Yet he wanted to fight.

Under a flag of truce Nicolls and Winthrop met with the proud old man and the city magistrates, presenting them with a letter containing extremely favorable surrender terms. These Stuyvesant angrily refused, tearing the letter into bits and countering with elaborate and threadbare arguments about Dutch claims to New Netherland, and the twelve-month truce he had recently signed with Captain John Scott. Nicolls lost patience with such legal maneuvering. "I shall speak with you at the Manhattans," he declared. "I shall come—not as a friend, but with ships and soldiers."

Within a day, two frigates dropped anchor near Governor's Island, while the Commander marched three companies to the Brooklyn end of Fulton Ferry. Here he was joined by the Connecticut forces, and a small troop of cavalry commanded by none other than the quondam President Scott!

John was in at the kill, after all. For a second time in his life he had come, armed, to New Amsterdam, and this time neither Colonel Nicolls nor Governor Winthrop rejected his aid. At the head of his men, he watched the other two frigates come on past the city under full canvas, their guns loaded, ready to fire a broadside.

The sight was too much for Stuyvesant; brave as he was, the odds against him were too great. A white flag fluttered from the fort. Nicolls allowed the Dutch forces to march out with all honors of war, and embark for home on the *Gideon*.

On August 29th, 1664, the English took possession of the citadel with a corporal's guard.

Cartwright and Carr spent some weeks attacking Dutch forces upstate with some rather disgracefully brutal incidents, from which Nicolls had to extricate them. But within a very short time Holland's rule in America came to a peaceful end.

Thus was John Scott's Narrative fulfilled in a manner which even that swashbuckling rover could hardly have deemed possible.

CHAPTER XIX

JOHN STANDS BY THE PEOPLE

"... there is some ground to fear that the phancy of a
commonwealth is yet in some of their brains."
—Commissioner Cartwright to Secretary Bennet,
Feb. 7th, 1664/5, *N.Y. Col. Docs.*, III, 89.

THE CONQUEST OF NEW NETHERLAND, which almost doubled
New England's territory, was a barren victory for the local
participants, and John Scott, after all the hints and promises
of service to be rewarded, received no recognition for his
share in it. Instead the King sent him a directive to proceed
at once to Barbados with horses and ammunition and to
establish a garrison there.[1] The far-seeing Charles, realizing
that his assault on a Dutch colony would inevitably provoke
retaliation at sea where the Dutch were strongest, feared an
attack on the weakly held English islands in the West Indies.
The dashing Captain Scott had not only proved himself of
exceptional competence on Long Island but was already
familiar with the Caribbean. The royal command was therefore logical if costly,—however crushing to John, with his
mind running on rehabilitation and reward at home.

Gloomily he set about purchasing guns and horses; but he
was not the only one to be disappointed.

Governor Winthrop, in defiance of all reason, had followed
up his illegal imprisonment of John by announcing his own
possession of Long Island; and, in June 1664, had marched
troops into Hempstead to establish Connecticut's rule there.

He deposed all the magistrates John had appointed, and reappointed them again in his own name. But his triumph was short-lived.

Richard Nicolls, now Governor of the newly conquered territory, officially informed Winthrop that Connecticut's southern border ended at the sea. Long Island was definitely and irrevocably in the Duke of York's charter.

The blow had fallen at last. Winthrop's dearest ambitions were thwarted. Still, gallant gentleman as he was, he hid his disappointment and with a show of friendship sent the new governor sixty bushels of wheat and offered to "help mark his boundaries." The gullible commissioners accepted his aid. They had no topographical knowledge of America and their task was not easy, for, pursuing the policy of overlapping frontiers, the King had named New York's eastern line the Connecticut River, irrespective of the fact that Winthrop's charter extended to the Pacific!

It was inviting trouble. Most historians have now forgotten the "pious fraud" (as one called it) whereby the dividing line was made to pass south through Poughkeepsie, thereby adding a good twenty miles to Connecticut Colony! But the fraud was discovered, rectification was possible, and from Hartford came a letter admitting the error and expressing "humblest and most unctious apologies."[2]

But the incident pointed up the difficulties of the situation.

Governor Nicolls and the commissioners realized they were in a tough spot, operating as foreigners in unknown territory. For assistance they turned to John Scott, asking him to postpone his departure to Barbados until things were running more smoothly.[3]

Nicolls' confidence in John was based on what he had heard about him in London, and, more particularly on the fact that John's appointment as Long Island's chief magistrate had been made at the recommendation of the Lord Chancellor himself.[4] News of the arrest and imprisonment had not reached England when the expedition started, so

John, as far as the four commissioners were concerned, was still Clarendon's protegé. He had met and talked with them aboard the *Thomas and James,* in August 1664, had heard their plans for the taking of all New Netherland, and had been shown letters from Clarendon and the Privy Council, on the basis of which he had delayed his departure for Barbados, in order to be of service to them.[5]

Winthrop hastened to inform Nicolls of John's "changed status" and disenfranchisement. Nevertheless one of the new governor's first acts was to grant John and his servant a passport, guaranteeing safe return from New York, since he was still, technically, a fugitive from Connecticut justice.[6] Later, Nicolls learned that John's case was to be "further considered" and had written to Winthrop, expressing a hope that "your Court would have given some example of leneity (sic) to Captain Scott which was once the intention of the gentlemen attending you."[7] He added that he had "expected long since" a copy of the Hartford trial proceedings to prepare himself should John decide to appeal his case in the New York Courts.[8]

It was particularly on Long Island that Nicolls needed John's cooperation for he knew that the latter's truce with Stuyvesant had lightened his own initial task there, and he was well aware of John's great local reputation.* New regulations re-establishing ownership rights had had to be immediately devised for the changed conditions of this so greatly disrupted colony. And the Long Islanders were already showing hostility at the first reading of the Duke's Laws which Nicolls was introducing.

This new code provided for the renewal of all land grants, an edict which outraged the English communities, accustomed for thirty years to run their own affairs without Eng-

---

* "A man of great influence," says James Riker, Jr., writing of John in 1852 (before G. D. Scull had made known, in America, the Pepysian affidavits) "in the balloting for president, Scott received a unanimous vote." *Annals of Newtown,* pp. 60, 61.

land's interference; while the former Dutch settlers were horrified at the reversal of what they had been led to expect from English law. Nicolls' decrees permitted no free election of civil and military officers; these were to be appointed by the King. And, as crowning insult, taxes were to be imposed without consultation with the people's representatives. In fact the new measures meant less freedom under the Duke than under the Dutch.

Nicolls further convoked a general meeting in Hempstead, February 1664/5 and ordered all seventeen island towns to send deputies bringing deeds of their personal holdings and of their townships as well, and invited the Indian Sachems too. John Scott, his local reputation in no wise impaired by what most of his neighbours evidently regarded as a personal "feud" with Winthrop, appeared as the town's attorney to deal not only with Hempstead's boundary quarrel with Flushing but with every matter concerning this important center.[9]

In pursuance of royal instructions to "curb New England pretensions," Governor Nicolls was treating his province like a conquered country. He presented the Convention delegates with a formal address of submission which he requested them to sign—it was "wholly voluntary" he assured them, but reminded them that those who did not "must not expect the fruit and benefit thereof common with others."[10] The delegates were incensed by the servile tone of the document, and hostile to the idea of "submitting." As the Hempstead Convention dragged into its second week their sullen resentment mounted. Accusations of "unconstitutional government" were heard. The harassed governor, seeking to detect a ringleader, issued an edict forbidding all further criticism. But opposition to the Duke's Laws continued, led by Southampton,* which was particularly averse to paying new taxes.

---

* Southampton also refused to comply with the patent renewals; and in 1671 the New York Court of Assizes declared many Long Island titles invalid. Together with some eastern towns Southampton drew up a Remonstrance, which the New York Governor declared illegal and publicly burned. A year later Southampton petitioned Whitehall for permission to secede from New

Nicolls was counting upon Scott—as prominent South-ampton land-owner—to mollify that town's delegates, and to use his influence with the disillusioned Dutch. He treated John with every mark of confidence and friendship, promising him unlimited choice of office (as John's angry letter to King Charles makes clear).

For the second time in his career, John was fiercely tempted. He had but to comply with Nicolls' desires and both rehabilitation and honor were his. His fortune would have been made. Thereafter he could snap his fingers at Winthrop and, at an appropriate later moment, might well secure the return of his Long Island property. As geographer, navigator, friend of the Indians and the Islanders' trusted president, there was almost no service he could not have rendered the governor and his inexperienced commissioners. But to do so would have meant offending his principles and turning his back on his fellow citizens.

Remembering all that he, in the King's name, had promised these people, and watching their determined resistance to the new legislation, John must have begun to realize the magnitude and implications of the choice before him.

BIBLIOGRAPHICAL NOTES

1. S.P. Dom. Car., II, 29, No. 419.
2. Egerton MS., 2395, f 432v.
3. S.P. Dom. Car., II, 29, No. 419.
4. *Ibid.*
5. *Ibid.*
6. *Early Col. Docs. L.I.*, p. 557.
7. Nicolls to Winthrop, original letter in Gardiner Memorial room of Easthampton Library, L.I.
8. *Early Col. Docs. L.I.*, p. 564.
9. *Ibid., Rec. N. and S. Hemp.*, I, 156.
10. Nicolls to Winthrop, *op. cit.*

York and join Connecticut. Refused! Many inhabitants, rather than endure conditions they considered intolerable, abandoned their homes and left for Holland! It was at the height of these disturbances in 1673 that the Dutch quietly sailed up the Bay and re-took Manhattan.

CHAPTER XX

JOHN'S SACRIFICE FOR FREEDOM

"Democracy hath taken so deepe a Roote in these parts
that ye very name of a Justice of the Peace is an Abomina-
tion."
—Complaint of Governor Richard Nicolls.
N.Y. Hist. Soc. Coll. (1869), p. 119.

By ACCEPTING THE DUKE'S LAWS and embracing the schemes
to subjugate the Long Islanders, John Scott could have made
himself solid with Governor Nicolls and the three commissioners.

But John would have no part in helping Nicolls subdue
the governments of New England. He stubbornly maintained
that "the people's liberties were being suppressed,"[1] and not
only on Long Island. He informed the King, the commissioners "opposed on all points" everything the royal charter
of 1629 had granted the colonists of Massachusetts[2] as well.

That he should identify himself with the resistance movement there was only logical. He had been intimately connected with this colony since 1662, serving it once as
agent, and would naturally have been among the first to share
its resentment at any "overhauling" carried out by English
officials.

In the long Narrative (Report) which members of the
Boston General Court sent the King[3] (together with five
hundred pounds worth of local commodities to sweeten their

arguments) they expressed their due respect for Charles II, but none at all for his commissioners.

While freely acknowledging that they themselves had erred in omitting the oath of allegiance, the members vigorously defended their other actions, and reminded the King of his own promises in the charter, granted them by his royal father and grandfather of blessed memory.

Indignantly protesting against Nicolls' recommendations of a local court of appeals (without jury!) they pleaded their ancient rights, not only freely to elect and be elected to all civil office, but more important, to be tried by their peers or by the law of the land. Here they were speaking not only as dutiful subjects but as citizens with a deep concern for the Law, as apart from *the laws*—a distinction sharp in English minds at this period.

The laws were made by men and could be found in any statute book. For New Englanders, Law had become deeper, self-evident, something derived from God, and enduring were every man-made statute wiped from the book. Such matters they held to be their inalienable right, vouched for in Magna Carta.

One wonders if John did not have a hand in drafting the ten pages of this Narrative. He was often employed for assignments like this. Its arguments and, in one instance, its phraseology, find a curious echo in the letter he himself sent the King. In this, his longest appeal to Charles, written in formal French, but with the note of easy familiarity which characterizes all John's correspondence with the world's great, he takes it for granted that in a matter of such magnitude the King would support the people, as against the lords and barons—those responsible, so he seems to have felt, for the commissioners' actions. There was an emotional background for this assumption: the Duke of York's ingratitude still rankled, and John was loath to see the Duke's power extend to Long Island. Nevertheless, his letter to Charles II proved to be a blunder most costly to his personal fortunes.

For if, as appears to have beeen the case,* the reduction of New England's independence was a fixed Stuart policy, then those who had to implement it would look coldly upon all those who opposed it. To Governor Nicolls, chief instrument in re-asserting royal prerogative, John's removal from the scene became essential to carrying out his instructions. John's loyalty to the American colonists was to cost him dear, not only in goods and land but in his good name as well.

Judging from several letters and his general conduct, John cared passionately for independence and for what we call today self-government. Together with Governor Winthrop and leading New England citizens, he had already debated this subject, two years previously, when the King's communication of June 28th, 1662, had first warned the Boston Court of royal dissatisfaction.[4] Gravest misgivings had been raised at that time, as to the future possibility of loss, or curtailment, of cherished freedoms.

It is no more surprising, therefore, that John supported Massachusetts in its clamor for liberty of Church and Commonwealth than to find him on the people's side in Long Island. There, too, he was against Nicolls, and seconded the General Court's opposition to Crown appointments of governor and officers; and this same unorthodox attitude had been apparent in his earlier championship of the Long Island English towns, where fear of religious coercion had, in part, prompted his aid. His stand put him among those first few who established the American tradition of protest, nonconformity and the right of the individual conscience over all corporate rights, even including those of the state.

It is idle to suppose he kept his views to himself. Endorsement by him was certain to be highly vocal, whether siding with the Court's demands or with the expostulating Long Islanders who refused to submit to Nicolls and who were

---

* Whitehall's secret instructions to the commissioners. *N.Y. Col. Docs.*, III, 57.

wearing the English governor out with their arguments and opposition.[5]

Few records have been preserved of that Hempstead Convention which John attended as town attorney. But a significant exception is a letter from the Southold freemen to Nicolls telling him what they had just voted in their plenary session, and stating, in forthright terms, what most Long Island citizens evidently felt about the new legislation.*

At this convention, John, together with the men of Southold, Southampton, Easthampton, etc., stubbornly argued, more than a century before the idea became a liberation slogan, that *there should be no taxation without representation.*

The reaction to his laws both baffled and angered Nicolls. Many settlers in these rebellious towns had originally come from Yorkshire and had retained, along with their sturdy political realism, a blunt broad dialect the Governor found almost unintelligible. It was possibly to win them over that he rechristened Long Island Yorkshire. But this flattery of native pride did not change their attitude nor persuade them to sign any written submission. They considered it offensively obsequious, and, to his great astonishment (as he afterwards wrote to Winthrop), he could not bribe them into submitting.

Nicolls had encountered a new type of man—the free citizen —and did not know what to make of him.

The governor was a polished courtier of more than average experience, travelled, a scholar delighting in Greek and Latin. Puritans he had met at home, and he had been quite prepared to cope with these rugged idealists of the English Reformation who had chosen to transport themselves "beyond the sea." But he expected to find them just like other Englishmen—in an overseas England.

---

* Among the various matters Southold's delegates were fully empowered to conclude was clause 7, which reads: "That there be not any rate, levy or charge, or money raised but what shall be with the *consent of the major part of the deputies* in a general court or meeting." *Southold T.R.,* I, 358. (Italics added.)

Years of pioneer existence, however, and three thousand miles of salt water had transformed these petty tradesmen, clerks, laborers, or whatever they had been formerly, into a different breed—unpredictable, as far as the governor was concerned, and almost foreign. He was, in fact, meeting for the first time a native product—the American (or, as the Indians said, trying to pronounce the word English, "Yenghee!"). This was what John, for all his royalist ties and Court experience, had become. And he was treasonably encouraging other Americans, so Nicolls believed, to resist the new policies and assert native rights.

The governor first resorted to blandishment, trying to win his chief opponent to his side.

"The commissioners showed me various letters they brought from Lord Clarendon and from your Majesty's Privy Council," wrote John angrily to the King, pouring out his grievances to one whose ear he felt he could always reach. "And Colonel Nicolls offered me a signed, *carte blanche.*" (John could have written his own ticket!) "In truth they made me very fine propositions in the name of His Royal Highness the Duke of York. But it was for suppressing the *New England peoples' liberties* which Your Majesty's grandfather and father of blessed memory, accorded them with the advice and blessings of Parliament, and which Your Majesty yourself, had confirmed by letters under your sign manual, and by your gracious message which I myself brought over only six months ago saying that Your Majesty would never curtail their liberties, but to which the commissioners *were opposed on all points.* I wished to have no part in this and said I would not serve them in this affair. Having no positive orders from Your Majesty I told them that they must excuse me if I refused to engage myself with them and said I would follow your direct orders to go to the Barbadoes and ready its defences as I had every reason to do, considering that the designs they had would inevitably bring about open hostilities. At this reply (which I trust Your Majesty and his counsel would consider reasonable) Colonel Nicolls and the other Commissioners were so furious that they impugned my loyalty and threatened to disgrace me with the Lord High Chancellor. . . ."[6] (Italics added.)

The threat showed clearly the degree of Governor Nicolls' fury over the Long Island deadlock. Resistance to his edicts, which he rightly attributed to John's influence, reflected upon himself. This amiable despot, though no more sympathetic to popular government than Stuyvesant, nevertheless, by his tact and good sense was, in many quarters, overcoming the obstacles inherent in his difficult task. Of all the commissioners, he alone had any success or got any good results. Failure on the Island marred his record.

But against him stood the majority of the inhabitants led by John.

Scotts had always served their sovereigns loyally, they were good public servants, but did not bow the neck supinely to authority. John Scott began and ended as a free agent. This he had proved when, as President of the Five Towns, he had dared make a choice, first American patriot to raise the standard which was later to rally a nation. So, faced with a second fateful decision, he felt obliged to defy the commissioners, let them say or do what they would.

"For my loyalty and integrity," he wrote to the King, "I told them that I was assured (whatever overbold souls might impute) that Your Majesty would never doubt me. As for the Chancellor's favor, it is something I would highly esteem, he being your Majesty's first minister; and I cannot believe that a man of such justice and judgment could in honor and conscience listen to such trifles (*badineries*) about a gentleman and a Christian. My honor could never be corrupted even through fear of all the world's evils; it being the only thing to which I lay claim. My soul belongs to God, and my life to your Majesty, but my honor is my own which nothing can subvert, God be praised!

"I beg Your Majesty to pardon me if I have done anything

to merit your disgrace, and to protect me with your royal vindication from those who would try to arouse your anger against me by the accusation of Colonel Nicolls and the other commissioners, who, (as they themselves told me), have preferred charges against me; false charges which contain information contrary to that which I am sending your Majesty."[7]

John had good reason for imploring royal protection: Nicolls had developed still another grudge against him. He blamed John for involving him in a dispute of historic implications resulting in the peculiar circumstance that New York has never since controlled both shores of its own magnificent harbor.

Among the first grants by the new governor was a vast region—known today as New Jersey—which Nicolls deeded to John Ogden to settle. But to the governor's intense annoyance, he learned that the Duke of York had already conveyed this territory to Sir George Carteret and Lord Berkeley of Stratton, who immediately assumed jurisdictional rights over it as well, and sent out a new young governor to take possession of what Nicolls fondly imagined to be still under *his* authority.

He was incensed at the treatment of his own patentee* and turned furiously upon John Scott, accusing him of ruining the Duke's New York holdings by this partition trick. In scathing terms he reported John's "infamy":

> "and I charge it upon Captain Scott, who was born to work mischief as far as he is creditted or his parts serve him," wrote Nicolls wrathfully to the Duke of York. "This Scott, it seems, aimed at the same patent which Your Royal Highness hath, and hath since given words out that he had an injury done him by your Royal Highness, whereupon he contrived and betrayed my lord Berkely and Sir George Carteret into a design (contrary to their knowledge) of ruining your Royal Highness' territory."[8]

---

* Nicolls' grant was declared null and void in 1688 and a century of litigation followed. Harleian MSS. 7001, f 299.

It is exactly what John might have done, and none knew better than he New Netherland's topography and rich possibilities. Disappointment could have prompted this ingenious revenge, but the facts do not bear out Nicolls' accusation.

That John felt injured by the Duke is true, but that came *after* the English had taken New Netherland when he, all unrewarded, was on Long Island and could not possibly have advised Berkeley and Carteret whose New Jersey patent was granted them in England on June 23rd, 1664, before the Duke had even secured the land, when Nicolls was still on the high seas and John himself was in jail.[9] And before that, at the time John was in London early in 1663, discussing the invasion or hearing it discussed around the Foreign Plantations Committee, though he most certainly could have suggested that the lush patroon country west of the Hudson would be a fitting reward for the two titled Cavaliers, he had no reason then to spite the Duke by recommending drastic partition. Indeed, at that moment he was an ardent ducal supporter, even boasting he was the Duke's agent, and having great expectations of some settlement for himself.

Actually, had the new proprietors not made their property a separate colony, this grant would have been no more detrimental to New York than Nicolls' grant of the same land to John Ogden. It was the two noblemen's highhanded assumption of governmental status that resulted in Manhattan's loss. As a matter of fact, for this conduct, both Berkeley and Carteret soon fell from royal favor.* But who remembers that? Nicolls' charges have thundered down the centuries, though impartial examination shows they were unfounded.

Nicolls, however, could not be impartial. He was indignant and bitter over the incident and over the unpopularity of the

---

* "Lord Berkeley is under a cloud, and out of all his offices and offers to surrender up the patent of New Jersey; Sir George Carteret . . . his partner is in Ireland but it is thought he will likewise surrender and New York will be enlarged." (Samuel Maverick to John Winthrop, 1668). *Mass. Hist. Soc. Coll.*, 4th ser., VII, 315. But despite Maverick's supposition, both noblemen retained their patent.

Duke's laws, which, despite their name, he himself had drafted. He wrote complainingly to Winthrop of the "greate Tryalls and exercises of Patience" he had had to endure from these "disobliging persons."[10] He did his best to appease them with minor concessions. All to no avail. The few delegates who did sign his submissive address and accepted his laws became, themselves, a target of reproach and were forced to issue a "Remonstrance" repudiating their fellow citizens' accusation of being "betrayers of our liberties and privileges."[11]

At this juncture Nicolls lost all patience and resorted to the arbitrary use of power enforcing the royal will. He threatened with prison sentences, or worse, all those who railed against the conforming delegates. Yet this made no difference to the heroically stubborn majority. They continued to oppose the Duke's Laws—particularly as they affected land. Not all the lawyers' big words could make them believe that the wilderness lots they had tamed and subdued were not their own property, nor that grants to acres cleared by the sweat of thirty years' toil should be paid for a second time—or pass to other hands. Patent renewal they felt was iniquitous.

Deed of purchase and court registration had always constituted proof of ownership; very few Long Island landowners held the English title to their lands. John Winthrop himself, for all his extensive estates, could not produce an English title to everything he owned. Not until 1680, four years after his death, did his son obtain from Governor Andros English deeds to the Setauket land Governor Winthrop had sequestered from John Scott to ensure the payment of fines which his own courts had levied.

Scot's Hall was sold, although it stood in New York, outside Winthrop's jurisdiction—but he had obtained Nicolls' promise to respect Connecticut's decrees. All John's extensive fencing was carted away and his goods stored in neighbor John Ketcham's house and carefully itemized "that he be in nowayse inbesseled."[12] The records show that his old mother and her servant Thomas Feis were allowed "three cows for their present condition,"[13] but there is little mention of Deborah other than that she was left in a "mean and pore" way,[14] as well she might with all her husband's possessions seized.

And still Nicolls had not finished with John Scott. He ordered him to bring to New York assizes, an alleged "perpetuity,"[15] i.e. the nine hundred and ninety-nine year lease (standard legal tenure in English conveyances) for the Setauket twenty square miles. This perpetuity, he declared, John had used to further his purchases, or to threaten those reluctant to sell. Nicolls had never seen the document, *indeed its very existence is only a matter of hearsay.* It does not figure in any of the numerous deeds John ever drew up, neither for the Setauket property nor anywhere else. But Winthrop had written Nicolls that John's claims to all this land (i.e. Scott's grant from the Indians) "would be destructive to the whole plantation,"[16] although when Winthrop bought John's Setauket land it appeared that private ownership was not so destructive.

Nicolls, in response to Winthrop's complaint, ordered the "perpetuity" into court. When John, following the example of other Southampton landlords, failed to comply, Nicolls issued a warrant for his arrest. And when John persistently disobeyed, the Governor turned Winthrop's sequestration orders into outright confiscation and seized all John's other lands, goods and chattels.[17]

In high dudgeon, Nicolls sent a letter to Secretary Morrice, in London:[18] "Scott, by a pretended seal affixed to a writing . . . hath horribly abused His Majesty's honor in these parts and fled out of the country to Barbados."*

---

* Only a month previously, Nicolls, intent on ruining John as he said he would, wrote Morrice that "Mr. Maverick's petition had been stolen from Lord Arlington's office by Captain Scott and delivered to the Governor and council in Boston—though Scott said Williamson had given it to him." *N.Y. Col. Docs.,* III, 136.

It will be remembered that Boston had a special fund for agents to obtain information from the English Ministers, and had once employed John.

No wonder that John had written the King that only royal protection could save him! The governors of both Connecticut and New York had undertaken against him proceedings not only arbitrary but from which both stood to gain—Winthrop in land, Nicolls in much needed prestige. That their intended victim was one of the first pawns in what was to become the struggle of the American colonies for freedom and independence has passed unnoticed in American history.

For John the issue was clear: power and return of his property for siding against the people; loss of material possessions, of a brilliant future and a growing reputation, if he stubbornly upheld the people's rights! But he had made his choice and there is no evidence that he ever repented of it.

With a warrant out for his arrest, he could take no further chances. Memories of the Connecticut jail presumably undermined his confidence in New England courts. The two ships were in readiness, horses and ammunition stored. With a King's order and a job ahead he set sail. . . .

BIBLIOGRAPHICAL NOTES

1. S.P. Dom. Car., II, 29, No. 419.
2. *Ibid.*
3. *Mass. Rec.,* IV, prt. 2, 219-29.
4. *Ibid.,* 166; *CSP. Col. Ser. Am. and WI.,* 1661-68, 125.
5. Nicolls to Winthrop, MS. letter in the Gardiner Memorial room at Easthampton Library.
6. S.P. Dom. Car., II, 29, No. 419.
7. *Ibid.*
8. *N.Y. Col. Docs.,* III, 105.
9. Brodhead, *Hist. of N.Y.,* II, 82.
10. Nicolls to Winthrop, *op. cit.*

At this period there were always *two* Secretaries of State, and not infrequently personal rivalry led one to undo the work of the other. (*CSP Dom. Car.,* II, 1665-66. Preface by Mrs. Everett Green.) Williamson (who was secretary to Henry Bennet Lord Arlington), and John's friend may quite well have "leaked" the letter to him. It is significant that Nicolls, instead of writing Arlington, whom the matter concerned, made his complaint to the rival, Morrice.

11. Br-haven *T.R.* (1924 ed.), II, 76, 152.
12. *Ibid.*, 98.
13. *Ibid.*, 76, 152.
14. *Ibid.*, 153.
15. *N.Y. Col. Docs.*, XIV, 590.
16. *Ibid.*, III, 86.
17. *Ibid.*, XIV, 590.
18. *Ibid.*, III, 136.

PART TWO

CHAPTER XXI

GET-AWAY

"Man is not born for himself or to confine his times within the narrow compass of his own poor pleasures or advantages, but being a creature of celestial extract ought ever to be looking upwards from whence he came."
—John Scott, Preface, Histories. Sl, MS., 3662.

DID JOHN SCOTT KNOW, as he left Long Island, late in 1665, that his life as pioneer was over and that all the hard-won acquisitions of ten strenuous years would soon be lost and forgotten? That he would never set foot in North America again?

Did the old Scott prophecy of family downfall ever occur to his mind as he mulled over his shattered career or raged over his lost possessions? For the second time his life was violently wrenched from its course. Or was this voyage the beginning of a new chapter of achievement with golden opportunity beckoning from a fresh quarter of the globe? Surely he could not have thought he was departing forever, leaving all that he loved and cherished behind. He must have believed that fate would relent and that one day he would come back, for it is on record that he rented to a friend some of his recently acquired Hempstead property until March, 1669.[1]

Deborah had long been schooled to his sudden departures and prolonged absences; they were all part of his exciting personality. John was too restless and ambitious ever to have been a good family man, and back of his mind must always have been the thought that her father would look after her, as he had done when John was in jail. At first Deborah would have been relieved to know that the immediate job took him out of the commissioners' vindictive clutches. She may also have consoled herself with thoughts of his success abroad, of his approaching triumphant return, when, like some fabled troubadour, he would entertain her with world gossip and fascinating details of his richly varied experiences. But the months slipped into years. His sons became young men, and the little girl, whom he had hardly seen, grew to a demure little maiden in hanging sleeves, and still there was no word of return.

Things might have gone hard with Deborah, but for Nicolls' long overdue repentance of his harsh treatment of her husband. He gave orders that part of John's sequestered property be sold for her benefit,* and a little committee, under her brother Joseph Raynor, was set up to look after her interests.[2] To compensate her for the loss of Scot's Hall, the governor ordered Daniel Gotherson's two houses to be taken down and re-erected on a lot for her. That he thereby deprived an English widow of her property meant little to Richard Nicolls. He had no time for Dorothea Gotherson, nor her petition concerning her Long Island holdings.

"He did me all the mischief he could," wrote that distressed lady to Colonel Lovelace. And being a spirited creature of more than usual enterprise, she insisted, when Nicolls returned to London in 1668, on having a hearing before the

---

* "Confirmation of the estate of John Scott, granted for sale unto George Hewlett and William Osborne, for benefit of his wife Deborah, lands, houses, privileges which John Scott bought of Hope Washbourn; also lands, houses, fences in Hempstead; also lands formerly belonging to John Scott in Matiniecock and Madnans [Madans] Neck. December 1667. Signed Richard Nicolls." From Original records in Office of Secretary of State, Albany, N.Y. Patents I (1664-67), ff 97, 99.

Duke of York. And Nicolls "acknowledged before the Duke to me" that her case had been shelved for lack of information, but that "now it is known" she might get back some of her land (confiscated together with John's) after all![3]

On the advice of Secretary Arlington she also made a sworn statement denying the damaging gossip Nicolls had started about her personal relations with Scott. In none of her numerous letters and affidavits[4] is there any accusation of John, or the slightest suggestion of fraudulent dealing on his part. They remained on good terms to the end, as these letters show.

"I have been informed but not by himself (i.e., John) that he had much wrong done him by the New England people, so I know not where to send or write to him . . . concluding him not in a capacity of doing me right or himself either as to the particular concern of possessing the land . . ." she assured Colonel Lovelace. And again: "I am satisfied I might have enjoyed the Indian and English interest if I had gone thither,* but having many children and not very healthy . . . I never went."[5]

In all fairness to New York's governor, it must be remembered that, along with the Gotherson claim, there were hundreds of other complicated land suits simply beyond his competence to settle, or so we must suppose, judging from the number of his decisions subsequently voided in law.†

But for the gentle Deborah he was always available and found time to make much of her. It was surely with his permission that she sold some of her husband's horses. In the Town Clerk's office in Southampton the original Earmark Book records, on tattered yellowing pages fragile as dried

---

* Some years after writing this she did leave for the New World. In the Egerton Parish Register, in Godmersham, Kent, there is a note that Dorothea Gotherson married a Mr. Hogben about 1680 and emigrated to Long Island.

† Nicolls himself begged Clarendon to recall him and to send "some other fitt person" to take his place. N.Y. Hist. Soc. Coll. 1869, II, 126.

moth's wings, that on May 21, 1667, she sold to Richard Burrett a six-year-old bay for six pounds, a four-year-old black horse, a three-year-old mare and a yearling. These must have been draught horses, where looks did not matter, for John's mark, registered there, was "a right ear completely severed."*

With her brother and father to look after her, Deborah did not lack for friends and funds. And after a few more years had passed, there is a recurring entrance of one Charles Sturmey's name in connection with hers. He was a tanner, one of Southampton's richest inhabitants,[6] and it is consoling to think of his taking an interest in the fatherless boys, giving one a pony, the other a piece of land. "To my best beloved stepson,"† reads a later entry.[7] So Sturmey finally married Deborah. Desertion was grounds for divorce in New England (although not in New York), but after much delay, Governor Lovelace granted her her freedom. Gossip had it John divorced her, writing one of his rare letters from abroad. But it is far more likely that she took the decisive step. She had always known what she wanted, and losing her first husband she solaced herself with the next best choice.

Not that John left his family entirely without resources. When grown, both boys inherited much of his land.[8] Nicolls must have still further relented or his orders were subsequently voided. One may be interested to learn that the elder son, John, went into the army, then sailed the seas, like his father. His will, proved in 1692, in London, left all his prop-

---

* Other horses of his, registered among the town records, bore a small slit in the right ear.

† The entry actually reads: "to my son-in-law"; but as Sturmey had no daughter, and John Jr. never married, it can only be supposed this means son *by* law, or stepson. Sturmey is known to have married Deborah for she is listed as his widow in his will, probated December 31, 1691. S-ampton Red Book of Deeds, ff 225-26.

erty to his brother Jeckamiah, who from his earliest days apparently was always a man of means.*

It was Jeckamiah whose colorful career most resembled his father's. Flamboyant, gifted, turbulent, constantly buying and selling land, his name is splashed all over Southampton's town records. His ornamental blue slate gravestone (and the plain one of wife Mary) are still standing today in the town's Old North Cemetery. He lived to the ripe age of eighty-six, rich and full of honor, the father of three sons, and Justice of the Peace.[9]

Legend has it (and this was told me a few years ago in Southampton, by the late Clarence Scott, one of Jeckamiah's direct descendants) that when Jeckamiah was named to the Bench and went to receive his commission from the Governor in New York he rode there on the back of a bull and came home brandishing his warrant aloft, shouting as he galumphed down Main Street: "Now I will make the town to fear me, and North Sea to tremble!"

But our John hardly knew his sons as men, and their careers and fortunes he could not have guessed in 1665, as his little ship slowly ploughed its way southward towards Barbados.

BIBLIOGRAPHICAL NOTES

1. *Rec. of N. and S. Hemp.*, I, 158-59.
2. Br-haven. *T.R.* (1924 ed.), II, 154.
3. Rawl. MSS., A 175, f 144.
4. *Ibid.*, f 148-49.
5. O'Callaghan, ed., *Doc. Hist. of N.Y.*, II, 536.

---

* Jeckamiah was evidently not convinced that all the land his father John Scott left him had been released from sequestration and confiscation. For in his will he specifically leaves to his son Thomas "all my lands, meadows, goods or chattels that of right may apertain or *which should any wise descend upon me* either in Easthampton, Southampton, Seatacott, Brookhaven, Smithtown or Hempstead. And so either in Old England or New England." (Italics added.)

Dated 24th March, 1747 in Surrogate's Office Hall of Records, N.Y. City, copied and recorded in Record of Wills Liber 16, ff 465-66.

6. S-ampton Red Book of Deeds, ff 255-56.
7. S-ampton *T.R.*, II, 73.
8. Somerset House, London: Prerogative Court of Canterbury, Register Fane, f 120; April 19, 1692.
9. S-ampton Yellow Book of Deeds, Liber C, f 170.

CHAPTER XXII

EXPLORER OF THE SPANISH MAIN

The increase of any estate must be upon the foreigner, for
whatsoever is somewhere gotton is somewhere lost.

—Francis Bacon.

I am not ignorant that many sober gentlemen are of the
opinion it had been better never to have planted colonies
. . . in regard we have not half people enough at home.
. . . But notwithstanding this loss by sending abroad, yet
let none be discouraged from new undertakings or have
little opinion of the colonies. For the most important advantages . . . which the world now enjoys have had rise
from very small beginnings.

—John Scott, Preface.

STILL FUMING over the rebuff he had received in New Jersey,
Colonel Nicolls wrote to the Barbados Governor, Francis
Lord Willoughby. "Such men should have a brand on them,"
was his indignant conclusion as he expatiated on John's
capacity to make trouble. To soothe a fellow-governor, perhaps, Willoughby assured him in reply that he would arrest
the man and send him to London.

He did no such thing, however. Instead, he greeted John
in the friendliest manner. Not only did the *Hopewell* bring
much needed horses and ammunition, but John's London
reputation was well established, his contacts with Secretary
Joseph Williamson known, as well as his relations with the
Committee on Foreign Plantations, of which important body
Lord Francis himself was a member. Besides, the Barbados

governor, a man of "versatile mind and impetuous character," admired courage and initiative.

"All the metall'd lads were for me," he once wrote Clarendon, informing him of steps he had taken to quell certain Barbados disorders. And whatever else John might be, he was certainly a man of mettle. Moreover his youthful escapade at Turnham Green and subsequent sufferings in the royal cause struck sparks of sympathy among local inhabitants, many of whom were also former Cavaliers, refugees from England. The Civil War had been passionately fought out on the little tropical island in a few dramatic incidents between Cavaliers and Roundheads, and in 1660 the thirteen baronets and knights there celebrated the Restoration amid mad rejoicing. They welcomed John as one of themselves. One eminent planter, John Crowe, put him up at his own house; prominent townsfolk came to call on him.

To one of these, Colonel Lewis Morris, a noted Quaker (intending shortly to return to New England), John sold a Hempstead property he had acquired just before his own departure, and among the Hempstead Town records there is a little entry of the arrival of said "Lues Mores" to take up the Scott land.[1]

Slightly restored in fortune, John now embarked upon one of the most important adventures of his life.

While in Willoughby's service he explored the West Indies to map some of the lesser known parts and begin making notes for his *History of the Coasts and Islands of America*.

He had (he explained in the *Preface* to this manuscript) always been a great lover of geography and history, and intended, somehow, sometime, to make these his life work. Preparatory studies over the previous eighteen years had convinced him that these things "may be both of some reputation to myself and a general advantage to the English nation."[2]

Evidently he considered most recent geographers outdated.

Even the observations of "his countryman Mr. Gages,"* were of little use, lacking perspective, or what John called "the great circumstance of distance between place and place." He himself would neither consent to write about places he had not visited, nor "cloy the world with long discourses about old matters. I choose rather to content myself with what my own eyes have seen and much of what my feet have trodden and my senses brought, or make exact inquiry."

It is easy to see that the new spirit sweeping England, particularly since the foundation of the Royal Society (1660), had affected Scott's thinking. He possessed both a mind freed from preconceptions, and a conviction that observation and experimentation were the only trustworthy means of securing data. To these, in dealing with data, he added the inductive method, thereby reaching what philosophers of the age were beginning to call the "timeless element."

All his writings show a strong mercantilist viewpoint. Like other leaders of this period, John was aware of the interrelation of economic and political factors, but his almost nationalistically expressed devotion to his native country, his desire to increase England's trade and power, were colored by knowledge of the way other countries coped with common problems. Most unusual for that time was his compassionate concern with people.

"If we could find a way for the employing of our poor, and setting able people to work for the public advantage, as is practised in the United Provinces . . ." he wrote at one point, suggesting that he had done a great deal more than just *trade* with the Dutch on Long Island ". . . for these Netherlands having five times more people than the innate growth of this country will feed and maintain, live better than the English that have three times more provisions than they have mouths to eat. . . . 'Tis not the multitude of poor people that makes

---

* The *English-American,* or *A New Survey of the West Indies,* by the true and painful endeavours of Thomas Gage, now Preacher of the Word of God at Acris, in the County of Kent, 1648.

any nation unhappy, but a nonimprovement of these people to a right end. . . ."

He supplemented his travels with wide reading, "Herera Ovida* and Acosta,† among the Spanish, Thunis among the French, John Delaet,‡ among the Dutch, and many other authors and curious manuscripts that came to my hands."[3]

During the years 1665-67, he covered, by small ship, thousands of miles along the Atlantic coasts "from New Foundland to the Amazon," putting in at one hundred and five islands. He also explored part of the mainland, namely Guiana and other places between the Tropic of Cancer and the Amazon. Some of this was already familiar to him from his buccaneer days, but much was new territory and his preparations had been scientifically thorough. Having this work in mind, he had, during his London trips, looked at Patent rolls, examining grants of Atlantic islands for original ownership, and customs-books, to evaluate their trade returns. Moreover he had bought all the best aids to mapmaking he could find and had learned to master them— "Quadrants, Terestanes, Bowes, Blowes, Astrolabes, Sextiles, and the like" as he wrote. Amazing for that early period were his efforts to give his maps "true direction and distances" because, as he explained, "by oblique and cross falling into the parallels, all *small* charts and globes are distorted by the curve of the meridians," so that many places are out of proportion and not clear. (Italics added.)

Since it was not until the twentieth century that aerial photography made such facts visible—most nineteenth century maps showed Greenland almost as big as Africa—John's concern over diminishing lines at the poles show either a pro-

---

* Luis Antonio Ovida y Herera, *Condé de la Granja*, 1636-1717.

† José d'Acosta, *Historia naturale e morale delle Indie*, Venice, 1596.

‡ Joannes Delaet, *L'Histoire du Nouveau Monde; description des Indes Occidentales*, Leyden, 1640.

found understanding of geography, or a very original mind. As experienced navigator he procured the very best compasses, "both azimuth and others calibrated for several meridians" (modern indeed!), "for the truth is without good instruments all observations are but deceivable guessings."

Colonel Morris's introductions to personages in the region made his travels easier, and John's own discoveries were supplemented by documentary information (he tells of examining all the Barbados records). Two years later, for each of the places visited, he wrote a short historical outline. He plunged into vivid lavish particulars of every aspect of travel: what the countries looked like and the population figures; the animals he saw, wild cattle and beasts of prey; the numbers of good eating fish and the abundance of edible roots and fruits; he mentions local commodities and products, tropical diseases and the curious "phisickall" drugs cultivated by the natives for their own use. His work is an example of the detailed reporting which was so rare in those days.

Compared with the meager ill-informed reports the King's commissioners were sending back from New England (on all Massachusetts they included just four descriptive lines) John's work readily explains Williamson's high opinion of him.* He had a lively eye for the strange and unusual. Indeed the very unlikelihood of some of Scott's statements to those unfamiliar with the byways of seventeenth century commercial history turned out to be one of the strongest guarantees of his veracity, for these peculiar individual facts met constant unexpected corroboration in Dutch and Spanish documents of the period.[4]

In Guiana, where he duly noted the failure of the first five Spanish attempts at colonization, he ran on traces of the great Dutch explorer and governor, Captain Groenewegen,† dead

---

* Scott's use of contemporary information sources makes this all of additional interest to historians.

† John spells this variously Cromwegel, Gromwegel.

at eighty-three only a year before John's arrival, but to whose son, the succeeding governor, John listened at length, absorbing many of Groenewegen's "ingenious observations."

For forty-eight years this remarkable old man had lived among the Carib Indians—"the first man who took firm footing on Guiana by the good liking of the natives, whose humors the gentleman perfectly understood," wrote John, paying tribute to the Dutchman's expert handling of these ferocious cannibals who had repeatedly massacred previous Spanish settlers. Groenewegen erected a fort on a small island twenty leagues up the River Disseekeeb (Essequibo) "which looked into the two great branches of that famous river," he was the first to open up the South American interior to trade and settlement. "All his time the colonies flourished; he was a great friend of all new Colonies of Christians; and Barbadoes oweth its first assistance both for food and trade to this man's special kindness in 1627, at what time they were in a miserable condition," wrote John.

Several times, in his "history," the author refers to the necessity of dealing fairly with the natives and Sir Walter Raleigh won his particular admiration on this score with "his judicious treatment, leaving so great a name behind that the English have been obliged to remember with honor."

A particularly lucky coincidence furnished John with exceptional sources of information on the whole Essequibo region. Two of the greatest travellers ever in Guiana—Hendrikson, a Swiss, who served the Dutch for twenty-seven years, and Captain Mattison, twenty-two years in Spanish service —were both, after a short military engagement, prisoners in John's hands for days on end. Insatiable of detail, he pumped them of all they knew.

He also sailed the lower Amazon, passing through straits not three quarters of a mile wide, convinced that two forts could command the whole waterway and noting that it was possible to sail in both directions, with a favorable current one way and a constant east-northeast wind which blew "good gales" in the other; he gives directions "for sailing the right channel," and how to enter the river with safety. The sun, he noted, rose and set every day at the same hour. Much of the fifty-seven pages devoted to this section, however, had been related to him by Captain Mattison, including piquant details of the armed women who headed some of the Indian troops, drawn up in crescent formation at the river's mouth.

He gave a tantalizing glimpse of Trinidad and the feuds of Carib and Arawak Indians there, and mentioned the mysterious "wasting away" of the natives in these parts—probably from syphilis, for it was from this Caribbean paradise that the white man allegedly brought back the scourge he so poetically christened and bestowed upon Europe. Gold was the lure throughout this region, the Spaniards sought it before all else, far more than trade, colonies, or propagation of the Gospel.

Chile is the southernmost spot he mentioned, quoting from voyages of other explorers—Magellan, Sir Francis Drake, and Sir Thomas Cavendish. His personal contribution was a single pithy comment on the native character: "most stout and warlike of all Americans, but most resembling Europeans, with such civility and gentility." The manuscript breaks off here, as though more were intended.

Unfortunately, these *Histories* have been practically ignored in America.[5] English scholars,[*] on the other hand, have appreciated them as valuable narratives by a contemporary, both familiar with the localities and conversant with all the literature on the subject.

The Hakluyt Society in London published the *Description of Trinidad, Tobago, and Guiana,* in 1925, and various Brit-

---

[*] Notably Arthur Percival Newton, who refers to Scott as the "most detailed English historian of the West Indies in the seventeenth century." *The European Nations in the West Indies,* p. 194; also Vincent Todd Harlow, who endorses the evaluation of Scott's work made by Edmondson, *History of Barbados;* p. 5; and the Rev. George Edmondson, in his exhaustive analysis of Scott's Histories, *The Dutch in Western Guiana,* EHR, 1901, XVI, 640-75.

ish and colonial journals have transcribed and printed excerpts from Scott's works.

Most English historians, who deplore the derision Scott has met in some American quarters, were impressed by this Restoration writer's contacts with men intimately acquainted, over long periods, with the countries about which he was writing. "The just conclusion would seem to be that his writings are a real authority on the evidence they describe, filling a gap in the record caused by the disappearance of original documents with which he was familiar, and the absence of written memoirs of pioneers from whom he received oral narrative."*

The extent of John's travels can be gauged not only from his *Histories* (a portion of which exist in the British Museum and the Bodleian Library) but from the maps seized among his papers (May 18th, 1682), maps which he had either made himself or collected and worked over—a list of which are now in the Record Office in London.[6]

These products of John's talents or industry were not only beautiful, but judging by one extant example, remarkably accurate. His map of the Scheldt Estuary, drawn (1673) on the basis both of personal survey and the combined testimony of local shipowners, pilots, bargemen, etc., and complete with depth soundings, compares favorably with charts of the British Admiralty currently used by the American Navy.

In short, a fellow such as John Scott was a godsend to seventeenth century English military commanders in the Caribbean, engaged in a four-way struggle (Britain, France, Holland, Spain) over largely uncharted seas and archipelagoes. For though he may not qualify as a scientific explorer in the modern sense, he exceeded most of his predecessors and contemporaries in the range and reliability of his observations.

---

* James Alexander Williamson, *The English in Guiana*, pp. 67-70.

BIBLIOGRAPHICAL NOTES

1. *Rec. of N. and S. Hemp.*, I, 270.
2. Sl. MS., 3662, f 785.
3. *Ibid.*, f 772.
4. Edmondson, *The Dutch in Western Guiana*, EHR, XVI, 645-75.
5. Scott's histories were not known to be in existence in 1859 when Brodhead published his History of New York.

   In 1883, Gideon Delaplaine Scull published (privately) his sketch, *Dorothea Scott otherwise Gotherson-Hogben*, in which he makes passing mention of Scott's work, calling it *undated*, although the Preface states that it was written in 1669, and dismissing it as an "attempt to play on a very limited scale the role of biographer and historian somewhat in the manner of Sir Walter Raleigh." Scull was unacquainted with any of Scott's other writings, or of the exhaustive work on the Scot's Hall Scotts, published (in 1829) by James Renat Scott.

   Wilbur C. Abbott published a few excerpts from Scott's Preface in his Life of "Colonel" Scott (Yale University Press, 1918, pp. 44, 45, 46. Reprinted in *Conflicts of Oblivion*, Harvard University Press, 1924, and a revised version in 1935). He wearisomely belabors charges of plagiarism, asking where Scott could have got his history and description, thereby proving that he himself had overlooked Scott's constant references to his source material. Abbott had not read the Hakluyt Society's publications, although these were available before he revised his life of Scott in 1935. As this is based almost entirely upon Pepys' affidavits, or upon the authors Pilling, Scull, and Palfrey, who also drew upon the affidavits, one cannot blame too severely the many inaccuracies in Abbott's little volumes.

   Scott's notes relating to New England, Massachusetts, Maine, Canada, Plymouth, New Jersey, Maryland and Virginia, etc.: a version of this appears in the Massachusetts Historical Society Proceedings First Series, vol. 13, p. 132. This was possibly taken from an English transcription in the Calendar of State Papers, Colonial series, American and West Indies, 1661-68, No. 1660.
6. List of John's maps:
   (1) A large chart of Barbados with detailed description of its coastline, harbor and fortifications.
   (2) Charts of the rivers Orinoco, Amazon, Curenteen (Corentin), Berbier and Cheyenne.
   (3) A large map of the gulf of Venezuela de Cora and Lake Maracaibo.
   (4) A large map of the Island of Providence.
   (5) A chart of Nicaragua Province, with the great lake in its midst emptying into the sea.

(6) A very large and excellent chart of Hispaniola with a description of the towns and the exact soundings of many rivers (this probably dated from his first visit in 1654-55).

(7) A large chart of the Island of Quarasoa (Curaçao—seventeenth century spelling was highly individualistic) a copy of which was sent to the Dutch West India Company by Governor Mynheer Becks.

(8) An exact plan of Cartagena, and a map of Jamaica with harbors and rocky approaches.

(9) A very large map of Surinam, an exact duplicate of which was sent by the Dutch governor there to the State of Zeeland in 1672.

(10) The Island of St. John de Portrico, and city of the same name both in "plan and prospect" with fortifications and harbors.

(11) Plans and charts of the French West Indies.

(12) Maps of St. Christopher (St. Kitts).

(13) A plan of St. Ann harbor on Curaçao with fortifications.

(14) Map of the island of Granada with its harbor fortifications.

(15) Map of Bermuda, with castles, forts and harbors sketched in.

CHAPTER XXIII

MAJOR-GENERAL SCOTT ON
ACTIVE SERVICE

"Plantaçon trade is one of the greatest Nurseries of the
Shipping and Seamen of this Kingdome, and one of the
greatest branches of its trade."
—Col. Office Records, 1/42, 60; 324 ff 56-58.

"Fishing is the nursery of their seamen. . . ."
—John Scott, speaking of Holland, in his
Preface, 1669.

WHEN THE SECOND DUTCH WAR between England and Holland was officially proclaimed in 1665—the two countries had
been skirmishing along the West African coast for nearly a
year—John obtained a commission under Sir Tobias Bridge,
Commander of the Barbados forces. As Captain of a small
fleet of six vessels and three hundred and fifty men, John was
sent to attack the Dutch-held island of Tobago, lying between Barbados and Guiana on the South American mainland.

He arrived late in October, only to find that a party of
eighty privateers had taken the place a few days previously.
Shades of Henry Morgan! That former Caribbean acquaintance was still going strong and his uncle, Edward Morgan,
was in charge at Tobago—called himself Admiral too, with
a commission from Sir Thomas Modyford, Governor of Jamaica, where Henry Morgan and his brave boys had one of
their headquarters.

They had come to Tobago to pillage, but John, who must have felt at home with the band, demanded, in the name of Governor Willoughby, that the island be proclaimed for the King of England. The privateers, "who were all masters and reckon what they take to be their own," as Willoughby ruefully reported later,[1] told John they operated under Modyford's commission. The situation was precarious, for the men were wild and mutinous and had taken possession of all the Dutch supplies, vast quantities of small arms and ammunition, guns and powder. But apparently they presented no problems to John, whose early experience with the Brethren gave him a confidence few commanders enjoyed. While Governor Willoughby sent urgent word to King Charles entreating orders as to how he should behave under similar conditions in the future,[2] John made a deal with the men and took over the island from them.

Tobago had the best port in the Antilles; it was one of the most fruitful isles—plenty of fresh water, a wonderful climate, had been well settled by the Dutch and excellently stocked with Negroes, cattle and horses.* These assets he would have purchased from the occupants, but Willoughby's resources did not run to such expense, so the privateers set fire to the eighteen sugar plants, and began stripping the houses of their lovely Delft tiles, destroying all they could not carry away "which hath been their custom in all places," as Willoughby lamented.

However by ceding them a plantation near the fort, and promising them they could sell their plunder at Barbados, John obtained possession of the fort, which they left standing, together with five guns and the governor's house, where he was able to quarter a hundred men detailed to clinch possession of the place and guard the King's flag which he planted with due ceremony. Some three hundred Dutch in-

---

* This is the island where the Swiss family Robinson is supposed to have been cast.

habitants were sent away, and the remaining English, Scotch and Irish settlers took oaths of allegiance to Charles II.[3] It must all have seemed very much like a repetition of his Long Island campaign.

Then John pulled up stakes and sailed away and within six months had captured "Boromeo and Issikeob" (Paramaribo and Essequibo) on the South American mainland and these victories, as well as the successful expeditions sent out by Lieutenant-General Byam (Antigua's governor) resulted in England holding all the Atlantic Coast of Guiana from Cayenne on the southeast to northwest Orinoco where Sir Walter Raleigh had once dreamed of finding gold.

A glowing account of these operations is found in William Byam's Journal, preserved among the Ashmolean manuscripts in the Bodleian Library.[4]

"In November 1665 there arrived from his Excellency (Lord Willoughby) his Sergeant-major* John Scott after his victory at Tobago with a small fleet and a regiment of Foote, under the character of Major-General of Guiana, Chief Commissioner and Commander-in-Chief by Land and Sea;† in a few months his great fortune and gallantry, prudent and industrious conduct, made him master of all the great province of New Zealand and Desseceub; settled a peace with the Arrowayes (Arawak Indians) and left both Collonys in a flourishing condition and well garrisoned for the King of England."

Both Byam and Willoughby used John to write up military reports and make official "relations" of events, and it has been suggested that Scott himself might have inserted this generous praise, tossing a bouquet in the copy he made. Comparison of the two existing versions, Byam's signed Journal and John's (which is in the British Museum) would seem to

---

* This was a senior officer in the seventeenth century.
† These were expeditionary titles.

disprove this implication, while there was never any question of his victories, which are officially recorded.[5]

True, combined with his sensibilities as writer, John exhibited a flash of grand gesture in everything he did. This—lest we forget—was the age, or very nearly, of The Three Musketeers, with all its tendency to theatrical bravado. John, like D'Artagnan, was full of exuberance. "He will tell you some truth, but not all gospel,"[6] wrote another Willoughby (William) to Sir Joseph Williamson, well aware of John's tendency to boast. But both public-spirited Willoughbys appreciated John's very real qualities; there were few men who could not only command a raid but write a competent report of it.

"The bearer, Major Scott, will make a better narrative of most affairs here and at Leeward than Willoughby can write," the Governor assured Lord Arlington.[7] And indeed Scott's "Relation"[8] is far in advance of the military reports of the day, giving in logical sequence the general situation, strength of the friendly and enemy forces, the actual battle operation and how field operations were carried out, with details of losses and a summary of the negotiation terms. No wonder bluff Sir Francis, a plunger and gambler and every inch the Colonial High Commissioner, ready to back his policies with his personal fortunes, was only too glad to have such an able pen at his command. Personal relations between them seemed excellent; Nicolls' plans to ruin John had failed.

After his success at Tobago and elsewhere, John returned to Barbados, where he learned that France, bound by treaty obligations to Holland, had declared war on England. He did his best to persuade the governor to combine all the newly acquired South American garrisons—Moruka, Barima, Wacopaw, Essequibo—into one stronghold, urging that this was the best way to meet the threat of combined powerful Dutch and French amphibian forces. But Lord Willoughby, now His Majesty's Lieutenant-General of the entire area, was of another opinion. He gave orders for the individual provisioning and garrisoning of these outposts—orders which proved ineffectual, for within a year all the places, after suffering great misery in a long French siege, were recaptured by the Dutch.

Sir Francis, meanwhile, embarked on his ill-fated voyage to reduce the well-settled French-held section of St. Christopher, in the Leeward Isles (the English called *their* half St. Kitts). But his ship was lost *en route* in a violent hurricane, and he perished with most of his men.

BIBLIOGRAPHICAL NOTES

1. *CSP. Col. Ser. Am. and WI.,* 1661-68, Nos. 1124-25-26.
2. *Ibid.,* No. 1125.
3. *Ibid.,* No. 1124.
4. Ashmole MS., 842, ff 109-22; John Scott's copy of this Sl. MS., 3662, ff 349-62.
5. *CSP. Col. Ser. Am. and WI.,* 1661-68, No. 1657.
6. *Ibid.*
7. *Ibid.,* No. 1581.
8. *Ibid.,* No. 1524.

CHAPTER XXIV

THE BATTLE FOR ST. CHRISTOPHER

"Of all the Colonies which these three nations (English, French, Dutch) have planted in America, those that settled themselves in the Caribby Islands are of greatest account, and the most frequented by Merchants, as being the most advantageous upon the score of Trade."

—Davis, *History of the Barbados, St. Christophers, London,* 1887, p. 158.

THE ENGLISH DID NOT, however, abandon their attempt to storm St. Christopher and John was soon in the thick of the fighting.

A strong expeditionary force had been sent to the Caribbean under Barbados' new royal governor Sir William Willoughby, younger brother of the late Francis, whose loss with his fleet had given the French momentary command of the sea.

Without waiting for all his ships to arrive, Willoughby decided to carry out the hazardous attack on the island, and dispatched a large contingent commanded by his son Henry. But the result was disappointing.

"They had an ill brush there," Lord Willoughby subsequently reported. "Captain Stapleton, Captain Cotter hurt and taken. Williamson's friend Scott escaped, who will give a true account of the business."[1]

The French had proved unexpectedly prepared for the attack, and the English initial surprise maneuver of landing under cover of darkness, as described in Scott's "Relation,"

186

failed. Next day, they tried again. Almost without casualties, English boats put into a flat beach, Sandy Point; but access to the enemy was up steep, almost perpendicular cliffs. A group of volunteers for the desperate task of scaling the heights (the "forlorn," Scott calls them) under the Irish officers, Stapleton, Cotter and others, began the ascent. Lt. Col. Stapleton led, and after a struggle at the top with M. de St. Lawrence's cavalry, succeeded in saving the English flag, only to surrender later, along with Captain Cotter. The rest of the English, Scott among them, fought doggedly "till most of them found graves." ("Relation": Appendix G.)

"The bravest English attempted the cliffs but were vigorously repulsed by the French cavalry who hurled them headlong down the precipice, showering them with boulders till they were forced to take shelter behind the rocks," is how the contemporary French historian, Monsieur R. P. du Tertre, described the attack.[2] This same writer, whose account of the battle is by far the fullest and clearest of all contemporary reports, gives a surprising reason for the English defeat— something which Scott's "Relation," somewhat understandably, does not mention.

"The Lieutenant[-General] Henry Willoughby," wrote du Tertre, "who was drunk and slept through much of the fight, when he saw his men surrendering, ordered a fusillade on the deserters which so infuriated the French, who by this time were mingled with them, that, had they not been restrained by their own officers, would have made short work of their prisoners. . . . The Lieutenant-General, having assuaged his chagrin or rage by all the cannonading, which he trained on his own men, against all the rules of warfare, decided on even more dishonorable conduct . . . to retreat . . . leading with him more than 1,500 men who had not put foot to land . . . with whom he could have made a diversion, dividing our forces, which could have given him the victory."[3]

A few days after the English repulse, Commander Tobias

Bridge entrusted Scott with a mission to visit the island, take money to the imprisoned British officers, negotiate an exchange of prisoners and bring back whatever information he could concerning French strength. Scott made his estimates, but was shocked at the fraternization going on between the Irish officers and the French governor, de la Barr, who had come from Martinique and was trapped on St. Kitts.

Scott's own behavior towards the enemy reflected only too strongly his feelings. "He had the effrontery," recorded du Tertre in his history, "to ask M. de St. Lawrence to surrender all his territory, if he were desirous of sparing French blood; adding that if he did not surrender amicably he would have to do so by force, indeed, give up the whole island."[4] (John must have thought he was talking to Stuyvesant!) "He offered to exchange Sieur Nouel, governor of Sammary, near Cayenne, for Lieutenant-Colonel Stapleton; and he said, insolently, that if M. de la Barr had been on his flag ship as he should have been, they would have captured him too and offered him in exchange for the governor."[5]

John said all this with such extreme arrogance that St. Lawrence called him down sharply and told him if he continued in that strain he would throw him into the sea.[6] The French commander was particularly incensed by John's slighting reference to de la Barr's recent attempt to intercept the English fleet before it reached Barbados, and to his attack (with fifteen French ships and four Dutch, under de Crynsens) on Captain Berry's much smaller squadron.

"Scott returned (from St. Christopher) with little satisfaction," Commander Tobias Bridge reported from Nevis,[7] "but complained of Captain Cotter's great familiarity with the French governor and says that most of our soldier prisoners, especially the Irish, have taken up arms with the French."

Retaliation for this statement was immediate. Next morning a messenger arrived from the governor of St. Kitts with letters from the British officers: Captain Cotter, and others, "complained much of Major Scott's imprudent carriage in the message and ill deportment in the engagement."[8]

This exchange of compliments is authentic, for it is calendared in English state papers, and John's arrogance was noted, too, by du Tertre. But there is an amazing sequel to this accusation and counter-accusation.

Among Samuel Pepys' private papers there is an unsigned unofficial account of a court-martial held on Nevis, January 4th, 1668, at "My Lord Willoughby's Command," before "Sir Tobias Bridge and seventeen other officers, on a charge against Captain John Scott, late colonel of Sir Tobias Bridge's regiment." Captain Cotter himself initiated the proceedings by stating flatly that "it is well known that Scott is a notorious coward."[9]

Of all the affidavits Pepys collected about him, this is the most damaging, for it has not only been repeated by all of Scott's biographers, but has been used as a yardstick to assess his every action with deplorable results.

Actually, such a court-martial never happened. Outside Pepys' notebooks there is no mention of it anywhere. In all the voluminous Admiralty papers, wherein the most trivial routine details are meticulously entered, there is no record of it. Among the, literally, hundreds of references in state papers to Nevis and everything that happened there—including courts-martial—not one word. In Lord Arlington's report to the King on officers of the Barbados regiment, cashiered by court-martial (or pardoned) Scott's name is nowhere to be found.[10] Even Pepys' version of the alleged court-martial mentions no verdict handed down—a most revealing omission.

Governor Willoughby, writing *officially* to Arlington after the defeat, says he got nothing but obedience and diligence from Major Scott. "He will give an account of all transactions at Leeward, where he did his part better than some that may pretend to have done more. I have no complaint against him, but against some others."[11] (Appendix H)

Various official records offer glimpses of John's further West Indies adventures. A communication to Williamson from one John Corney, a ship's surgeon, speaks of an encounter with the Dutch who attacked with five men-o'-war "and were warmly handled by Major Scott."

Action against the Dutch and French was largely a series of raids on their coastal towns, burning and destroying enemy settlements, forts, goods, wrecking plantations. John had his fill of it, daringly carrying out one hundred and sixty thousand pounds worth of damage for the glory of England; while he spent "73,788 pounds of Muscovado sugar on His Majesty's Service." He was wounded in the arm, breast and shoulder.[12]

The exact figures of his depredations are listed in a petition John made to the King for reimbursement, accompanied by the tactful suggestion that the amount be charged up to the Barbados four and one-half per cent customs duties.[13] But one wonders if he were ever paid. A second petition[14] reiterates his request, stating that he was out of pocket one thousand six hundred and twenty pounds, and that a sum which the King had ordered Willoughby to pay him, namely seven hundred and thirty-eight pounds, charged on the local customs, he had never received. Moreover he had lost his ketch worth five hundred pounds in the hurricane which took Lord Francis Willoughby's life; while on the Guiana coast he had been forced to pay for his soldiers' provisions out of his own pocket. It is a sorry picture of English finances, and John was not the only one who suffered.*

BIBLIOGRAPHICAL NOTES

1. *CSP. Col. Ser. Am. and WI.,* 1661-68, No. 478.
2. du Tertre, *Hist.* IV, 267.
3. *Ibid.,* 271.

---

* As late as 1668 Sir Tobias Bridge was complaining to the King that from the beginning of the campaign he had received little more than a month's pay and that his soldiers and officers were "very naked and necessitous." But there was no money to bring him, and his troops home . . . The Barbados Assembly proposed that the Governor employ him on the island (at £300 p.a.). This was refused but Bridge was offered "a gratuity of £100. *CSP. Col. Ser. Am. and W.I.,* 1661-68, No. 1760, No. 1856; *C.E.B.,* XI, 173-77.

4. *Ibid.*, 302.
5. *Ibid.*
6. *Ibid.*, 303.
7. *CSP. Col. Ser. Am. and WI.*, 1661-68, No. 482.
8. *Ibid.*
9. Rawl. MSS., A 175, f 149, r,v.
10. *Col. Pap.*, XXVII, 31.
11. *CSP. Col. Ser. Am. and WI.*, 1661-68, No. 1580.
12. *Ibid.*, No. 1531.
13. *Ibid.*, No. 1525.
14. *Ibid.*, No. 1526.

CHAPTER XXV

ROYAL GEOGRAPHER

> "In perils by sea, in perils by land, I have passed through
> good reports and ill, as is the lot of all who charge fortune
> boldly. But I bless that God who so often saved me . . .
> never suffered me to return from beyond the seas so much
> in love with other countries as to retain any prejudice, by
> what I have seen abroad, to the land of my nativity."
>
> —John Scott, Preface.

BLISSFULLY UNCONSCIOUS of Cotter's charge against himself,
John proceeded to London to report to the King, glad of this
chance to press his personal claims as well. But just as he
seemed about to reap the reward of two years' service, misfortune dealt him an entirely gratuitous blow. He was "surprised at his lodgings by four bailiffs who forced him into a
coach and clapped him into Gatehouse prison," for a debt
incurred at the time of his last visit.[1] His anguished appeal to
Lord Arlington reflects the first hint of bitterness that
haunted his belief that he was being used, then cast aside.

His long letter recapitulates the details of two former petitions to the King for reimbursement. He tells of resettling the
islands of Montserrat and Antigua, and how, before he had
been thirty hours at Barbados, he had re-embarked for England upon Lord Willoughby's orders, to give His Majesty an
account of affairs in the West Indies. He had saved the royal
ships from the fury of the hurricane by persuading them to
put to sea, while ten merchantmen, that stayed, were beaten
to pieces . . . he had served a gracious Prince, yet for thirty

pounds and ten shillings and *that not due*, he is hurried to a jail, and without influence upon his Majesty for release, must be carried . . . on the morrow . . . by a *habeas corpus* to the King's Bench![2] Even the self-centered Arlington was touched by the plea. Scott was released, and actually awarded one hundred pounds.

But it would have been a monstrous double wrong had he been left in prison, for his debt had been incurred over the sixty pounds worth of curiosities he had bought to prosecute the Atherton case for Winthrop and his friends, a sum the interested parties had promised to refund. He had had to raise the cash in London with a bill of exchange on one Thomas Alcocke, a member of the Atherton Company. John's futile efforts to collect the money, as detailed in the Chancery suit[3] he finally brought against those involved, give a vivid insight to the chain of ill luck that hounded his every financial transaction.

London itself presented a shocking spectacle as he left the prison and picked his way through the charred ruins of the Great Fire. The double horror of plague and conflagration had shattered the nation's nerves, and a vast uneasiness gripped the popular mind. Rumors were rife, fears of popish arsonists and wholesale massacre swept the City. There was a smell of revolution in the air, mobs broke the windows of the new Piccadilly palaces, sacked shops, clamored for parliament's recall. What the people wanted was a scapegoat for all the recent troubles, and their natural target was the Administration Chief, the Earl of Clarendon. The violence of their protests against this minister must have rejoiced John's heart. For it was to this potent figure that governor Nicolls had once complained of John's determined opposition to the new colonial policy that he, Clarendon, was trying to impose upon New England. That fact had been grimly recorded in the Chancellor's tenacious memory.

"The unkindness of the Earl of Clarendon and my zeal to my king and country have been my ruin," John once lamented to Arlington[4] while reviewing his own conduct in Long Island and Massachusetts. The significant political changes inherent in the great man's imminent downfall looked as if they would coincide with a fresh start for John Scott.

The old pilot was finally dropped, impeached, and banished from England, to be replaced by a new ministry—the famous Cabal—so-called from the initials of its five members. Scott's patron, Sir Henry Bennet—boyhood friend of Charles II and one of Europe's most skillful and experienced diplomats—was one of the five, under his new title, Lord Arlington. Two others were the Duke of Buckingham and Anthony Ashley Cooper (afterwards Earl of Shaftesbury), both of whom looked kindly upon the talented and forceful John.

The latter's reports on the West Indies situation were noted, and, we must presume, appreciated, since John was immediately given a new assignment to investigate the Newfoundland Fisheries, which for some years had been threatened by the French. His survey,* a thoroughly competent bit of work, was submitted in July 1668; and, perhaps because of it, or as a general vindication of all his past activities, a special reward awaited him.

By the end of August, 1668, a royal warrant, countersigned by Arlington, conferred on John Scott a government appointment, the post of Royal Geographer. It must have been the proudest moment of his life: it wiped out, in a blaze of glory, the losses and disappointments of the previous years.

CHARLES R

Our Will and pleasure is that you give order for the swearing of Our Trusty and Well beloved Major John Scott to be our Servant in quality of Geographer unto us, and that he be admitted thereunto as Our Servant in Ordinary, and receive and enjoy all Rights, profitts, privileges and advantages thereunto, belonging. And for so doing this

---

* In Bodleian Library.

shall be your Warrant. Given at our Court at Whitehall the 29th day of August, 1668 in the Twentieth year of our Reign.

To Our Right Trusty and Right Well beloved Cousin and Councillor, Edward Earl of Manchester, Lord Chamberlain of Our Household.[5]

With what satisfaction John must have read and reread the precious document. His gifts were finally recognized, the King's nomination was positive proof of his industry and skill, he had his place at Court.

But there was no money in it. The post carried no stipend, nor were any "profitts" discernible. John was as hard put to it as ever to make a living, and his country seemed to offer little or no opportunity, at that moment, of acquiring an honest livelihood. England's finances were hardly better than John's. The royal exchequer showed a constant deficit as Commons voted annually less and less. The King dug deep into his private purse to eke out the costs of his growing navy. Even so, many of his seamen went unpaid and were tempted to serve on foreign ships, while his ambassadors abroad chafed under the galling restriction of salaries long overdue.

Obviously the Royal Geographer had little to expect from Royal quarters.

BIBLIOGRAPHICAL NOTES

1. S.P. Dom. Car., II, 233, No. 74.
2. *Ibid.*
3. Collins, Ch. Pro., 221.
4. S.P. Dom. Car., II, 493, No. 70.
5. Warrant copied in Rawl. MSS., A 175, f 158.

CHAPTER XXVI

COLONEL SCOTT IN HOLLAND

"It seems we no longer understand war."
—Colonel Bampfield to De Witt, April 1672.
Petrus Johannes Block, *Hist. of the People
of the Netherlands,* IV, 336.

LIKE SO MANY impecunious English officers of the period, John turned to the Continent to try his fortune. There was, at this period, little sense of nationalism; men passed easily back and forth across the Channel, seeking outlets for their talents, finding employment where they could: they officered foreign regiments, served at different Courts. Only the budding industrial skills were sacrosanct, and artisans and technicians were strictly forbidden to "pass beyond the seas."

France was Europe's mecca. The court of Louis XIV, the "Sun King," surpassed all others in magnificence and wealth, and John's first thought was of Paris. He must have made some move in this direction for he is the subject of official correspondence, judging from a letter in the Quai d'Orsay archives.

This is from Charles Colbert de Croissey, newly arrived French Ambassador to England, and brother of Louis' exceptional administrator, the "great" Colbert, as he is known in France.

De Croissey had installed himself in London (1668) in sumptuous style, keeping open table, celebrating Mass every Sunday with ten richly garbed priests. No foreign ambassador had ever enjoyed such prestige and power; he had a secret understanding with the principal advisers to the Crown, and busied himself in national policies as though he were an English Cabinet minister. He was a man who could well have helped John.

But the latter's appeal to serve in the French West Indies was fruitless. "It is very difficult for us to make use of John Scott in America," wrote Colbert to Pomponne* at St. Germain early in 1669.[1] "That country being very well known it would be dangerous for us to use an Englishman there."

John did not give up all hopes of serving the French, and after a year came back again to the Marquis de Croissey with a proposition for gun-casting in France. According to the ambassador's subsequent letter, and the two *mémoires* concerning this project,[2] it aroused considerable interest which was later to bring results.† In the meantime John looked elsewhere for a position.

His Long Island background and knowledge of the Dutch language made him seem useful to the United Provinces.

"I was commanded to go to Holland," he stated, in his Chancery suit,[3] "then returned to England with the Prince of Orange and on his business." This was when the Dutch Prince, then only eighteen years of age, ignored by the Republican government at home and rigorously kept out of all public office, was visiting his English royal uncle and seeking to fortify his position. He was in very short order to be made Captain-General of the United Provinces' military forces.

Once again John crossed the Channel, still "on the Prince's

---

* Simon Arnauld Marquis de Pomponne, formerly French Ambassador at The Hague, adroit diplomat of the incomparable Mazarin school, became Secretary of State for Foreign Affairs in 1671.

† In this second letter of the French ambassador, he does not mention Scott by name, but the identity is unmistakable. He refers to "the English officer, who for this project, proposed making some sample 7-lb gun models." In France, John Scott, with the help of D'Alliez de la Tour, French Purveyor of the Navy, made some 7-lb models of his guns, Mit. Ch. Pro., C8, 638, No. 61.

affairs." And soon we hear that John is officially attached to the Dutch army, to recruit and train troops in Holland and Zeeland—no unusual procedure at all, for English "younger sons" often acquired similar commissions abroad.

The Hague municipal archives of 1669 show that John Scott, sergeant-major (a senior officer at that period), appointed a certain Englishman, Wilhemus Akers, as lieutenant in his company and made him recruiting officer to round up and deliver soldiers for Scott's regiment at Berg-op-Zoom.[4] A little more than a year later John was sworn in as sergeant-major and captain; and by February 16, 1672, he is full colonel of infantry and captain.*[5]

John had seven companies, two in s-Hertogenbosch, a big garrison town in the southeast; two at Goringchem in central Holland, the main defense of the so-called water line and usually winter headquarters; one at Schoonhoven, not too far from The Hague; and two in Zeeland, the next most important province (after Holland), of all the seven United Provinces.[6] This entailed constant traveling. He was in the *Lichtung* [administration]; i.e., he had no command in the field, but was responsible for the supervision of the officers, discipline, and training. (Among the papers confiscated from his London chambers in 1682, were Dutch manuals, drill instructions for musketry practice, etc., all considered very modern at that period, where it was customary, even in the famous French army as late as 1680, to attach a youngster to a regiment and let him pick up what he could, without military instruction.)

John's work was gruelling for the United Provinces were

---

* In the seventeenth century commanders of regiments were often called not colonel, but sergeant-major. A commander-in-chief was sergeant-major-general. In the military organization of that period, the colonel (or sergeant-major) was also captain of its senior company. The officer who actually led that company was, by title, only captain-lieutenant. However, not too great precision was observed in *naming* rank. Commander Bridge, for example, referred to John Scott as both major and captain in one and the same dispatch.

regrouping and realigning their entire forces.* After the
Treaty of Aix-la-Chapelle, 1668, the Dutch had considerably
reduced their army, their magazines were empty, their officers
undisciplined, their fortifications neglected. Grand Pensioner
de Witt began to change all that. He appointed expert foreign
officers, and hoped to raise 100,000 men to meet the expected
attack. He was well aware that Louis XIV longed to duplicate his former brilliant victories and take over still more
Spanish possessions in the Low Countries.† He knew that
the French king was forging the weapons for this calculated
aggression with all the vast resources of his country's riches
and military genius. But de Witt counted on Holland's alliance with France to delay this calamity and he refused to
believe in England's secret negotiations with the latter country. But King Charles, despite his treaty with Holland, was
on the verge of a yet more comprehensive agreement with
his cousin in Paris. This was the famous (or infamous) Treaty
of Dover. So urgent was Charles' desire to be financially independent of his parliament, that, in return for substantial
French subsidies, he promised to aid France militarily, declare himself a Catholic, and restore Catholicism in England!
The fatal character of this document was the key to Europe's
foreign policy for the next decade, and its torturous implications, so alien to the hearts of most of the King's subjects,
would have surpassed their shocked understanding had they
grasped but a fraction of the terms. ("There is a mystery in

---

* Dorothy Temple, wife of the British Ambassador, Sir William, in her
voluminous correspondence writes on October 31st, 1670, that Holland intended raising fourteen new regiments of foot, and six of horse, and that
all the companies—new and old—should comprise 150 men, instead of 50;
and every troop 80, instead of the former 45. "These new levies please everyone—are talked of everywhere." In the same letter she mentions Major Scott
receiving certain news from Williamson "and so, you probably know it too,"
she adds to her husband, as though there were cooperation between the two.
John gave the Ambassador an autographed copperplate reproduction of one
of his West Indies maps—a beautiful thing which Sir William, much to
Pepys' surprise, hung in his dining room.

† Louis claimed these Spanish possessions in lieu of his Spanish wife's
unpaid dot.

this, more than I dare speak of," declared John Scott, half sensing the awful truth, as he spoke in the House of Commons years later.)

The preparations for this momentous change were carried out in the very strictest secrecy. In the Cabal cabinet, only Clifford and Arlington, both Catholics, knew about it. Even Buckingham, the King's confidant and playmate, never guessed what was afoot, although he was chosen to negotiate a *traité simulé*, or mock treaty with Louis. While the keen-nosed Ashley was so far from sniffing the odor of popery this time that the King (when finally signing the Dover Treaty in 1670) created him Earl of Shaftesbury in a mood of almost mocking prodigality.

It was against this background of political maneuvering that John tackled his technical job. There was a great deal about the Dutch Republic which appealed to him; its spirit was quite unlike that of New Netherland. He speaks of his close friendship with Jan de Witt, in several instances calls him "brother," although at the crucial moment when he was forced to choose, John remained a loyal Englishman.

De Witt had been in office since 1653, a skilled, upright, highly intelligent public servant. His prominent eyes and large hooked nose lacked the appeal of Louis XIV's handsome features, but this aristocratic Republican, who went on foot through the city followed by a single servant, was one of the most eminent statesmen in Europe. He had a consummate sense of political balance, steering for long years a safe course among the French, Spanish and English. He was a magnificent orator, who despised the mob and prayed every day to preserve his country from the fury of Kings—his country, whose century-long fight for independence may have burnished in John's mind bright memories of his own brief stand for freedom and human dignity.

The United Provinces, a mere hand's breadth of territory on the North Sea—with seven practically autonomous little states differing from one another in language, manners and race—had become a nation only owing to its early heroic struggle against unparalleled Spanish tyranny and persecution. In this epic conflict of eighty years, facing one of the greatest European empires, the Dutch themselves had become great—a vast naval and commercial commonwealth, with their own empire girdling the earth.

And just as their great leader in the sixteenth century, William the Silent, brought them independence and union by his courageous resistance, so his noble descendant in the seventeenth century, the young Prince of Orange, met invasion with the same indomitable assurance which halted the enemy, saved the homeland, and eventually put him on the English throne.

Such blazing issues appealed to John's sense of drama, compelled his admiration and zeal. He made countless friends among Dutch senators and governors.

"He is very kindly used in this country and is in great credit with de Witt and all the principal ones of the States," reported James Vernon to Williamson in January 1672, "and in many cases this good will is reciprocated."[7]

"He is one that hath great trust from these people,"[8] Gelson (Pepys' friend) wrote of John from Amsterdam to a London merchant, Zachias Thorn. "He knows affairs of Holland as any man in the Netherlands. He was chosen governor of Roos, but they impose an oath of abjuration against the King (Charles II) and his generals, which no honest man can do, let his condition be never so desperate."[9] John's nonconformist conscience again stood in the way of easy advancement.

Dutch service was not without its drawbacks, however. Life in garrison towns (outside The Hague) was dull. While others gambled and duelled John worked on his histories and maps, sketching points of strategic interest.

As commanding officer, he was responsible for provisioning and advancing money to his men, and the States were not always punctual in repaying their commanders, a failing by no means confined to the Dutch. Army financing was a personal affair in Holland: customarily the military authorities granted regimental concessions to certain private individuals —a sort of banker-solicitor-paymaster—who advanced the necessary sums and then collected from the War Office. This was an investment on his part; he bought a regiment as he might buy a block of municipal bonds, and he charged interest, money which was frequently deducted from the men's pay. When troop expenditures were met irregularly the commander could either shoulder the loss or cashier a few men and recuperate by drawing their expenses later. Horses and military equipment were his own property; but an incoming new colonel had to take over the regiment just as it was— whatever deficits of pay or materiel formerly existed were his to cope with. On the other hand, he had certain perquisites; twelve horses at his disposal, a following of secretaries and servants and a large wine allowance. During the winter months colonels were sometimes made governors of a fortress or of a town, so that despite the exasperating financial system, commissions in the United Provinces' forces were eagerly sought by the Dutch nobility, and by younger sons of wealthy or noble German and English families. There was a rectitude and integrity, especially under the high-minded William of Orange, which excluded adventurers. Unlike most other nations, the Dutch Republic forbade the purchase of commissions; and bribery for promotion in the army was unknown.[10]

But the tedium of garrison life told on John's thirst for excitement. "Colonel Scott, that mercurial man, rests not one day in a place, to the wonder of the English since all officers are commanded to their garrisons" is a report among the Holland state papers.[11] He was drinking heavily too, a sure sign he was in low spirits. "Major Scott, riding-master Van Hill, and Strongh, smash things up in the coffeehouse of Matheus de Bruyn, at the Hofsingel" reads an entry in the Yearbook of the Historical Society "Die Haghe."[12]

He seemed to care little for his reputation. Even on his

trips back to London he acted with reckless insouciance, punishing real or fancied slights in an outrageous manner.

"It is possible you have not heard of the disaster of the Earl of Anglesey the other day," wrote Sir William Gower to a friend in the country. (Anglesey was Treasurer of the Navy, a good worker, but so venal people said he had sold himself too often to be worth anything.) "His coach being stopped in the street, Major Scott came to him and told him he had received injuries from him of a high nature, that he must come out and fight. The Earl answered he was no swordsman, professed it not, he might seek another way of remedy. Major Scott replied his [i.e. the Earl's] power was too great in those ways; he would take that where there was more equality; in short, pulled him out of his coach and with a boisterous cudgel beat him in an extraordinary manner. Sober men look upon it as the action deserves, others make sport of it."[13]

No one could feel very sorry for the slippery Anglesey. He was universally unpopular at the moment for he was suspected of lining his pockets at the expense of the Navy. But the fact that John could go unpunished after such violence to a Minister would seem to show that either public opinion considered the assault justified, or that John was exceedingly well protected by the Cabal, particularly by Buckingham.*

John's was a complex disarming nature, his unbridled exuberance steeled with commonsense. He was a great resenter with a deep-seated craving to be of value and to serve. An inordinate touchiness kept his temper at flame point, making him many enemies. But his was a character to attract and enchant, for his temperamental excitability was offset by sparkling whimsical talk which won him immediate friends.

Occasionally this charm and captivating talk made him enemies too. But in this case his enemies would be women.

---

* "My Lord Anglesey was Buckingham's enemy and the best head in the Council." MSS. Fr. Corr. Pol., V. 92, f 137, Colbert's gossipy letter to Louis XIV.

BIBLIOGRAPHICAL NOTES

1. Cinq Cents de Colbert, MS., 204, f 210.
2. Aff. Etran. Dip. Corr. pol. Angleterre, 102, ff 167, 166, v.r.
3. Collins Ch. Pro., 221.
4. Not. Arch. Hague. Mun., Protocol of notary C. Dispontejn, No. 592, Dec. 21, 1669.
5. Arch. Raad. v. St. (Counsel of St.): Resolutions, No. 92/93, Mar. 12th, 1672; Ten Raa, *Het St. Leger,* V, 489; John's signature in *Oath Bks.,* No. 1928, 154, 170.
6. Arch. Raad. v. St., No. 1928, inventory; Resolutions: 92/93 inventory, Ten Raa, *Het St. Leger,* 278.
7. S.P. Holl., 84/188, f 76.
8. *Ibid.,* f 77.
9. S.P. Fr., 77/40, f 73.
10. Information contributed to me personally by Colonel Siersema and Colonel Wijn, historians of the *Krijgsgeschiedkundige Afdeling van de Generale Staf,* The Hague, August 1955.
11. S.P. Holl., 84/188, ff 244, 289.
12. Johanna Beck, *'Eene Wandeling door s-Gravenhage in 1679,* p. 157.
13. *HMC MSS. (Var. Coll.,* of Sir George Wombwell, bart), II, 127-28.

CHAPTER XXVII

DEBORAH EGMONT AND THE
RECRUITING OFFICER

"These golden stars, these fragrant flowers,
Eventual glories and delights
Bright spirits in their golden bowers
Are still ourselves in various Lights."
—John Scott.

IN THE MARKET SQUARES and other public places of Berg-
op-Zoom during the early spring days of 1671 one could often
see a tall, handsome, lusty fellow, accompanied by a few
robust veterans, making a rousing speech to the crowds, and
jingling a purse of coins in his pocket.

This was Willy Akers, English lieutenant in the Dutch
forces, and John Scott's recruiting officer.

The States-General had no national recruiting. It was all
done locally, and Akers was an old hand at the game; had
been with John for nearly two years. When on the job, he
usually had a pretty girl or two around and saw to it that
some of his followers would be brandishing a loaf of fine
white bread or gnawing on a succulent roast fowl, just to give
an idea of how well one fared in the army.

Actual enlistment was concluded between a couple of
drinks in a local tavern, and if the new recruit later regretted the step or felt he had been "overpersuaded," there
was no drawing back, for there were always plenty of witnesses to swear they had seen him drinking the Prince's

health. Those who wavered were very few, however. The prevailing mood was determined and belligerent, for no one expected peace to last.

John was pleased by the way Akers "brought them in"; he was a fine lad. And he had an eye for a wench, too. There was a certain girl John had noted once or twice—who was she—that blonde with the inviting smile?

"Deborah van Egmont, a friend of my sister, Madame de Saint-Amoer," Akers told John. "A lively piece. Her father was a servant in the Prince of Orange's household. She lodges here in Druart's house with the Saint-Amoers."

John wanted an introduction, so Akers brought the two together and John visited Deborah at her friends' lodging.

He was full of compliments about her father, asking all about him, flattering her by insinuating that de Witt himself had said that her old man must be related to *the* Egmonts, one of Holland's first families. She giggled and blushed and lifted great blue eyes to him, asking what his name was and what he was doing. He told her he was Royal Geographer to his Britannic Majesty King Charles II. (But she was not so simple as to believe that!) He stayed by her side all evening and whispered that he was moving his company from the Berg-op-Zoom garrison to Gennisperhuys camp, a fort near Gennep. Wouldn't she come along, and visit him there? She and her friend, Willy Akers' sister, of course?

When the troops left town, Deborah went along. Saint-Amoer was one of John's sergeants whose wife followed the colors, so Deborah had every reason for going with her friend.

This sentimental Dutch interlude is fully documented in two long affidavits Deborah subsequently made. The first, in 1672, before a Dutch notary, concerned John's dealings with his recruiting officer and army solicitor, Dispontejn. It was made at the latter's request and Deborah was under no pressure at all in her sworn statement.

The second, made in London in 1680, covering the same incidents seem to show that Deborah had been "got at," and brought into the Pepys-h plot! It introduces a great deal of John's alleged conversation revealing him as planning to "ruin and spoil England," "lead a company up the river of London to make England dance"; and urging his officers to "land, and burn and plunder the English shores."[1] As some of this evidence is self-contradictory, disproved by official records, and all of it pretty silly, there is no need to go into it at any length. But the incident with Akers and Dispontejn as revealed by Deborah receives confirmation in Dutch law courts and belongs in the story of John's life.

It was more fun at Gennep than at Berg-op-Zoom. Big, fashionable Dordrecht was nearby, and Deborah went to Court there and met the dashing Major Scott again, who entertained her in company and asked her to visit his rooms where he promised to show her some pretty drawings.

But it was in an upper chamber of a Schwindrech tavern, where they had all gone to drink, that Deborah first saw John's "pictures." The table was strewn with colored charts and drafts, and one of John's men, Richard Adams, a former seal engraver at the Hague, was working over them.

"What is he doing?" asked Deborah.

"He's a copyist, a really fine draughtsman. He's making a copy of one of my maps," said John.

Deborah looked wonderingly at the large sheet with its bewildering lines and colored sections. "Is this the river of London?" she asked at last. "Yes," he whispered, "that's the river of London. Pretty, isn't it?" he observed turning to address Admiral Van Putten, de Witt's brother, who had been inspecting John's troops that afternoon and who had just entered the room and was glancing at the maps. But the Admiral only wanted a word with the major and had no time to examine the drawings, for he was on his way to a big "do" at Utrecht.

The friendship progressed. John often took Deborah out, but always with friends. She became more and more interested in everything the troops were doing in order to find out where her major was. She was like a child with a new toy. Forgetting her former infatuation with a Sergeant Nederway, she had eyes only for the tall English officer and felt personally aggrieved when he left Gennisperhuys—as he often did. "You go away and no one knows where," she pouted. "Three times you've gone and don't say where you've been."

He never told her about his other companies. He never told her anything that mattered. She was a little goose, but a pretty goose. An inquisitive one, too. She pried into his affairs, took delight in all the regimental gossip, scandal and squabbles, and, since several of the men were quartered with the Saint-Amoers, had plenty of opportunity of indulging her curiosity.

"That Akers is a rascal," she told John one day. "He's not loyal at all. I have often heard him say he is sick of serving the States. He says he'll be damned if he'd stay with them any longer . . . he'd rather be with the French. . . . They pay better, he says. Do they pay better? When he was going to be sworn in as lieutenant by the States' Councillors, he said the oath didn't mean a thing to him; he'd keep his fingers crossed, for he didn't care two hoots about it. It was no more to him than drinking a glass of wine, he said."[2]

This would have been bad enough news about such an indefatigable recruiting officer. But John was having other troubles with Akers.

During John's absence, the army solicitor, Dispontejn, had visited Berg-op-Zoom with two hundred florins for the troops. "I saw him pay the money to Akers," Deborah told John. "It was at our house, and Akers showed me the receipt dated April 23rd, 1671, written by Dispontejn. But Akers changed it to April 28th, because he said that was the date he got the money."[3]

John asked Akers about the consignment, complaining that the lieutenant was always putting him off when asked for an accounting about his recruits.

"The men are beginning to complain about you, Akers;

they say some of them are not getting paid at all or as little as four pennies—six at most—and others are getting short rations—they don't get enough bread."[4] There were continual disputes and charges over this money. On one occasion John flew into a rage and drew his sword, threatening his subordinate, but Deborah calmed him down and got the sword back into its sheath,[5] though she did little to improve relations between the two men. Recriminations and angry scenes were constant. The troops openly declared Akers was swindling them, giving the money to his mother, a camp scrounger.[6] But although John cursed him out, calling him scamp and scoundrel, he did nothing about it. He was careless concerning money. Or he may not have been convinced that Akers was really at fault. Perhaps Dispontejn was responsible for the shortage. The latter's very function was an exasperating one likely to invite ill feeling or resentment and the major was not one to forget a grudge. This could have been a reason for blaming the solicitor for the deficit, rather than his able compatriot, Akers.

A week after they arrived in Gennep there was another incident. "You received five hundred florins from Dispontejn in May," Scott charged his lieutenant. "You get this money and you keep it a secret from me. Moreover you changed the receipt date on this too . . . it was May 15th. I saw it on the document before you altered it to May 17th. . . ."[7]—which was two days after the books had been balanced.

Akers was defiant. "You altered that date yourself, Major," he said, "or had it altered by someone else, to harm Dispontejn. You want to get him in Dutch," he added with a laugh.[8]

Still John took no steps against Akers, but apparently started to build up a case against the army solicitor. He talked with young Johan van der Pijll, Dispontejn's assistant, needling him into derogatory statements about his superior.[9]

One day, as Deborah started out for a visit to The Hague, she was overtaken by one of John's corporals, sent after her with a message from the major and the request that he might accompany her as far as Nimeguen, which was on the way, so he said.

Within a quarter of an hour John himself came by riding a magnificent white horse which he turned over to his corporal when Deborah accepted his escort. They went slowly on their way together, and when they reached Moke they found an obliging wagoner who let them climb up behind and ride on the hay.

John slipped his arm round Deborah's plump waist. He held her comfortably against him and with practiced fingers began to unbutton her gown . . . the scene is not hard to imagine—we have John's several references to his casual affairs, and the girl was so very willing.

The scene in the wagon stems from the 1680—the doctored —affidavit . . . Deborah never even mentioned it in 1672. And her account of John's offered bribes—if indeed he actually made them—sounds as if he were trying to get her to promise something very different from what she said he wanted.

"Do you know how Dispontejn has been dealing with my men?"[10] asked John.

"Yes, he has always paid the company very well and advanced you more than your due and you go away with it so as nobody could find where you were.* When the Company needed their pay Dispontejn advanced the money to Sergeant Nederway who brought it from The Hague to Berg-op-Zoom; I saw it at Druart's house, in the room where Lieutenant Akers and his mother and I were together."[11]

John had replaced Nederway in Deborah's affections and she never let him forget the sergeant's name—possibly to stir his jealousy.

"What have you to do with that?" answered John. "I would not have you say anything of your seeing that money, but give

* Deborah was unaware of the existence of John's other companies.

me a note under your hand declaring you never saw it, I'll take you to a man who will write it [for she could not write herself] and then you can set your hand and swear to it."[12]

"Then I must swear my soul to hell, for I saw the money. I believe Dispontejn pays the Company very well, the company could not have a better solicitor than he,"[13] insisted Deborah.

"You don't know how matters stand between Dispontejn and me," retorted John, "For he pretends that I have set my hand to his book of accounts, but he is a rogue and a rascal and I must make him a liar; and if you will swear what I would have you, that you never saw that money, I will give you four hundred guilders and your choice of some new French stuffs which I have in two trunks at The Hague, the like of which no one has ever seen."[14]

"I am in want of no stuffs nor anything else and therefor would not be tempted to swear to an untruth."

"What about a very fine ring?"[15]

Deborah peeled off her glove and showed John the very fine one which the Duke of Gloucester had given her when he left for England with the King. John tried to persuade her to change her mind. "Mine will be a much better ring than the Duke's," he whispered.[16]

She continued her refusals, but he would not take no for an answer. Then, since nothing would satisfy him, she began to relent and said she would ask the advice of an uncle she had in The Hague. This seemed to please him and nothing more was said in the wagon until they reached Nimeguen, where, as Deborah distinctly remembered eight years later, they spent the night at the *Sign of the Smoked Salmon*.

The next morning John was the conscientious officer back on the job again, inquiring about ships to Rotterdam. Nothing till late afternoon. He invited Deborah to go with him over the water to a place where the wagons stood for Utrecht. She agreed, but his attitude seemed to have changed, he paid little or no attention to her on the trip. He was busy measuring the *pund,* or flat-bottomed boat they were in, questioning the ferryman about other possible *punds* locally available for transporting horses and baggage. (If he had to bring his men this way he would need a good many.)

The two passed the day together and then John took his leave, asking her, at parting, where she would be staying at The Hague, for he certainly would not fail to visit her, he said, just as soon as she arrived.

BIBLIOGRAPHICAL NOTES

1. Rawl. MSS., A 175, ff 6, 7, 8, 19.
2. *Ibid.*
3. *Ibid.*, ff 13, 14; Not. Arch. Hague Mun., No. 392, f 323.
4. *Ibid.*
5. Rawl. MSS., A 175, f 13.
6. *Ibid.*, f 15; Not. Arch. Hague Mun., No. 392, f 324.
7. *Ibid.*, "John Scott and Akers quarrelled about change of date."
8. Rawl. MSS., A 175, f 23; Not. Arch. Hague Mun., No. 715, ff 343, 395.
9. *Ibid.*, f 396.
10. Rawl. MSS., A 175, f 12.
11. *Ibid.*, f 13.
12. *Ibid.*
13. *Ibid.*
14. *Ibid.*, f 14.
15. *Ibid.*
16. *Ibid.*, f 15.

CHAPTER XXVIII

DISPONTEJN GOES TO JAIL

"When in doubt, win the trick."
—Edmond Hoyle, 1672.

THERE IS NO RECORDED REASON for John's treatment of his army solicitor. The disputed sum was comparatively trivial—seven hundred guilders in all, or roughly one hundred and forty dollars, though it was worth much more then. The fact that he decided to take legal action about it points to the basic honesty prevailing in the Dutch army. For in November of 1671, while garrisoned at Wesel, John authorized an attorney, one Willem Lissart, to institute, before the *Gecommitterde Raden* (Deputy States of Holland), proceedings against Dispontejn for forging his, Scott's, signature.[1] A few months later, also at John's orders, Lissart proceeded against Abraham Arents, a Jewish moneylender at Gennep, for making unauthorized loans to Lieutenant Akers and Sergeant Nederway.[2]

Pending trial Dispontejn was imprisoned in The Hague Stadhaus. And almost immediately he was caught up in a perfect *opéra-bouffe* quibble over jurisdictional procedure between The Hague High Bailiff (magistrate) Rudolph van Paffenrode, and his political opponent, the Attorney-General. Van Paffenrode believed Dispontejn guilty and wanted him put to the torture to wring a confession from him. But the Attorney-General did not agree and was ready to free the prisoner—if only to spite his rival. Alternately they released

213

and reincarcerated the man. When the Attorney-General demanded his freedom, or that at least he be transferred to the Court jail,[3] van Paffenrode promptly raised objections. Dispontejn continued to languish in the Town Hall jail while the matter was referred to the cause-list session.[4]

John, often absent from The Hague on military duties, retained Johan van der Heyden, L.L.D. to press the case;[5] but Lissart, examining Dispontejn's books which had been requisitioned[6] and comparing John's alleged signatures with a genuine one, could establish no forgery. He sensed the possible cause of the trouble, however, and urged Dispontejn to relinquish the company and hand over the military account to van der Heyden. This Dispontejn would not do.[7] The unfortunate man's wife, Maria van Hulst, now appeared on the scene and requested an order that van der Heyden appear before the Commissioners for questioning.[8] When nothing came of that she demanded that a copy of the court order to imprison her husband be sent to the Attorney-General for examination and reconsideration.[9]

Dispontejn, becoming more and more uneasy as his prison days lengthened into months, decided to do something about his defense himself. He asked permission to bring witnesses to testify in his favor. He requested that Deborah van Egmont be subpoenaed and brought for a hearing. The court agreed.[10]

Deborah was staying with her brother-in-law, Peter van Cortenhoven, who lived on the leafy old Spui Allee near the Palace. But her Hague visit was proving very disappointing. She had had a hundred gay projects in mind for her reunion with Major Scott, but had hardly seen him since arrival.

He had called once, as he had promised, but his visit was exasperatingly formal. He had discussed the political situation with her brother-in-law and only once talked with her. He had wanted to meet a certain state deputy of Middelburg, from Walcheren Island, a man of "great understanding and influence," said John.

"Do you think you could arrange this for me?" he asked

her, turning on the charm. "His nephew, a lawyer named Dakers, lives in this neighborhood, perhaps you may know him and through him reach the deputy." John promised her a present for her pains. "For," he added, "if we can bring this man over to our side, we shall be doing very well."[11]

Deborah did not know what he meant, nor have any notion of the struggle de Witt was having with the pro-Orange Walcheren politicos. But she was glad to have something to do for John and did her best to please him. She met Dakers and arranged with him to bring his uncle to a well-known tavern, The Old Docke, where the rendezvous was to take place.

Then gleefully she ran to Scott's lodgings at the *Sign of the Golden Boat* to bring him the good news.

He was at work on his maps when she arrived, but began rolling them up and putting them away when she entered the room.

"Isn't that the map of the river of London?"[12] she asked. All maps looked alike to her. He smiled. "Surely," he answered teasingly, "that's the map of the river of London. I'm making it for my brother de Witt; I'm seeing a great deal of him now; we do a lot of business together."[13]

Deborah flitted about the room looking inquisitively at everything, trying to make out what was written on the envelopes on his table. But she could not read and her curiosity was baffled.

He took her arm and they went to the café together to meet the deputy, but she did not understand what the men talked about.

That was practically the last time she ever spoke with John. Although she waited eagerly for another visit, he never came. He had, it seemed, left The Hague; departed on one of those trips that she now chose to regard as highly mysterious and suspicious. She heard that he had been seen going into the *Binnenhof*, the Dutch Foreign Office, but she did not dare seek him there. She also knew all about Dispontejn being in jail and John's efforts, through van der Heyden, to keep him there. She was becoming increasingly indignant over his neglect of her, and his treatment of the solicitor struck her as infamous.

Then one day, quite unexpectedly, she espied him going into the British Embassy. A crowd was waiting around to see the new British Ambassador, Sir William Temple, make his first entry to Maesson House, the official residence. Among his retinue was John Scott.

Deborah sprang from the table where she had been standing to get a good look at the procession and ran at him, trying to detain him from entering, calling him a rogue for keeping a good man in jail, and saying he ought to come at once and get Dispontejn released.[14] But John gently disengaged her arm and disappeared into the building. Enraged, Deborah rushed to the Town Hall and asked to see Dispontejn, telling him what had happened.

"He is not a diplomat, he is not attached to the Embassy," Dispontejn assured her.

"Then he is just hiding there,"[15] Deborah exclaimed triumphantly. "You should get a State warrant for his apprehension."

With energy born of wounded vanity she herself took the warrant and went to Maesson House with the intention of serving John with it. But the servants knew of no Major Scott; there was no one of that name among the Embassy attachés.

"I saw him enter, with my own eyes," she expostulated. Convinced he was up to no good, she was more than ready to comply with the subpoena to testify in Dispontejn's favor.

And before the Public Notary, Pieter van Swieten, on June 23rd, 1672, she told all she knew about Akers receiving the money, altering the dates on the receipts, and Scott's efforts to put the blame of its loss upon Dispontejn.[16] She also told how, shortly before Scott was made colonel, he tried to induce a certain notary, Johan van der Pijill, to make a detrimental statement concerning Dispontejn, to throw as much suspicion as possible upon the solicitor.[17] And how he had even offered *her* inducements to accuse Dispontejn, only she had refused because she knew it was not true.

She included further accusations against Akers, quoting some of Scott's men.[18] So William Cowley, cadet, was called and acknowledged that Scott, one day at Wesel, had tried to persuade him to give false evidence against Dispontejn, and that he and Scott had had angry words over this.[19] Cowley later recanted some of his testimony concerning the whereabouts of Akers at the time the army accounts were made up.[20]

From the combined statements of men and officers, Akers' dishonesty was established and it looks as though Scott, to protect a fellow Englishman, was determined to make Dispontejn bear the blame.

The Hague Aldermen acquitted the prisoner and ordered his release. Van Paffenrode made one final effort to keep him in prison, appealing to the Court of Holland, but the Court Committee upheld the Aldermen's judgment. The Bailiff himself was removed from office for political reasons.

And on February 10th, 1673, exactly one month after Deborah married Sergeant Nederway, Dispontejn was a free man.

The whole affair was the kind that could easily have happened among foreigners serving in any European army, and it was swallowed up, anyway, in much more explosive national events.

There would have been little point in recounting it but that it returned to plague John in later years; and shows, moreover, what mountains were made from molehills.

BIBLIOGRAPHICAL NOTES

1. Not. Arch. Hague Mun., protocol of Notary Ennis, No. 522.
2. *Ibid.*, 523.
3. Arch. Hof v. Holl: Criminal Docs., No. 5291, Dec. 26th, 1671.
4. *Ibid.*, Sentences: No. 788, Jan. 15, 1672.

5. *Ibid.*, Verbals: No. 1354, Feb. 3, 1672.
6. *Ibid.*, Petitions: No. 4565.
7. *Ibid.*, Verbals: No. 1354.
8. *Ibid.*, Petitions: No. 3026, Feb., 1672.
9. *Ibid.*, April, 1672.
10. *Ibid.*, June, 1672.
11. Rawl. MSS., A 175, f 18.
12. *Ibid.*, f 19.
13. *Ibid.*
14. *Ibid.*, f 24.
15. *Ibid.*
16. Not. Arch. Hague Mun., protocol Pieter van Swieten, inventory No. 392, f 323.
17. *Ibid.*, f 325.
18. *Ibid.*, f 326.
19. *Ibid.*, ff 337, r, v.
20. *Ibid.*, ff 340-42.

CHAPTER XXIX

JOHN IN THE THIRD DUTCH WAR

"Is it possible that the descendants of a nation which laid
the foundations of our freedom, so feebly defend what
their forefathers obtained with so much glory?"
—De Groot, Pensionary of Rotterdam. 1672.
Hist. of the People of Netherland. Petrus J.
Blok, p. 369.

BUT WHAT HAD HAPPENED to John and Akers during Dispontejn's trial? International events had swept them off the
scene. The dreaded French invasion erupted, and England,
shackled to France by treaty, declared war on Holland in
March 1672, to the disgust of the English people who bitterly
resented fighting with Catholic France against the Protestant
Dutch Republic.

Charles II issued a proclamation calling home all British
subjects serving with the United Provinces,[1] but some ignored
the royal command, choosing to keep their jobs and fight
against their own country—John Scott was not one of these.[2]
He received a personal summons from England[3] and immediately relinquished his post, although he lingered a short time
on the Continent and visited the Dutch Ambassador in
neutral Brussels.[4]

Dutch military files refer to Colonel Scott's "desertion,"[5]
but also to his statement that, as an English subject he could
not, once hostilities broke out, remain in the service of the
States-General.[6] For the record the Assembly voted a formal
Resolution requesting the *Raad van Staat* to proceed against

him for deserting,[7] but the resolution was never carried out, and shortly thereafter John was honorably discharged from the Dutch army.[8] It is highly probable that the temporary charge of desertion masked a diplomatic move on the part of some influential Hollanders who were desperately anxious for England's neutrality and who were counting on Scott to convey their last-minute peace proposals.

A letter by a well-known German secret agent in London, addressed to his opposite number in Spire (and intercepted before it reached its destination), reads as follows:

"London June 1672 . . . Yesterday I saw unexpectedly in the Park, Colonel John Scott, recently in the service of the United Provinces; of whom some say he quit Holland, and others that he is expressly sent hither by some Dutch lords (who desire peace with the English) to make propositions for that purpose. He was yesterday conducted by Sir Joseph Williamson to My Lord Arlington's house where he stayed a long while, which makes the latter the more credible."[9]

Whether or not the Dutch did entrust him with such a mission, they were certainly sorry to see him leave Holland. When John bade farewell to Van Beverningh and to the Wesel state deputy (as he wrote Williamson later), "the deputy spoke respectfully of His Majesty (Charles II) only in discouraging me from going. He told me that they were confident the King would meet great troubles. I told them that induced me the more to go, being resolved to run the utmost hazards for my own Prince. Van Beverningh intimated to me what unkindnesses the Duke of York had done both to me and to himself and also to the Prince (of Orange). I only replied that that was no excuse for my allegiance and that I did not question to convince His Highness he was mis-informed; and that in point of love to His Majesty's person I would vie with His Highness himself."[10]

John does not seem to have wavered for a moment about giving up his good job. Writing Williamson from Ghent, in May 1672, Gelson (one of Arlington's agents), reported:

"Nothing can tempt Colonel Scott from love and loyalty to King and country. Necessity and some ill offices made him take service with the Dutch which hath been much greater in all respects than he could expect. Yet when it comes too near of the service to the one, it must be the service of the other, and of that which he loves above all things he chooses; to leave a certain noble employment to throw himself upon the country and goodness of his Prince; and is now writing his farewell to the States-General. Please to give me directions what I may say unto him. I think him a person very fit and willing to serve His Majesty."[11]

For once John's sacrifice of position for principle was appreciated and his loyalty recognized. A note in Sir Joseph Williamson's journal indicated the nature of the job: "Major Scott taken for Intelligence."[12]

John had already given ample proof of his ability to make a sound report, and it became a British Foreign Office tradition to employ writers of repute as agents abroad. Walsingham began this system under Queen Elizabeth, Sir Walter Raleigh contributed his quota of "special information," Daniel Defoe once served this way and, in modern times, Somerset Maugham did a stint. So John joined a goodly company when he departed for his field of operations in neutral Flanders (today's Belgium), at that moment a Spanish possession. Arlington placed him in Bruges but his reporter's instinct took him all over the country: his dispatches are headed Ostend, St. Omer, Nieuport, and Brussels; his recent contacts with well-known Dutchmen favored his quest for news, and it was amazing how many of them still talked frankly with him.

Typical of the man was his serious preparation for the assignment. "To inform my mind for His Majesty's service,"[13] as he wrote, he immediately spent two months inspecting the Dutch coastline and all the ports and harbors of North Holland, Zeeland, Friezland and Groeningen. When James

Vernon* visited him, to look over the situation, in late March, and again in April and May, John surprised this eminent official with his intimate grasp of the situation. Already he had a general idea of the Dutch Fleet's strength. Though he had not procured a complete list, he knew the number of capital ships, their names and commanders and where most of them were stationed, together with the revealing item that Admiral Van Ghent was counting on holding Texel (the chief naval base) with fourteen men-o'-war and twenty fireships.[14] The Dutch, according to John's estimate, did not question their ability to command the sea, though they counted on creating a diversion for England by arming Scottish malcontents (anxious to resume trade with Holland); and had ordered their West India Fleet to put into Spanish ports, "if they can't make it home."[15]

John's knowledge went beyond military and naval intelligence—he had a nose for related news. From the neutral Spaniards he had learned that they intended seizing all English effects in Spain; and that a certain French Huguenot, Du Moulin (once a clerk in Arlington's office), had now turned agent for the Dutch, was corresponding with de Witt and van Beuningen, tipping off the Dutch Smyrna Fleet as to English movements, and boasting that he was worth at least forty thousand troops to the States![16]

John accompanied Vernon to Zeeland, where, since the latter spoke no Dutch, John spent half an hour alone with the Middelburg Pensioner, chatting about Willoughby in the West Indies, and Dutch designs there.[17] They ran into Everson, Vice-Admiral of the Zeeland Squadron, another of John's acquaintances ready to talk at length with him. John also took the occasion of visiting Lampsinn, a Caribbean associate, now a big merchant busy outfitting Dutch privateers. Altogether John proved an invaluable guide for Vernon as the latter's *Relation* of events discloses.[18]

---

* Secretary of State under William and Mary.

This report was quickly followed by John's own dispatch, May 26th, in which he completed the list of ships in the Dutch Fleet, with their complement of guns, together with the rather ominous news that the confident de Ruyter and his admirals were spoiling for a fight, despite the Dutch War Council's Resolution to avoid all action if possible. The Fleet's exact position, John added, had been six leagues west by north of Ostend at nine the previous morning.[19] A prize bit of information the English Navy did not heed, to its cost.

England began this Third Dutch War by an attack on the Dutch Smyrna Fleet returning from Constantinople laden with riches which Charles II hoped to capture to finance his desperate war. But it had been well warned, and instead of anchoring off the Isle of Wight (as originally planned) it fought so doggedly that only six prize ships were captured and the English were badly mauled in the engagement. Had not the first of King Louis' promised subsidies—six hundred thousand pistoles (roughly five hundred and twenty thousand pounds)—arrived that moment in London, the English King could scarcely have put his Navy on a war basis. As it was, his hard-working Clerk of the Acts, Samuel Pepys, performed miracles to outfit men and ships, with stores practically exhausted and sailors none too keen to fight. "The Fleet," as Prince Rupert put it, "was huddled out!"

Almost at once the situation became critical. In mid-May some Dutch were sighted off Harwich, but the British Fleet missed them in the fog and put into Sole Bay to ride at anchor. Here, twelve days later, May 28th (June 7th, new style), it was caught napping by de Ruyter.

A furious battle ensued. The Dutch Commander, staking everything on this his first encounter with the combined fleets of two great powers, had addressed his captains before the fight, speaking in rousing terms from the bridge of his flagship, *The Seven Provinces*. Then, with a fine southeasterly gale behind him, he had fallen upon the unsuspecting English and French, driving off the latter and concentrating on the great ship that carried England's Lord High Admiral, the Duke of York; while Van Brakel, with a smaller vessel, attacked Lord Sandwich, Vice Admiral on the *Royal James.*

The ships were drawn up in fine battle array and thundered broadside after broadside across the water; the peaceful countryside for miles around reverberated with the deafening cannonading—guns could be heard all the way to London, people said. Frantic crowds of spectators surged along the Suffolk coast trying to catch a glimpse of action through the mist, watching horror-struck as great vessels with torn sails and shattered rigging sank in flames. The wind dropped and Dutch fireships closed in on the two flagships while the stricken English gallantly sought to fight them off and beat back Dutch sailors trying to come aboard. Twice the Duke of York was forced to shift his flag as ships beneath him foundered; and near the end of the day the *Royal James* exploded with a terrible roar, filling the air with blazing wreckage, and catapulting the Admiral into the sea.

This historic although indecisive battle was the subject of John's first military report; and it was a European scoop.

He returned to London to dictate it personally to James Vernon. His arrival was awaited with some impatience judging from Williamson's Journal: "Most details, at this period unimportant, such as arrivals of ambassadors . . . but the following seem worthy of note; *May 24th/31st* The Duke of Buckingham returned from the fleet; June 3rd/10th Major Scott arrived last night from Ostend."[20]

He had done an amazingly prompt bit of intelligence work —here was first-hand news of enemy losses before the English even knew their own! John gave lists of Dutch ships sunk and of others, towed, shattered, into Flushing and Pasgrecht; he had the numbers of the mortally wounded and killed including Admiral van Ghent and van Brakel ("he that broke the chain at Chatham"); he told where the ships had set out from, who furnished some of them and where they now rode; that Ostend claimed it was an "entire victory" although the action (given in detail) was very confused and variously reported. The Dutch, he said, confessed that the English fought well and admitted many of their own men had not; while few French fought at all.*21

Considering that nearly ten days passed before the Admiralty knew with any certainty the fate of Lord Sandwich, John's scoop can be appreciated. It was something that Pepys should certainly have read—one of his wartime tasks was to correlate information. He wrote Williamson begging for frontline news, but either the Secretary ignored him, or there was no communication between government departments, for Scott's *Relation* never reached him. A thousand pities, for had Pepys read it he would have learned at first-hand something of John's identity and qualifications, and the disastrous struggle that was nearly to ruin one and destroy the other's reputation for centuries might have been averted.

John stayed in London only briefly, but he had made his mark. He dined several times, "very magnificent of habit" (as an observer noted) "at the Duke of Buckingham's table and was addressed as Major-General Scott."22 Two days later, back in Ostend, he was writing Williamson about scurrilous Dutch pamphlets proclaiming the "great English defeat."23

BIBLIOGRAPHICAL NOTES

1. *CSP Dom.*, 1671-72, No. 253.
2. Archives Staten-Generaal. Sec. Res., No. 2322, f 630, r, v.
3. *CSP Dom.*, 1671-72 (*Journal of Sir Joseph Williamson*), p. 2.
4. SP. Holl., No. 2921, f 167 (May, 1672).
5. Ten Raa, *Het St. Leger*, p. 283.
6. *Ibid.*, 491.
7. Res. of St. Pro of Holl., No. 105, f 74 (June 2nd, 1672).
8. SP Fl., 77/40, f 110.

* The French received contradictory orders which halted their action. This could have been due to a language error on the part of the English commander. Or might have been the result of the "daily graving jealousy against the French," noted by a Dutch intelligence officer. Besch. Mit Vreem. Arch. De Groot Nederland. Zeevorlegen, pp. 125-27. RCP Kleine Seria.

9. SP Holl., 84/189, f 17.
10. SP Fl., 77/40, ff 110, 111.
11. *Ibid.*, f 73.
12. *CSP Dom.*, 1671-72, p. 608 (*Journal of Sir Joseph Williamson*); SP 29/319, A.
13. SP Fl., 77/40, f 201.
14. *Ibid.*, f 42.
15. *Ibid.*, f 42 v.
16. *Ibid.*
17. *Ibid.*, f 43 v.
18. SP 29/319 A (*Williamson's Journal*); SP Fl., 77/40, ff 42, 43, r, v.
19. SP Fl., 77/40, f 105.
20. *CSP Dom.*, 1672, p. 683.
21. SP Holl., 84/189, f 7, r, v.
22. Rawl. MSS., A 188, f 262.
23. SP. Fl., 77/40, f 110.

CHAPTER XXX

THE SECRET DOINGS OF
JOHN SCOTT

". . . If it be true which the most approved Philosophers have told us and among others Hugo Grotius and Descartes, that nothing is in the intellect which passes not through the door of some Sense, then certainly their Intellects may be most improved and possess the largest streak of knowledge whose Senses have traffiqued and been entertained with the greatest Variety of Objects. . . ."
—John Scott to Sir Francis Rolle, 1678.
"No Man's knowledge here can go beyond his experience."
—John Locke, *On Human Understanding*, 1690.

AND NOW BEGAN a year of feverish activity. Nothing so clearly reveals John's capacity and quality as his dispatches to the Secretary of State. Indeed no understanding of his complicated personality is possible without a reading of these pages of troop movements, fleet maneuvers, defense plans and, predominantly, political analysis—all in his fine skimming artist's handwriting, difficult enough for modern eyes to decipher, but with hardly a single correction or erasure, although obviously he was working under extreme pressure. He speaks of taking the mail aboard personally, sometimes, "to prevent any miscarriage," or riding post haste on horseback to catch the Channel packets.[1] He never spared himself; he mailed two reports the same day from Bruges and Nieuport, towns some twenty miles apart.[2]

At the very beginning he wrote Arlington of a most daring

227

project—to hire a small boat and go to Walcheren Island, right through the Dutch Fleet! "I shall sail between the land and the Fleet to view in what condition the shore is for defence, by guards or otherwise; from thence to Jorveer—to Jorgoos—and to Philipeen; then back to Bruges."[3] To an old Caribbean sailor such a trip presented no difficulty. A few days later he had made the excursion and told how he had taken "eight of His Majesty's Declarations to as many captains, directed them to one Van Putta, a captain from Jorveer in Zeeland, a man bold and loving to communicate news."[4] Evidently someone after John's own heart and a valuable target for English propaganda!

It was astonishing that John could get into enemy territory this way; he may have sailed with a privateer's pass or disguised. He had a boyish delight in putting on wigs of a different cut and color from his own; darkening his eyebrows, wearing peasant's clothes. Or possibly he was able to conceal from the Zeelanders the fact that he was no longer in the Dutch service.* Wartime news travelled slowly to the outer islands, and many English officers despite the King's orders, were still with their Dutch commands.

John was always on the go. "These particulars I drew up at Antwerp and communicated to the Earl of Arlington," he wrote Williamson. "I crossed the country from Blankenburg to St Omer, and this morning came from thence afoot and was, before 7 o'clock, on the barge for Nieuport, where I write."[5]

His incessant travelling did not escape local comment, and various interpretations were put on his activities. The English Consul in Ostend, Stephen Lynch, reported to London in August, 1672: "Colonel Scott is at present in this town and, as I understand, the Spaniards do not love his company being

---

* So complicated was the political machinery among the seven Provinces that John's formal discharge from the army did not come through till June 6, 1672. S.P. Fl., 77/40, f 110.

sometimes suspective of his so often coming hither this much."[6]

Not that he was the only one thus coming and going. The English government had several agents on the Continent— William Carr, Silas Taylor, William Bulstrode, James Puckle, Gelson—some of them, like the last two, just picking up odds and ends of information with no fixed salary, "only somewhat for expenses" as Puckle pleaded;[7] while Carr proved to be unreliable, working for both sides, abjectly confessing to Arlington later, begging forgiveness and another chance.[8]

Among these agents rivalry was inescapable. They wrote to complain of each other; Gelson admitted he was jealous of Scott[9] while Scott both to Williamson and to his other London correspondent, Sir John Bankes, the East India merchant prince, slighted Gelson and his "inability to gather very much for all his travels. I was in his company two or three times and could hear very little news."[10]

John's professional knowledge of ships and armies put him in a class by himself; his former service and friendships gave him an entrée the others lacked. His dispatches are full of "names": "one of my former officers"—"a man very near the Prince"—"the Mayor of so-and-so"; nor did he overlook tips from fishermen, privateers, and canal bargemen. But most important was his knowledge of Dutch politics—he understood what was going on and knew all about the old rivalry between the Regents—those merchant-princes who, under Jan de Witt, practically ran the country with a broadly decentralized form of government—and the Princes of Orange, who would have abolished the cumbersome, complicated governmental machinery and established themselves as hereditary monarchs.

John clipped the highly polemical speeches of de Witt and the young Prince from local news sheets and translated them (copies preserved among his papers);[11] eleven volumes of Party lampoons (mostly anti-Orange) he collected and forwarded to Arlington.[12]

For more than thirty years the two respective political parties had struggled for power* and de Witt considered this internal strife far more dangerous than any foreign enemy for it threatened to destroy the very structure of the Republic.

Fear of this was back of his search for peace, as John was well aware. De Witt had made his country invincible at sea—Holland was a great prosperous counting house protected by a Fleet ready to tackle anyone—but his army was hopelessly outnumbered and he was forced to rely on powerful alliances and diplomatic negotiation to stave off war by land. His efforts had the support of all the wealthy cultivated citizens of the Seven Provinces, interested mainly in commerce and the arts. But the country had its malcontents: soldier squireens eager for war's opportunities; fanatical Calvinists; all the masses, envious of the commercial aristocracy and ever-ready to swarm out of their slums to support a Prince whose regal paraphernalia pleased them far more than the heavy pomp of stiff-necked merchant-Regents.

De Witt had had to appoint Orange Captain-General of the national forces although the young man had little military experience and no luck. After the Dutch made such a brilliant showing against the combined British and French fleets, their army crumpled before French soldiers at Woerden. John's vivid battle report revealed that the Prince did not dare publish his losses lest the public be discouraged, and the youthful leader had to re-group his men fearing to take French-speaking Walloons into his regiments.[13] Dutch morale

---

* "There is civil strife in Holland owing to popular tumults fomented by the House of Orange . . . July 1653," *CSP. Ven.*, XXIX, 98.

Stadhouder William II (the young prince's father), had made a surprise *coup* on Amsterdam with troops from other provinces, capturing its civilian head and de Witt's father, the Mayor of Dort, and holding them in Lovestein prison. It was to prevent a repetition of such tactics that Jan de Witt, and his so-called *Lovestein* party, abolished the title of Stadhouder, and decreed that no one person should hold supreme military and civil power. Political administration of the country he kept in his own hands, excluding from office the young Prince who, in revenge, began inciting the populace against him. De Witt, *Mémoires*, pp. 250-53.

was sinking together with the national credit; there was a run on the Amsterdam bank, government securities dropped: "The greatest securities Walcheren has now are the eight ships that lie at anchor in the Veer Gate," wrote John.

French troops overran several Dutch provinces, and Catholics in these occupied territories occasionally assisted the enemy. The untraditional severity with which the Prince dealt with them "has made them his implacable enemies," wrote John.[14]

Many of John's Zeeland informants were, obviously, staunchly republican de Witt partisans, and, as he himself recognized, "they endeavor to traduce all the Prince's actions and render everything he does suspect."[15] John's own reporting was impartial for he went on to describe these citizens' somewhat unpatriotic efforts to get their money out of the country "by bills of exchange and vessels that trade with the Spanish Netherlands."[16] These were the men who groaned under wartime taxes, "trying to suggest the necessity of coming to terms with the French." The alternative, they grumbled, looked like "self-destruction" which they feared would end by bringing the Prince of Orange to sovereign power, "something his family has always aspired and could not attain."[17]

Once again John put his finger on the crux of the matter, for he realized that the Prince was aiming at making himself supreme, and that the Dutch domestic struggle could easily become the old one of popular rule versus "absolutism—that lion let loose," as de Witt called it. The wise old statesman was a sturdy believer in the sovereign power of the people and of the cities, and was utterly opposed to a would-be monarch making and enforcing law alone.

Now this was the same issue—on a grander scale—that had fired John's ardor in New England, and had led to the decision that had cost him so dear. His deep admiration for de Witt indicated how very firmly his convictions were rooted, but in this case it was not merely political preference which prompted his devotion for the Grand Pensioner. John's dispatches clearly show that he considered de Witt's policy much more advantageous to England. And he wrote to Arlington and Williamson quite frankly of his own efforts to further it. "I dined last night at Bruges with some Middelburg Senators (Zeelanders) and had a deal of discourse with them when I drank them to a mellow and good talking strain."[18]

After listening to their laments on wartime's restrictions and implications of urging peace with France (leaving England in the lurch, as John realized), he pointed out that France was far the greater menace to them, and reminded his listeners that for twenty years the French had blocked their trade in the Caribbean and with Virginia; that the growing naval power of France tied up Dutch warships, excluding them from exploiting one of the richest most profitable areas. Here John was speaking from wide personal knowledge and as the convinced mercantilist his writings show him to be. His political sense was sharpening as he plunged more and more into politics and it is easy to understand his association with John Locke. "Their [the French] injury is great to merchants, greater to the States, and insupportable to the traders and husbandmen of Walcheren and Zeeland," he went on. "French troops are now threatening Berg-op-Zoom,"[19] and if that fortress fell, warned John, the outer islands would be captured and not only would the inhabitants "lose their liberty and *freedom of conscience*" but be in no position to seek good terms with England. (Italics added.)

"They (the Zeelanders) timing their business well, might put themselves into a better condition of freedom . . . than ever they were in since they were a Republic . . . that this might more easily be brought about because their Province had never disobliged His Majesty [Charles II]."

In this long dispatch John added that he had assured the Senators he was speaking only for himself, though he was "confident he might do them a service as well. They date our ruin about a year or two after their own," he continues, "but I soon put them out of that humor. I left them . . . inclined to be protected by England, but remaining entire [faithful] to their own government."[20]

Several dispatches return to the delicate political possibility of inducing this practically autonomous Province to make a separate peace. "There are in Zeeland many hundreds of people that wish England well and His Majesty sovereign of the place, if they knew how they could only, with safety, bring it about. A Middelburg man, entrusted with His Highness' most secret designs in that and other towns of their Province, told me a few days ago, with tears in his eyes, that one misfortune more would ruin the Prince and his party, and did wish 8000 English well landed on Walcheren."[21]

This Dutch prediction that the Prince was approaching ruin, was, however, wildly inaccurate. William of Orange, a thin asthmatic stripling with hunched shoulders and hollow, pockmarked cheeks, bore in his frail body one of the most valiant spirits that ever breathed, and a strain of political shrewdness which amounted to genius. Nothing could shake his phlegmatic determination or the courageous tenacity with which he faced almost insuperable disaster.

In June, 1672, King Louis had begun a massive offensive with his customary spectacular luck in surmounting obstacles. A certain little-known ford over a branch of the Rhine was exceptionally low that dry season and while French cavalry under the great Prince Condé held back the current, one hundred and twenty thousand French soldiers poured across, marching on Amsterdam to threaten the whole country with extinction. It was at this moment that the indomitable young Dutch leader stoically declared: "We can die in the last dyke."

And opened the sluices. Cold brackish water rolled over the rich countryside. Opulent mansions and lovely gardens vanished, crops and fat flocks were engulfed, but Holland was saved. Amsterdam stood above the waterline, a grim fortress surrounded by gunboats, and the besieging armies had to stop.

Orange sued for an armistice, however, and when this was refused his undaunted insistence on continuing the fight steeled the nation to heroic resistance. The precarious military situation brought to a head the long-smouldering domestic revolution which John had described. De Witt and his government resigned, and the Prince was proclaimed Stadthouder, amid the frantic rejoicing of his followers and certain "bloody seditious uprisings and magistrates threatened with death" when they hesitated to confirm him.[22]

Political passions ran fever-high, inflamed by the country's desperate plight. Wildest anti-Republican rumors fanned the mob to violence. Admiral Cornelius de Witt was imprisoned on a trumped-up charge of trying to poison the Prince and was cruelly tortured. While Jan was visiting his brother in prison, infuriated mobs burst in, dragged both men into the street, tore them limb from limb and gibbeted the remains. It was one of the most brutal political murders in history.

A rumor, treasured by Pepys, and given wide credence in England, had it that John Scott was hanged in effigy in 1672.* It is quite possible that at the time of the de Witt lynching John's effigy did suffer similar outrage. He was known to be Jan de Witt's friend, and, in the estimation of the Orange party, was identified, as far as any foreigner could affect national policy, with de Witt's "peace party." In numerous Dutch towns there were scenes of indescribable ferocity.

The mob challenged a certain Sir Michael Livesey (one of the regicides hiding in Holland under an assumed name), and cut him to pieces for much less reason than it might have felt against John at this moment of savage panic. (Appendix I.)

---

* "It seems he swindled £7000 from the States-General and was hanged in effigy in Rotterdam," says the English Dictionary of National Biography, parrotting a typical distortion of the Dispontejn case and even citing erroneously its dubious sources. DNB, John Scott, XVII, 979-80.

BIBLIOGRAPHICAL NOTES

1. SP. Fl., 77/40, ff 116, 127, 225.
2. *Ibid.*, ff 303, 306.
3. *Ibid.*, f 194.
4. *Ibid.*, f 202.
5. *Ibid.*, 77/41, f 117.
6. *Ibid.*, 77/40, f 281.
7. *CSP. Dom.*, 1672-73, No. 458.
8. SP. Holl., 84/191-2, ff 277, 278.
9. SP. Fl., 77/40, f 240.
10. *Ibid.*, f 127.
11. Rawl. MSS., A 175, ff 188, 191; *Ibid.*, A 176, ff 62, 100, 101, 110.
12. SP. Fl., 77/41, f 53.
13. *Ibid.*, f 63.
14. *Ibid.*, f 52.
15. *Ibid.*, f 87.
16. *Ibid.*
17. *Ibid.*
18. *Ibid.*, 77/40, f 201.
19. *Ibid.*
20. *Ibid.*
21. *Ibid.*, 77/41, f 87 v.
22. *Ibid.*, 77/40, f 108.

CHAPTER XXXI

BRITISH AGENT

"What I have done I have done for the present age and for posterity, who whatsoever envy or ignorance may say now, will have occasion to commend it because they will in time find by their own experience, that I have performed the work with justice and honesty, having separated truth from falsehood, things real from things fictitious or imaginary, as he only can that writes not barely, from hearsay, but hath seen the greatest part of what he is to treat of."

—John Scott, *Preface.*

IF JOHN HEARD ANY RUMORS concerning himself he did not record them; nor did they deter him from pursuing a course that went far beyond the office of mere agent.

Dutch civil strife did not cease with the Prince's seizure of power and John pleaded at home more urgently that England exploit this rift in the United Provinces, split off Zeeland and bring it over to the English side.*

"In all parts of the Dutch territories great disorders," he reported; "the commonality" (as he termed the Prince's lowly supporters), "now lead in Holland and Zeeland, God knows"; and such was their attitude that all wealthy patricians, irrespective of political affiliation, were ready to forfeit thirty per cent of their estates, "to be well out of Zeeland and its present government."[1] He furnished gruesome details of the

---

* A strong pro-English sentiment had existed in this Province ever since the reign of Elizabeth I, when the Zeelanders had formally requested the English queen to take them under her jurisdiction.

mutilated de Witts; told of Rotterdam magistrates narrowly escaping the same fate; of young de Witt, beaten and abused by the crowd for wearing mourning "for a rich traitor" while no onlooker dared say a word; and of the "mutinous, unsettled, disturbed condition of the common people, neither pleased with nor without the Prince."[2]

In two dispatches John deplored his lack of a code, for he was bursting with "things I dare not write." Then "the people are still very proud, strangely elevated with hopes of what they will do next summer, but their game at home is not so secure as they imagine," and he hints at "strange alterations" and tells of rumors that the enemy might continue fighting France but *make peace with England.* Many Dutch troops in Middelburg were kept there more on account of "the rabble," he revealed, than for defense; and once again he urged Williamson to take advantage of this crisis, naming points for a possible English invasion which could be effected "even without big ships."[3]

His political counsels, however, did not interrupt his flow of routine military intelligence. He sounded and measured the extent of the "drowned country" and sent details concerning movements in the several armies he was watching. Besides the Dutch, there were the French and their assorted German allies; the few English troops under the Duke of Monmouth, as well as the neutral Spanish forces commanded by the Count of Monterey, one of whose "greatest confidants" dined with John and imparted the startling fact that Spain could not possibly continue long at peace with France, an important tip John passed on to Arlington with the modest suggestion that His Lordship would be best able to judge its worth!

From one of his "stringmen" in Middelburg, John learned that the Zeeland States had felt compelled to pass a Resolution declaring it treasonable for any single Province to make peace overtures to either France or England. Nevertheless certain persons continued to put out "feelers" and one of them

wanted to know if John had a commission to "treat" with
them. If so, he was willing to meet Scott and discuss details.
Two of the men involved, John assured Arlington, "through
the Prince's influence have overall direction of the colonies
and are above temptation." Of the others, he was not so sure.
However, he thought he might be "creating His Majesty's
interest" in listening to them. "They have trusted me this
far because they know if nothing comes of it I shall not betray
them."[4]

It was not unusual, at this period, and even later, for
private individuals to undertake such missions; they provided
opportunities for a noncommital exchange of views without
loss of face if they came to nothing.

John was right in saying the Dutch trusted him (to this
very day his reputation is ace-high in the Netherlands). But
he scrupulously reported all such overtures, writing to the
Secretary of State personally, rather than to Williamson; as
in October 1672, when he told Arlington of a letter he had
received from the Commander of the Dutch troops at Cadzunt, requesting a meeting in a Spanish *sconce* (blockhouse)
near St. Donai.

The messenger bringing the letter first fed John news of
prime value: that the Prince intended putting his fleet into
winter quarters (places mentioned); that Cadzunt was adequately defended and could always get reinforcements from
adjoining garrisons; that Spanish troops would be available
for Walcheren (a scoop!) though the Dutch did not want
their help except as a last resource; and that if the English
attempted a landing, the Dutch possessed "very ingenious
means" and gear for blocking it (details given).

Then he came to the point of his visit. The messenger
suggested that John go over to the Dutch! He urged him to
work for people "who loved and trusted him rather than for
those who undervalued him," for even "to perish," among
his admirers was better than to live "sneakingly" (as the
messenger put it), among men who failed to appreciate him.

(His undercover role evidently irked John a little.) This was clearly what the Cadzunt Commander had in mind.[5]

John answered him frankly that as long as war continued such a course was unthinkable; that he was "resolved to have no such complications." "How can a man do anything against his own country?" he demanded indignantly of Arlington in a second dispatch, à propos a similar incident.[6] To the messenger he refused all exchange of information as to the position of the English fleet, or its invasion plans. But he repeated his conviction that Zeeland should seek separate terms and put itself under England's protection, saying he himself "would be glad to be instrumental in such an affair."[7] Indeed, so convinced was he that this was England's most propitious moment to negotiate, that twice he wrote Arlington requesting that "some ingenious person" be sent over to arrange the surrender.*

"I have no greater ambition in the world than of being an instrument to dispose the States to give His Majesty all reasonable satisfaction."†[8]

---

* The French, too, were considering a similar strategy, as is shown by a memorandum among French archives, by a Mathurin Pélicot (Colbert's agent) who outlines the possibilities of Zeeland's surrender. "Practically all the magistrates of certain Dutch towns are of the de Witt faction and enemies of the Prince of Orange. It would be easy to win them over and make them submit . . . with a foot in the country the rest is assured." Fr. Mar. Docs., B-4, V, f 56.

† In this, and in another long dispatch to Arlington, John discusses world affairs and analyzes Dutch party politics, with the people torn between loyalty to their Prince and fear lest his prolonged war lead to domination by Catholic France. Fundamentally, John points out, it all boils down to "Who Should Govern"; but he sees in the Prince's ascendency, parallels with Cromwell's trend to dictatorship, against the will of the Dutch people, "rivetted in their desire for a Commonwealth."

In somewhat the same rather lofty tone of political philosophy is John's essay: A King Ought to be Instructed to Rule Well (among his private papers in the Public Record Office, SP Dom. Car. II, 29, No. 419, ff 50, 51), in which he quotes Plotinus, Cominius and others to support his own theories of a monarch's responsibilities toward his subjects.

It is quite impossible to reconcile the author of these writings with the shabby caricature made of him by Abbott, Bryant and other historans who have relied chiefly on Pepys' affidavits for their views on Scott.

What John did not know, of course, was that the devious English King was even then considering shifting sides and marrying his niece to the Prince of Orange in order to cement a new alliance. Naturally Charles did not want Dutch bargaining power weakened, as it inevitably would have been, had its principal Province quit.

The Dutch made still another effort to seduce John. He reported to Williamson he had received "an odd message out of Zeeland menacing me to have a care of England where I can expect nothing but unkindness—and in time to resolve to take my fortune with them."[9] Apparently the proposition was not even considered. John mentioned it only casually in a long dispatch devoted to other matters. There was more pressing business at hand.

The war had settled down to a winter deadlock. The French forces were closely invested by freezing water and when they tried to attack The Hague, over the ice, a sudden thaw plunged their troops waist deep in heavy mud and did more to save the country than all its combined military forces. Dutch luck was on the mend.

And now Dutch privateers went into action redoubling their efforts and wrecking wild havoc on allied merchant shipping. Darting out of Flushing, their little armed *capers* infested the trade routes and lay off every port in the West of England in such numbers that English and French frigates could not deal with them; one sailed right into Plymouth Sound and before the astonished townsfolk could even register their fury, impudently flashed her colors.

These were the renowned "Sea Beggars" of Zeeland, ever the foremost province in outfitting daring raiders. In England, Samuel Pepys pleaded for a convoy system to end their shocking depredations, but merchants were unwilling to assemble in port waiting for accompanying warships, and with the scanty number at his disposal Pepys could ill protect the nation's trade.

From Flanders, John's specialized reports tell of the new peril England faced.

"Zeeland's men of war, bound for the West Indies are not fully manned," but "in ten days, at longest, they may be ready to sail, the privateers that go with them from Walcheren are these:

The Catzunder, 100 men, 16 guns;
The Otter, a ketch, 70 men, 8 guns;
The English ketch, that came from Barbary, 80 men, 10 guns;
The . . [paper torn] frigate, 100 men, 14 guns;
The Clock, 60 men, 8 guns;
The Castle Ardyne, 150 men, 25 guns;
The Summer, 50 men, 16 guns;
The Sucher, 50 men, 16 guns;
The Maria, 100 men, 16 guns;

. . . on the 18th here came three Commissioners from a Zeeland money-company backing the privateers, to treat with some Spaniards and some Bruges and Ostend merchants about transporting English and French prize goods in Spanish bottoms."[10]

At Bruges John ran into an "intelligent talking" captain of a Spanish privateer whom he accompanied to Ostend, to learn of the shipbuilding and outfitting on Walcheren Island; of ship's carpenters busy in Zeeland, of fat prizes captured from the English, and ever more and more movements of ships and cargoes. There had always existed a freemasonry among privateers and buccaneers, and it must never be forgotten that John, in his youth, had belonged to the Brotherhood. This Spaniard told him of a certain De Vrees, of Amsterdam, who was sending out seven of his own privateers:

"They carry blank commissions," wrote John, "they may be of the most pernicious consequence to our ships trading to the Straits, to Spain and Portugal and to French ports on the Great Bay. I thought it my duty to be particular in this, in regard to the insupportable damage our nation suffered in the time of Cromwell's usurption by those very people who may do us more hurt (we not being at war with them) than if we had open war with Spain."[11]

What would Pepys have given to have read these reports and been able to give precise instructions and warning to English colliers and merchantmen, sailing on their gallant but foolhardy course?

"Dutch capers are the flower of their seamen," lamented John, "and there are still about 4000 of them abroad,"[12] while a "great man in the Zeeland government" boasted to him that "these were the men who might bring England to reason and force her to Breda a second time to seek peace*. . . . The vanity and insolence of the Dutch are almost insupportable!"[13]

There was every reason for the Hollanders' bravado. It detracted attention from their own domestic plight; and while hitting the Allies in their most vulnerable spot, focused attention on allied pressing problems concerning France's military predominance. "The Emperor and the whole House of Austria are apprehensive of French designs on Maestrich," reported John, "and the German princes fear they would be beggared if the Rhine trade is stopped."[14]

Dutch courage and statesmanship were paying off. So great were the Allies' perplexities over the war's ravages and the possible outcome, that, finally by common consent, hostilities were suspended, and a Peace Conference, to re-examine all claims, was called at Cologne.

On the eve of his departure to attend it, Sir Joseph Williamson, Great Britain's delegate, received from the noted diplomat, James Vernon, a significant report: "The States-General are ready for peace with France and England—all the people of Walcheren and Zeeland are saying, "We must be English next summer."[15]

John had been plugging this separatist policy for a whole year!

---

* After the Second Dutch War, unfavorable terms had been imposed on the English at Breda, in 1667.

BIBLIOGRAPHICAL NOTES

1. SP. Fl., 77/40, f 300.
2. *Ibid.*, 77/41, f 39 v.
3. *Ibid.*, 77/40, f 302 v.
4. *Ibid.*, f 225 v.
5. *Ibid.*, 77/41, f 39.
6. *Ibid.*, f 196 v.
7. *Ibid.*, f 39.
8. *Ibid.*, 77/41, f 39 v.
9. *Ibid.*, 77/40, f 302.
10. *Ibid.*, f 225.
11. *Ibid.*
12. *Ibid.*, 77/41, f 110 v.
13. *Ibid.*, 77/40, f 302 v.
14. *Ibid.*, 77/41, f 31 v.
15. *Ibid.*, 77/42, f 104.

CHAPTER XXXII

FRANCE LOSES AN ALLY AND
JOHN LOSES A JOB

"On the 6th at midnight I had the answer of a letter I had
writ to a friend in Flushing . . . and the truth is the
language of the Gentleman's letter is much like that of
Rahab the harlot to the men of Jerico when they examined her about the two spys."

—John Scott to Lord Arlington,
SP. Fl., 77/42, f 143.

INTERSPERSED WITH JOHN'S DISPATCHES are the inevitable requests for money, "without which, no man can do business,"
as he wrote, half humorously, at first.[1] Then, becoming more
serious, he complained that money was three months in
arrears.

There is a single item in the English Consul's accounts of
forty pounds paid to John Scott, a small enough sum if this
had to cover travelling expenses, to say nothing of the drinking to loosen his informants' tongues. (The former English
Ambassador in Holland, Sir William Temple, had been
urgently requesting that his own salary be paid, with the
same negative results.)

For nearly a year John's zeal and ardor remained un-
diminished though he seemed to be getting a little wistful
about his recompense. "I trust His Majesty will be pleased to
think of something in proportion to what I have frankly
written. I hope I shall not be forgotten," he suggests to

Arlington; and another time dwells on his own exceptional qualifications, "no man living knows better the humors of the Dutch and the advantages that might be made from them; had my advice been taken a good part of Zeeland might now well be in His Majesty's hands"; reminding the Minister that he had sacrificed a very good job rather than take an oath against his King whom he had always served "with justice" at considerable personal risk.*[2]

Arlington's replies are not among the State Papers (nor indeed are all John's dispatches . . . he refers to several that are not in the Flanders collection) but evidently there was some criticism of his judgment, for in one dispatch John excuses himself volubly for having suggested that the French advance would be checked at the Rhine. "But my opinion was guided by probabilities and reason," he almost wails, "I could not foresee so dry a season . . . as it was, I was the only man who knew how the French came over."†[3]

Lack of encouragement and promotion set him brooding over past injuries. He blamed "the business of America and the injustice done me by persons who could not justify their ill-service to His Majesty and have for several years made it their business to traduce me by all means possible. I shall think myself fully recompensed if by some honorable action I should remove these false suggestions some ill persons have insinuated to His Majesty and His Royal Highness."[4] For all his dashing assurance on missions, John was such a passionate partisan that he craved an enthusiastic response—a word of praise was sufficient to re-ignite his boundless devotion.

But from London apparently came no hint of approval; and his behaviour reflected his growing depression. He grew defiant, began drinking, making scenes and embarrassing the

---

* John never did realize one cardinal fact of British Intelligence—that an agent is neither rewarded nor recognised—or at least not until much later.

† The French secret agent, Count de Montbas, told John that it was he, Montbas, who revealed the shallow ford where a crossing was possible.

English authorities. Stephen Lynch (always suspicious of John's influential connections and his free-spending swashbuckling ways) wrote Williamson from Ostend: "Colonel Scott is looked upon here most strangely having committed some insolency in his drink . . . the Governor sent for me to know what he was and what he did here. I told him all I knew of him was that he was a gentleman that expected orders from Whitehall . . . with all desired there be no affront put on him."[5]

A week later Lynch gave full details of the scandalous incident. John had gone to an English merchant's house on business, but being refused admittance—the man was at supper with his friends—he had stoned the windows, abusing the company with ripe oaths. The merchant and his brother protested to the magistrate and governor, but John, with drawn sword, had gone rampaging up and down the town threatening and beating up the inhabitants. Next morning when the Consul accompanied him to the city gates, he remembered nothing. "So it is but drunken business," Lynch wrote.[6]

The story of John's uproarious behaviour caught up with Williamson while he was at Cologne. His Whitehall clerk, Robert Yard, wrote him July 4, 1673, "Several complaints have been made of Colonel Scott in Flanders, who, it seems, does the King all the ill-service his capacity will give him leave."[7]

Williamson, knowing his friend's weakness, may not have been too concerned. Especially, as though to offset his boisterous conduct, John forwarded him an unusually valuable dispatch, nothing less than details of Dutch preparations to suppress any possible Anglo-French invasion. This long document (written with his usual good-humored *bonhomie,* "as one gentleman to another"), is illustrated with an enchanting little map, an exact outline of the Scheldt estuary with all the sea approaches to Holland and Zeeland![8] Evidently tossed off quickly, from a larger map he retained, its delicate nervous strokes show speed in every line (and his dispatch closely followed a previous one and was almost immediately succeeded by another), yet it is painted in blue and rose-red with faint touches of gold and details of deep green, so that it has something of the charm and quality of an illuminated missal. At one side is a decorative motif in blue, red, and gold to mark the scale, which was 2 English leagues, or 6 miles to the inch; "it is twice as large as any draft extant," wrote John when he sent the key in a subsequent report. All the neighboring towns are shown and their church steeples painted red (for navigators' easy identification) and, most precious of all, there are several marked passages through the shoals with the soundings given in fathoms or feet; information about which he had collected "from the experience of the most knowing pilots and fishermen of these parts" whom he contacted precisely for his purpose.[9] Williamson may well have thought that such a treasure more than made up for a few brawls.

The Cologne Peace Conference dragged on and the Minister's Journal discloses how very pessimistic he felt over England's chances of a speedy settlement. "How peremptorily and indeed saucily, the Dutch Ambassadors have demanded an ultimatum!"[10] he wrote. They would listen to no suggestion of a separate peace now; demanded that all their towns be restored, and confidently predicted that in five years time their country would recapture all its old trade pre-eminence; "their incredible pride and insolence . . . we are like to lose the peace after such condescension on the part of His Majesty."[11]

At home the English people were protesting angrily against the French, whose military ambitions they blamed for all their troubles. The *maladie des coalitions* was asserting itself, to rupture the thin veneer of friendship imposed by Charles' secret treaty with Louis. British naval losses had been very high and could not quickly be repaired. Pepys was even sending out merchantmen as warships.

What galled the men at the Admiralty—well aware of the current superiority of the English Fleet—was that they had not only to show their French ally "the manner and order of their fighting at sea" (as a well-known Dutch agent gleefully reported to the Hague), but had "to teach him all the secrets of their coasts, their sands, their banks, their avenues of approach, in fact, the very strength and weaknesses of their kingdom."[12]

It was a situation that might bode ill for the future and the English King was only too well aware of it. To cap all misfortunes, while the Ambassadors haggled around the green table, His Most Christian Majesty, Louis XIV, wishing to show the world he could make war without help of allies or of his own famous generals, ostentatiously laid siege to Maestrich, a key fortress, and took it in a week: June 27, 1673! All Europe was aghast at this sudden revelation of the overriding supremacy of French military might and realized anew the menace which a single dominating power—Catholic at that—presented.

Ranks closed. The very alliances which de Witt, before his death, had been negotiating, came into being. A coalition against France was formed, with the King of Spain and the Duke of Lorraine joining the Prince of Orange. When the minor German princes (whom Louis believed he had bought) broke with him, France stood alone against all Europe.

England, worn out by hostilities which ruined trade and in which de Ruyter threatened to destroy her Fleet, made a separate peace with Holland, though without formally abandoning the French alliance.

For English subjects this war was over.

And John Scott's assignment with it.

BIBLIOGRAPHICAL NOTES

1. SP. Fl., 77/40, f 201.
2. *Ibid.*, f 234; *Ibid.*, 77/41, f 53.
3. *Ibid.*, 77/42, f 110.
4. *Ibid.*
5. *Ibid.*, 77/41, f 102.

6. *Ibid.,* f 109.
7. W. D. Christie, *Letters . . . to Sir J. Williamson,* I, 85.
8. SP. Fl., 77/42, f 142.
9. *Ibid.,* 77/41, f 97 v.
10. SP. For., 105/224, f 282.
11. *Ibid.,* 105/226, f 71.
12. Colenbrander, *Besch. mit Vreemde arch.,* pp. 125-6-7.

PART THREE

CHAPTER XXXIII

A BOURBON AS PATRON

"I know some are apt to say we have maps and charts of
these countries already . . . to those I answer, my history
and maps are not calculated for their mean meridian but
for men who are able to judge, gentlemen who have seen
the world, the brave merchants, commanders of ships and
mariners, who . . . are able to put a difference between
things that differ, things of art and labor and things of
error and show."

—John Scott, *Preface.*

WITH ENGLAND OUT OF THE FIGHT John realized he must look
further afield for a career, "for I suppose I shall not stay
here,"[1] he wrote Arlington, possibly hoping for a further
English assignment, which, however, was not immediately
forthcoming.* "I should have been glad to have done His
Majesty the best service I could, for I wish the prosperity of
the Nation with all my heart; and as long as I have anything
to buy me bread with shall still wait with impatience, till
necessity compels me to seek my fortune where the providence of God shall direct me."[2]

There was nothing for him in Holland, now, for he was too
well known as a de Witt partisan to be *persona grata* with the
Prince of Orange. That grave young ruler had never forgiven
de Witt for keeping him in humiliating obscurity during his

---

* "It is a pity to lose him," Secretary Williamson had said of John, Parl.
Deb. 1667-1694, VII, 311. But John's repeated suggestions concerning policy
probably irritated Arlington.

youth. Even after the shocking murder of the eminent states-man, Orange made no effort to apprehend and punish those responsible for the crime. It indicated, only too clearly, how he felt about his Republican predecessor.

France was then the country which rewarded most hand-somely those who served her, and John had never relinquished a hope that one day he might do so. Now was his opportunity. England was still allied with France despite the withdrawal of her fighting forces, and here in Flanders were all the greatest French marshals at his disposal. He lost no time in getting an introduction to Prince de Condé—he always be-lieved in beginning at the top. A meeting between the two men is most flatteringly described by another secret agent, a Madame d'Arbey (writing about it later to William III of Orange) in 1679:

"You must absolutely have recalled from France a certain Scott who was once infantry colonel with Your Highness' troops; he is known to the King of England . . . and is one of the most famous engineers there are; he has the plans of all the rivers, canals and sluices of the United Provinces; also places in the West Indies both Dutch and English, drawn on a very large scale by himself with all the ports, harbors, entrances, exits. . . . He showed them all to the Prince of Condé in my presence at the Hienem camp" (Quiévrain, one of Condé's headquarters). "Prince Condé said he had never seen such beautiful maps and sent him to Paris to sell them to Monsieur Colbert."[3]

Louis de Bourbon, prince of the blood, and first cousin to Louis XIV, had been winning great military victories for thirty long years. Now, at the end of his career and wracked with gout, he dreamed of retiring to the lovely château Man-sard had just built him at Chantilly, there to devote himself to art and letters, which were his passion.

A true Condé, he had a streak of fantastic genius and was violent, careless, charming. John evidently pleased him and kept his friendship till his death. Not only did the prince recommend him to Colbert, France's First Minister, but wrote personally to introduce him.

"This Englishman, Scott, a man of quality . . . came to see me with the object of serving the French King, he being desirous to attach himself to His Majesty, rather than to the English King, with whom, he says, he is on good terms, although on bad terms with the Duke of York.

"He believes he can render very valuable services . . . he has been in the West Indies and he showed me maps of them, the loveliest in the world. As I do not know anything of these countries, I will not comment on them. And because he does not speak French very well he had some difficulty explaining himself, and I in understanding just exactly what he wanted to say. I cannot tell what he is capable of, however he struck me as a man of extremely good sense.

"It was he who had several disputes (*combats*) with M. de la Barre* and came off victorious.

"I trust he can be as useful to the King as he promises to be. I am sending him to you to examine more closely and to see what he can do."[4]

Without such backing John would surely never have met, or would have spent endless hours in *antechambres* waiting upon, the busiest man in all Europe.

Jean-Baptiste Colbert was one of the greatest statesmen France ever produced. Not only was he Controller-General of Finance but he held five other portfolios, including the Navy. He was governor of several provinces and responsible for all their fortifications. Such overwhelming occupations he accepted with joy. It was his incredible energy and love of work (plus a very good marriage) that had brought this petty

---

* This reference to the French commander who refused to restore St. Christopher to England, indicates John's very close knowledge of colonial politics. Acrimonious Anglo-French correspondence concerning this disputed little island continued for nearly two years between de la Barre and Willoughby, between the French foreign minister and Arlington, finally culminating in Charles II's appeal to Louis XIV himself. Corr. Pol. Angleterre: Vols. 88, 89, 91, 92, 93, 94. Quai d'Orsay.

tradesman's son to his high eminence as all-powerful First Minister to Louis XIV.

Colbert's personality was harsh and cold, his "savage manners" in piquant contrast to the suave servility of the Versailles Court. But this "man of marble" had a single weakness; he wanted at all costs to be accepted as a descendant of the ancient Kings of Scotland. He even went to the length of arranging the "discovery" of a tombstone at Reims bearing the inscription, in half-effaced Gothic characters: "Here lies the valiant knight, Richard Colbert called the Scott . . . 1300."[5]

A harmless enough vanity, typical of his *milieu,* too, but one to which John responded with an actor's pliancy. For it is noticeable that in documents of this period John makes constant reference to his own Anglo-Scottish ancestry and signs himself Lord of Mornamont—something he never did before or after. Colbert's predeliction may have been the reason.*

The great man received John and examined his maps carefully, exclaiming over both the geographer's art as well as the detailed knowledge of the Low Countries' strategic areas. He had seen nothing so original, nor so up-to-date. In fact John's latest drawing of the Bruges fortifications had been rudely interrupted when French troops had suddenly overrun the Spanish Netherlands, and John, surprised upon the outer walls, his sketchbook in hand, had been forthwith ordered to leave town within twenty-four hours—resulting in a hurried departure with consequent loss of valuable copperplates of other maps (including the one he dedicated to Sir William Temple), personal belongings, and a "great painting" which could have been his own portrait, never, unfortunately, recovered.

---

* When Samuel Pepys had all the affidavits concerning Scott copied out in fair hand, he sarcastically named the lot "My Mornamont Papers" to mock John's pretensions. How surprised he would have been if he had known that John, with his self-styled title, was adopting exactly the same attitude towards Colbert!

The business of selling Colbert the maps, however, proceeded slowly. It seems to have confronted John with a tormenting problem. For there was one map "he held dearer
than a place might be corrupted for," as an English correspondent wrote to Secretary Williamson, informing him of
these Paris transactions. "He [Scott] says he will not sell a
whole country [Holland] unless he can make his fortune
by it."[6]

Though John had no obligations toward the United Provinces, evidently his deepest feelings were stirred, and he
seemed beset with scruples. His maps in the hands of France
—Holland's enemy—might prove detrimental to Dutch national safety. Should he disregard his qualms, make his fortune once and for all?—he was reputed to have asked £10,000
for the collection, "secured on Hamburg."[7] Apparently his
better nature won—or was it M. Colbert's avarice that tipped
the balance? The French Minister did not want to pay outright for the treasures, but offered an annual pension for
them—a proposal which instantly aroused John's suspicions.
Nothing in his professional career had ever given him cause
to trust princes and ministers; indeed (in his cups), John had
been known to confess that he suspected every man he knew![8]
The idea of surrendering his precious original charts for an
initial sum of three hundred pistoles was not tempting. What
if payments ceased after the first year? Any good draughtsman
could have copied them in that time.

The negotiations fell through.

Prince Condé, learning that someone whom he had recommended had failed to achieve his purpose, interceded in the
matter and John was presented with "fifteen hundred crowns
in gold and silver"; roughly some $1800. He was able to
renew his badly depleted wardrobe and invested in one particularly lavish suit, with silver buttons and buckles.

He finally sold his Dutch maps to an Englishman, a lord
of the Trade and Plantations Committee, and it looks as if
he definitely intended to keep them out of Colbert's hands,

for when the latter, a year later, asked to see them again, John told him they were already sold. Colbert suggested he make fresh copies from the rough drafts he had kept, but John replied that such an undertaking would require at least five or six years—a polite way, it would seem, of refusing.[9]

BIBLIOGRAPHICAL NOTES

1. SP. Fl., 77/41, f 53.
2. *Ibid.*, f 153.
3. Japikse, *Hol. R.H. Arch.*, No. 2650, II, 292, 293.
4. Mél. de Colbert, 165 bis. (Letter of Louis Bourbon, Prince of Condé to Colbert, 1673.)
5. Boulenger, *The Seventeenth Cent.*, p. 323.
6. SP. Fl., 78/138, f 178.
7. *Ibid.*, f 145.
8. Morn. MS., I, f 319.
9. Japikse, *Hol. R.H. Arch.*, No. 2650, II, 293.

CHAPTER XXXIV

A CURIOUS EXPERIMENT

"Princes, Courts and Camps are very improving, but he
that trades there had need be fraught with wit and Virtue, or else he may confound both Body and Minde . . ."
—John Scott, Rawl. MSS., A 175, f 182 v.

FRANCE REMAINED John's home for several years.

He had brought over with him one of his most precious
belongings, a travelling desk especially fitted to carry his
pencils, fine pens, compasses and special tools to grind colors;
everything, in fact, needful for making maps. He was lodging
in Paris in the *rue de la Monnaie,* and his work brought him
in contact with a certain M. de la Pointe, draughtsman and
copyist, and also a Mr. Butterfield, the celebrated mathematical instrument maker. Both assured him he could get
good lodgings with John Joyne, an English watchmaker. So
over to Joyne's John moved his belongings, and thereby
hangs a tale.

For two and a half years John was in and out of Joyne's
house where the impecunious young craftsman-concièrge had
his shop, though his business was almost nonexistent, where
he kept no apprentice, and whose occasional watch repairing
was surely not enough to keep him and his family alive. Yet
he managed to live, by his wits or by other means John never
knew. Later generations have learned, however, to Scott's
infinite detriment.

But Paris did not claim all John's time. (Or was he still

acting on orders from Secretary Williamson?) His exceptional connections with the French may have tempted the English to employ him again as intelligence officer. Whatever the reason, he accompanied one of the French armies when it went off on the spring campaign of 1674.

With English troops out of the war, France was forced to maintain three large armies in the field; Condé held the Dutch and Spaniards in Flanders; Turenne faced the Imperialist forces in Alsace and Lorraine; while Louis reserved for himself a showy offensive in Franche-Comté.

Here John joined him. "They have invited me to go with them to Besançon and treated me very handsomely,"[1] he wrote his M.P. friend, Wentworth, in London. He went as observer, not commissioned officer, since, as usual, John refused to take an oath of loyalty to a foreign sovereign.

King Louis favored a war of sieges, at which he was always successful for he took along with him his master of fortifications, "Sieur Vauban," of whom it was said: "A town defended by Vauban is impregnable, a town invested by Vauban is taken."

This famous military engineer had invented an entirely new technique—trench warfare, and his clever use of cross fire to enfilade covered ways and bastions was but one of the modern methods about which the English were anxious to learn.*

"I shall tell you more of this when Besançon is French," John's letter continued. He was in the thick of the mêlée and was wounded, but the campaign was over in six weeks.

John returned to Paris, and right after his recovery embarked upon an entirely new career. His experiment as military engineer and gun manufacturer revealed him as a true "virtuoso" in the Renaissance sense, yet fantastic as it seemed it was not a haphazard undertaking. He had carefully

---

* Among Scott's papers, together with his letter about the siege of Besançon was the plan of the siege of Neuhausel, invested by the Turks, 1663.

prepared the ground in London, taking advantage of a brief trip there in 1670 to talk with the French ambassador, who not only listened to his plans with interested consideration, but secured him a retaining fee of forty pounds.

Now the moment seemed propitious for action since he had just the right connections beginning with the King's First Minister.

Colbert, over the previous twenty years, had encouraged France to master all the most renowned specialties of other countries—the fine weaving of Holland, England's steel making, Sweden's tar production, and so on, and to this end subsidized factories, granted monopolies to likely entrepreneurs, and ordered his ambassadors abroad to recruit skilled foreign craftsmen.

About 1665 he turned his attention to the Navy, which Louis was neglecting. Two years fighting with the British Fleet (1672-1674) had revealed the extent of France's maritime deficiencies. There was nothing wrong with the human material—only recently a crabbed old sea-dog of sixty-six, named Duquesne, had twice soundly beaten the famous De Ruyter off the coasts of Spanish Sicily.

But the French lacked fire-power: Colbert wanted better cannon.

With audacious vision the Minister embarked on the stupendous task of creating a national industry. He set up royal foundries at Nevers (and elsewhere), established a new ordnance company under the noted Swedish technician Abraham Besch, and entrusted the entire undertakings to his *homme de confiance,* Samuel D'Alliez de la Tour, a Gascon financier whom he made Purveyor to the Navy and whose outstanding activity and capacity matched his master's, as he organized, purchased, travelled, kept in motion all the ramifications of this great new state enterprise.

Installed at Nevers with French technicians were groups of Swedes and Spaniards, busily experimenting with different production methods. Artillery had developed over the years without much scientific application, there was every variety of calibre, and Vauban was always complaining of the lack of good guns. "They break like glass," he roared.[2] So far nothing had been successful; there were so many unwarranted explosions that, at one moment, French naval officers, in charge of local operations, had unanimously refused to be present at gunnery tests.[3]

Into this highly competitive field, John, as promoter and gun manufacturer, had the good luck to appear just when Colbert had promulgated his first great *Règlement* concerning naval expansion. And although John had no qualifications other than a single formula and some willing colleagues, his personality was so engaging, and he talked so convincingly that he not only gained the interest of all who listened, but won the support of the very highest officials in the land.

Colbert, remembering, perhaps, his brother's letter from London about Scott's guns, turned our enterprising young man over to his eldest son, the Marquis de Seigneley, who, since 1669—when he was just eighteen—had been State Secretary for the Navy.

Seigneley was as handsome and pleasure-loving as his father was harsh and cold, but the lad's qualities were outstanding, and he soon acquired the parental capacity for hard work. Under his ministry French squadrons became the foremost in Europe.

Negotiating with him was no easy matter however. By temperament violent and overbearing, this tradesman's grandson was so lofty that he even (as Voltaire said), "managed to show civilities haughtily."

Arrogance was something John could also assume when he wished, especially towards the French, as Du Tertre had already noted. The pair were well-matched.

The Secretary listened attentively as John described "the greatest curiosity of polished cast-iron guns that for beauty and service would equal the standard brass cannon,"[4] and granted him permission to proceed. With this initial encouragement John began the necessary formalities for permits and patents with the Navy's Treasurer-General, M. de Pélissary, hoping (as he wrote the latter's secretary) that Seigneley would remember to send him the fifty *louis d'or* he had promised. "When I dined with the Treasurer-General two days ago he said nothing about it. I shall not forbear to carry out what I have promised in hopes that they (the Ministry) will do the same on their side."[5] For despite his astuteness, John was strangely gullible. If a proposition interested him, he went ahead with dedicated energy, no matter how often he was let down.

For the technical side of the venture he engaged two men whom he had known in Holland—a Captain Manning, and Edward Sherwin, the English gun manufacturer who had worked with Prince Rupert, when the latter's experimental quick-firing gun was being tested at the English Royal Society.

John now rented a large room in the *rue des Fosses* at St. Sulpice, both to conduct his affairs, and to display his maps. John Joyne's lodgings lacked elegance and the watchmaker was proving a sodden drunk and an inquisitive bore. He had his uses, however; he knew Paris well and spoke fluent French, something in which John was still not proficient though a dictionary was seldom out of his hands.

Preliminary negotiations were carried on at M. de Pélissary's house, or in the *rue des Marais,* at that of Mademoiselle des Moulins—one of the amazing feminine business types the century was beginning to produce and who missed no detail. Here the Navy-Treasurer on several occasions brought along Monsieur Le Goux, from the Nevers foundry, a man of experience who really knew gun-casting. When consulted about the "reasonableness of Scott's proposals" he seemed somewhat doubtful of the method's success.

But John swept all objections aside. Pélissary was finally convinced, and signed a document (duly witnessed by Mademoiselle des Moulins and M. de la Pirogérie, officer and technical interpreter) giving full consent to the undertaking and the permission to import Englishmen to work on it. This was the first hurdle.

The strictest laws prohibited skilled artisans from leaving England. Sherwin, trying to get out of the country, ran into great difficulties, arriving at last, incognito, at the little port of St. Valléris, where John met him. Some of his men were arrested at Dover; one, on the King's orders, stopped in London. John, hastening to assure his patrons that all would be well, wrote Mademoiselle des Moulins that his cousin, the Earl of Winchelsea, would provide a pleasure yacht ("at my orders") to bring everyone over.*6

Four or five English workmen finally reached France under false port declarations: one came as a pastrycook, another as a milliner, two declared they were engravers; there was Harrison, an office clerk, and one signed "unemployed." In Paris John engaged Butterfield,† the mathematical instrument maker, whose new-type compass was already used by the Navy.

It was a modest beginning, though John spoke of more coming later, and enthusiasm made up for lack of numbers. They all had the highest hopes; judging from the agreements they signed with John, and with one another, they must have imagined they were going to make millions. John was equally elated; his generosity boundless. In high-flown legal documents (all attested by the King's own notary, Noel Duparc) he made the handsomest offers to Sherwin and Manning and

---

* In 1680 when the Navy Department was being investigated for misuse of the King's ships, Winchelsea naturally denied this. He also wrote Pepys he knew nothing of his own relationship with Scott. But John had a professional knowledge of his family tree. "Cousin" was perhaps too close a claim —except as term of address—but the Winchelseas were connected with the Scotts through Isabella Finch, Sir William Scott's second wife, (m. 1433). This widow of Sir Moyle Finch, was created (by James I) Viscountess Winchelsea and her male heirs made Earls of Winchelsea. In the Scott Memorials there are five letters addressed to George Scott Esq., in 1711, all signed, "your very affectionate kinsman, Winchelsea." Scott Mem., pp. 105, 116, 117; XLIII, XLIV.

† John Locke, the philosopher, writing from Paris, in 1677, mentions visiting this eminent man and examining his instruments for astronomical observations; a levelling instrument; a perspective glass or telescope, etc. Fox-Bourne Life of Locke, pp. 375-76.

seemed to believe that he himself would be created a Marshal of France, at least! He was in closest touch with the all-important D'Alliez de la Tour, who was enthusiastic about the formula and facilitated the casting of some little seven-pound sample gun models, and also presented John to another key figure, the Duc du Lude, no less than Grand Master of Artillery, begging the latter to favor Scott with his protection and recommend him to the King. The Duke, realizing the advantages of such guns, was delighted at the prospect, and urged all speed ahead in production. John, with visions of his guns being adopted by the Army as well as the Navy wanted to reward La Tour for his good offices. But La Tour (who like all of his kind at that period, probably made a very good thing out of purveying), declared that he was only serving his country in procuring the best possible guns. However John insisted on settling upon him a pension of three thousand pistoles—countersigned Lord of Ashford and Mornamont! Even John Joyne "for several services rendered" was to get thirty *louis d'or* out of every one hundred ton of metal Sherwin cast.[7]

John was indefatigable. Back and forth he travelled, from Paris to Nevers; from Abbeville to look at Colbert's new factories, to Rochefort, where Seigneley was founding a magnificent arsenal.* He made elaborate and beautiful drawings of his guns; the least detail received his personal attention and he was always ready to solicit further patronage of his scheme.

About this time an old acquaintance, Sir John Bowles, arrived in Paris, and heard all about the new venture. John entertained him lavishly, placing a coach at his disposal to go to Versailles, hoping that his friend would put in a good word for him with the French King. Bowles did more; he took John with him and presented him at Court, and for the

---

* It is quite possible that John, all this time, was still doing intelligence work for the British. His gun-casting scheme would have provided un-rivalled opportunities for reporting on French naval expansion.

first time they both beheld that stone and marble miracle of comfortless splendor and mingled with the fashionable crowd who daily paid homage to the *roi soleil*.

Paris officials began watching the experiment with increasing interest. Colbert wrote D'Alliez de la Tour asking for precise details concerning the number and calibre of the English cannon;[8] he ordered Besch to visit Nevers personally and try to get the secret of this formula for cast-iron so that John's guns could be duplicated in other foundries.[9]

From Nevers, in August, John wrote Joyne in extravagant praise of his workmen, "all masters of their craft."[10] Only a dispute with Sherwin over the engraving on the cannon—each thought his own name should be immortalized—broke the close harmony of those busy days.

At last the guns were ready. Late in 1675, they were brought to Paris to be tested, just outside the city, in the presence of Seigneley, other Cabinet Members, and "certain great lords."

Alas for all the high hopes. John's guns were no better than all the others. He had used the same acid brittle ore; his furnaces, too, lacked heat enough to "work" his material sufficiently; and like all cannon of the period, his barrels were outlandishly long. At each firing the strain on the tail was too great, and the pieces gave way under the powder's force. Only two out of his five resisted; the others broke to bits amid terrible explosions and clouds of smoke.

It was a bitter disappointment; John was humiliated as never before. He simply could not face his old acquaintances. The gun makers quarrelled fiercely among themselves, heaping reproaches on each other and upon him, challenging him to a duel, making the wildest accusations of bad faith and botched opportunities.

John's hopes of making a fortune had foundered. In his dejected mood he talked wildly of turning counterfeiter—making all the money he wanted, and flooding Europe with it. He would unload it on the coasts of England, Scotland and Ireland, operating from the Isle of Man . . . so very convenient, right in the midst of the countries which would distribute it.

And it must be true, murmured the others, credulously, for when we looked at the map, there was the Isle of Man, right in the middle, just as he said it was!

As a matter of fact among John's papers—which reveal the man's almost universal interests—there is a formula for blanching copper. It was invented and published by Rudolf Glauber, of Glauber Salts fame, a German chemist living in Amsterdam whose fantastic claims earned him an international reputation as a second Paracelsus. But one cannot help suspecting, reading testimony about this counterfeiting talk that John was indulging in the very American practice of "kidding" his companions. Contemptuous and furious with himself over his Nevers failure, he was not above poking a little bitter fun at his workers, gullible enough to fall for any crazy scheme. But was Glauber's magic formula for transmuting copper any less extravagant than the cast-iron process he himself had just tried?

He might have felt less gloomy could he have read the reports French officers were making on other gunnery experiments; and how, for two long years, they continued to deplore efforts both of their own countrymen and of foreigners, to produce cannon heavy enough to fire a charge without exploding.[11]

BIBLIOGRAPHICAL NOTES

1. SP. Dom. Car., II, 29/419, No. 28.
2. Min. of War, *Fr. Artill. Mem.*, XIV, p. 934.
3. Fr. Mar. Docs., B³, XX, ff 164-65.
4. Morn. MS., I f 406.
5. *Ibid.*, f 339.
6. *Ibid.*, f 341.
7. Morn. MS., I, f 563.
8. Fr. Mar. Docs., B-2, XXXI, ff 31, 423 v, 424.
9. *Ibid.*, f 303 v, 304.
10. Morn. MS., I, ff 353-54.
11. Fr. Mar. Docs., B-3, XX, ff 164-65; 294-95.

CHAPTER XXXV

YEARS OF MYSTERY

> "It has always been accounted prudence before a man im-
> barkes himself in any designed Enterprize, to consider
> well the event of issue that it is like to arrive unto, for
> the want of this has often proved the ruin of many a
> glorious undertaking; for where one Design has been
> gravelled in to the sands of a little delay, thousands have
> been split on the Rocks of Precipitancy and Rashness."
>
> —John Scott to Sir Francis Rolle,
> Rawl. MSS., A 175, ff 181, 182.

NOW FOLLOWED THE LEANEST PERIOD of John's life, for whatever fees he had received for his gun-casting experiment were
exhausted. He had to give up his grand rooms near St. Sulpice; the silver buttons and buckles of his satin suit found
their way to the pawnshop. Shabby and down on his luck, he
turned again to map making as a means of livelihood. The
maps most prized by buyers were his brightly colored enlargements with decorative figures and designs surrounding
different towns to commemorate battles or special events.
Delving into local histories, he would dig up odd bits of information and ornament his charts with imaginative skill.

Much of this work he did in a "greate chamber" lent to
him by the Earl of Berkshire, a former Catholic Cavalier, living in self-imposed exile in Paris. Berkshire had been one of
the very earliest to support Charles I and in all probability
knew John's father, also among those first valiant few. Hence
the offer of this vast room where John could handle his great

rolls of drawing paper, undisturbed by the prying eyes and pilfering fingers of his concièrge, Joyne.

Monsieur La Pointe, a Paris draughtsman, testified that John employed him for months at a time, copying a number of maps (with a Mademoiselle Jaquelon to do the coloring). There was an elaborate one of the Magellan Straits; another of the St. Lawrence River and other parts of Canada which John had worked over from old Jesuit charts; as well as one of his favorites—the River Thames (Deborah's River of London). All these took a very long time to do as there were so many details to insert, said La Pointe. One of them was destined for the Prince of Condé.[1]

It is probable that during this period John compiled a survey of New Jersey for an English publication promoting emigration. *An Abstract of Testimonies** (now in the British Museum) was printed in London in 1681, but as John's contribution included French source material and mentions Frenchmen whose names also appear in a letter he wrote from France in 1678, it suggests he did the New Jersey piece while living in Paris.

It is a typically competent Scott report, based on personal observations from several trips there, and on information drawn from "the Collections I took from the English, Swedes and Hollanders."

He considered the Virginia Company very ill-advised in not settling in this delectable country. Had Lord Delaware (Virginia's governor), after his visit there, 1611, prevailed upon the Lord Commissioners to remove their colony to New Jersey he would have prevented the deaths of "thousands of the English Nation who found graves in Virginia by reason of the many Boggs, Swamps, and Standing Waters which corrupt the air." Dutch trappers and merchants thought so too.

---

* *An Abstract or Abbreviation of some Few of the Many Testimonys from the Inhabitants of New Jersey and Other Eminent Persons who have Wrote particularly concerning the Place.* London. Printed by Thomas Milbourn in the Year 1681. (C 114, b. 7.)

John dwelt lengthily on "the agreableness and kindness of the air," and its many natural blessings—divers fish, fruits, vegetables, medicinal herbs "Puchamines, Malagotoons; and a vast large creature called a Moose."

He wrote of the abundance of wild grapes from which wine and brandy had already been made, and predicted that with the transplantation of vine-stocks from Greece, Calabria and Cyprus, New Jersey could possibly rival those countries in wine production, and be "even the envy of France and Spain." He dashed off statistics of wine-growing in Languedoc and Provence, quoted M. Le Tellièr (Louis XIV's Secretary of State since 1643) on silk manufacture, and could not refrain from giving a brief history of the whole business of silk making since its introduction from the Orient! No detail escaped his darting mind.

Remarkable was his news of the iron mines in the province and the presence of various ores, coupled with "great conveniency of wood and a multitude of Brooks for iron mills."

Since the Tinton Falls Iron Works—the first in New Jersey —were established in Monmouth County only in 1675, John showed how very alert he was to American colonial conditions. Evidently his French friends (particularly Monsieur Gallane, son of Nantes' governor, whom he mentions) had been boasting of their iron in the Mesabi range around the French-held Lakes. This probably prompted John's revelation of New Jersey's deposits which were actually extensively used until the Revolution.

There is no record among state papers that John at this period was employed as British agent in France—this time in all secrecy. There is however some reason for thinking that he may have been: his frequent comings and goings throughout that country fit well into such an explanation. Certain it is, however, that he was sedulously keeping up his official contacts, English and French, and closely following the war situation. The information in one of his letters to Sir Francis

Rolle, Republican MP, reads very much like ammunition for foreign policy debates in the House.

"If this can be used as a Spurre," he begins, "draw the necessary consequences and the result that is fallen out, is unavoidable."[2] And he proceeds with an account of France's withdrawal from Sicily after her 1676 Mediterranean successes, and suggests she is concentrating her forces at home in preparation for an attack on England. He analyzes the military situation for two pages with a background of the historico-political intrigue at the French Court.

His pithy thumb-nail sketches of high-ranking officers show not only inside knowledge but a nice sense of irony. The Duke of Vivonne, for instance, "great by birth and greater by the Meritt of his own Virtue," had conquered and long held Messina, gaining thereby "abundance of Reputation and is determined to keep it, as also to have the Duc de la Feuillade" (his creature) "appointed as his successor. La Feuillade, though not, peradventure, a man of the first or second thoughts in great Affairs," writes John, "yet I who know him as well as I know myself,* know him to be a Man that will be apt to say: 'Had Monsieur Vivonne stayed there, the place might have held out longer.'"

An admirable successor for a momentarily vanquished hero!

But it is not so much John's professional knowledge that this letter reveals—however competent his reporting—as the nature of the writer himself. Leaving politics and war aside for once, John described his visit to Rolle's only son—a Paris student who had evidently, to his parents' anger, married without their consent, and without a marriage settlement! It is a very human little story John tells, gently reminding his reader that wealth, after all, is not everything. "Pursuant to My Lady Rolle's and your Commands, I was with the un-

---

* The Duc de la Feuillade was stationed in Bruges at the time John was British agent in Flanders S. P. For Arch. 105/224, f 43.

happy Couple, and aggravated the Crime so to him that he wept and promised he would do anything you or your Lady his Mother would command him, . . . I informed myself well and find he follows his studys with great diligence. . . . You cannot expect him to be a Philosopher nor a Politick-man. . . ." (and here John digresses for several paragraphs on the philosophy of knowledge, then comes back again to the lad).

"You may, after his wife is brought to bed, dispose of him how you please. I must assure you that the People where they lodge take me for a man of a very severe nature, for the whole family was in tears, and the poor young Gentlewoman —near her time—wept with that vehemency that I could do no less than sympathise with her, and promise my utmost as-sistance; and I am confident had Sir Francis Rolle seen the condition she was reduced to, within a few days of her time, you would have had so much humanity as to forgive a thou-sand greater injuries than is committed to your Family. If my request is able to move you and My Lady, since none can say one word of her not being unspottedly vertuous. Have not so much regard to the Goods that perish, nor to the Extraccount which is not to be distinguished in death. And if she has a son pray own it as one that is like to keep up your Name, for Providence does seem to barre other hope. . . ."[3]

At least once, and possibly twice, during these lean years, John returned to England. Crossing the Channel and enter-ing his own country was a simple matter for a former govern-ment agent. Many a Searcher must have known him by sight and passed him with a nod. He was certainly in London in the spring of 1677, but still fortune did not favor him. Both his former patrons, Shaftesbury and Buckingham, were pris-oners in the Tower. In the mortal struggle between Charles II and his lawmakers, these two powerful ministers had dared to assert that the current parliament was illegally constituted. For this heresy they were temporarily banished from office.

John's luck had never been lower. He was lodging in an

unfashionable part of town, at the house of an iron-founder, one Hill, when an extraordinary incident occurred, which, for all its seeming insignificance at the time, was to shed a curious light on John's career, and to have repercussions of a most sinister nature.

BIBLIOGRAPHICAL NOTES

1. Rawl. MSS., A 190, f 117; *Ibid.*, A 175, f 161.
2. *Ibid.*, f 181.
3. *Ibid.*, ff 181-82 r, v.

CHAPTER XXXVI

PEPYS APPROACHES JOHN

"... no guard can defend a man from an envious eye."
—John Scott, *Preface.*

IT WAS A BLUSTERY DAY in April, 1677, when John came back
to his Houndsditch lodgings in a towering rage. He had been
accosted by a stranger in Covent Garden, who had dogged his
footsteps all the way to Lincoln's Inn Fields and then followed him home. "And the fellow seeing me come in here,
went to the grocer's opposite to spy on me," roared John.

His noisy indignation attracted a neighbor, a Major John
Gladman, who came over and whispered to John that his fol-
lower was none other than the notorious Popish priest, Dr.
Coniers.

"How do you happen to be acquainted with a Romish
priest?" inquired John, for papists were anathema in England, those days. Even knowing one was enough to make you
suspect.

Popular distrust of the King's indulgence to Catholics and
the Duke of York's open conversion to Rome had stirred terrible misgivings throughout the country. A Bill introducing
a loyalty test had been forced upon Charles—all office holders
and members of the armed forces had to take the Anglican
sacrament and forswear the Catholic doctrine of transubstan-
tiation.

The nation's eyes turned questioningly towards James.
Would he renounce his religion to keep in office? The answer,

when it came, rocked the nation to its foundations. The King's heir laid down his post as Lord High Admiral rather than take the Test!

That meant the crown of England would pass to a Roman Catholic! Protestants throughout the land closed ranks; political tension deepened; John's question was almost a threat.

"How came you to know a papist?" he repeated.

Major Gladman was very happy to account for his acquaintance with the Jesuit Coniers. "I was in the army with his brother Christopher, a harmless Protestant, with whom I became friends," he explained. "That's how I know George, who sometimes visited his brother, but who's lived in Rome these last seventeen years." Coniers, catching sight of Gladman, came over to join the two men and, together with Hill, they all went to Gladman's quarters.

Coniers suddenly asked John if he had ever heard, in France, of Mr. Pepys, and of his corresponding with the French to the prejudice of England.

"That's an odd question to ask a stranger," growled John, on the defensive at once.

"I do it in order for your good," answered the priest smoothly. "For I come from Mr. Pepys to offer you his services in order to the getting you into some honorable employment at sea. For he hath great power to do kindnesses by reason of his interest in him who was a Barr [sic] to your Fortune" (meaning the Duke of York, who since Long Island days had been John's nemesis.) "Mr. Pepys will serve you frankly and effectually; he can do you a great kindness."

The mysterious stranger left, and Hill wanted to know "why John would not embrace Pepys' friendship and offers to him by Coniers."

But John continued to fuss and fume. "You don't know what I know," he answered surlily. "I'll have nothing to do with those rogues, Jesuits and Papists; I wish it were in my power to prevent what I know concerning these villains who hate our religion and government and People. And so doth their Patron"[1] (meaning the Duke of York).

This entire scene was sworn to by these Londoners, three years later, when Samuel Pepys sent an investigator to find out what they had remembered of it. Gladman, possibly aware of its political implications, declared that he had not heard everything, merely "something mentioned about France."

But Hill was more explicit. . . . And the great Mr. Pepys himself, possibly in some trepidation, came all the way to lowly Houndsditch to meet the humble tradesman and to hear again what he remembered of the curious encounter.

Hill, "a harmless ignorant fellow, minding his own business but reasonably well considered locally," told his story, without mentioning, however, that Coniers had said he had been sent to Scott by Pepys.

Pepys asked him point-blank if Coniers *had* said this.

Hill hesitated, professing that his memory might fail him . . . he "was but a tradesman," he said diffidently. "But now you put it into my mind," he admitted, "Coniers *did* say he was sent by Pepys."

The great man thanked him and withdrew.[2]

Had he really been willing to induce the Duke of York to help John in 1677? If that were so, and his offer a genuine one, it would have marked a turning point in John's life, and could have averted the misfortune which was to overcome him. John always considered that the Duke of York had blocked and blighted his career. In 1674, for instance, during the Third Dutch War John had had a promise to command the frigate *Jersey,* but Esquire Pepys hindered him of it. The only reason was "the place was too good for him," and Pepys told him the Duke of York said it was; it was a command for the best Knight in England. The command was never settled upon anyone."[3]

This *Jersey* was the ship John had already hoped to command in the Caribbean when Willoughby had brought her

where the anniversary of Guy Fawkes' Gunpowder Treason was celebrated by official act.

Persistent rumors of French gold in English hands increased the national terror. The Third Dutch War was dragging on, with Holland so hard pressed that many Englishmen now urged helping the Prince of Orange, even at risk of war with France. The House of Commons, panicked by French military successes in Flanders, hastily voted six hundred thousand pounds for a small expeditionary force; and Louis XIV, anxious to stop this British intervention, doubled his bribes to certain parliamentary friends to veto further supplies; while to his royal cousin and secret confederate he offered another subsidy to remain neutral and dissolve Parliament.

When negotiations for a general peace began, Charles withdrew his troops from the Continent, but he did not disband them. He kept them camped at Blackheath, within striking distance of London, thereby increasing the fears of those who said he might use them—as his father had done—to enforce his will on his own rebellious subjects.

Relations between Crown and Parliament had never been worse. Even buttressed with French funds, the English King's position was precarious, and that of his enemies growing stronger. Public clamor against the Catholic Duke of York and concern over the succession were uniting the most divergent political groups. Anglicans as well as Dissenters, remnants of the armed Cavaliers, with thousands of Cromwell's old Ironsides, outright Republicans even ready to abolish the monarchy, all found themselves together in a formidable Opposition. John Scott, for all his royalist tradition, was irresistibly drawn to this camp. And upon the passions and convictions of these distraught people, the greatest parliamentary tactician of the age piped a daemonic tune with all the skill of a political virtuoso.

Public opinion, as it is understood today, did not exist in the seventeenth century. History could literally be made by a single man, and the Earl of Shaftesbury, leader of the militant Country Party, emerged as instigator of ways and techniques to mould men's minds and manipulate votes. And despite the rigged elections and packed juries of this unhappy period, the impetus given by the "great little Lord" led eventually to the Glorious Revolution and constitutional government. This was a transformation of incalculable historical importance and John Scott played an active part in it.

The stage was set for dramatic upheaval. The national mood was tense and turbulent; inflammable as summer brushwood, it needed but a spark to kindle a flame. And on a sultry day in 1678 the match was set. Charles II was walking in St. James' Park on August 13th, when an old acquaintance, a certain Christopher Kirby, approached him and warned him not to leave his companions as there was a plot against his life. He could be killed on that very walk.

The King ordered the man to Whitehall that evening with fuller information, and continued his stroll.

That night Kirby brought along with him a well-known, somewhat hare-brained Protestant clergyman, Israel Tonge, author of countless anti-Catholic pamphlets, who gave the King details of an alleged Jesuit conspiracy. He begged leave to introduce the man who had uncovered it all—a man himself educated by the Jesuit Order and until but recently a devoted adherent, when, reeling under the discovery of unspeakable infamies, he apostatized and was ready to reveal the whole infamous plot. Charles was inclined to pooh-pooh the matter, but the Duke of York, who felt he was implicated in this, insisted upon a public inquiry.

So in the Privy Council, before the King and his Ministers one late September morning stepped the sinister figure soon to be hailed as Saviour of the Nation, Titus Oates, whose outrageous story produced a veritable reign of terror wherein the merest hint labelling a man a Papist could wreck a career or end a life. His perjured testimony blocked parliamentary business for two years, brought notoriety and riches to him-self, caused death and ruin to literally thousands of victims and split England in two, leaving scars which only centuries effaced from minds and hearts.

Squat, bull-necked, bow-legged, his face a livid purple from high blood pressure, Oates' small sunken eyes were dominated by a huge wart on one brow. But most memorable was his chin—that vast expanse of flabby flesh which made his mouth seem the exact center of his face. From this slit came a voice at once shrill and affected, the voice of a toady and a bully; it smote the ears with the impact of "a bray and a bleat."

To support his monstrous charges he exhibited letters which had been entrusted to him by unsuspecting English Fathers corresponding with Catholic seminaries abroad. This highly subversive correspondence alluded freely to Jesuit treason in Scotland and Ireland, a second burning of London, with wholesale massacre when French troops landed, and, crowning horror, the assassination of Charles II, decision for which had been taken at a secret Jesuit congregation—"the Great Consult" he called it—held at London's White Horse Tavern April 24th of that year, at which Oates—so he said—was present! He had all the details pat. Coniers, the Jesuit, was to plunge his foot-long knife into the King; the Queen's own physician was to furnish poison should the knifing fail; Papist members of the new government had all been chosen and were ready to take their places when the Duke of York ascended the throne. Sole witness for all these horrors was Titus Oates—lately starving in the London streets. He had sworn out the whole narrative before a London magistrate on September 6th, he said, but nothing had come of it. Now he felt compelled to tell all.

Open-mouthed at the revelation, his listeners sat silent, for-getting the man's unsavory reputation. Not once, but three times, Oates had changed his religion. His entire twenty-nine years were a tissue of failure and fraud. He was a self-confessed perjurer, had been dismissed from a Jesuit seminary for sodomy, and from the Navy—as chaplain—on the same charge.

Yet one or two notable details in his interminable recital were startlingly true and precisely confirmed certain facts known only to a very few. Such an obscure creature as Oates could never have learned them had he not access to some important source. Moreover the tale he told was so perfectly attuned to the hysterical fears of Protestant England, haunted as it was by memories of the Great Fire and by distorted news leaks of the Secret Dover Treaty, that more than one figure at the Council Table realized what Party profit could be drawn from exploiting such sensationalism.

Chief among these was the Lord Treasurer, Danby, anxious to divert attention from his own unpopularity and his dubious relations with France; and now fighting a bitter political battle with Shaftesbury, who, too, was equally aware of how the Popish Plot could be used to serve Party ends.*

When Oates left the Council Chamber he carried warrants for the arrest of various Jesuit priests and lay brothers. And, with his unfailing flair for the spectacular, he was soon hammering on doors at midnight, dragging victims from their beds, rifling letters and papers.

The great witch hunt had begun.

Almost immediately seeming confirmation of the Plot came from the highest quarters. Edward Coleman, private secretary to the Duchess of York, was implicated and his papers sequestered. The bulk of these he had already destroyed, tipped off by the very man who had taken Oates' original deposition. What remained was sufficiently incriminating: there were letters from the French King's own confessor, Père La Chaise; embarrassing lists of English on the French pay-

---

* "Let the Treasurer cry never so loud against Popery" said Shaftesbury, "and think to put himself at the head of the Plot, I will cry a note louder and soon take his place." Sitwell, *The First Whig*, MDCXCIV, p. 50.

roll;[1] detailed intrigue spread over long years.* Coleman was imprisoned and, to his own bewilderment, for the foolish young bigot obviously expected a reprieve, shortly thereafter hanged.

Any doubt in the Plot after that sentence vanished overnight. Mobs lit bonfires throughout the city, exulted over the execution. And a blind unreasoning panic swept the land.

BIBLIOGRAPHICAL NOTE

1. Aff. Etran., Nov., 1678, No. 131, f 203.

---

* "Mr. Coleman's letters have given us much more trouble (than Oates' accusations), matters treated in these papers are of very high consequence"— Secretary Coventry to Charles II, Oct., 1678 (Add. MSS. 32095, f 119).

CHAPTER XXXVIII

"BUCKINGHAM'S JOHN"

"Go flattering hope, by whose uncertain fire
I cherish my tyrannical desire.
Grief is a less unwelcome guest than Care
And my state's such
That t'will cost as much
To doubt as to despair."

—John Scott.

SHORTLY BEFORE THE PLOT'S tumultuous outbreak, John Scott
emerged from his Parisian obscurity and returned to London
to join his one-time patron, George Villiers, Second Duke of
Buckingham, recently released from his Tower penance and
restored to public life if not to royal favor.

England's former Prime Minister and State Secretary, member of the Cabal, once richest man in the kingdom, childhood
friend of the Stuarts and intimate companion of his amorous
monarch's "most remiss hours," the jolly Duke of Bucks had
been a resplendent figure at the Restoration Court and was
still a potent voice in the House of Lords. Vigorously and
audaciously he had devoted his life to the pursuit of happi-
ness, fame, and fantastic ideas. Handsome, witty, of most versatile gifts, his frivolity and vanity masked a dual nature
struggling with itself, for he was also of keen speculative
mind, musician, playwright, friend of poets and philosophers,
a true modern in this budding Scientific Age.

Dryden's satirical genius does him infinite injustice. Never
has he lived down that poet's biting caricature; and, stripped

—in verse—of his essential qualities, the Duke has been almost as much maligned as Colonel John Scott himself. For beneath the quick-witted ebullience, the glaring indiscretions and follies, lay a core of disinterested idealism, an aspect the Royal Court never saw. In an age of religious intolerance, Buckingham led the fight for liberty of conscience, risking political fortune with impassioned pleas that men might worship as they chose.* William Penn, the Quaker, was his friend; persecuted Dissenters everywhere looked to him as leader, a paradoxical position for this gilded worldling. But it helps explain his association with John. For the latter, too, had a deeply serious side and profound concern for the individual. He too could drink and wench with the best (or worst), turn a pretty sonnet—indeed, no one not a lively talker could sit at the Duke's table. But throughout his life ran a dominating theme, and a curious one it proved to be in as resolute a Royalist as John had been.

Time had brought the Kentish boy full circle. Politically he was reaching the summit of his life, he had matured to the role he had to play. New England had first opened his eyes to the rights of common people; the high-minded de Witt, with his painstaking genius and determination to maintain the Dutch Republic, had completed the transformation. Now with England's faith and liberties in danger, John's place was logically within his patron's orbit. And very close, too, for he was known, at this period, as "Buckingham's John."

When he arrived in London, early in 1678, the Duke was still under a cloud, sulking with the Country Party. Peeved at being out of office, he was also smarting from the unparalleled affront the Cavalier Parliament had spitefully put on him. In that notoriously profligate society with cuckoldry a

---

* Buckingham's great speech when he introduced his Bill for *Tolerance of Protestant Nonconformists* (1675) was regarded then as rankest heresy. Though much of it reads today as merest truism, its opening line still strikes a powerful response: "My Lords, There is a thing called liberty. . . ." (Proceedings H. of Lords. (1742, Ed.) 1, 164-65.)

universal pastime, it had officially censured him for his adulterous life with the ravishing Lady Shrewsbury whose overweening cupidity had exhausted even his vast fortune. Despite his formal appeal for forgiveness (together with that of his magnaminous wife, no less) he and his mistress were forced—like any common fornicators caught in the act—to give sureties for future good behaviour and were let off with a "caution" to the tune of ten thousand pounds each! Never had peer of the realm been so humiliated. He had retired to his Cliveden estate to lick his wounds.

Back again in London, he bought a mansion at Dowgate, and here John found him installed. "Alderman George," the King dubbed the Duke jovially, but kept a sharp eye on him, all the same. The City had never lost its Cromwellian flavor, it was boisterously anti-Court; "the Republic at the side of the Throne" some called it. Now it teemed with all the Opposition sects, busy with pamphlets and propaganda, active in the Clubs and Coffeehouses which were fast becoming a feature of contemporary political life. Among them, veteran plotter of half a century, was Buckingham's solicitor, trustee, and close friend, Major Wildman. Soul of the Republican Party, this "flamey" dedicated creature, loyal alike to colleagues and ideals, conspired—in a constitutional manner—to bring about a democratic Commonwealth. Through five successive reigns he had defied kings and dictators, spent more than half his life in jail, finally helped bring about the Glorious Revolution, and finished—not on the gallows, as his foes had confidently predicted, but as Postmaster-General, knighted, and one of London's richest Aldermen.

Sporadically the three, Buckingham, John and Wildman plotted and talked strategy, though the Duke's credit was far too low to finance his manifold schemes. And his fortune did not improve when he supported—in the Upper House—the first move to exclude the heir-apparent from the King's counsels and presence, a defiant challenge bringing himself perilously near impeachment.

The former royal favorite's defection to the Opposition had been duly noted across the Channel. The French King had always had a weakness for the flamboyant Buckingham —"the only gentleman in England," he had commented flatteringly on the latter's ambassadorial magnificence, doing much to win the Duke's Gallic sympathies. Louis saw in the present changed circumstances a means of infiltrating the House of Lords comparable to his pressure on the Commons. He had no scruples about supporting an opponent of that English monarch with whom he himself was still secretly linked!

Bucks had a ducal disdain for personal bribes, but was not averse to accepting funds for the Country Party, especially if money conferred leadership, outranking his ally and rival, Shaftesbury. He decided to ask Louis for a round thousand pounds annually—paid to the City Treasury, to be sure—to be distributed among City magnates to win their friendship for the King of France.

So complex were Anglo-French intrigues at the time that the mercurial Duke saw nothing paradoxical in a situation whereby the champion of English Protestants appealed to the French head of the Catholic Church to support the Whig Opposition whose avowed policy—at that moment—was war with France and exclusion of the Catholic heir-apparent!

To Paris in those sultry days of 1678 flitted the three conspirators, Bucks, Wildman and John, while fashionable London wondered what the Duke was up to. Barillon, the French Ambassador there, who had encouraged the *démarche*, begged him to make his journey openly. But it pleased Buckingham to go incognito, play a hush-hush role, pretend he was "busy with his wenches," and, instead of lording it at Versailles or Fontainebleau live modestly with his confidant, Sir Ellis Leighton, or in Picardy at the place Monsieur Gourville, Prince Condé's Intendant, placed at John's disposal.[1]

Negotiations for the money were tedious, protracted and in the end unsuccessful.[2] Louis found the masquerade little to his liking and, when a general pacification of the Continent began, his interest lagged still further.

Somewhat crestfallen, in mid-September the trio returned to London, where their escapade was quickly forgotten in the furor over the Popish Plot. Buckingham retired again to Cliveden, there to fête King Charles's French mistress, while John did a little courting on his own.

Women played a minor role in his life, casual affairs seemed to satisfy a nature as furiously energetic as his. Three women only had ever held his interest for long, but their qualities reveal something of his own, for each was a creature of spirited distinction: Deborah, his wife, now divorced; Dorothea Gotherson, preacher and author whom only just recently he had been squiring around London; and the last who attracted him, Lady "Constantia" Vane, staunch Republican partisan and widow of that Sir Harry who more than any single man, perhaps, brought down Charles I and perished on the scaffold for his pains (1662). Vane it was whom John, as a little boy in London, quite possibly had heard haranguing Guildhall crowds, little dreaming that the speaker's widow would one day be captivated by himself. But the lady, still in her prime, with a shrewd political head on her shoulders, indulged in romantic fancies about the dashing John. He bore his forty-six years lightly with the slim grace he kept right to the end. She declared "the sight of him fed her soul," the merest glimpse "but once a week" was strangely satisfying.

They wrote each other in high-flown terms, using classical pseudonyms in the current literary fashion. She was his everfaithful "Constantia," he, her "Artaban"—mere mortal to others but later revealed to her as Prince. She dated her letters from "Suspendance" a mythical country retreat, and he responded with poems, many the graceful competent verses which every proper gentleman of the age could pen at will, but a few marked with real feeling and definite poetic quality. He did not, of course, overlook the advantages of such a relationship. But fortune-hunting was quite respectable in the seventeenth century, no marriage was ever contracted without lengthy talk of settlements. The greatest love-match of the age, that of Sir William Temple and the vivacious Dorothy Osborne, was postponed seven mortal years simply because each family considered the other too little endowed with worldly goods.

The impecunious John began dreaming of independence, with means to enter public life, get even with his slanderers, fulfill personal ambitions instead of living the hand-to-mouth existence his current jobs imposed. Fashionable clothes tempted him, he sported a fur muff, mingled with rake-hell poets and pamphleteers in the political clubs. Alternately he provoked, then seemed to repel his lady, as his poems to her wavered between ardent joys of the flesh and spiritual counsel.

Fundamentally, friendship between the two was based on a consuming interest in public affairs—no mean bond for a middle-aged pair. John, like any troubadour, thrilled his Constantia with news and political gossip, and poured out his heart concerning his likes and dislikes, real or imagined slights, the ever-haunting conviction that his honorably accomplished services went unrewarded. Evidently he broke a long silence when he returned from Paris, and from her country house came an answer. For all its stilted tones and classical allusions it gives a fair indication of her mellow worldly good sense and the way they felt about each other:[3]

Suspendance: Sept 25th, 1678
 I was very agreeably surprised last night with your most excellent lines, for as much a hermetess as I am, and lover of solitude, yet I am very sensible of your great act of charity, in giving me so pleasant an entertainment, and by that, almost restrained some growing fears that you had received some ill-impressions of Constantia as well as of others.
 Certainly, Sir, as dull as I am, I am not so lost to gratitude and insensible of all your favors nor so little capable of

judging persons as to mistake you, whatever others have done, whose faults I would excuse since the greatest part of the world judges without evidence and by appearances.

I confess your profound silence made me sometimes guess at the cause, yet find I was there mistaken till I found it in yourself. I cannot condemn your caution, were that person your enemy, which in no discourse with him could I ever find; nor does any speak less ill of the absent than he, nor of yourself in the least degree. This injustice to an old friend I must beg leave to affirm. What has passed between yourselves I know not, but I never discerned him your enemy, and I would fain be a peacemaker between you if you would permit it. If not, you two are not the only opposites I have a respect for which I can preserve without injury to either. My long experience in the world has taught me greater tasks than that.

Sir, I am extremely obliged for the particular informations you please to give me on public transactions. Certainly these Peace-Maker rumors in *Casa Corydon's Caban* and his fellow shepherds will be at a loss how to deal with Sylvander. . . . [These are cryptic allusions to tentative peace offers between the respective allies of Holland and France.]

I believe peace will be sought by the Emperor upon the death of the Duke of Munster . . . I thought the wind was turning and do expect a new face of things there. Sir, all your notices are extraordinary in their kind and have given me a more pleasant diversion since I left the Town; and you have made an effectual amends for your long silence in giving so large a pleasure, and yourself a trouble. None has the art of obliging as the Great Artaban [John himself] whenever he pleases. Time will do him great right in the minds of those who at present mistake him, but to them that know the grandeur of his mind and his true zeal for his country, they know what estimates to put upon all the hazards and fatigues he has put himself to, which I daresay he has, and will acquit himself with honor.

The news from Scotland . . . [etc., etc.]

I suppose the sitting of Parliament and the Cabal of the Capital will so wholly engross you that it were cruelty to you to invite you into the country. And you have not only destroyed my hopes of that, but of hearing from you, a pleasure I cannot quit without regret. I must confess your entertainments there more worthy of you and that active public soul of yours, than when discoursing with a poor solitary, who yet has no small concern for the country and what part is yet like to be acted upon the stage of it. If you have anything *di nuova* which you care to commit to paper, if but two or three words, you may please put it in the characters of the alphabet, for I am a little curious, at this juncture, to know how things are. But if this be too much for me I will excuse you when you have assured me you had no particular dissatisfaction; or if you have, what it is, for that is the honest way to preserve friendship, and not so to do as La! Dor!, take offence, and never tell what!

My great innocency and certain knowledge of the true respect and esteem I have ever had for Artaban makes me enlarge on this matter that nothing but a clear understanding may remain between him and

Your most humble and faithful servant,

Constantia.

BIBLIOGRAPHICAL NOTES

1. Longleat MS., Cov. Pap., XI, f 506.
2. Aff. Etran. Sept., 1678, No. 130, f 25; No. 131, f 77.
3. Rawl. MSS., A 176, f 107, r, v.

CHAPTER XXXIX

THE PLOT THICKENS

"If old Nick Machivel . . . were charged to invent a
charm . . . to conjure . . . the people into . . . insan-
ity . . . would not he have said: Have you never a Magistrate that is popular and some way concerned about this
Discovery? If you have, take and kill him and expose the
body in a manner as may be most apt to stir the Passions
of the People, for if you can fill them with anger and
Terror all at once, any work, you would have, is done."
—Roger North, *Examen,* p. 198.

LADY VANE might beckon from her country seat but her
Artaban belonged definitely to the world of daily politics.
He was too much accustomed to being part of history in the
making to relish rural existence, unless, of course, it would
prove a springboard to greater prominence. Anyway he was
due to leave England again, on a mission.

There was no time for fond farewells since his departure
turned out to be dramatically precipitous, owing to the
tragedy which befell Sir Edmund Bury Godfrey, the distinguished magistrate before whom Titus Oates had sworn his
original narrative. The Popish Plot gathered a terrible mo-
mentum!

Missing, in mid-October, from his London home, Godfrey's body was found five days later in a ditch near Primrose
Hill, run through with his own sword (as if he had fallen
on it), but with dark marks on his throat and chest that suggested foul play rather than suicide. The latter was not ex-

cluded, however, though his relatives did all they could to hide evidence of it, a suicide's estate being forfeit to the Crown!

Sir Edmund's father had committed suicide, and Sir Edmund Bury Godfrey himself was a moody neurotic creature known to have brooded fearfully over his own unconscionable delay in reporting Oates' confession. During those fateful weeks, he had, moreover learned from Coleman that the Jesuit meeting which Oates attended—the so-called Great Consult, reputedly held in the White Horse Tavern—had, in reality, taken place at Somerset House in the apartments of the Duke of York himself! Such a damning fact, were it known, would be grounds for impeaching the heir-apparent. And the honest magistrate had groaned in spirit under the burden of his knowledge.

Did he kill himself to end his predicament? Contemporary medical evidence points to this, no matter what politicians said.[1] Or did the Papists murder him to shut his mouth? Whatever caused his mysterious death—and at least twelve different theories have been advanced during the last two hundred and eighty years—Shaftesbury seized upon it to whip up public frenzy against the Jesuits. Godfrey's funeral was staged as a huge Protestant Manifestation. The corpse was paraded through the London streets and lay in state while the City went wild (under skillful mob-management) and the violent death was hailed as proof positive that all Titus Oates' horrendous predictions would every one be carried out. Almost overnight the unfrocked clergyman became the country's benefactor, arousing England from its sleep to an awareness of dangers in its midst. Honors were showered upon him, he was lodged sumptuously at the King's expense in Whitehall, was rewarded with money, regarded with awe. Admiring crowds surrounded him whenever he appeared in public; his highly sensational sermons drew record attendance when he preached on Sundays; his merest hint of accusation was fatal.

The London jails became jammed with men of every condition, entirely unprepared to meet his wholesale charges; forced to face packed juries before judges who did not attempt to be impartial; threatened by howling mobs who would undoubtedly have stormed the prison and lynched the victims, had they been acquitted.

Nearly thirty thousand Papists, or suspected Papists, were driven from home and employment by a decree banishing them ten miles from London. Teachers were investigated and harried; many stood mum in court refusing to incriminate themselves. National hysteria reached unprecedented heights. Trained bands and militia patrolled the streets against possible attacks by "Popish cavalry," cannon were placed before public buildings, ladies of fashion carried pistols in their muffs, men wore quilted "silk armour" and flourished "Protestant flails" when they walked abroad. Many of the wildest rumors that kept London's nerves on edge originated in the Green Ribbon Club which met at the King's Head Tavern overlooking Temple Bar, and which was headquarters of the Opposition.

Just two days before Godfrey's body was discovered, John Scott, who was preparing for his mission to France, left London very suddenly. By the grapevine he had heard he was wanted and was to be "clapped up and starved."[2]

This was a moment when no man stayed to investigate a rumor; if he could get away he did. Abandoning his leisurely travel arrangements John fled, telling his Cannon Street landlord he would be gone a month, but, curiously enough, returning the next day to impress upon him that should Major Wildman or Mr. Wentworth M.P. call, he was to say that John would be back in three or four days.

He did not know that it was the Jesuit Coniers, "squinting in both eyes," who was being searched for in the City—John's sudden flight merely attracted attention to himself. And the misunderstanding was further complicated by the fact that yet once again he had been mistaken for William Scott "son of the regicide," that convicted conspirator whom a Government agent, Colonel Blood, had just reported as "contriving an assassination."³ Though all this only came out later, the rumor was sufficiently disturbing to affect John's behaviour. He arrived in Gravesend, his horse all in a lather and he himself somewhat wild-eyed. A simple-minded local butter merchant took him at first for a highwayman in his great light-colored periwig and cloth coat with silver lace on it.⁴

He stabled his horse—a fine black creature with a good saddle holsters and pistol—with a certain John Skelton who sold drinks at the Gravesend Fair. There John ate supper and afterward, since he had departed in such a hurry that he had no greatcoat with him, went to the Fair and bought one, for it was a wet night.

The salesman, by an odd coincidence, was a man who usually worked in London, at an inn in Cannon Street, and he claimed to recognize his purchaser by sight, declaring that it was a Mr. Godfrey.

Since all England was agog with tales of escaping Jesuits, John's harried actions began to attract attention, and a junior member of the Clerk of Passage decided to have him watched, confident that he could not possibly get away since no outward bound ship could leave Gravesend unless searched and cleared by a port official.

After dinner John visited a certain Cresswell, one of the Searchers he had known from his British Agent days; and shortly thereafter he was noticed at the local *King's Head* inquiring for the master of the *Assistance*, due to sail next day for Portugal.

Sure now of his plans, John stayed drinking late at Cresswell's, talked volubly of his Republican friend Sir Francis Rolle, a Whig member of Parliament, at whose country house he had recently been staying. A health was drunk to the prosperity of the nation and all responded noisily. Then John proposed another for the noble Duke of Buckingham. But when someone toasted confusion to those concerned in the

Plot, John (so it was related afterwards) was observed to dally with his glass and only lifted it to avoid a scene.

Next day, easily evading his shadower, Scott disappeared. He joined some sailors rowing out to the *Newcastle* but had no difficulty in bargaining to be put aboard the *Assistance*. By the time his flight was discovered the latter had sailed, cleared privately by the obliging Cresswell.

But John did not go to Portugal. Bad winds prevailed and he left the ship at Margate; most fortunately for him, since Samuel Pepys, alerted as to the mysterious traveller's movements, had sent orders that the *Assistance* be followed and searched, and the man arrested. The Admiralty Secretary now suspected that the Irish Jesuit Father Suiman (or Simmons) was fleeing the country under the alias of Godfrey (as he actually did.)[5] There was a hue and a cry after him. Pepys' men hounded the suspect from Gravesend; then rode pell mell to Deal, and, missing him there, tried Dover. Not a sign of him! John had escaped the dragnet. He coolly doubled back on his tracks. Finding he could get no direct passage, he took horse for Folkestone, hunted up a fishing vessel whose owner he knew, and set sail for Dieppe. In no time at all he was safely at his destination, Paris.

BIBLIOGRAPHICAL NOTES

1. L'Estrange, *Brief Hist. of the Times,* pp. 154-234.
2. Grey, *Parl. Deb.,* VII, 311.
3. SP. Dom. Car., II, 405, No. 91.
4. Rawl. MSS., A 175, ff 114-15.
5. Cobbett, *St. Trials,* VI, 1443-69.

CHAPTER XL

JOHN WARNS KING LOUIS; AND
RECEIVES A STRANGE CONFESSION

". . . French and Papists, two terms of art in every malicious mouth, completing revenge on whomsoever either
can be pinned, and considering the easy credulity of this
uncharitable age, it seldom fails to stick."
—Colonel Ed. Cooke to Ormonde, 29th March,
1679. *HMC Ormonde*, V, 7.

IT WAS A NEW John Scott who appeared in France at the end
of October, 1678. He lodged in the fashionable Faubourg St.
Germain, was in "good equipage" and rode in a fine coach,
and once again seemed "very full of guineas." He paid off
some of the money he owed John Joyne, though he was far
too busy to spend any time with his former landlord. He was
on a secret mission. Buckingham had sent him over with a
message to the King of France.

Paris refused to take the Popish Plot seriously. The Court
treated it *"en ridicule,"* laughed at England's fears, openly
sympathized with "poor Coleman" who was executed, it declared, simply because he was a Catholic. Even the British
Ambassador was piqued by the prevailing skepticism,* and
in such an atmosphere of scoffing distrust John readily understood why Louis found nothing disturbing in England's cur-

---

* Henry Savile, British Ambassador in Paris, wrote to Viscount Halifax of
"the horrid impertinence and obstinacy of all here as to their disbelief in our
Plot." (*HMC Ormonde*, V [1678], 459.)

rent anti-French attitude, and was consequently unwilling to part with any money to counteract it.

Buckingham's clandestine visit and subsequent efforts to obtain subsidies had failed because he had not realized how little the Plot impressed the French. It was exceedingly hard to bring home to Louis the full impact of England's belief in Jesuit intrigue. Something was evidently needed to convince him that their violent and determined conspiracy would spare not even the King of France himself.

Such was the background of John's mission. The Duke provided his agent with credentials and wrote personally to Louis of the awful matter John was about to reveal. "That Time presses more than can be readily conceived is shown by the new incident which the bearer, Mr. Scott, is charged to inform you. And I beseech him (Louis) most humbly to give faith to all he (John) will say from me. . . . Do me justice on this score for the love of God and rest convinced that I am with my whole heart and soul, your very humble, very obedient and much obliged servant, Buckingham."[1]

John also carried a letter from Buckingham to the French Secretary of State, the Marquis de Pomponne, who was to secure his audience with the King. "There are many things which it is necessary you should be acquainted with but which would be too wearisome to send you by letter. The bearer will inform you of them in detail, therefore I beg you to conduct the gentleman bearing this note to the person in the world whom I honor and love the most, and to believe me [etc., etc.].[2]

John went to Versailles, but if he was granted an audience, he had no opportunity for private conversation and a personal warning to the King. He was, in all likelihood, requested to put his message in writing, no easy matter for John. He could be eloquent in English, with a gift for a deft phrase and fine shades of meaning, but his French was far from perfect, and he must have had a hard time composing, on the spur of the moment, a missive of such import. But write it he did.

And duly filed among the Quai d'Orsay official documents is his recognizable script, a short letter on a double sheet of writing paper, unidiomatic, even somewhat ungrammatical, but conveying quite adequately, in its bald terms, a startling enough story:

"A person of quality and one of the best accredited and most intimate friends of the Duke of Buckingham and the Treasurer told the Duke of Buckingham that the Duke of York and the Treasurer had resolved to shift the Government of France into other hands. And that several persons had taken the Sacrament on it to assassinate Your Majesty. The Duke of Buckingham considered that it was his duty to communicate the matter to Your Most Christian Majesty and he begs Your Majesty to beware of strangers, and in particular of Irishmen."[3]

Whether the Duke actually believed this political gossip, it is impossible to tell. These were desperate times with men seeking desperate remedies. More than likely he was reporting a sensational rumor of the Plot's ramifications in order to frighten Louis and thereby spur his generosity toward the Opposition leaders.

But there certainly were links in the whole shady business between England and France. Shortly after John accomplished his mission he himself received a curious confirmation of sinister designs involving men on both sides of the Channel.

He had returned from Versailles to Paris and went to visit his friend the Earl of Berkshire. The old man was an invalid now, plainly nearing his end. He had missed his young companion; there had been no one to bring him news of the outside world, no gay gossip of the latest plays as in former times. Now when John appeared, the Earl was interested but little in these and talked in troubled whispers of the Plot. Evidently something was worrying him; he feared that innocent blood had been shed.

One night in March, 1679, feeling very low, he asked

John's advice about a doctor, and John told him he knew a good one, an Englishman from the London College of Physicians, but that he was no Catholic and surely the Earl's friends would not approve a man who was not only a strict Protestant but one who had publicly declared that the prosecution of English Roman Catholics was just. The Earl, who was plainly no bigot, said it mattered not; "such a point he would not dispute nor did he value any man the less for differing from him in judgment, therefore he did commit himself to the charge of Dr. Budgeon."[4] But it was too late. The doctor quickly recognized how serious was his patient's condition. Visiting John afterwards at his lodgings he told him that the Earl greatly desired to speak to him, adding that the old man in all probability could not last long. John went back to him next morning and when all the servants had been banished from the room and forbidden to return until he called, the Earl made the following confession:

"Colonel Scott, you are my friend; I must commit a secret to you; there has been a foolish and ill design carried on in England: I don't tell you the Roman Catholic religion is a foolish business for it is the faith I will die in, but 'tis the giddy madness of some of that religion I blame. I knew nothing on't till my Lord Arundel, Mr. Coleman and others told me the business could not miscarry, and that I should be looked upon as an ill man if I came not in in time, and truly I believed them. I was none of the contrivers, I was not consulted with till towards the latter end of the day, nor did I ever hear anything mentioned about killing the King; if I had, I would have discovered it; and so indeed I ought to have done what I did know, as well for the personal obligations I had to his Majesty, as that which my allegiance obliges me to, and every man to; for my Lord Bellasis is an ill man; he and others were accustomed to speak ill of the King, indeed very irreverently."[5]

John begged the old man to say who these "others" were, but he said he would not, though, in the way of old men, he ultimately did. "Good Colonel, ask me no questions; if I had known of approaching dangers to the King, I should have told him."

He then sighed and wept but presently continued:

"Friend, I see things will go as you will; for God's sake promise me you will find some way to tell the King every word I say, and that though some passages in letters of mine may look a little oddly, I would have run any hazard rather than have suffered any injury to have been done to His Majesty's person. 'Tis true I would have been glad to have seen all England Catholic, but not the way of some ill men. My Lord Stafford* was all along a moving agent, and was here in France about the business; the man of himself is not very malicious. My Lord Powis,* his covetousness drew him in further than he would have gone. I believe and hope there will hardly be found matter against them to take away their lives, but pray the King, from a poor dying man, not to have to do with any of those four Lords I have named, for they love not his person.

"My Lord Peeter* [Petre] has always had a great love and reverence for the King's person; 'tis true this last wife of his is foolishly governed by priests and influences him; but he was ever averse to all things of intrigue in this matter. I need not desire you to be secret, your own safety will oblige you."

Lord Cardigan and others then came to call, the servants were given orders to let them in, and, in their presence, the Earl repeated: "Pray don't forget the hundredth we spoke of. . . ."

Once more John was with him, accompanied by Dr. Budgeon, but the Earl was sinking fast. He had grown exceedingly deaf, and could only whisper: "Colonel, don't forget what I said to you, for God's sake."[6]

Yet instead of returning immediately to England, John

---

* These were the Catholic lords imprisoned in the Tower, for whose lives the Earl of Berkshire feared.

lingered in Paris, publicising the Popish Plot. His old acquaintance Dallais, a language teacher, helped him translate news of it which he received from London and circulated among prominent people and in the French press. There was nothing secret about this activity; the British Embassy seemed to know what he was doing. Ambassador Brisbane reported home, 1679, that "The Duke of Buckingham has his agent here, Colonel Scott";[7] while John, as was his wont, talked freely of everything he undertook and was volubly resentful about Samuel Pepys' attempt to arrest him as a Jesuit.

Much of his time was his own. France was no strange land to him, and he could pick up many broken threads. He went to Burgundy and Picardy to do a surveying job for the Prince of Condé. That gallant old warrior who had never forgotten the charming high-spirited English officer, paid him a thousand pounds for his pains.[8] Gourville, the prince's *Intendant*, reported that John was working on maps again, hoping to solicit the latter's aid in selling some to the Prince. John also looked up D'Alliez de la Tour, Colbert's *alter ego*. The gun-casting fiasco, was, after all, a thing of the past, John had regained his self-confidence and was ready to meet anyone. La Tour, however, was still grimly of the opinion that the Englishman had promised much more than he had ever accomplished.

The months slipped by; John was never idle. Sometimes he was seen in the company of Mr. Benson, the Earl of Shaftesbury's Paris agent, but more often he played a lone hand. It seemed almost as if he were marking time, waiting for something to happen.

*   *   *   *   *

However skeptical France might be about it, the Plot in England was going full blast. Investigations of Godfrey's murder overshadowed all else.

Titus Oates had expanded his original testimony. At the bar of the House of Commons and again before the Lords, he came forward with fresh "recollections" and accusations, brandishing aloft a list of new suspects each time he appeared, in tremendous pomp. Prisons throughout the country began filling with Catholics; scares and rumors poisoned public life. All Papists were barred from sitting in Parliament (the Duke of York, excepted) and "priest-codding" became a brutal popular sport with tough gangs hounding the unfortunate holy men from hiding place to hiding place.

Legislative business was practically at a standstill except in the investigating committee of the Upper House, presided over by Shaftesbury and Buckingham, who held hearings, sifted evidence, browbeat witnesses.

The aims of the Opposition had been immeasurably advanced by Godfrey's death. From that moment the Popish Plot "was rooted in the mind of the nation." When General Elections were finally called in 1679—the first in eighteen years—the King's political enemies swept the polls. This Whig landslide was due in part to skillful Party organization, but also to the unstinted use of innuendo—a whisper of Popery unseated the staunchest King's man.

The Duke of York's situation worsened ominously. Married to a foreign and Papist princess, stubbornly claiming leadership of the Catholic faction, he was regarded, by nine Englishmen out of ten, as the most dangerous man in the country. The politically sensitive Charles, noting the Commons' first tentative movement towards exclusion from the throne, ordered his brother to quit the country, temporarily, for fear of civil war. Huffily, James left for Flanders, but attacks against him did not cease. A circle was tightening around the heir-apparent, though his foes approached him obliquely at first, striking at his subordinates in the hope that the latter would incriminate him. His long term as Lord High Admiral brought the Admiralty Office under fire, always a safe move, anyway, for the Ministry was thoroughly unpopular and the Fleet's poor showing against the Dutch still rankled in the public mind.

Now Samuel Pepys had risen to power on the Duke's favor. As Admiralty Secretary and political protégé of James he began to realize how very vulnerable he was. True he had retained his parliamentary seat in the election, but his constituents seemed strangely suspicious. They circulated most damaging libels about the money he was supposed to have made in office, and revived an old charge of Popery against him, an accusation which but a few years previously he had formally and brilliantly refuted. But the political atmosphere in 1679 was such that no amount of oratory could wipe out so deadly an indictment.

Like all men of humble origin whose unremitting industry brought them to prominence, Pepys had accumulated a number of enemies; men who resented his power and self-important airs, who envied him his fine coach and his handsome Admiralty barge. Nor did his unfailing habit of assembling damning facts to rout his tormentors hinder their fixed determination to destroy him politically, and to take his job. For Pepys served not only the Navy. He was Treasurer of Tangier and during his years of office in this capacity carried on transactions of more than a million pounds sterling for this British overseas possession. In less honest hands than his such emoluments would furnish very rich pickings.

Already the Opposition had struck at him through his clerk, Atkins, accusing the lad of complicity in Godfrey's murder. The unfortunate wretch was hustled to Newgate prison, kept in chains for months, alternately bullied and wheedled by the Committee who tried to get him to denounce his master. But for Pepys' own undaunted efforts to defend the prisoner, Atkins would surely have perished.

Shaken by the near-tragedy and thoroughly apprehensive about himself, the little Secretary went back to his administrative vigilance, to build more ships for the King's Navy and to set about devising a system for disciplining British tars. He confided his fears to his intimate friends, for he felt himself slated to follow Coleman to the gallows. But he took consolation in his own cast-iron alibi, for during the very days that Godfrey had met his violent end, Pepys had been summoned to Newmarket by the King. As long as he enjoyed his monarch's confidence and Parliament was in session, Pepys believed he could weather the storm.

Then, on April 20th, an event occurred that was simply beyond his comprehension. The government fell. Neither civil war nor revolution provoked the change, but the King could no longer struggle against a hostile parliamentary majority backed by frenzied masses howling for Papist blood. Charles dismissed his Ministers and invited leaders of the Opposition to take their place, though he retained Pepys on the Admiralty Board. It was a constitutional experiment, ultimately to become the basis (and the glory) of British Party government, with its permanent Secretariat. But for Pepys it was sheer disaster. With Shaftesbury now President of the new Council, the Admiralty was delivered into the hands of those who had always been its bitterest critics. Within a week they appointed a special committee to inquire into the Miscarriages of the Navy.

And on that very day, April 28th, 1679, Colonel John Scott, acting on Shaftesbury's orders, landed in England.

BIBLIOGRAPHICAL NOTES

1. Aff., Etran., 17th Nov., 1678, CXXXI, f 183.
2. *Ibid.*, f 187.
3. *Ibid.*, f 186.
4. Longleat MS., Cov. Pap., XI, f 397.
5. *Ibid.*
6. *Ibid.*
7. *HMC. Round MSS.* (1679), p. 404.
8. Grey, *Parl. Deb.* (1678), VII, 311.

CHAPTER XLI

JOHN ACCUSES PEPYS

It is upon the Navy under the providence of God that the
safety, honor and welfare of this realm chiefly attend.
—*Articles of War,* Charles II.

JOHN STEPPED OFF a fishing smack at Folkestone, but the
arrest-warrant which Pepys had issued the previous October
for "Godfrey" was still in force, and the port authorities,
while according him kid-glove treatment, would not let him
proceed. He was on secret orders—hence his informal entry—
and he gave his name as John Johnson. But to the Dover
Commissioner, to whom he was sent for examination, he was
jovially frank. "My father's name was John and I am his son,"
he explained, telling who he really was and adding that he
had been recently commissioned by Prince Condé to survey
his Burgundian estates, and was now coming home to revisit
his native land. John was completely at ease, said he was a
soldier by profession and offered to take the oaths of supremacy, allegiance and the Test.[1] He was quite unruffled
when his trunks were opened and found to contain several
elaborate suits, worth hundreds of pounds; a footman's new
livery, as well as personal papers he had retrieved from
Joyne's lodgings, including many maps, among them one
handsomely fringed in blue silk.[2]

The Commissioner was baffled by his self-confidence, and
subsequently wrote the Secretary of State for instructions. No
sooner was John escorted to the Dover jail, than he called for

paper and pen and sent a letter to the Earl of Shaftesbury, who was now virtually the head of the government![3]

Shortly thereafter a mysterious rider, a Mr. Cavendish, arrived to inquire after him, and finding him in detention, seemed most uneasy and immediately rode away.

Prominent townsmen came to call on the prisoner: a Scott could hardly go unnoticed in Kent. They knew that this was no "wanted" Jesuit—"not squint-eyed at all," testified one observer indignantly, "a proper handsome person."[4] His visitors included many of the leading Quakers and other Nonconformists, attracted, doubtless, by his association with their idol the Duke of Buckingham, but brought there also in remembrance of ancient loyalties. For was it not the Quaker Mayor of Flushing, Elias Doughty, who, years ago, had helped John escape from another prison, where Governor Winthrop was holding him for having signed a truce with the Long Island Dutch? The Friends did not lightly forget such ties. They sat up drinking all night with him, talking of brave past days; and one of them supplied him with money for his needs.

Four days later the Secretary of State, Sir Henry Coventry, ordered his immediate release, and John set out for London.

His first task was to unfold to the King and to the investigating Committee the Earl of Berkshire's confession. He told the story of the old man's last words and his remorse at not having spoken sooner. But John's statement was little to the Committee's taste. Its members were far less interested in establishing sober confirmation of conspiracy than in dramatizing and exploiting its sensational aspects, in order to widen the breach between the Crown and the people. Titus Oates' trump card was the King's assassination by Jesuits. Berkshire never mentioned the Order; and his words practically contradicted this all-imposing detail. John told his story simply, almost casually;[5] it lacked all the lurid particulars with which other witnesses—many of them professional informers—spiced their concoctions, when they appeared before the Committee to point an accusing finger at some chosen victim.

Yet there was no gainsaying his facts. At the time John gave his evidence, Berkshire's correspondence with Coleman was not publicly known; and Coleman himself was dead. The incriminating letters, read during his trial, contained nothing from Berkshire. The only other persons who could have known of the Earl's correspondence were those officials now holding all the letters—a source to which John had no access. Certain passages in the writings must, indeed, have looked "a little oddly" (as the Earl put it) to the investigators, and certainly contained matter technically treasonable. But not one of them suggested any personal danger to the King. They tended rather to support the contention, confirmed in other quarters as well, but paradoxically not stressed by the Opposition, that there was indeed a fragment of truth in the Popish Plot.*

Oates must have picked up hints of the *real* Popish Plot—the Secret Treaty of Dover—visiting Jesuit seminaries in Flanders and Spain, although his vast superstructure of lies involving fire and bloody murder was fashioned to stun an irresolute public greedy for horrors. And to serve his own personal ends of course, for it had not escaped the cunning impoverished Oates that denouncing Papists was a very profitable business. Only three years previously a young French

---

* "The truth is, that after searching over every man's sack of papers (to a degree that we are all harassed) there is but little found to corroborate Mr. Oates' assertion as to the point of killing. But Mr. Coleman's papers . . . do notoriously explain his contrivances with France and Rome to extirpate heresy, route all Parliaments and establish the Catholic cause." (Sir Robert Southwell to James Duke of Ormonde. *H. M. C., Ormonde* IV, 458-9, Oct. 15th, 1678.)

The King told Reresby that though he did not believe a word of the Plot, or that there was any design on his life, it was plain from Coleman's letters that there had been a design to introduce Popery. (Reresby, *Memoirs*, p. 23-25th, Oct., 1678.) Coming from one who signed the secret Treaty of Dover promising to introduce Roman Catholicism, this was quite an admission!

See also Sir Edmund Bury Godfrey's statement that "there would not be bloodshed or cutting of throats, but there would be an alteration of government." *H. M. C. House of Lords* (1678-88), p. 48.

Jesuit—wanted for forgery in Paris—escaped to London and preached a hot sermon in the French Protestant Church at the Savoy, inveighing against Papist error. His congregation accepted his apostasy with joy and fat donations. For a while he lived in princely style, but the young man was unskilled in lying. Avid to wring more money with further fabrications, he was soon trapped in a web of self-contradiction, and ignominiously thrown out of the country.

Titus, on the contrary, was one of the most accomplished liars of the century. Caught repeatedly in flagrant untruth, he could recover his equanimity and launch upon a flood of plausible detail that confounded his listeners and sent victim after victim to the gallows and the quartering-block. London mobs, like tigers, licked their lips at the obscenity of these ghastly executions, applauding alike the spectacle of castration and disembowelling, and the zeal of those who vaunted that they were saving England from political peril and the domination of Rome.

Oates was their Saviour—he dressed like a Bishop and was dated for months ahead for all the public City dinners given in his honor. Parliament made the Duke of Monmouth responsible for his safety; the Lord Chamberlain for his lodgings, the Lord High Treasurer for his diet and necessaries. Three servants were always at his beck and call; he walked abroad with a guard of honor; the House of Lords publicly thanked him, the Archbishop of Canterbury recommended his promotion in the Church. Whispering and gesticulating at his side was always his tame counsel, Aron Smith —an agile lawyer, devastatingly inventive but of dubious character.

In an atmosphere of such hysterical excess John's moderation precluded further testimony before the Committee, though he was slated to be Crown witness when the findings of the Navy were reported to Commons.

Samuel Pepys had meanwhile passed an excruciating three weeks justifying to the new Council his every act in office.

Armed with his books of minute entries he was able to stand off much of the searching criticism, though it was impossible to satisfy such implacable probing. Overwrought and exhausted, he was ready to resign from the Board in the face of concerted enemies.*

The Opposition Lords had no intention of permitting such an easy exit. William Harbord, powerful member of Thetford (and he who most coveted Pepys' job), rose before the packed benches, and outlined the Secretary's crimes: popery, piracy, felony and treason.

He was sorry, said the suave Harbord, to accuse a man he liked well, but Pepys was a secret Papist; he had trafficked in privateers, procuring a royal grant to the sloop *Hunter* for Sir Anthony Deane and his brother-in-law Balty St. Michel; and, worst of all, had sent to France, by that same Anthony Deane, naval secrets and confidential maps which he had offered to the French King for a vast sum . . . To confirm these horrid charges, Harbord said he would bring a witness to the stand. And before the bar of the House of Commons, he ushered in Colonel John Scott, a splendid figure in satin and silver lace.

In such a setting John was in his element; a captive audience and a cause to plead! He began by informing the Committee that he had had the opportunity of knowing several great men belonging to the French Navy, and by their death he was discharged from obligations of secrecy. He stated "that Monsieur Pélissary, Treasurer-General of the French King's Navy showed him several Draughts of Models of Ships (sent him from England); the Government of the Admiralty; the Number of Ships; the Strength and Condition of the Navy; Methods of Sea-fights, collected from the best Sea-commanders; the Satisfaction of the Seamen, those bold fools who for money will do anything; Maps of Sands and Soundings of

---

* ". . . and Mr. Pepys, however prepared, must certainly be destroyed." Sir R. Southwell to the Duke of Ormonde, April 28th, 1679. *H. M. C. Ormonde* IV, 506.

the Medway, and the Kent shore; the Isle of Wight; Remarks upon the present condition of Plymouth; the Plans of Sheerness and Tilbury. He who brought the Yachts for the Canal of Versailles was Captain Deane who could give a further account. All these papers were signed by Pepys.* M. Pélissary had orders to use Captain Deane with great kindness. Pepys would not part with these things but for so good an end as forty thousand pounds. But there is a mystery in this, more than I dare speak of,"⁶ added John.

Pepys sprang to his feet, heatedly, full of denials. Never had he been a Papist; and there had never been hearings at the Admiralty concerning the *Hunter*. "I know neither the ship nor share in her, nor the cause there depending. As for the charge of Captain Scott—I know neither his name nor quality, where is his abode or dependencies? He is an utter stranger. This House made not the Committee a Secret Committee. I overheard a Gentleman say 'Is not this Colonel Scott, he that gave information at the last Parliament?' I know not.

"The story is this, There was an information about the breaking out of the Plot from an officer at Gravesend—that a stranger came thither on Saturday night and walked about Sunday, and would have hired a boat to carry him away anywhere. He set up his horse without the town. (I will do nothing with malignity.) This man made his escape before he could be seized; he was pursued to Deal and to Dover; this man could not get passage directly but goes to Sandwich and so to Rye under the name of Godfrey." (Pepys had evidently had a time following John's traces.) "The House commanded me to seek after him. The Lord Mayor found out his lodgings and found papers of ill-importance which were de-

---

* The piracy charge was for fitting out a sloop, the *Hunter*, out of His Majesty's stores in the year 1673, making her free of the French ports, procuring her a French Commission in order to cruise on the Dutch; she also made a prize of a free English ship called the *Catherine of London* which, though English, the checkmaster of Portsmouth sent to Paris to get condemned.

livered to the Speaker and are now in the Secret Committee's hands. I would not have troubled you with this story without some reflection. If the same be true of this gentleman (Scott) you will find that these papers, found in his lodgings, *were just such papers as he accuses me of.* What construction you will make of it I will leave to you. Now, whether Scott does this to quit scores with me I do not know, but this I am sure of, for writing into France, to the Ambassador, or any French Minister, or for communicating any of these weighty secrets, it is out of my province, for the fashions of ships, etc., are entirely out of my watch. In these Papers you will find all Representations, as reported from the Navy Officers to the House, word for word, and the Ordnance transcribed. He tells you, 'That the Papers in France etc. were signed by me.' Tis Scott's 'Yea, by Report'; tis my 'No before God Almighty.' "[7] (Italics added.)

The House listened in silence. The little Secretary was an emphatic speaker, but there were too many present, intent on his downfall, to be impressed by his oratory. In vain Pepys rebutted the testimony of his butler, James, called as witness of his Popish leanings; it availed him nothing. There were members who mocked his misfortunes sneering that even Pepys' servants, who could best observe his behavior, supported the Popery charge.

Anthony Deane spoke equally heatedly in his own defense, denying all but the charge concerning the *Hunter.* Curiously enough, he admitted he had had an eighth share in her, but the captain had swindled him, he received not a penny of profit, and he seemed to think that this exonerated him from any suggestion of piracy. As to Scott's other accusations, never had he conversed directly with a single Frenchman during his whole visit to France. His son had been with him every minute, to act as his interpreter, for he himself spoke not one word of the language, he was dependent upon his boy. And he wept at the thought of his innocent child . . . of all his twelve innocent babes. But the House was unmoved by the spectacle—Party discipline triumphed over any personal qualms.

Sir Joseph Williamson rose to add one detail: "I remember one thing that Deane forgets—there was a time when the French sent the Marquis de Seigneley who took his way— affectedly out of his way by Portsmouth. I remember Deane laid a counterplot against the Marquis to prevent any information he could get of the Navy." But Mr. Harbord would listen to no such defence . . . the Duke of York himself had laid down his post of Lord High Admiral, by act of Parliament yet these men, he declared . . . Pepys and Deane . . . are directed by the Duke to put the Navy into Papists' hands. The ships are riddled with Popery. . . ."

This was an echo of that month-old terrible threat! "I will prove Popery in the Fleet at the Bar!"

Sir Henry Coventry rose to speak in Scott's favor and to wipe out the counter-accusation which Pepys had just made against him, explaining the misunderstanding which had caused that former inquiry and ignominious arrest. "It was Conyers the Jesuit who was searched for in the City," he said, describing the comedy of errors. Mr. Harbord added his word of Scott's defence, too, quoting Williamson, who knew John better than any present.

"He is the ablest man in England for a West India voyage . . . Scott has a testimonial from the great de Witt, he commanded eight regiments of Foot for the relief of Flanders. A great man in England told me that Scott was attempted to be corrupted to bear false witness against him. And Scott detested it." (For John's high-principled action in Flanders was remembered by the well-informed.) "Though the matter is not treason against Pepys, yet it is felony."[8]

And felony the House believed it to be. Pepys and Deane were led away and committed to the Tower.

That night cheering crowds assembled around the Green Ribbon Club and there were triumphant bonfires and wild jubilation.

BIBLIOGRAPHICAL NOTES

1. Longleat MS., Cov. Pap., XI, ff 393-96.
2. Rawl. MSS., A 188, f 137.
3. Longleat MS., *op. cit.*
4. Rawl. MSS., A 138, f 114.
5. Pollock, *The Popish Plot,* p. 63.
6. Grey, *Parl. Deb.,* VII, 303-04 (appendix 311).
7. *Ibid.,* 305-07.
8. *Ibid.,* 311.

CHAPTER XLII

COUNTER ATTACK

"In probability of a war 'tis best to begin."
—Duke of Buckingham,
Commonplace Book.

OVERWHELMED BY THEIR HORRIBLE SITUATION Samuel Pepys and Sir Anthony Deane sank down in their Tower prison quarters. For four days they lay crushed and speechless.

The Opposition had been devilishly clever in preparing its case to entrap the man who had dared, many times, to bypass parliamentary sanctions when he considered that these blocked his efforts to build more ships.

The taint of Popery, of course, Pepys knew clung to him from his Catholic friends, beginning with the Duke of York himself: it was guilt by association. But treachery to his beloved Navy! How could a man whose lifework had been creating England's sea defenses face such a charge?

Yet innocent as Pepys believed himself to be, he could well see how damningly facts could be twisted against him. He must have known, only too well, how much material the Admiralty had furnished France during the two-year alliance, 1672-74, when a British Admiral commanded the combined Fleets. Even at the time these revelations had aroused the greatest apprehensions at the Admiralty. But the King, however grave his own misgivings in this period of shifting alliances, was captive of that secret Treaty of Dover. Salve his conscience as he might with the thought that he had no intention of keeping its terms, yet certain concessions Louis could exact of him. And did.

There were all the Duke of York's most explicit instructions (and when he resigned, 1673, those of Prince Rupert) concerning the union of the two Navies, with eighteen pages of rules and diagrams of the fighting order—that close-hauled five-mile array: England's "wooden walls"—and exact position of all ships of the line; the discipline (*gouvernance*) to be observed both night and day; the methods of attack, etc., secrets no nation gives away lightly unless bound to another by the closest ties. All these documents (now in the Paris *Archives Nationales*)[1] John might very well have seen, for in his expanded notarized testimony his descriptions tally with the original French.

In addition to these memoranda there were the related geographic details to which that Dutch agent, in 1672, had already referred: "the secrets of their coasts, their sands, their banks, their avenues of approach"[2] the kingdom's very strength and weakness, as he gloatingly related, that the English had had to make known to the French. Was this all down in black and white, too? Such matters were not Pepys' department, but he must have quailed as he thought of the record. When a former ally becomes an enemy—and England was practically at war with France in 1678—does not such information look like treason? In the fevered climate of those days it could very well be made to.

Yet how could the Secretary defend himself, and disclaim any part of this without implicating the Crown?

Samuel Pepys was being framed by the Opposition. Miscarriages of the Navy there might well have been, but prime target in this attack was the popish heir-apparent. By bringing the Admiralty Secretary within the shadow of the gallows his adversaries hoped that he would "fetch himself off" by incriminating the Duke of York.

Pepys did not scare easily, but he had always demonstrated a marked political insensitivity. His mind was a rich store of the multifarious technical details that made him the greatest naval administrator England had seen, but broad lines of national policy were beyond the compass of his vision. He reacted to the present dilemma as though it were a purely personal challenge: John Scott's wicked plot to revenge his attempted arrest!

But Scott himself, was he perfectly convinced that the papers he had seen had been *secretly* conveyed to France? "There is a mystery about this," he had testified, both before the House and in his subsequent sworn affidavit. "More I dare not say." Had he dared say more would not his evidence, too, have thrown suspicion on the King? No one has ever explained this point. Who actually was responsible for the telltale documents? It remains as much a mystery today as John confessed it to be.

In the House of Commons, John was no docile witness. He had not slanted his Berkshire communication to fit the Investigating Committee's requirements, and even now as Crown witness for this most important issue he would not suppress an honest doubt that all was not clear as to how those papers came to Pélissary's hands. The Lord High Admiral's orders were obviously official, but we do not know what else John saw. French Ministers are permitted to keep and dispose of their papers (when they quit their posts) and the Paris Archives are not complete.

Had there been more than the authorized communications? Had Deane taken over anything extra from the Navy files, or made verbal communications? He could well have argued that since France already had so much, a little more could not matter, relations between the two countries were so very cordial in 1675. Then Louis, too, was universally regarded as the fountainhead of European cash. Was it possible that the sturdy shipbuilder had tried to make a little on the side when he accompanied the miniature ships to Versailles? One viewed such conduct more or less indulgently in those times, and he certainly would not be the first to have taken French money.

All this and more must have occurred to Pepys as he looked long and questioningly at his fellow prisoner.

Deane had admitted the piracy charge; and even Pepys himself may have felt a little uneasy on that score, though his hands were clean in the matter of the *Hunter*.*

But secret information was another matter. Deane had indignantly countered the accusation by swearing that he could not possibly have had intelligence with the French since he spoke not a word of the language and his son who interpreted for him never left his side. Could a father betray in the presence of his child?! But here again, the Paris documents tell another story. There are so many entries about interpreters for the English captain that it looks as if indeed Deane had, as John's testimony averred, had a great many "explanations" to make.[3]

Colbert's directive to Monsieur Vauvre† is precise on this point: "I heartily approve of all that you have done concerning Mr. Deane. I will give him an interpreter so that his son will not be obliged always to be with him, I will let him have M. Danois,‡ until I come back to Paris, after which I shall see if it will be necessary to put some other man with him."[4]

Intendant Arnoul reported to Colbert that "Mr. Deane will be very happy to have an interpreter with him so that his son does not always have to be with him."[5] Obviously Deane was not telling the truth by insisting the lad never left his side.

The gifted ship builder had been overwhelmed by his

---

* During the Second Dutch War of 1666-67, Pepys became joint owner, (with Admirals Penn and Batten) of the *Flying Greyhound,* granted them by the amiable Charles II, and referred to (in his Diary, Mar. 14, 1666/67) as "our privateer." (VI, p. 223) Pepys was concerned lest news of this irregularity leak, especially as certain men with "orders under our hands," as he wrote, demanded payment for sailing her. "The thing upon recollection, I believe, is true and do hope no great matter can be made of it, but yet I would be glad to have my name out of it, *which I shall labor to do;* in the meantime it weighs as a new trouble on my mind." Wheatley *Diary* VII, 347.

† Commissaire-Géneral of the Marine at Le Havre.

‡ Secretary of the *Intendant* of the Marine at Le Havre.

friendly reception in France, in 1675; courtesies and presents
were showered on him[6] bringing to a triumphant conclusion
his two years' labors building the yachts, aided by French
sculptors and painters, and paid more money than he had ever
seen before. The two little ships were Charles' "gift" to his
royal cousin, but it was Louis who bore the cost. Thirteen
thousand pounds Deane had asked and received for the Commission;[7] was it unpardonable to think that such a golden
source might provide even more?

Why, if Deane was innocent, did he lie about his interpreters? Was he afraid that they might be subpoenaed to tell
what they knew of his "explanations"?

Had Pepys any inkling of his colleague's possible indiscre-
tion; could he have guessed what might creditably have trans-
pired in Paris? His capacity for acquiring gossip was phe-
nomenal, however garbled the facts might sometimes be.

Deane had surely told him about that memorable dinner
with Pélissary, where, walking in the garden beforehand, his
host had informed him that doubtless he would be delighted
to know that a fellow-countryman was joining them. On
hearing that this was none other than John Scott, Deane was
appalled. On no account did he wish Scott to see him there;
he had had positive orders about this. So Pélissary, astonished,
but obviously most anxious to hear what Deane had come to
"explain," prevented the encounter by having John served
dinner privately in another part of the château.

Was this the reason that Pepys had promised to help John
Scott get a naval command, back in 1677—to insure his silence
about that disturbing contretemps? A hazardous undertaking,
but the Secretary was quixotic enough to risk anything for the
sake of his King and Navy.

Only John had not risen to the bait. "You don't know what
I know," he had answered those who marvelled at his refusing
such good services. And Pepys in his grim confinement, must
have remembered, in agony surely, his rash message sent to

John's Houndsditch lodgings, by Coniers* of all people! What would the Opposition make of that?

For four days Samuel Pepys was crushed and helpless; at a loss as never before. Then his resolute spirit asserted itself. He would carry the offensive into his enemies' territory. He would destroy their prime witness. He would show that Scott "was a scandalous person not to be believed."[8] And more. He would discover evidence to back up his own wild counter-accusation that Scott himself, not Pepys, was the traitor.

In a burst of energy he seized pen and paper, writing to everyone he could think of at home and on the Continent, carrying into his private affairs the meticulous technique he had devised for Admiralty administration. A spate of letters poured out of the Tower, conveyed and posted by a friend. While Deane still lay in silent consternation, Pepys was his old industrious self, building up the biggest case of his life.

"What do you know of the ill practices of John Scott?" was his standard inquiry, supplemented with suggestions along the lines of reply he needed.

The British Embassy in Paris was driven frantic by the avalanche of mail both to the ambassador and to Brisbane, the Naval Attaché. Pepys listed every detail of John's accusation of himself and, in counter-accusation, asked about John's "ill-usage of the States-General"; demanded to know about "his more private negotiations with France; whether he did sell to the King of France, or to Prince Condé maps and papers relating to the world in general as well as England in particular"; etc., etc. For good measure he added that although Scott was "wholly a stranger to him," yet he was "so well known to others as to give me little fears of having the credit of my evidence outweigh his. I hope to lay at his door the very crimes he accuses me of."[9] (He probably hoped, too, that by flatly denying, at the very outset, all knowledge of

* Oct. 30, 1679 George Coniers apprehended as guilty of the plot. Luttrell *Brief Relation*, 1, 36.

John that his own embarrassing offer of help would never be known.)

Fat, good-natured, indolent Ambassador Savile, goaded into action by these long epistles, with Pepys' anguished postscript that his very life was at stake, finally took time to reply that "Scott is a fellow who I thank God is not of my acquaintance." Then, drawing upon his correspondent's lurid insinuations, added, "but he is of so despicable a vile reputation in all places where he has lived that a real criminal would be fortunate to suffer by his means." A statement which would not be too helpful before the Investigating Committee.

Brisbane replied that he, too, did not know John personally though wrote at length about his work. (It was, of course on account of John's maps that Pepys hoped to pin on him the proof of treason.) But Brisbane's letters were disappointingly negative. He said that he had indeed heard that John furnished some maps of English and French ports to Prince Condé but that he, Brisbane, did not think they were original, but copies of old English or Dutch prints, "to be bought cheap and publicly allowed. . . . [His] maps of large scale, variety of colors and ornaments of designing . . . might pass upon Prince Condé's *seasmanship* for all his vast and unparalleled abilities in all other things."[10] For evidently Brisbane seemed to consider that there might be lovely pictorial charts, not necessarily of strategic value, nor even very accurate. (Italics added.)

"Someone else told me about Colonel Scott's work," wrote Brisbane, in a second letter. "Lord Arlington's brother and some others had been examining an unfinished map of the English and French coast, and Arlington said Scott was asking for some printed books to copy the part not yet drawn. He agrees with me that Colonel Scott did perform the part of copyist. . . . except we think the ornamenting and enlarging the scale of a map to be a piece of great art. Neither of these gentlemen could say he (Scott) expressed any intention of giving that map to the French; it rather seems he designed to tempt *their own* curiosities than to impart any worse designs to them."[11] (Italics added.)

Brisbane was entirely noncommittal and was obviously irked by the insistent demands that he approach Colbert and Seigneley and get from them "public statements" exonerating the Tower prisoners. In vain he pointed out that no Englishman could possibly believe the testimony of French Catholics. Pepys simply refused to be put off with excuses. And at last Brisbane, profiting by a casual meeting with the supercilious Seigneley brought up the embarrassing matter of Pepys' alleged correspondence with him, assuring the French minister that he would not have done so had he imagined it would "cause the least pain," since he was convinced that the "answer would prove easy to him and satisfactory to me," as he wrote Pepys.[12]

It was anything but satisfactory to Samuel Pepys. The answer must have tended to confirm all his own tormenting memories. For Seigneley told Brisbane he had never had any manner of correspondence with Pepys either good or bad "since the time he [Seigneley] had been sent to England to regulate the common affairs of the Fleets [1671]" and that Pepys "did *then communicate the number and strength of the ships to which the French squadron was to join.*"[13] (Italics added.)

Which information was exactly what Pepys must have feared the Opposition was using to base its case against him.

It was even more difficult to get anything out of Colbert. Pepys had enlisted the help of his brother-in-law, Balty St. Michel, sending him across the Channel to gather whatever evidence he could. Brisbane was outraged when this young man, accused as he was of piracy, turned up at the Embassy expecting introductions to the French First Minister![14]

Though the egregious Balty got to Colbert, the great man did not deign to answer him, and if he replied to Pepys, his letter is not with all the others preserved in the Rawlinson

collection. But after the visit he sent somewhat startling instructions to Barillon, his Ambassador in London.

Referring to Balty's request that he "justify the innocence"
of the two men accused by Scott, Colbert asked Barillon if
Deane "is that same man who brought over the yachts for
King Louis, and in that case, tell him that when he gets out
of prison . . . if he wishes to come over to France [*passer
en France*] he will be very well treated."[15] A curiously
ambiguous offer, for the Opposition might easily construe
this as a reward for past services to the French.

Undaunted by his initial lack of success, Pepys redoubled
his efforts. Letters flew all over the Continent, suggesting
avenues of crime to explore: to James Houblon, a Whig
merchant friend in Amsterdam requesting "confirmation" of
John's "counterfeiting a deed or some kind of forgery,"[16]
appeals to Sir John Werden, the Duke of York's secretary in
Brussels, concerning John's "infamy and being hung in
effigy,"[17] to Captain Gunman, in Rotterdam, for news as to
Colonel Scott's "debts, cheats and other villainies, public or
private";[18] even to strangers he addressed urgent requests
and would not be rebuffed. Three letters went to Mr. Grey de
Stamford, the Earl of Berkshire's heir, who replied curtly, at
last, that he had indeed seen the map with a blue silk fringe;
that the Earl his uncle had known John a very long time and
that John visited him very often; but that he (Stamford) had
met John only twice.[19] This was of no assistance whatever to
the prisoners in the Tower.

These first replies indeed furnished nothing of an incriminating nature. The writers assured Pepys of their full sympathy, their dismay at his plight, they promised to help Balty
to the best of their ability. But evidence, such as Pepys
wanted, there seemed none.

Balty labored in Paris, costing his brother-in-law hundreds
of pounds. It was the first time he had ever been abroad on
an expense account and the experience went to his head. He
rashly spoke of engaging a French tutor for his small son

. . . a suggestion which threw the economy-minded Pepys into a fury of apprehension. As to Scott's business, Balty admitted "he could find little or nothing in the matter."[20]

Then one day in June his watch stopped and he was directed to a small shop off the *rue de la Monnaie*. Talking garrulously about his affairs to the watchmaker, he learned, to his unconcealed amazement and delight that the man not only knew John personally but that John had actually lived in his house for nearly two years, and had left—"without paying all his rent," added the watchmaker, whose observant eye could not have failed to take in his visitor's good cloth coat. Some of John's papers and maps were still in a drawer, and the man suggested that Balty might like to look at them. "You may find something for your purpose,"[21] he proposed significantly.

Balty had stumbled on John Joyne.

BIBLIOGRAPHICAL NOTES

1. Fr. Mar. Docs., B⁴, V, ff 26-39; 42-51, r, v.
2. Colenbrander, *Besch. mit. Vreemde arch.*, 125-6-7.
3. Fr. Mar. Docs., B², XXXI, ff 279, 297, *passim*.
4. Clement, *Lettres Instructions Mémoires de Colbert*, III, Pt. I, 556.
5. Fr. Mar. Docs., B³, XIX, f 256.
6. *Ibid.; Ibid.*, B², XXVI, ff 280, 285.
7. *Ibid.*, XXXI, f 253, r, v.
8. Rawl. MSS., A 188, f 317.
9. *Ibid.*, A 194, ff 1, 2, 6, r, v, 7, 12, 13.
10. Morn. MS., I, f 151.
11. *Ibid.*, f 152, 153.
12. Rawl. MSS., A 188, f 151.
13. *Ibid.*
14. *Ibid.*, A 194, ff 91, 93.
15. Fr. Mar. Docs., B², XLI, f 538.
16. Rawl. MSS., A 194, f 5.
17. *Ibid.*, f 5 v.
18. *Ibid.*, A 188, f 313.
19. *Ibid.*, f 181.
20. Mit. Ch. Pro., C 8, 376, No. 69.
21. *Ibid.*

CHAPTER XLIII

THE AFFIDAVITS

"An honest use of one villain to discover the iniquity of another."
—Samuel Pepys to Balty St. Michel, Rawl. MSS., A 194, f 50.

THE ENCOUNTER with Joyne proved of lasting consequence to John Scott, for this shady character was the fount of most of the legends which tarnish Scott's name. Balty was overjoyed at his find.

He promptly paid fifty pounds for John's back rent and assured Joyne that "he would be thankfully and liberally gratified and rewarded" for anything he could disclose about his former lodger.[1] Joyfully he wrote his brother-in-law about the great discovery and within ten days came Pepys' letter to Joyne, thanking him and inviting him to come to London as defense witness.

But Joyne, who had at first professed the greatest readiness to help "an innocent man in distress," and had immediately volunteered astounding revelations, now became exceedingly cautious, realizing, perhaps, that he would have to substantiate his tales. He could not possibly leave his business he pleaded, he had a wife to consider, his five children to provide for, the trip was out of the question. Pepys, pressing for trial and with the last days of Trinity Term fast approaching, was frantic with impatience. He dispatched to Paris a colleague, Monsieur Denise, a supply merchant to the French Navy, who managed (with what means we do not know) to overcome

Joyne's reluctance, and made arrangements for bringing over the obsequious watchmaker to whom Pepys' promises now "went beyond all that Balty had assured him."[2]

While waiting for Joyne, Pepys followed up the latter's leads and tried to pinpoint Scott's movements during the month he said he had seen the incriminating papers. But who had kept track of the Colonel's travels? Back and forth he had ridden, between Paris and Nevers those busy days, who could possibly say with certainty where he was, and above all, when? Pélissary's widow, disdainful and ailing, fearful of answering any questions, had, after endless hesitations, stated merely that John did not dine with her husband the night Deane had been there. But she would not swear, as Balty urged her to do, that John had no familiarity with Pélissary.*[3]

And to complicate Pepys' difficulties, his Counsel made clear to him that English law did not permit written evidence from living witnesses: they were required to appear in Court for cross-examination. How could he possibly bring over this diffident aging gentlewoman? He felt on much surer grounds with a co-operative type like Joyne.

In a long deposition the watchmaker swore out everything he knew of John's activities between 1673 and 1677, as well as everything that John, so he said, had ever told him! True it is that Joyne had occasionally acted as Scott's interpreter; but for the most part Joyne relied upon his own friendly sources, the Duke of Buckingham's barber, and Pélissary's (discharged) porter, Moreau. With such fountainheads of information, he could furnish Pepys with unlimited suggestions of wrong-doing: the gun-casting experiment was all a "cheat"; the chemical formula discussions branded as outright "counterfeiting"; John's making and selling of maps,

---

* La Fontaine, Pélissary's footman, swore that Scott often came to M. Pélissary's house, concerning the making of cannon. And that he, Fontaine, sometimes fetched Scott to come and speak with Pélissary at Mlle. des Moulins' house in the *rue des Marais*. Morn. MS., I, f 485.

always for evil ends. On this last subject Pepys pressed his most searching inquiries.

There was one map particularly, deposed Joyne, of the English coast "looking towards France" about three yards long and one and a half wide, fringed on the upper and lower edge with blue silk; "showing all the harbor-soundings, the islands, rocks, sandbars; their approaches and dangerous places, . . ." These markings were "all in French." Monsieur La Pointe had worked over this with "great earnestness"; and when it was ready, John had taken it by coach to St. Germain; and on his return Joyne noted, he was "very flush with money."[4]

But Pepys' very zeal to prove John both a traitor and a cheat defeated his own ends. He found a witness to swear (*"at your request"*) that John had borrowed the deponent's map of *Shereness,* copied it, and offered it to the Prince of Orange saying he had made it expressly "to discover England's weak places."[5] Yet if it were only a copy of an already available map John could hardly be selling *secret* information. Other witnesses, solicited by Pepys, obligingly swore that John *told* them he prepared maps of fortifications for the King of France; or *showed* them estimates, as well as the famous blue-fringed chart, telling them these were destined for the French King and worthy only of him!

But would a traitor *tell* other people about his nefarious doings?

And the indisputable fact remained that when John's trunks had been opened at Dover, there, among his papers, was the map with the blue silk fringe![6]

In the face of such conflicting stories Pepys implored Balty to get a definitive statement from the man who knew John's work best, La Pointe.[7] And this celebrated copyist finally confirmed what Brisbane had already volunteered, that John's maps were of historic rather than maritime interest.[8] In a frenzy of disbelief, Pepys wrote Brisbane again, asking if John could draw at all!

It is curious he did not know that the man was Royal Geographer. For the rest, it was an age of geographic ignorance; even an Admiralty Secretary seemed unaware that map-making entailed some scientific surveys. John had never sailed around the English and French coasts as he had in New England, in the Caribbean and through all the waterways of the United Provinces. Nor had he sought the specialized information of local pilots, fishermen, privateers, who had furnished much of the data that made his Netherlands maps so valuable. Apart from these, and from his own New England masterpiece, John's work was not original. Most of his charts were beautifully colored and decorated enlargements, to *"horoscamotter de l'argent,"* as Brisbane put it.[9]

Pepys was equally in the dark about John's work as foreign agent. Had he talked with Sir Joseph Williamson, he could have learned all about John's activities in the Lowlands. Or he could have consulted his old friend Sir John Bankes—the City merchant-prince—for there are at least half a dozen of John's letters to the latter among the state papers—the two men seemed well acquainted. But relying upon Joyne's keyhole peepings and concièrge gossip, Pepys wrote to the insignificant James Puckle, in Flanders, and to the self-confessed double agent William Carr, who both retailed, about their former rival, stories that the record shows as false.

From Holland, too, came some very uncomplimentary affidavits from certain Dutch citizens. These last, having been implored, by Captain Gunman, to recollect (after an interval of nearly ten years!) "the ill-behaviour of John Scott," may be pardoned for confusing him with William Scott, son of the regicide, who had also been an officer and a British agent in the Netherlands.[10] This Scott had a long criminal record, had served prison sentences in Holland and England, and was convicted of treason both to his King, and to his fellow countrymen.*[11]

---

* Wilbur C. Abbott confused these two in his *"Colonel" John Scott*, and *Conflicts with Oblivion*.

With such encouraging material in his possession, Pepys began maneuvering his forces for the hoped-for trial. He made arrangements for bringing into England some foreign witnesses—a maddeningly expensive task, for trial date had not been set, and the Opposition was gleefully doing its best to prevent any decision. First to arrive as his guest was Deborah Egmont Nederway (now a servant at a Hague Inn), delighted no doubt at the chance to get even with the faithless Scott, and bubbling over with remembrances of all his doings—his wild tales of buccaneering and fighting in the West Indies—incidents that were to be twisted into charges of his "attacking and burning the English coast."

From Paris, Pepys invited some of the gun-casting crew, but here he ran into fresh dangers. His desperate plight was becoming known, as was the fact—due to Balty's indiscretions—that money could be made by speaking against Scott. Henry Fielding, one of the group, was brutally frank on the subject: "though I know enough of his [John's] villainous practices in Holland as well as in France to hang him, yet by God, I will discover nothing unless I get something for it," he wrote. And he urged his colleague, Sherwin, that "this is the time and occasion to make his fortune . . . that he was a Fool and an Ass if he did declare anything of his knowledge touching the ill practices of said Scott without being first assured of the advantage he should make to himself of it."[12]

Fearful of what his brother-in-law was up to, Pepys sent M. Denise to France again, to warn the feckless young man to be extremely cautious in dealing with money-seeking applicants. Balty bitterly resented this seeming distrust. True, he had always failed in everything he undertook and had been hoisted from job to job by the good-natured Pepys. Naturally he was eager to repay past kindnesses, but Balty was also extremely anxious to stay in France, well out of reach of any possible investigation. That piracy charge still hung over him, and this second arrival of Denise looked like a prelude to his own recall—something he was determined to prevent at all cost.

The indefatigable Pepys had meanwhile managed to get himself and his fellow prisoner discharged from the Tower and recommitted to the old Marshalsea prison in Southwark. Much more uncomfortable and undistinguished than in the aristocratic Tower quarters, he was, nevertheless, now beyond the power and privileges of the dread Parliament and his professed enemies, and could make an appeal under common law. Very soon the Court yielded to his demand for bail. And on a surety of thirty thousand pounds each—a sum which strained their resources to the very uttermost—Pepys and Deane were released during the Long Vacation, to the fury of London mobs who greeted their freedom with vicious lampoons; while Lord Justice Scroggs (who let them out) when next he ventured into the City, had a dead dog, with a rope round its neck, flung into his coach.

Deprived of all official duties, the disgraced Secretary retired in seclusion, and lived for the purpose of destroying Scott. It was an all-consuming passion to which he devoted the detailed methodical attention he had formerly lavished on Naval Affairs. Repeated postponement of Court proceedings did not deter him, nor the fact that so many of his correspondents did not know John and could not have testified personally. In defiance of all law (and logic) he tenaciously accumulated his unique collection of affidavits.

Trial was once again denied him: this time because there was no one to present further evidence. John Scott had left town; he had gone off to France again with Buckingham.

The Duke, with his unfailing political bad luck, chose to leave England at the very moment the Opposition's fortunes seemed brightest. In August, 1679, the King caught a chill and suffered a slight stroke. Everywhere the cry arose he had been poisoned, and the nation was flung into wildest confusion. The Country Party's hopes soared. Their candidate for the throne, the Duke of Monmouth, the King's eldest bastard, made a regal entry into London; and Shaftesbury, who appeared to have the country well behind him, began preparations for a nationwide insurrection in favor of the charming young man. The government responded by bringing the Duke of York back from Brussels; and, with so much at stake, Buckingham and John came hurrying home. But the magnificent royal constitution defeated all expectations. By September the King was himself again, and the struggle over the Stuart succession resumed its old ferocity.

In an effort to regain lost territory, Charles sent both claimants to the throne out of England, and, after a haggling deal for a subsidy from Louis, prorogued parliament. He was seizing the offensive and fighting back against the Opposition: Shaftesbury was still too powerful to be struck down, but an arrest warrant was issued against Bucks "for alienating the hearts of the King's subjects."

Now this was a charge Pepys might rightly have levelled against John. Lobbyist or publicity man (as we should call him today) for the Opposition, his job was carrying to the people's level all the republican talk which so appalled Charles as he stalked Westminster galleries. The Parliamentary Record—Hansard—dared hardly mention such antimonarchical sentiment. One must read the Venetian ambassador's dispatches to realize how virulent this was, how far the Exclusionists went, and how many foreign dignitaries were expecting a republic in England.* The King knew he could never check this torrent in full flood. It was for this same reason he left open field to Titus Oates:—Full gallop, give them their head, they were easier to rein when tired, was his policy. And by skillful play of prorogation and dissolution he resisted exclusion, fought off civil war and brought his rebellious parliament under control.

This same tolerance and political acumen saved Buckingham: his arrest warrant was never served. The Duke retired

---

* "Unless something very vigorous be done within a few days, the monarchy is gone." Duke of York to the Prince of Orange. *HMC Foljambe*, p. 131.

for a while to his little 'Versailles' at Cliveden, and was soon back in London again, to squander his talents on one of the most incongruous roles of all his checkered career.

To whip up waning anti-popish fervor and to keep the political pot a-boiling, the Green Ribbon Club organized the first of its famous Pope Burnings; and the Duke, experienced in theatrical matters, was credited with having written and staged this macabre pageant. Nor is it unreasonable to suppose that "Buckingham's John," himself no mean showman, assisted him.

For five hours the torch-lit actors and mechanized puppets paraded from Aldgate to Temple Bar, followed by one hundred thousand Protestant fanatics. So great had been the build-up for the show that the King himself and the French ambassador were among the spectators, cautiously disguised and hidden. Godfrey's death was sensationally featured; a waxen bloody corpse on a great white horse, supported by the Jesuit Murderer, complete with crucifix and crimson sword. Black-robed bellmen tolled the story; monks, friars, cardinals, streamed through the streets, distributing pardons, brandishing phials of poison; the darkness rang with shouts of "NO POPERY! EXCLUSION! A Shaftesbury! A Buckingham!" The Pope's effigy in triple tiara raised the mobs to delirium. Borne aloft in his golden chair, his sceptre blotched with guilty bloodstains, his right hand (clockworked) raised in jerky benediction, he was surrounded by waxen nuns—his *Courtesans in Ordinary;* while the *Pope's Whore* attended the Inquisitor-General, in full panoply of revolting torture instruments.[13]

A crude mock trial climaxed the procession; then the Pope was suspended above a giant bonfire. And as the "flames of hell" shot upwards, shrieks and wails rent the air as the myriad cats, stuffed in his vast belly, burned to death in hideous agony, providing the final thrill for the maddened crowds. The spectacle of popery thus triumphantly destroyed was designed to fortify Protestant belief and spur the people's continued resistance to tyranny. But Samuel Pepys made no effort to join the throngs; he had lost his old relish for street shows and plays. He paid no heed to politics of the day, if, indeed, he was aware of impending constitutional changes. He had never been a Party man and regarded partisan intrigues with disdain. He served the King, the rest were rogues. And just now he was, he felt sure, about to catch the greatest rogue of them all.

John Joyne had finally arrived in London and had consented to shadow John Scott.

Pepys was teaching him how to keep a diary.

BIBLIOGRAPHICAL NOTES

1. Mit. Ch. Pro., C 8, 376, No. 69.
2. *Ibid.*
3. Rawl. MSS., A 194, f 73.
4. *Ibid.,* ff 232-33.
5. *Ibid.,* A 175, f 22.
6. *Ibid.,* ff 231, 163.
7. *Ibid.,* A 194, f 139.
8. *Ibid.,* A 190, f 117.
9. Morn. MS., I, f 152.
10. Rawl. MSS., A 194, ff 6, 118, 158, 109, 111, 118.
11. SPD Entry Bk., 28, f 11; *CSP Dom.,* 1664-65, pp. 383, 500; *Ibid.,* 1666, pp. 318, 342, 457; *ibid.,* 1672, p. 24.
12. Morn. MS., I, f 583.
13. Chapman, *Grt. Villiers,* pp. 257-60.

CHAPTER XLIV

JOYNE'S JOURNAL

For among friends 'twere inequality
To think one should be blind and 't 'other see.
—Duke of Buckingham.

THIS CURIOUS DOCUMENT,* preserved among Pepys' personal papers in Cambridge, covers the days Joyne trailed Scott, and has been described by the historian who first used it† as "a unique record of a rogue's own view of the London underworld . . . almost as though Lockit or Filch had kept a diary."

As it is the only eyewitness account of John's activities it is certainly worth studying in detail, although whether it really reflects the underworld is open to question. True, there are scenes in certain low political taverns and coffeehouses. Joyne never fails to mention them and tell at length when and what John drank, and where they all pissed against the wall, but similar habits—and worse—are down in Pepys' Diary too, and surely this did not constitute the underworld.

How much credence can be given these pages is a much more interesting question. These are the jottings of a paid informer, of a needy, ignorant man who could best please by recounting the worst, yet who so little understood the purport of his job that there are endless passages of his own meagre

---

* Morn. MS., I (Pepysian MS. 2881), ff 285-328. Published by the University of California Press, June, 1959.

† Bryant. *The Years of Peril*, XI, 294-302.

adventures in London on the days that he failed to spot his quarry. But Pepys, in this fight for his life, could afford to overlook no possible weapon.

The Journal begins as the two men met in Drury Lane on November 26, 1679, and the first thing Joyne noticed was that John was without his sword—an unusual (perhaps significant?) occurrence, since, after an absence of four years this is what immediately caught his eye. There are mutual greetings, Joyne explaining he has come to London to collect a debt, and they stroll through Covent Garden to Major Wildman's house in Queens Street where John had spent the night. Joyne does not recognize the name nor what Wildman stands for (he tells Pepys it was Major *Williams*) but one observation does reveal John's familiarity with the place, for while drinking with Wildman's son, John calls for a crust of bread. The men sit till midnight, talking colonial affairs, . . . "relating to East or West Indies," writes Joyne, obviously out of his depth, though he devoted several lines to John's introduction of himself as "an old friend and the best watchmaker in the world."

Their relationship is quickly established: John sends Joyne on an errand—the fellow always made himself useful. After some hesitation and time spent disguising his handwriting, John gives Joyne a letter to deliver to Lady Vane (follows a wordy paragraph about her house-porter at St. Giles Churchyard and the tip Joyne is to give him). Then, after drinking the lady's health "in a pott of ale" the two part agreeing to meet next day at 3 o'clock.

That afternoon they walk through Paul's Churchyard to Cheapside, greeting four or five young dandies who ask Scott what he has done with his periwig . . . he having pulled it off and crammed it in his pocket, declaring it was too hot. "Why," said John, "to show you I have not lost it, here it is," patting his coat while one of them, to make sure, tries to get at it. Two of them accompany our pair to Bow Lane, then leave, calling good night to Scott. "Who are they?" asks

Joyne. "Young parliamentarians," says John. Lord Wharton's son was in black, and the other was Lord Sand's son. "I preserve my interest with the sober men of Parliament by espousing the interest of the People and with those mad fellows by drinking," and John lifted his hand to his mouth in vivid gesture. "And so, I have all Parliament to espouse my interest." (This does not sound too much like John's verbal style, but his spy was of limited education and vocabulary.) Joyne remembers "at length," however, all that John had told him about Lady Vane, and about that letter he had sent, unsigned, for it was supposed to be an anonymous confirmation of the story Lady Vane's daughter invented that John "was that Colonel Scott* that commanded the Duke of Monmouth's regiment in France and who was so be-poxed that he was not able to stand before his company. "Now when this is done," explained Scott, "I shall find ways by My Lord Arlington and otherwise of proving I was *not that* Colonel Scott, then I shall come the sooner to the end of my desire with My Lady when I shall have brought it about that this story shall be thought to have proceeded only from the daughter's malice." For daughter highly disapproved of her mother's "particular kindness" for John, who, apparently, was confident he could get Arlington to second his little jape with the romantically inclined Lady Vane.

Joyne and John do some shopping, then call on William Penn, the great Quaker, who is out; John leaves a message he will be at Appleby's that night (one of the much-frequented political coffeehouses where he lobbies) though Joyne, of course, hasn't a notion of what his work is. At the *Dog and Dripping Pan* John inquires of his landlord if he has had any callers, then repairs to Appleby's where he makes his host sit and drink with them; whispering to Joyne how he uses this man to repeat everything he's told. Talk turns of course to

---

* *CSP Dom.*, 1675-76, p. 101; *Entry Book* 41. *Lt. Col. Scott of Royal English Regiment in France, Archives de la Guerre* A¹ vol. 476, No. 253; Vol. 473, No. 237.

politics. A Doctor of Divinity "who showed great servility to Scott" brought the latest news and they all fell to discussing chances of Parliament's recall—"the Salve [sic] of the Nation," Joyne notes. An old Cromwellian commander was with them; and a curious individual—coming to summon John to Penn— joins them, without removing his hat. "What sort of rascal is that?" asks the astonished Joyne. John explains it is the Quaker solicitor of Penn—"the King of the Quakers. For Presbyterians have Kings, and Anabaptists have their Kings and so we have a great many Kings in this country and all very great ones, I can assure you," replies John, who sounds a mite sarcastic about the self-importance of the varying Sects. Joyne gossips over his sweet wine with the messenger, then everyone leaves, John going to Penn, and Joyne—late as it is—to report to Pepys. So we never learn what the future founder of Pennsylvania talked over with John Scott, though it is pretty safe to assume it was about conditions in North America.

Next morning Joyne is again at Pepys', catching up on his delation. He now describes in detail the room in Wildman's house (he has the name right, too) and how young Wildman had told John his father was at Westminster but if John would stay to dinner there would be a piece of good venison— matters of no interest at all to the worried Secretary, who, together with Deane, M. Denise, and a Captain Brown, spends the whole day coaching Joyne as to the kind of information they want.

John is out when Joyne calls next day, but the landlord recognizing him, sends him over to Newman's Coffeehouse, one of John's regular haunts in Talbot Court, and here Joyne finds him with a thin-faced man in an old blue-trimmed campaign coat breakfasting "on Purle and three or foure small redd herrings,"—a detail of vital importance immediately noted in his journal! The talk is all of the Pope-Burning and the Pope's great speech before the bonfire. Joyne, agog with zeal and curiosity, asks who John's visitor is, and, while easing himself downstairs, addresses this stranger and hears John order him "to give satisfaction about a horse." "You have a horse?" he asks. But no, says John, he had left one at Gravesend the time he was mistaken for a Jesuit and he wants to know when the man is returning there. It was the Chief Gravesend Searcher, "a rogue," John tells Joyne, "but fit to be made occasional use of" and he asks Joyne if the man had mentioned Pepys.

Then off the two go together, to a laundress—John's cravate is dirty but the woman tells him he can't have another till tomorrow—down Cannon Street, all the people asking John for political news and he telling them that Parliament is about to sit "very suddenly," writes Joyne. Some are delighted and promise John a quart of sack, were it true. "I can assure you it's true and will be the salve [sic] of the nation," replies John. On they go—to a furrier—John leaves an otter skin for a muff; to a chemist, "a Roman Catholic . . . but an honest fellow," volunteers John, and Joyne puts down this fact twice; it is the nearest he can bring John to treasonable utterance. The red-faced doctor they greet belongs to the College of Surgeons—John tells everything—the disjointed diary is crammed with trivial detail—and so they arrive at Lady Vane's, where John gives his companion sixpence to deliver another (anonymous) letter, urging him to wait first "a large quarter of an hour." (It looks almost as if he were testing Joyne's dependability, for John was visiting the lady when the letter was brought in.)

Joyne, writing up his diary, recalls their preliminary conversation about the lady's good estate. John said he could have been chosen M.P. in three counties, but with no means he would never be elected, though if he were, "he was sure he would be able to do more than ever was done by any one man yett—or words to that purpose," writes Joyne. And here his description really sounds like John!

The young reporter hangs around Lady Vane's noting that two men entered, a Mr. Wentworth, M.P. (whom Joyne had once overcharged for watch repairs in Paris) and one Harring-ton, whom Joyne recognized as the priest-clad figure known, across the Channel, as Benson and sometimes Wilson. It was in fact the Earl of Shaftesbury's personal agent, a good acquaintance of John's, familiar with all the latest Paris gossip about the latter and ready to assure Lady Vane that Scott was certainly not the rogue certain fellows there were reporting him to be! (Whatever must Pepys have thought of this entry?)

John gave Joyne the slip after leaving the party and Joyne, finding Pepys out too when he called, ambled forth again to seek Scott, ending the night somewhat unaccountably at Southwark, dead drunk, we must suppose, for next morning the fastidious Pepys, seeing him so bedraggled and dirty, sends him home to shift and shave. But Joyne was worth his pay: he did dig up news. That day he surprised John reading a letter from France, which had reached him indirectly. (John had his own means of communication just as of travel.) The letter warned that Balty St. Michel had offered the writer, D'Allais, a Parisian language teacher, two thousand pounds "to make discoveries and help him to John's maps." D'Allais had assured Balty he "would not betray a friend"; while Foster (a debauched young Englishman of very good family) in the same manner just laughed at Balty's questions about John's affairs, and his visit to St. Maures with the D. of B. D'Allais gave further information about Sherwin's "dis-coveries" touching John's vilification of the English King and Balty's assurances that for the two thousand pounds in ques-tion he could give good security on Paris merchants "for P. and D. were worthy gentlemen" that B. St. M. could well aver.

Joyne had to read this letter three times and then have all the puzzling initials explained to him by John who angrily swore St. Michel was a rogue, a Quartermaster in the Fleet, or something, and that he would have the place taken from him just as soon as parliament met, he would be revenged, by God! and would claw off these dogs!

Fuming and furious, John goes to his M.P. friend Wentworth, who was at Westminster, it being last day of Term, exchanging greetings en route with Sir John Narbrough. John, to Joyne's inevitable question, declares that "this is the greatest sea captain in the world . . . he made the map of the Magellan straits" (Joyne writes Mogdelaine). "That you copied?" asked Joyne accusingly. (Like Pepys, Joyne seemed to think that any map based upon an existing map, was a "cheat.") "Yes," answered John ("as I have heard him say at other times" adds Joyne). "I sold that map for £500; and My Lord Arlington cheated the King and sold it for £1000." They walk to St. Giles and John goes in to Lady Vane, telling Joyne to wait. The latter awaits for an hour and a half, buys a drink, but John does not reappear.

Joyne did not spot his quarry again till Friday, December 5th, when he found John on his lodgings staircase talking to a young wench. Joyne goes up to John's room where the latter puts on a fine velvet coat, talking the while about his periwig and pulling from his pocket a small bag containing a brush with which he blackened his eyebrows and beard.

Amazed, Joyne asks why, and John explains it's a kind of disguise. Taking off his fair wig he puts on a black one, and even Joyne, prepared for a change, was astonished to see such a transformation.

Joyne informs him he is leaving soon for France and John good-naturedly says he will get him a passage on some ship, and, in that case, he forbore to change the black ribbon on his muff for a red one as he had intended, for, he explained, he could not go among those shipmasters looking too gaudy! John says he is dining with Wildman and would meet Joyne later, but he did not keep his appointment, and Joyne, though he visited John's lodgings several times, did not see him again until Dec. 11th, when their private talk was interrupted by Newman's boy whispering to John that *Benson* is waiting for them at the Coffeehouse. They go over and Joyne effusively greets Benson and they all fall to talking of old Paris days. But in come the news sheets and the others switch immediately to politics. Newman regales them with gossip of Samuel Pepys, who "once made everybody stoop to him and now he was grown very humble"; but John was pitiless and called him and Deane rogues; railed at the two thousand pound bribe again and swore he would "claw them off."

Joyne, to stress his own importance, tells Newman that "nobody knoweth the Colonel better than I do," and Newman replies that the Colonel "was a very honest gentleman who loved his country." Joyne then offers his "services" to Benson—anything in France he could do he was ever ready, and leaving Monday—but Benson does not need him.

They drink three bottles of sack together and Benson and John go off in a coach with two women. Joyne, who had stopped to buy a lobster, tries to accompany them, but they drive away, laughing. To those two professionals, his clumsy spying must have been all too obvious. Joyne is left behind crestfallen, clutching his lobster.

But the watchmaker-detective is undaunted. Back he goes to Newman's next day. No Scott—but he smokes a pipe of tobacco with mine host and a stranger, all three gossiping about John. This seedy third individual says his name is Jacob Milbourne and that he'd like to get better acquainted with Joyne, whom he bids tell Scott that his *friend* is here. (Milbourne was no friend of John's, but of Nathan Seeley, the Hartford marshall who, years before, had arrested John at Setauket!) Milbourne had watched John's trial in 1664 and later had had a glimpse of him in Barbados where Milbourne, who formerly had been Thomas Olcott's servant, had been transferred to John Crowe, Scott's host there.

Milbourne takes in all the talk about D'Allais' warning John of those "trying to do him an injury," and later pumps Newman for further information. Joyne learns of this when Newman cautions him that Milbourne is a rogue. Follows a long tedious account of Joyne's drinking with Harrington, and nine further pages of just how and why he did not see John. December 14th Joyne calls at the *Dog and Dripping Pan* where the maid tells him that John's lady (meaning Lady Vane) is dead! She died the day before and Scott had immediately gone out accompanied by the landlord—(here follows an interminable story about this honest fellow whom John had once set up with four hundred pounds from a charity fund).

No sign of our hero till late on Monday when he comes into Appleby's, very melancholy. Joyne sympathizes over his loss. "It's the greatest loss in the world, a Devil of a loss," laments John, and Joyne comforts him with a Portugal orange, "he telling me that the palate of his mouth was down." Even so, he does not forget about Joyne's ship and goes to a broker next door to make arrangements about it, promising to dine with Joyne another time. That dinner was a memorable event (of which much more later). It was the culminating point of all Joyne's efforts to entrap John, and showed John at one of his most lamentable and reckless moments.

He broke numerous subsequent appointments, obviously disgusted at being trailed. Besides there was work to do—even if marriage hopes were shattered.

Joyne (after a boring account of his departure plans) arrives at Newman's one evening when John is speaking at a "conventicle." Here might have been trenchant material for Samuel Pepys; this could have revealed what John was doing and how far he was committed to Opposition policies or anything else of a serious political nature. But Joyne naturally muffs this opportunity—he was incapable of seizing essentials. From a neighboring room he heard little and could only report that the talk was "sometimes about the King and sometimes about Parliament and sometimes about Law but I could gather nothing from it." John comes out after his speech, shakes Joyne's hand, but will not drink with him.

There is another broken rendezvous and, at the last moment, Joyne, surrounded by his baggage, waits nearly three hours in Billingsgate for John to appear. He never comes and Joyne, after a fruitless search, learns he is once more with Major Wildman. The two never meet again till February 13th when Joyne espies John "by chance . . . at a distance, twice in the same day but spoke to him not."

So ends this remarkable writing, with its pretentious promise of "all that past between myself and Colonel Scott," and its puerile ending on a note of failure.

Two items of interest Pepys had learned: Balty was betraying him in Paris with open bribes, and Milbourne looked like a very promising witness.

But in the great struggle with John Scott, Joyne's Journal was only a blunted sword.

CHAPTER XLV

THE LEGEND OF JOHN SCOTT

*He that questioneth much shall learn much . . . especially
if he apply his questions to the skill of the persons whom
he asketh.*

—Francis Bacon.

THE AUTUMN MONTHS of 1679 were full of turmoil and upheaval, though Samuel Pepys, still held at the mercy of the
Court, seemed unaware of the shifting political scene.

In late October Charles dismissed the Earl of Shaftesbury
as President of the Cou..cil, and "little Sincerity" as he was
nicknamed, went straight from Whitehall to his "Republican" residence in St. Giles, there to be rapturously welcomed
by the City, and publicly banqueted by Prince Rupert, who
had no use for the King's financial dependence upon France.
To many Englishmen the Country Party was the Patriotic
Party, the side which defended liberty, property and the
people's rights against royal prerogative and possible foreign
domination. With Shaftesbury now giving it his undivided
attention, he quickly out-maneuvered Buckingham, and
claimed full direction of its policies. Whereas the Duke had
maintained his position by erratic brilliance, Shaftesbury was
the diligent committee chairman, the untiring reader of endless reports; and John Scott and Major Wildman, while the
Duke was still under a cloud, began working more closely
with this other great leader.

Shaftesbury had encouraged John's suit with Lady Vane.
It was just the thing, he declared, to set him up with the
material backing for a parliamentary career (the Earl should

surely know—he had made three most advantageous mar-
riages). Under his remarkable administrative ability, John
met the principal Party men, sat in on all their "consults and
cabals" and participated in Party rallies.[1] He saw the rise of
the Green Ribbon Club to such significance that it almost
usurped the functions of parliament.

Meeting in the King's Head Tavern, at the Strand corner
of Chancery Lane, club members were drawn from every class
and condition: landed statesmen, country gentlemen, constitutional Republicans—pious forerunners of the revolution as
well as outright seditionists like Ferguson the Plotter, sworded
pastor and virulent pamphleteer, who lived only to plot, and
outlived them all. The Club was the source of most of Charles'
troubles. It could make and unmake politicians, sway elections, muster and manipulate the Thames-side mobs—Shaftesbury's ten thousand "Brisk Boys" wore green ribbons in their
hats for "street engagements." But the Club's most powerful
weapon was moulding public opinion. However dubious this
last activity—and when the Licencing Act expired, its libels
knew no bounds—it was, nevertheless, preparing the way for
popular self-government. Shaftesbury's agents swarmed into
the halls and lobbies of parliament, whipping up waverers to
a division, feeding members trenchant argument for debate.
They acted as a clearinghouse for all the latest news, received
and issued orders, starting rumors in the coffeehouses that
spread like quicksilver through the whole country. The
Opposition maintained an overwhelming parliamentary majority. Three times it brought in the Exclusion Bill until
silenced by prorogation. Now it was flooding Westminster
with petitions for reassembly of parliament, and it was from
this monster petition campaign, countered by addresses from
those who "abhorred" the appeal, that arose the party names
—Whig and Tory—we remember to this day.*

---

* The petitioners called the "abhorrers" Tories, a slang term for Irish
Catholic highwaymen; the Tories counterattacked by calling petitioners
Whiggamores or Whigs, after the Scottish fanatical Convenanters, whose
rebellion Monmouth had just put down at Bothwell Brig.

Unrecognized, almost unseen behind this creation of party politics, was the modest figure of John Locke, Shaftesbury's personal physician, companion, and political mentor. From their Oxford student days, when the young nobleman had recognized the other's promise of brilliance and lack of fortune, an affectionate intimacy existed, which deepened when Anthony Ashley Cooper (as he was then) felt he owed his very life to Locke's daring surgical intervention following a serious accident which almost terminated the noble career.

Lord Ashley took Locke permanently into his household and let him handle the correspondence of the important Board of Trade and Plantations. It was while Locke was thus employed that Ashley's attention was drawn first to John Scott, when the latter had impressed Board members with his vivid knowledge of colonial affairs. Scott and Locke, then, may have known each other as early as 1663.

The bold navigator, merchant seaman, youthful Long Island landowner and magistrate could have been a resounding anvil on which the cloistered, dependent Locke might have hammered out some of the ideas which Scott developed independently.

When Ashley, as Earl of Shaftesbury, was raised to the Chancellorship Locke labored with him more closely, and John's contact with the two men—the restless ambitious statesman and the lofty, clear-thinking philosopher—was a highwater mark in his own political career.

Shaftesbury, struck by John's energy and virtuosity, "made frequent use of him, promised him great rewards and preferments, that he should be Governor of the Isle of Wight with a settlement of £1200 annually."[2] He made John what we should call today public relations officer for the Duke of Monmouth, let him manage the Irish Witnesses (of which more later), and publicize the History of the Black Box which would have ended forever the Succession crisis. Such dazzling promises were sufficient to kindle John's customary ardor in this mighty conflict whose outcome would decide the future of the kingdom, and the fate of world Protestantism.

And all this while, Samuel Pepys was preparing the legend of John Scott's life. It was ludicrous—as well as tragic—that at the very moment of John's participation (as however minor a figure) in events of national importance that his life story was being written by humble creatures avid for gain. Jacob Milbourne so delighted Pepys with "his readiness to give evidence" and discover John's "infamy" on the other side of the Atlantic, that after hearing the story he sent the man to the Duke of York.

Overawed by the illustrious presence this ignorant servant liberally sprinkled his truly fantastic recital of John's early life with extenuating "so I heard"-s and "so it was generally discoursed." It was he who furnished the piquant detail that John "cheated an Indian queen of a tract of land whose name was Sunksqua,"[3] an item that has found its way into every history book mentioning John.

Colonel Edward Sackville, Pepys' old friend, interrogated Milbourne at length, then fashioned his own version of the Long Island saga, featuring John "on the gallows, a rope about his neck but saved by his hopefulness and brisk parts."[4]

Matthias Nicolls (secretary to, not a relative of, Governor Nicolls) added his quota to John's boyhood exploits, endorsed by Pepys as "a historic account."[5] In ten long pages which trail off illegibly and are finished in another's handwriting with apologies for "repetitions, etc." we are treated to reminiscences of someone describing events allegedly happening twenty years previously to a man the writer hardly knew. John was "admired and adored by the people," was "somewhat of a seaman, had a nimble genius though otherwise illiterate." There is a garbled account of the trial at Hartford —the only time Matthias ever saw John—also damaging allegations of John's Long Island land deals including reference to that phantom document, his "pretended perpetuity." At the time Matthias wrote, he himself owned some of John's former land, and would have been the last to say anything that might lead to a scrutiny or possible rectification of the deeds.* (Appendix L).

More special pleading came from Governor Thomas Lovelace, unexpectedly back from America on his own affairs. His affidavit concerning John was accompanied by an abject appeal to Pepys for help, together with a petition to the Duke of York which Lovelace begged Pepys to forward and to foster. The writer stated he was "suffering and indigent" . . . was "willing to do anything" owing to the loss of his Staten Island estate, seized for debt. He enclosed the deeds of the Gotherson land purchases and other papers, previously procured by his brother, the late Governor Francis Lovelace; and included an abstract of them which was practically a lawyer's brief proving a case against John. In some instances he departed from the facts even contained in the very papers he forwarded. On many details—particularly John's alleged treatment of Gotherson's son—Lovelace's testimony contradicts that of Dorothea Gotherson—the only one among all the persons questioned by Pepys who really knew John. Her long letters[6] answering specific questions were naturally ignored by Pepys at the time, since they disturbed the picture he was building. They have been curiously overlooked by historians, following the lead of G. D. Scull, first American writer to make use of the Pepysian affidavits. He disposes of Dorothea by suggesting she was distraught and did not know what she was talking about.

To elicit information, Pepys did not hesitate to refer to his own great "power of appointment," especially when dealing with Navy Personnel. He wrote peremptorily to Captain Dyre ordering him to "collect the legend of Scott's life"[7] and enclosing the details furnished by Matthias Nicolls. Dyre fulfilled the command without difficulty, naturally, and returned

---

* Matthias received a grant of the Setauket land as a "gratification." Thompson, *History of Long Island*, I, 411.

it with most obsequious assurances of duty, etc., etc., adding, on his own account, that John had also "most miserably deluded, deceived and abused Lady Vane."[8]

Pepys' former clerk, William Hewer, deposed that "John Scott held dangerous correspondence with foreign powers and that he made draughts of several of His Majesty's seaboard towns in order to the destroying of the same,"[9] information that any court would disregard as incompetent and immaterial for Hewer had never met John, had no familiarity with his correspondence and maps, so could not possibly tell for whom, or what purpose, they were intended.

In his painstaking efforts to prove John wrong on each and every count, Pepys himself makes curious errors. On the back of two deeds concerning John's sale to Gotherson of one hundred, and fifteen acres of land respectively, Pepys endorses it as fifteen hundred acres . . . quite a slip.[10] He questions John's alleged possession of Ashford, confusing Ashford, Kent, with the Long Island town, known also as Setauket.[11] "And was Scot's Hall ever a castle?" he queries indignantly forgetting that, as a younger man, he himself had often mentioned it in his Diary,[12] had visited Thomas Carteret, who married a Scott of Scot's Hall; and that his old friend Evelyn had described the place as a "right noble seat."[13]

It was to a collateral branch of the Scotts that Pepys addressed these family inquiries (to the Rookes, not the Scotts—there was an Admiral Rooke among them, which perhaps prompted this choice). Ignoring his frequent requests at first, they finally wrote that "they did not know but did not 'think' John was kin to them since he had only appeared at Scot's Hall and been heard of *some years after the Restoration.*"[14] This was inexact. Dorothea Gotherson stated she met John at Whitehall, in the presence of the King, early in 1661.

But since John, as a young boy, had disappeared during the Civil War, ignorance of his existence or whereabouts is understandable.

Mr. Pepys, while never failing to refer in most derogatory terms to "our villainous adversary," "Satan Scott," "his hellish rascality" etc.[15] was, however, becoming somewhat suspicious of the sudden influx of incriminating information concerning John. Why, if all this were true, was the villain still at large?

"Very much do I wonder how he has been able to appear in Paris after the practices I find laid to his charge," he wrote Balty.[16] And once again he urges his brother-in-law to have a care as to what he "discovers." "So remote an evidence . . . a hearsay of a hearsay will never convince or be suffered to be read in Court," he complains.[17] One of the "obliging" affidavits in this collection is heavily scored across in red chalk as though Mr. Pepys' credulity had been strained beyond all limit![18]

John Joyne was quick to note Pepys' incipient doubts (doubts which increased over the years). Fearful of losing so lucrative a job—he had made three hundred pounds during the first five months as private detective, more money than he had ever earned in so short a time—Joyne made a proposal to Pepys. The Secretary should judge for himself John's wicked ways, listen to "a narrative of his own Villainies." Joyne would inveigle John into some chosen meeting place where Pepys should already be hidden, to hear with his own ears the utterances of the man's evil tongue.

So the stage was set for the Great Revelation to take place at St. Clements in the Strand, in a little public house kept by Joyne's sister. In a dark closet up on the first floor the great Mr. Pepys crouched for hours, while the other two sat over a dinner of calves' head and bacon, for which the embarrassed listener had previously forked out thirty shillings.

And now we come to the famous drinking scene always cited as conclusive proof that John was indeed everything that Pepys wanted to believe him to be. It is all down in Joyne's Journal.[19] And one wonders how much Joyne—with his job in the balance—egged John on to incriminate himself

—and if any of the scene were really written down by Pepys, for Joyne had proved he could only report short encounters; anything longer got him entangled and unintelligible.

It was just two days after Lady Vane's death; John, at the dinner table, "being mighty full of expressions of his grief," was still bemoaning this tragedy, expatiated "on the excellency of her wit and spirit and her extraordinary love to him," ("and so ran on from one thing to another impossible to set down," wrote Joyne). John read aloud a letter she had written him, then burst into a song "which was a kind of a satyr [sic] upon Lady Vane's family, her daughters and their husbands who all pass under feigned names, among which was Proteus, a person who often changed his shape, but whether it was himself or no I cannot tell." (It would be too much to expect Joyne to follow Lady Vane's classical and literary conceits.)

John mentions "a well-turned whore he had seen and did fall in with in hopes that it would take away his melancholy," and Joyne assured him "that if anything would cure melancholy that would." But apparently it had not availed, for John's mind still ran on his beloved.

He told Joyne that Lady Vane had three thousand pounds a year which she would have settled on him, since she had said that if she could see him "but once a week it would be content enough to her."

"God damn him he would go on in the line and marry her sister who's a widow," burst out John, and added that now he had got the affections of all the people of England he lacked only marrying into parliament; and if he could but marry her, there would be a great alliance for him, with M.P.'s [who would of their own accord] make it their business to support him for their honor . . . if he could marry her, he swore, by God he would poison her; he said she was a bitch and looked the kind who would give crooked pins in bread and butter to children . . . and if the child [meaning a niece, upon whom Lady Vane had settled three thousand pounds] should ever have smallpox and die, he would bring witnesses out of France to swear she had poisoned it. . . . "And a great deal more in the same vein about that family," comments Joyne.

But affairs of the heart never occupied John for long. Drunk as he was, politics were uppermost in his mind. "He had words of praise for Sir Thomas Player" (republican merchant on the committee examining Navy Office irregularities), "a very honest worthy man," and Joyne asks him if it was true, as people said, that the King had taken some office away from Sir William Waller (the notorious Whig magistrate). John said no, not yet, but added that Waller was a rogue.

John said he might be going to France again soon, to which Joyne begged him not to, it would be more to his advantage to stay in England, he declared. Well, yes, agreed John, unless the people of England should desire him to go there for their service. . . . "He lacked nothing now" he explained, "but to be thrown into the pool of Bethesda . . . for he had got an interest in the People . . . and nobody knew the several interests of every sovereign Prince of Europe better than he. . . ."

The rambling talk turned to past events. Scott called Sherwin a rogue, said he was a fellow made of soft wax "who always took the last impression that was set on him, whether it was that of a well-cut seal or of an ordinary farthing." He talked of all his gun-making associates, said they were mere tools, and if his tools failed him he could not help it; but if they had been worth anything the business might have proved a great one. . . . He readily confessed he was at St. Denis when he wrote letters to Mademoiselle des Moulins, purporting to come from St. Valois and Abbeville, cursing the rogues who told her otherwise. He had never valued himself among women on account of his being a *beau garçon*, he said, but upon "knowing himself to have some good humor and some sense above the common, and that therefore it was no fault in him, whatever it was that they liked in him, if he had the good fortune of prevailing upon them more than other men."

Parliament's chance of recall and the Great Petition campaign next engaged his talk. Nothing could hinder its success, John said, for it was not as if they were petitioning for anything unlawful . . . (even though *that* might succeed with the right men behind it) . . . but their goal was "agreeable to the law," and all they had to do was to observe the regulation numbers of delivery and not exceed the legal ten. The Petition had been drawn up originally in very forthright terms referring to the Damned Confounded Plot.

That, John insisted, was no way to address a King and he himself had rewritten it, smoothing its style. (Here Joyne adds a memorandum . . . something he had forgotten to tell Pepys before, though it was surely of more political interest than most of his trivial reporting. John had shown him that same petition weeks before, when he was at Newman's Coffeehouse with Harrington, saying that five hundred well-known men were going to sign it, and that it had been given him— John—to "draw it in better form.")

John had been put out that evening in Newman's Coffeehouse by the fact that some men had declined to drink the Duke of York's health, "for," said John, "I look upon the Duke as a great Prince and therefore it is not decent to deny his health, though God Damne! I love him as little as anybody else and have as much reason to do so." And after having revealed this lofty sentiment, John launched into a long tirade against the Duke, who had chea⁺ed him in New England, he declared. But this page in the Journal is so garbled as to be almost meaningless, and we have no way of knowing if this was Joyne's poor reporting or John getting more and more drunk.

"The Duke of York has some friends in England," continued John, "but not as many as he thought he had." Joyne, guessing full well the answer, asks who were "his most known friends," and John says "That rogue Pepys and the officers of the Navy and others." [Their numbers] "must be very inconsiderable," egged on Joyne. "No," said John, "since there were a great many officers under them—the port officers and others where the Duke had the benefit of them, though he did not execute them [sic]."

The two drank more and more, John calling freely for wine and tankards of ale, repeating with drunken incoherence, that he would marry the sister of his loved one, swearing and cursing to an excessive degree, harking back to his sorrow, praising again Lady Vane's great spirit. Then suddenly dropping into deep earnestness he said that from being perfectly well in appearance one day, while he was with her, she had died within a few hours and that by God he feared that they had poisoned her. . . . The thought seemed to inflame him. He began to rant and rage. He would get her body opened. He swore he would revenge her death. And growing more wild-eyed, John asked Joyne to go along with him now to set fire to the house, pull it about their ears . . . crash it in on that daughter and the other married one and her husband. . . . If he had him here he would cut him into a thousand pieces! Tossing off more wine, John tearfully remembered the little child "that used to hang about him," and when he had called, after Lady Vane's death, and the child came running to him as it always did, the unmarried daughter said: "I hope you will continue to love the child as well as you did before my mother died." To which John answered: "I hope you will not put crooked pins in its bread and butter."

At this juncture Joyne's sister came into the dining room, and John, "censoring strange company" (as Joyne puts it), told how he could hardly endure most people, and suspected every man of his acquaintance . . . justice was what he demanded . . . that was what he gave, and expected. In his City speeches, at the coffeehouses, John averred, he was as open in his talk as anyone, but always took care to keep himself "within the lash of the law." (This was John Locke's policy which both Scott and Wildman rigorously followed.)

Again he launched out about the Great Petition. He thanked God he had a stock of sense . . . whereupon Joyne, no doubt fearing all this political talk was getting nowhere, interrupted him by saying that no doubt John could carry off anything . . . "after imposing upon the ablest man in France, the Prince of Condé," he added suggestively. And John answered simply that, "yes, the Prince indeed was the ablest man in France . . . he did own it." Joyne artfully reminded John of the money Condé had given him, but John who even drunk seems suddenly to suspect Joyne's promptings broke into a little French song, *Les Pas Tortus* . . . whose irony was certainly beyond his host's comprehension.

Joyne reproached John for having been so little with him . . . John excused himself saying that he was driven to dine with Sir Thomas Player and other great men, "he could not command any time to himself," he explained. He boasted a bit of the speech he had made at the Guildhall trial of Harrington (Shaftesbury's agent),* all the nobility and gentry in town had come to hear him, and were amazed at the way he had addressed the Chief Justice. John sat silently, half an hour, brooding and drinking, then having "drunk himself into a high pitch" grew amorous, kissing Joyne's sister and the maid; declaring he must go to a ball at Newmans. . . . He went downstairs, where Joyne's father sat, drank a pot or two of ale with him, kissed the maid again, and so was gone.

"If an angel from heaven had recounted this, I would not have believed it," exclaimed Pepys pulling himself out of his cramped quarters and expressing due thanks to Joyne for the "horrendous revelations."

But what had he really heard?

Was this a confession of past "crime"? Could this possibly serve in a court of law to convict Scott of treason? Was it evidence of anything more than the coarseness of the age and

---

* ". . . 'twas proved that Mr. Harrington said the government of England consisted of three estates, and that any one making war against the other was no rebellion; you may guess at *his* opinion. . . ." *H. M. C. Report* 7, p. 470.

the hardly surprising circumstance, that a drunken man frequently mixes fact with fancy?

Pepys was no fool. He must have recognised what he was dealing with. His later conduct was to prove it.

BIBLIOGRAPHICAL NOTES

1. *SP. Dom. Car.*, II, 633, No. 15.
2. *Ibid.*, 432, Nos. 35, 15.
3. Morn. MS., I, f 118; Rawl. MSS., A 175, f 83.
4. *Ibid.*, ff 83, 92, 99, 157.
5. *Ibid.*, ff 101-110.
6. *Ibid.*, ff 1, 2, 49, 125, 126, 147-79.
7. *Ibid.*, A 194, f 58.
8. *Ibid.*, A 175, ff 77, 79-81.
9. SP. Dom. Car., II, 29/419, f 42.
10. Rawl. MSS., A 175, f 136.
11. *Ibid.*, f 116.
12. Wheatley, *Diary S. Pepys*, V, 34, 39, 78.
13. Dobson, *Evelyn's Diary*, Aug. 2, 1663.
14. Rawl. MSS., A 175, f 170.
15. *Ibid.*, A 194, ff 126 v, 139.
16. *Ibid.*, f 61.
17. *Ibid.*, f 129.
18. *Ibid.*, A 175, f 24.
19. Morn. MS., I, ff 311, 320.

CHAPTER XLVI

MURDER IN THE DARK

An evening with its sweetest light
Did close a day too fiercely bright
—John Scott, *Poems*, "The Fountain of
Verity in the Gardens of Beau-plaine,"
Rawl. MSS., A 176.

"STILL NO WITNESSES AGAINST PEPYS?" John Scott was asked
one morning as he strode into Appleby's Coffeehouse. He
looked up from the letter he was reading and flourished it
menacingly. He had witnesses, he assured his listeners, many
witnesses, but Balty St. Michel, he had just learned, was tam-
pering with them, offering them money not to sail.[1]

This was a strategic defeat that John had not expected.
News of Balty's bumbling machinations had previously
reached him from Paris, but it had never occurred to him
that the young man was a menace. Now it looked as if bribes,
after all, were to play a decisive role. He girded himself for
the coming confrontation. He knew that Pepys and Sir Anthony were pressing desperately for trial, but he was also
aware that the Attorney General kept blandly asserting that
witnesses against them would only testify before parliament.
And parliament, of course, was not in session. Time was still
on John's side.

Hoping that his Parisians might eventually appear, he
made shift to get a local man to second his accusation. He appealed to John Harrison, one of the gun-casting group who

had once visited Pélissary's house with John, in 1675, but Harrison refused. No one, during the Popish Plot hysteria, would, if he could possibly avoid it, risk involving himself in the contemporary politico-legal proceedings, where a man's life literally hung on an innuendo. John had to content himself with summoning his Houndsditch landlord, Hill, who was ready to swear, under oath, that he had heard the Jesuit, Coniers, relay Pepys' proffered help to Scott.

It is noteworthy, indeed, highly revealing, that at no time during the strenuous two years' struggle, did John pay the slightest attention to Pepys' wild countercharge of treason. That was something too wholly remote to warrant rebuttal: yet his dismissal of this factor gave an element of shadow-boxing to a deathly duel in which the life of one, and the reputation of the other, were nevertheless very shatteringly at stake.

Samuel Pepys, too, was preparing himself for the last round in their grim ordeal: he was maintaining *his* foreign witnesses in London at most vexing cost, and with waning hopes of getting them heard. He had retained John Joyne, too, hiding him in M. Denise's house and sending letters to Paris, to be posted back to John to substantiate the fiction of Joyne's departure.

Balty himself had warned his brother-in-law he should not be seen in public with this dubious character.[2] But without the glib watchmaker Pepys felt lost, his obsession with the fellow becoming notorious. The King heard of it, and was amused.

How strange it is that all his friends kept a tame rogue, observed Charles II about this time, struck by the prevalence of manufactured evidence. John Joyne was Pepys' rogue. From him he heard reports of Colonel Scott's political conversations with obscure conventicle preachers, of the red herrings and small beer he had for breakfast. The scoffing remark, duly related to Pepys, was but one of the pinpricks he had to endure—like the libels hawked through the streets screaming his dockyard "knaveries."

Then came a break from an unexpected quarter. A trio of shifty individuals, one of his own Admiralty clerks, Phelix Donluis, together with an ex-porter and an Admiralty messenger—all resentful at having been fired by Pepys—now wrote him, confessing that Harbord and other Whig leaders had paid them for furnishing material from Navy files. They told him, too, that James, his ex-butler, now a dying man, was anxious to absolve his conscience and recant the words that had fastened the popery charge on his master.

In a squalid back room Pepys met the perjured creatures. "They all knew enough," James whispered, "to stop Scott's mouth. . . ." But with the customary proviso. They wanted something in return . . . their jobs back, payment of arrears. . . . It was the same old story. The desired testimony had to be bought.

Claiming that he wanted "nothing but the bare truth," Pepys, nevertheless, skillfully managed to satisfy their demands without laying himself open to possible subsequent charges of bribery. But before he could make use of this promising material Easter Term had ended, again with no trial.

Colonel Scott was trumping Balty's ace.

"From beyond the sea," he sent to the Court, through his lawyer, Goodenough, copies of the treasonable material, but when called, did not appear. John was in France with the Duke of Buckingham, on business which may have possibly involved the quest of campaign funds for the Country Party. But in his absence, the Lord Chief Justice refused to have the matter read. And Pepys, in a torment of bitterness and indignation beyond measure was told he must hold himself at the Court's disposition for yet another three months! Bail, however, was this time disallowed, and he and Deane were subjected only to recognizances of one thousand pounds each.

Convinced he would never be able to make use of them, he

packed off his foreign witnesses, after taking all their depositions. And for years they continued to clamor for money![3] As
late as 1689 Deborah Egmont wrote to "Squire Pips" reminding him she had once "served him" and begging a job
for her new husband.[4] Even the reluctant Joyne Pepys finally
sent back to Paris, where he was speedily recognized as official agent of the once all-powerful Admiralty Secretary and,
as such, became the target of assorted rascals, particularly a
Portuguese, one Moralles, a man of forceful ingenuity. Together he and Joyne invented new Scott villainies which they
said threatened the Secretary and could only be averted by
the immediate payment of five hundred pounds! For three
more years they kept up this blackmail, pursuing Pepys to
London in 1683, where the sorely tried little man, throwing
caution to the winds, had Joyne imprisoned. The watchmaker
promptly sued Pepys, in Chancery, and Pepys responded by
a thumping rebuttal (which runs into thirty-three large
membranes) in the Mitford Chancery Proceedings. But that is
another story.

For the time being—in early 1680—Pepys' hands were full
with the "Revelations" of his three perjurers who now
showed signs of wavering; even his dying butler seemed under
fearful pressures and literally collapsed while still trying to
make a statement. In an almost inhuman disregard for the
unhappy man's last hours, Pepys, his lawyer, his colleague and
close friend Will Hewer, sundry Justices of the Peace and
the great Harbord M.P. himself, all crowded into the poverty-
stricken bedroom where James lay in agony, there to read
correspondence, take depositions, confront the tormented
creature with papers which he acknowledged to be true, and,
faced practically with delirium and death throes, finally to
obtain a signed declaration which absolved not only Pepys
from popery, but Harbord from bribery!

With his battle half won, Pepys sternly resisted opportunities for revenge in the tempting suggestions of the genial
Donluis that they now enter the world of plot and counter-

plot and involve Shaftesbury in a momentous "discovery." Shaken by his recent experience, Pepys was only too happy to retire, a spectator on the sidelines. High politics had never claimed his allegiance, and with so much evidence for sale he may well have begun to suspect how very fragile were his own defenses.

From Paris had arrived the first of Joyne's letters. Pepys, still feeling dependent upon him, sent him ten pounds and told him "to be easy with Moralles" and to continue his search for Scott's crimes. To Balty, he sent renewed instructions; to seek more sworn statements, there were still so many people to question: Seigneley's maître d'hotel; "that French boy, Doise," former servant of Mr. Wentworth, M.P.; and "him that was with the Duke of Buckingham and made the sweetmeats"; Javier, former barber to the Duke of York, now in France; Berkshire's two servants; Pélissary's porter and footman.[5] Pepys' truly heroic energy overlooked nothing . . . and he learned, at third, or fourth hand, innumerable remarkable details—that John had said he was a Dutchman; that he had killed the Duke of York's page, had pawned his map-plates; and, once, didn't pay his tailor.*

It was the last frantic gesture. All things considered, however, Pepys felt that his labors were paying off. "My adversary continues his old practice of keeping out of my way and giving no evidence . . . saying that his purpose is to respite it for parliament," he wrote John Joyne on June 18th, 1680. But it was something right outside both Scott's and Pepys' dominion that brought their business to a sudden standstill. The Opposition had overplayed its hand: it had not reckoned on Charles' successful counteroffensive. The

---

* Typical of so much of the "evidence" that builds John Scott's life story, is the testimony of a Captain Holland, who is relaying information of a Captain Brown, a sealgraver who worked on the gun-casting experiment. "He promises to inquire out one Poulsen that did belong to Lord Arlington who knows Scott very well and all his Practices, as having discoursed mightily with him against Scott but upon what particulars he knoweth not." Rawl. MSS., A 173, f 192.

Petition Campaign had backfired; the public was beginning to tire of violence and vilification.

The popular mood seemed reflected in the action of the Lord Chief Justice and the Attorney General. Trinity Term opened and Pepys and Deane put in their routine motion for discharge, hardly daring to hope for either trial or liberty. But the end came with startling brevity which surpassed their wildest dreams. For on June 28th, 1680, the Court, hearing that there was nothing against their motion, informed them they were discharged and bid them be gone. After months of humiliation, anguish and suspense, Pepys was a free man.

And a most cautious one, too. For the first time it looks as if he understood that "Satan Scott" was not the sole cause of his misfortune; that dangers of a vaster, more nebulous nature threatened him. Whether he knew it or not, he was caught up in a political maelstrom. With possible civil war in England and with Charles in full breach with Louis, the European situation was such that the King could not exist on his revenues. Supplies would *have* to be voted by parliament. And if parliament met and witnesses were brought over to testify against him, Pepys, to defend himself, would be forced to reveal the King's secret ties with France. To a man of such simple loyalties as the Secretary, the thought was intolerable.

His original intention of taking the offensive and wiping Scott from the political scene forever was abandoned. When Deane bluntly urged him to publish (under the assumed name of G. Bayley) the collected "evidence," he refused. Perhaps he saw how impossible it would have been to have substantiated any of this gossip. The affidavits—all the original ill-scrawled statements, as well as the copies in Paul Lorraine's exquisite copperplate, he locked away among his private papers. From time to time he added more villainies, supplied by the unquenchable Joyne. But the accusations were now becoming so far-fetched—with a whole new Popish Plot involving the Queen of England—that Pepys' original doubts returned a thousandfold; and he even reproached Joyne heatedly for his "impious and detestable machinations."

And not many years passed before he himself referred to the "silly charge" that had once sent him to the Tower and on which he had hoped to convict John Scott! "What a pother was heretofore made about the pretended discovery of our sands, etc. to strangers," he wrote; with scoffing memories of a certain British Admiral who for all his precise knowledge of their exact position still managed, at a most critical moment, to get stuck in the mud."*

But in 1680 Pepys was taking no chances. When John Scott, just back from France, was reported at Newmans talking to an Admiralty clerk, Pepys dispatched the faithful Hewer to fortify (with a little financial aid) the man's honesty against Whig assault! The danger was not yet over.

Though there had been no trial, and Pepys had never had to justify himself before them, the Opposition Lords were still very strong and cunning, and John was far closer to them than Pepys had ever suspected.

Shaftesbury was driving his party with terrible urgency. Racked by physical pain and in failing health, he never lost sight of his goal: a Protestant English monarch. He was always ready with new assaults, relying on John, among his partisans, to carry them out.

In the spring of 1680, the great little Lord announced to the Privy Council the existence of an Irish Plot, and insisted that his substantiating witnesses be examined, not in Ireland —as the Duke of Ormonde, the staunch Royalist Lord-Lieutenant demanded—but in England under his own control. So into the country poured a motley crew of "good swearers" ready to make Protestant flesh creep with the tried-and-true recital of fire and massacre. John, lawyer-like, was their "manager," briefing them for their courthouse appearance.

Hard on this exploit came Shaftesbury's Black Box rally,

---

* Lord Dartmouth, sailing to oppose the Prince of Orange in 1688, could not get his fleet off Galloper Sand, in the mouth of the Thames!

an ingenious attempt to bolster his candidate's claims to the throne. Late in April persistent rumors—which John circulated assiduously through coffeehouses and taverns—hinted at a mysterious box among the effects of the late Bishop of Durham, containing proof that Charles, during his exile, married Lucy Walter, thus making the Duke of Monmouth legitimate.

So successful was this rich vein, appealing as it did to all the romantic yearnings of simple folk for a disinherited Protestant prince restored to his rights, that the King had to make a public declaration denying the existence of marriage lines.

Even so the young Duke's stock rose very considerably. Shaftesbury sent John into the West country—always a Stuart stronghold—on a big campaign tour for the dashing young warrior; to arrange royal "progresses" and generally act as publicity man. It was the kind of work that suited John best. His ready charm, his easy line of persuasive talk, won friends and adherents wherever he went, and so impressed the powerful Member for Taunton, John Trenchard, that, on the strength of this visit, he put up Colonel Scott's name for the Green Ribbon Club. Within a short time John, duly elected, was free to swagger through the rooms of the famous King's Head Tavern; to come out on the balcony, his long pipe in his hand, and, at Pope-burning orgies or on bonfire nights, watch the delirious crowds, and take pride in knowing that for some of their antics at least, he and other members were pulling the strings.

But if Shaftesbury relentlessly pursued a policy to establish a Protestant heir-apparent, the King had never shown greater political sagacity in defending the hereditary principle. Burdened as he was with a childless wife he would not divorce, a papist successor whose rights he would not betray, and his unalterable refusal to place a bastard on the throne, he defied his angry Ministers, shrugged off all minor plots and dared flout public opinion by even turning against the still towering figure of Titus Oates.

Commons had already expelled two Members for expressing disbelief in the Popish Plot, but Charles put the first real
brake on the national hysteria by refusing any further to
grant pardon in advance to those whose testimony sent Catholics to the gallows. And Oates he sent packing and pension-
less from his Whitehall suite.

Response was immediate. The Duke of York was indicted
as a Popish recusant, and burnt in effigy. "T'is rebellion,"
Charles accused Shaftesbury to his face. But the little Lord
coldly maintained that he was within the law—a fact the King
could not dispute.

For behind this mortal duel the influence of John Locke,
"that great doctor of the Revolution," as Trevor-Roper calls
him, was still operating. More than ten years were to elapse
before he formulated in philosophical terms the ideas which
Shaftesbury professed and which John in a simple fashion
had both anticipated and applied. Unscrupulous as the use of
some of them might be at that date, they rested, nevertheless,
upon belief in the sovereignty of the people, and in the conviction that all peaceful beginnings of government must have
the people's consent.

But how long would ambitious men remain within the law?

In autumn Charles met his fourth Parliament; saw the Exclusion Bill triumphantly carried through the House—to be
defeated, after a terrific struggle, by the Peers. George Duke
of Buckingham made one of his great speeches and moved
that a committee from both Houses "consider the state of
the nation with regard to Popery."

It was debated two hours before being thrown out, but it
brought the unpredictable Duke into the political limelight
again. He had been feuding with Shaftesbury over choice of
the successor; the Republicans favored the Prince of Orange
—Dutch William—rather than the wastrel Monmouth; while
Buckingham, whose mother was a Plantagenet, considered
himself a more fitting candidate than either. Now the two
powerful Lords closed ranks again. The Exclusion Bill's

defeat had turned the tide against the Whigs, and both men scented an upsurge of royalist sentiment. Charles made a clever surprise attack by calling Parliament to meet at Oxford where, out of reach of the bullying London mobs, and with troops patrolling the road to the Chilterns, he faced and dismissed his fifth and last Parliament. Resolved neither to surrender to pressure nor risk civil war, *he had made a second secret deal with Louis.* Assured of the equivalent of one hundred thousand dollars a year, he could dispense altogether with the people's representatives and custodians of national destiny. And at last he felt strong enough to send Shaftesbury to the Tower.

With his rival out of the way, Buckingham seized control of the Country Party, and John came back to his old patron. The Duke, with his parliamentary motion defeated, indulged in a little direct action and now made overtures openly to the nation, declaring once again that arbitrary government was imperiling the Protestant religion. This clarion call was taken up with a will by John, Colonel Mansell, and others of the Duke's clan who urged all listeners that it was the duty of every Protestant to oppose the prevailing conditions "to the hazard of their lives and fortunes."[6]

Lacking his great rival's tactical skill and superb sense of measure, Buckingham rashly financed armed intervention. Obscure blacksmiths in London's East End, were commissioned to forge daggers with *Memento Godfrey* inscribed on their blades; all night long the lathes were turning out weapons; and, just as in the tragic days of '42, horses and ammunition were sent from Holland, landed on lonely beaches, hidden for the coming "Day." Buckingham, so it was reported, unable to exclude the Duke legally, intended, upon the King's death, to bring over Dutch help and impose his own choice by arms!

John, however, did not go along with this violence. He was a commonsense politician believing that government was a "noble art" and that "to keep order in the land" was a monarch's first and foremost task (as he wrote in an essay on how Kings should rule). Not only would his former royalist attachments exclude drastic measures but such an attitude was reinforced, at this period, by his contact with John Locke whose ideas on the mutual contract between sovereign and sovereign-people in the spirit of toleration and civil liberty Scott so demonstrably shared. And if, indeed, Buckingham had ever plotted York's assassination, this dark design was, to John's relief and possibly owing to his influence, dropped.[7]

Soon Shaftesbury was released by a packed grand jury who returned a verdict of *Ignoramus* (insufficient evidence). And together the two noble lords rode from the Tower to Aldersgate, their coaches followed by hysterically vociferous crowds. "A Buckingham! A Shaftesbury! No Popery!" they cheered hoarsely the length of the way. It was the last cheers the two were ever to hear, before they disappeared from the political arena for good.

But John was not there to witness their downfall. His own had come even more suddenly and from a source whose insignificance seemed to mock his whole existence. Yet it was not wholly out of character. John had never learned to discipline his passions nor check the turbulence that made his career a storm of sixty years. His intemperance proved his own undoing.

For one tranquil May evening in 1682 he was in the Horseshoe Tavern on little Tower Hill, in the company of one of Buckingham's lawyers, Mr. Warton, of Lincoln's Inn. The host had shown them into a back room whereupon John had been much offended and demanded a better, threatening the man with his sword. Apologizing profusely, the tavernkeeper gave them what they wanted, and brought a pint of canary wine. They sat drinking and talking, and then John sent a boy for a hackney coach to take them back to Temple Bar. The hacker, a George Butler, "who loved not that end of town," refused to take them there for one and sixpence and was dismissed.

"Am I to have nothing for my pains?" he demanded truculently.

Suddenly John was filled with suspicion; ("he had not God before his eyes," testified a witness later).

Why had the hacker come into the inn? What had he overheard of their conversation? Was he a spy in somebody's pay? Cabbies were notoriously venal, and John had been engaged in earnest conversation with one of the Duke's legal aides. Was the driver part of the offensive against the Opposition? Nobody knows; for there was never any adjudication. But it is impossible to believe that the dispute and subsequent tragedy were merely about the insignificant sum of one and sixpence.

Rising abruptly and following the cabby into the courtyard, John shouted: "I will give you something for your pains." And drawing his sword he ran the man through.

Suddenly the night was rent with screams of "Murder! Murder! You have murdered me!"

"You lie, like a rogue," retorted John. But the man lay silent and prostrate with a wound below his navel.[8]

Abandoning his coat and gloves, John disappeared, before the gaping crowds arrived.

A hue and cry was put out.

And in eighteen pages of formal Latin he was subsequently arraigned before a London Court. "The Outlawry of Colonel Scott for the murder of John George Butler," it read; but John was not there to hear the charge. Nor is there any record in the files of the King's Bench, or London Sessions, of any trial.

Two weeks later *Thompson's Intelligencer* published a story with embellishments which could only have come from someone very near Samuel Pepys. Now were made public all the spiciest details of the collected affidavits, a list of the "pranks" John was supposed to have played.

"This Great Vindicator of the Salamanca Doctor," shrieked the news sheet, hitting headlines by coupling John's name with that of Titus Oates, "cheated the States of Holland of £7000 and was hanged in effigy at the Hague. He went to Paris pretending to be a person of quality belonging to the Court and got several sea cards [sic] which he could shew them how to burn all His Majesty's navy in their harbors, but being discovered a cheat was forced to fly. Since the discovery of the Popish Plot he came into England and pretended he had those sea cards of Sir Anthony Deane and Mr. Pepys and that they would hand the ships burnt by the French King and employed him for this purpose . . ."[9]

It was all there, even more garbled than Pepys had it. But John did not see the sheet. Once again he had slipped out of the country and was safe abroad.

BIBLIOGRAPHICAL NOTES

1. Rawl. MSS., A 175, f 204; Mit. Ch. Pro., C 8, 376, No. 69.
2. Rawl. MSS., A 194, f 117.
3. Ibid., A 178, ff 49, 52, 54, 103, 115, 178, 182, 188.
4. Ibid., A 179, f 57.
5. Mit. Ch. Pro., C 8, 638, No. 61.
6. CSP Dom., 1682, p. 269.
7. Ibid., No. 110.
8. Rawl. MSS., A 178, f 238.
9. Ibid., ff 238-240; 260-62.

CHAPTER XLVII

LAST DAYS

Duty in my heart, not faction, shines.
—John Scott, "Lines on Courageous Talbot,"
Rawl. MSS., A 176, f 75.

York Buildings
May 13th 1682
Will Hewer to Samuel Pepys:

"OUR FRIEND COLONEL SCOTT, being fled for killing a coach-man, the Coroner having found it willful murther meanes are using to buy off the widow who has three small children; but we are considering what to do to prevent it, Sir Anthony Deane being come to town. . . ."

Pepys, from Newcastle on May 26th answered, "This leads me to the tidings you give of our friend Scott, whom God pleased to take out of our hands into his own for justice; for should he prevail with the widow for her forgiveness there is the King's pardon behind, which I suppose he will not easily compass, unless by some confessions which I am confident he is able to make, relating to the State *as well as us;* that might enough atone for this his last villainy. Nor do I doubt but to save his own life, he will forget his trade and tell truth, though to the hazard of the best friends he has, *which pray let Sir Anthony Deane think of.*"[1] (Italics added.)

Pepys' concern about Deane may have been no more than that of a good friend for a colleague who had shared his prison ordeal. But Deane's activities do little to enhance his reputation and seem rather to confirm the suspicion aroused by John Scott's accusation. No longer a Navy ship-builder, but engaged in various lucrative private undertakings, Deane was one of the three speculators who had purchased from the ruined Duke of Buckingham York House to develop as Admiralty offices, a vast commercial enterprise which must have called for the outlay of considerable capital. Where had he suddenly found all this money? And one is further disturbed by the man's apparent need to assuage his conscience by vehement self-justification over the excellence of his former service, insomuch that (as he wrote Pepys), "from his single care and industry in the place he served, he saved His Majesty above one hundred thousand pounds, and had saved further one hundred and fifty thousand pounds more," had his advice been taken.[2] Surely the gentleman did protest too much!

Pepys' fear that Scott would betray his friends and return "to tell all" was never fulfilled. Though John was privy to all the Republicans' last desperate ventures and knew where the smuggled arms were stored, he made no use of the fact. And his friends were equally loyal to him. Someone in the government allowed him a small pension during his exile, just enough to keep him alive, though the details of this period are very meager. His flight to the Continent came at the very height of his career and at a moment when he seemed about to renew contacts with his family. Apparently he had sent for, and was expecting his sons; and from the affectionate tone of a letter he had written from London in May, 1681, the correspondence had evidently been going on for some time. That he should consign Jeckomiah to the care of Captain Howell (of the distinguished Southampton family of that name) and send warm greetings to John Topping, another of his home town's first families, gives the lie yet again to the Pepysian affidavits. A man is, after all, known by the company he keeps, and on Long Island, John kept excellent company.

"My Deare Child,

I have sent to thy brother a hat, a suit of clothes, a pair of stockings, some Gloves, Cravats, Paper, a grammar . . . and have writ to Captain Howell to take you into his family." [The boys. in 1679, came into their share of "the great division of land formerly belonging to their father,"[3] and Jeckomiah's going to Captain Howells' may have coincided with Deborah Scott's marriage with Charles Sturmey.] "I charge you to yield to him exact obedience and be verry Diligent and let me find by a letter by Captain Bound what proficiency you make. . . .

"If you give me Incuragement I shall be very kind to you and take great care for your Preferment, and shall send for you as soon as your Brother has made one voiage to get the Practical Part of Navigation, that at his Returne to Southampton he may be able to give such account of himself that Render him useful and acceptable to his friends, and, if God preserve him, become master and merchant, of a ship and cargo. But I design you for another sort of Life, therefore do not, through want of an Industrious address, Injure your selfe by Destroying my hopes and Expectations. Had your brother come over *when I sent for him* he would have learned that which I find he is now uncapable of in great measure, and might have been back again before this time, and so has in effect, lost two or three years which I hope he will with great Industrey Retrieve. I have sent you a hood and Skarfe, and three Paire of Gloves for you to make a present on to your Mother to shew your Dutifull Respect to her. For whatever *Difference she and I have had, Remember she is your mother,* and you owe her a Duty of the greatest Tenderness. [Italics added.] I charge you keep close to your Book; the first good accompt you give me I will send you anything that you signifie to me you have occasion for; Captain Howell must be an evidence for you, of your civil Gentle behaviour, I trust God in his mersey will dispose you to have an eye to his service and not to think it Labour Lost, for it is the Interest of

Every Private Person to make search Into ye Nature and Quality of the Religion by which alone he can hope to be Eternally happy. My service to your uncle Joseph [Raynor, Deborah's brother] and all my friends, Wright upon Mr. John Topping and present my service to him and Pray his Excuse for not wrighting at this time; I shall suddenly, God willing, do him the trouble of a letter.

    I am your very affectionate
    Loveing father,
                John Scott"

Though a fugitive from justice, John neither forgot his family nor seemed to have lost hope that he might once again serve his country. By his own underground means of communication he began negotiating for resuming work as foreign agent, negotiations that were not, at that moment successful, though he writes hopefully to Lord Arlington, later. He had heard that the Secretary of State, Sir Leoline Jenkins, had had his papers and personal effects seized from his Chancery Lane lodgings, to be put with those previously confiscated from Cannon Street on Samuel Pepys' order. His elaborate suits he hoped to get back for his son. Many a Restoration gentleman put the best part of his fortune into his wardrobe and John's satins and silver laces were obviously of more value than the "little necessaries" he mentions.

His plaint that he was "traduced" to the Duke of York is partially explained by the fact that the Duke's informer, Colonel Thomas Blood (himself a soldier of fortune, who almost succeeded in stealing the Crown Jewels from the Tower and was pardoned by Charles for the sheer audacity of his crime) had recently reported to his master "dangerous conspiracies still carrying on against your person and interest."[4] He included evil doings of Colonel Scott (William, son of the regicide) who was active in an Irish rebellion. Since Blood never distinguished between the two Colonel Scotts, the Duke may also have entertained the same illusion, re-inforcing his Long Island memories of John.

But in his last letter to Lord Arlington, *our* Colonel Scott speaks for himself.

Teerveer, Zeeland, June 26th, 1682

The person I ordered to wait on you writes that it is expected I should set down particularly in what manner I can be servicable, and that I might write either to you or to him, and that it met with opposition. I had hoped for such an answer as might have encouraged you to favor me with two or three lines, but, it seems, no service I can do will balance the severity of my enemies. They that desire my mentioning particulars under my hand may consider that would bring me under great perils, before I have a pardon. Though its refused, I wish as great security to the government as I wish to my own soul, I should never have mentioned what I did to you, had I not intended the greatest sincerity and there had been something in it much more considerable to me than my own safety. Not many months ago a black design was touched gently and let go again, which was of worse consequence than was imagined and wants no improvement. You may remember I have expressed great dissatisfaction at the carriage of some persons, ever since before the Oxford parliament and had a great desire to be represented to his Majesty and His Royal Highness, to whom I have been traduced; and such was my misfortune more than my natural inclinations, which put me on some things and adhering to some persons, which otherwise I should not have done. I was never for *overturning** and my moderation may one day appear to have been of some service, as inconsiderable a person as I am looked on. If you judge it not advisable to write I pray say nothing to this young man, for, though I have writ to him to mind his own business, there are of that party that will not

---

* This was the Fanatics' classic expression, denoting complete constitutional change. Italics added by author.

endure that I should accept of His Majesty's grace if offered, and, till he gets out of England, I know not how they may be sifting for him. Since you have taken the maps, charts, and plans at my lodgings, I would entreat you to move Secretary Jenkins for an order that my son might have my clothes and little necessaries, which are of little value."[5]

John found nothing to occupy him in Zeeland. The Prince of Orange had all the United Provinces very firmly in hand, nor would he be likely to look very favorably upon one who, in 1672, had so persistently advocated a separatist movement in his kingdom. John quit Terveer and we hear next of him in Norway. In September, James Gelson, former Shaftesbury agent, wrote to Pepys from Skeen and Christiana, where he had met John, and heard from his own lips something of his work with the Opposition. It was John's fate to be described and interpreted by people of limited knowledge and intelligence, and one must remember that Gelson had been bitterly jealous of his Flanders rival in the old days, so we must accept his words with some reservation.

Skeen, Sept., 1683

". . . His Service was to insinuate evil against the government, His Majesty and His Royal Highness," wrote Gelson.

"He should cry up sometimes the Commonwealth, sometimes the Duke of Monmouth as he met with persons fit for impressions to beget a loathing to the government and governors and to divide the King's friends, the latter being only for that purpose; they desiring no King but tyrants under the pretence of a commonwealth. Oates was to have sworn in a fit time that the King gave commissions to the Roman Catholics to destroy the Protestant subjects. He knew the authors and spreaders of treasonable libels; they swore the King was to be killed by the Papists and put other things on them to aggravate the people against them and through their sides was the only way to wound and destroy the government and to raise parties and force on pretence against them . . . Their party consisted of enemies to the government and discontented and disappointed persons, and such as hoped for proferements, with fools and others deluded. He (Scott) was put upon informing against Mr. Pepys by a person that hoped to get his place and they designed to have taken away his life, but the person found he was not like to succeed if they proceeded."[6]

Again Gelson writes, Sept. 30th, 1683 . . . Skeen "My last acquainted you I was going to find Colonel Scott in hopes to prevail with him to make a full discovery of the late ill designs. I met with him at Lauvik and he promised to do it and put it in writing before I went to England, But I insinuated that expedition would be its life and therefore desired him to do it as soon as possible and I would convey it by good hand. But being sent for to unload a ship in this river I was forced to leave him before it was effected.

"He was present at many of the consults for overthrowing the government, at least for putting force on His Majesty. Very many late Parliament men were of the same conspiracy. He knows all the principal persons engaged in it. He was chosen to go into the West country to make parties for the Duke of Monmouth and practised it by private insinuations and public speeches . . . That they had been in action long before the *discovery* [presumably the Popish Plot—italics added] but that the Commonwealth men disagreed with the others and they were jealous of each other. He acknowledges he was a tool much used. As he pretends to know all of any consideration that were engaged I hoped to procure from him their names and the methods designed . . . and with such circumstances and proofs as may confirm what he declares. I insinuated that it would be very acceptable to God and might be servicable to His Majesty and be the way to insure forgiveness from both, and to kept strictly to the truth was all that was desired.

"I shall go over to him again in a few days to see what he

can and will do and shall endeavour to get it done with greater expedition because I hope the nation is a little come to itself and as soon as may be in a posture for His Majesty to have a parliament. . . ."[7]

But Parliament never met again during Charles II's reign though national passions *did* subside a little after Titus Oates disappeared. The infamous doctor of divinity was convicted of perjury in 1685, was pilloried, and actually survived the two awful floggings through London streets from Aldgate to Newgate and to Tyburn.

Tories gradually regained the ascendancy in public affairs; and the day a Tory Sheriff of London was appointed—which meant an end to juries packed in favor of Whigs—Shaftesbury (alias Johnson) slipped out of England, to die some months later in Amsterdam, a lonely embittered man. All that he had feared and tried to prevent came to pass when, in 1685, the Duke of York, as James II, succeeded his brother and proceeded to suppress local government and the civil and religious liberties so long defended by the patriots. George Duke of Buckingham made his last public appearance at the Coronation ceremony—stripped of his offices, to be sure, but a still commanding figure, his lively eyes and high-bred features unable to conceal the contempt and ridicule he felt for glum, dull-witted obstinate James. This new King he could not take seriously and within a matter of weeks he had outraged the royal sensibilities with an essay, *Reason and Religion*, his final plea for liberty of conscience.

But no one could cope with James II's political ineptitude, his stubborn blindness. After three disastrous years, his exasperated subjects rose and drove him from the throne. They drew up a Bill of Rights and invited William of Orange with his wife Mary—Protestant daughter of James—to sign it and to reign as King and Queen together. Major Wildman and Harbord were on the ship which triumphantly brought them from Holland, and John Scott may have hoped that on *their* return (after a voluntary exile during James' brief reign) they might hasten his own. He was disappointed. The Glorious Revolution had come about, but with Shaftesbury, Buckingham and Arlington all dead, John lingered in quasi-oblivion for a few more years, forgotten by the other two.

At Montserrat, in the West Indies (an island John had once "resettled" during his early travels), there is a parchment indenture, dated March 1st, 1694, of the sale of a hundred acre estate to him, with all buildings thereon. So John had returned to his old haunts and had become a member of the Leeward Assembly since 1691 and was Captain of the Montserrat Forts at the time he bought this, his last residence, listed as being in St. Peter's Parish, between Soldier's Gutt and the Old River.[8] But evidently he was only giving the place a trial; he did not stay long and the final sale was not recorded until 1697.[9] John, meanwhile, returned to Europe and was certainly in France once more about 1695. He was presumably again doing some kind of intelligence for the British government, and, returning unexpectedly in London one day, was arrested "for coming out of France without leave."[10] He surrendered to the Duke of Shrewsbury, but apparently his work was known and recognized; indeed he is credited with having exposed a Jacobite plot brewing on the Continent and threatening the royal family.[11] Whether he actually did so or not, King William's providential escape marked a change in John's luck. He was formally pardoned for illegal entry into England and this was followed by even greater clemency.

In April, 1696, the King sent a preliminary order to the Attorney-General, stating: "it is the King's will and pleasure" that a bill be prepared "for our Royal Signature . . . containing our gracious and free pardon unto John Scott Esq. . . . concerning the death and killing of . . . and of all indictments, convictions, outlawries, Paynes and Penalties . . . incurred thereby. . . ." With legal flourishes it ordered "all requisite apt and beneficial clauses be inserted" to make the pardon "most full, valid and effectual."[12]

Even in his most sanguine moments John could not have hoped for such complete forgiveness of his hot-headed killing. When the document passed the Greate Seale in July, 1696, John was once again a free man, to come and go as he pleased. Pepys and his friends caught up with the news only much later.

One of his innumerable correspondents wrote Pepys in November, 1696, "Colonel Scott came to England about 7 weeks ago in a seaman's habit, he was not seen by anybody I know till about 16 days ago and then he appeared in a pretty good habit and a bob wig and pulled out a parchment with a broad seal on it. . . . His person and carriage are not a bit altered."[13]

He had not changed. He was still the lithe, ardent figure he had always been, but the times had changed. He was alone and without patrons in an England ruled by a man to whom John "had always been obnoxious."[14]

What had he to expect?

When indeed had his expectations ever been fulfilled?

"A tool much used," Gelson had called him, but John Scott was no man's tool, though he had often served a cause. Perhaps he recounted to himself bitterly the many times he had kept the faith, and always to his own disadvantage.

Oliver Cromwell he would not serve, though "great employment" would have come if he had. Governor Winthrop's commission he resigned when its purpose would have imperiled religious freedom. The King's New England commissioners could not tempt him from what he chose to regard as his duty to his monarch and his monarch's overseas subjects. While in Dutch service he declined governorship of the town of Roos, since taking it would have entailed an oath of allegiance to Holland.

He abandoned this foreign military career at a word from his King; nor would he betray his side no matter what inducements the United Provinces offered him. Even John's work with the Opposition and his abandonment of royalist sympathies were founded on the assumption that Charles himself was betraying his better nature and degrading England by his financial dependence upon France. A summing up of John's feelings on this score (as his letter to Arlington suggests) was Shaftesbury's last desperate appeal that the King give heed to Whig proposals; and his assurance that the King would find loyalty enough would he but be loyal too!

"There must be, My Lord, in plain English, a change, there must be neither Popish wife, nor Popish mistress, nor Popish councillors . . . you may have anything from Parliament. Put away these men, change your principles, change your Court. Be yourself."[15]

Well, now it was all over. The Whig cause had sunk into conspiracy and perished, only to be gloriously revived to flourish for more than a century. But there seemed no place in England for John. Now he definitely took ship for the West Indies. Seven times he had sailed the Caribbean in his life's wanderings; he was as much at home there as anywhere. And it looks as if he were rejoined by his former wife Deborah, now a rich widow. Sturmey had died in 1691 and there is no further reference to her in the Southampton Records after the mention of her as sole executrix of his will. It would be pleasant to think of the two former lovers spending their declining years together; John's restlessness finally appeased, his flaming temper quenched by Deborah's placid ways. The possibility of reunion is strong; but it is only *conjecture*.

Public affairs claimed John's last years, and in that part of the world which, as he had written, he chose to make the scene of the greatest actions of his life.

He was appointed Speaker of the Assembly at Montserrat in 1698.[16] In the lists of names from which the respective Leeward Isles' councils were filled in 1699, John Scott, with others of the islands, was described generally as "of good sense, honesty, and repute."[17] As Council member he was also signatory of a petition in 1700 regarding a gubernatorial appointment, and the handwriting on this document (now in the Record Office), although somewhat subdued, is still the same distinctive signature of Scott as it appeared in the Preface of his Histories and on the New Amsterdam armistice agreement.

Then comes the final entry among the public records of Bridgetown, Barbados, in 1704: his name is listed among the deaths, and the following year, it was recorded in the British state Papers.

"And so," as his biographers invariably write, "nothing more is known of him." They had said that so often—when he had helped bring out that little catechism for the Indians; when he left Long Island to serve under Willoughby; when he feuded with Nicolls and took service with the Dutch.

"Nothing more is heard of him." That was the end of John Scott.

How wrong they were.

BIBLIOGRAPHICAL NOTES

1. Braybrooke, *Diary S. Pepys*, IV, 292.
2. Rawl. MSS., A 464, ff 88, 91.
3. S-ampton TR., II, 73.
4. *CSP. Dom.* 1681, 417, No. 207.
5. *Ibid.*, 419, No. 110.
6. *Ibid.*, 432, No. 35.
7. *Ibid.*, 433, No. 15.
8. *Montserrat Code of Laws*, 1688-1788, p. 30.
9. Add. MSS., 15, 556, f 120.
10. SP. Dom. Warrant Bk., 39, f 240.
11. *HMC State Aff.*, III, 483; *HMC Buccleuch*, II, 291-96.
12. SP. Dom. Entry Bk., 167, f 394; *Bk.* 345, f 436.
13. Braybrooke, *Diary S. Pepys*, IV, 26 (Edward Wright's letter to Pepys).
14. *Ibid.*
15. *CSP Dom.*, 1682, p. 494.
16. *CSP Col. Ser. Am. and W. I.*, 1697-98, No. 995.
17. *Ibid.*, 1699, No. 659.

EPILOGUE

"Give me leave to hope these Histories may be of use, in
the first place, to ministers of State who may now, without tedius examination of records . . . be satisfied in a
view both of what hath been disposed, and when. In case
there be any differences, as there have been between
colony and colony, by this means without trouble may be
adjudged and decided."

—John Scott, *Preface.*

FOR OVER TWO CENTURIES the turbulent spirit of John Scott
was stilled, but it was not extinguished. The world was to
hear more of him. He had swept through life like a high
wind, stirring and stirred by controversy; but his comeback
ultimately routed his enemies in a manner unexpected and
surprising, yet oddly in keeping with his character. And his
last appearance put the stamp of approval on his worth and
integrity, wiping out, with a typical Scott flourish, the unwarranted reputation his contemporaries had bestowed on him.

An urgent international crisis was the setting for his reappearance: war or peace was at stake. To a certain extent
John tipped the balance in a conflict over a boundary line.
So it was land—the disputed possession of land—which brought
him back. No occasion could have been more appropriate.
How he would have relished the situation! It fulfilled his
dearest hope as expressed in the Preface of his Histories!

British Guiana was the region in question. For a century
Venezuela and Great Britain had been wrangling over the

exact extent of their common South American boundary, each country claiming vast areas held by the other. In April, 1895, the Venezuelan Government brought matters to a head by arresting two members of the British Guiana police force for trespassing on Venezuela territory.

Shades of Long Island! How many times had John, in his day, adopted precisely the same tactics: charging trespass to challenge ownership by a Court decision.

But nineteenth century imperialism was in full flower: the two police officers reported to their government: Venezuela, foreseeing trouble, asked for United States backing. In July 1895 U.S. Secretary of State Richard Olney formally reminded Great Britain that the Monroe Doctrine must be respected. But his intervention could not lightly be accepted by Queen Victoria's ministers, and the following October Great Britain sent Venezuela an ultimatum. This was judged high-handed defiance of American rights, and in December, President Cleveland, invoking the Monroe Doctrine, sent to Congress his startling message that any attempt by Great Britain to enforce claims upon Venezuela without resort to arbitration would be resisted "by every means in our power."

Ominously the war drums began to roll.

Fortunately Commissions were immediately appointed— Great Britain's under Sir Frederick Pollock, that of the United States under Professor George L. Burr; and these, with a group of jurists and scholars, found themselves charged "at the cost of peace or war to find a true divisional line." Armed with quinine, bourbon, and a raft of maps they set off for the disputed area.

They found a trackless jungle of swamp and forest threaded by rivers no white man had navigated. The stakes along the so-called Schomburgk Line—which the British claimed—had long since disappeared and there was no hint where the two regions met. "There is and there can be, no true divisional line in the sense of the indubitable," declared the official American historical geographer.

Diplomatic correspondence of a century was sifted, only to reveal that during the entire controversy no single claim had ever been made by either save under the express protest of the other. Neither country had direct proprietary rights, but each based its title on its Spanish or Dutch inheritance. It was therefore to the records of Spain and the Netherlands, rather than to those of Venezuela and Great Britain that the Commissioners turned for light. They began searching for evidence of who settled there first.

And it was at this point that John Scott came into the picture. Scholars remembered Scott's account of his adventures in this obscure corner of the globe, now suddenly the proving ground of good faith and friendship between the two great Anglo-Saxon powers which had known him best.

Not only had he commanded an expedition there in 1666-67, and captured "Moroco, Wacopou, Boromeo* and Issekeob (Essequibo)," while together with Lieutenant-General William Byam, they "made themselves masters of the Atlantic coast of Guiana from Cayenne to North West Orinoco." But he had written about the Dutch West India Company's early trading stations and the Dutch claim, in 1621, to an exclusive right to colonize Guiana. A Dutch commander, the great Groenewegen, John wrote, "was the first man who took firm footing on Guiana by the good liking of the natives . . . he helped Barbadoes with food and trade in 1627 . . . and died in 1664 at the age of 83 having been governor forty years."

John's Histories were brought into the Arbitration Court as important contemporary writings, directly relevant to the

---

* Part of Guiana, renamed Surinam, the English restored to Holland, 1674, in exchange for Manhattan, which the Dutch had reconquered during the Third Dutch War. In 1814, the English acquired another 20,000 square miles of Guiana from the Dutch; the Schomburgk Line had taken in 60,000 more square miles of the territory. And by 1885 this had grown to 76,000 square miles . . . or altogether, 109,000 square miles. The area disputed by Great Britain and Venezuela had originally only concerned the Pomeroon region. (*Ven. Briefs.* Vol. VII.)

solution of the issue!*

The evidence was most upsetting to Venezuela's claims. John not only listed fourteen successive attempts—Spanish, Dutch, English, French—to colonize Guiana, but described Spain's continued failure to establish a settlement there. He quoted Hakluyt and his own contemporaries who refer to the same fact.

The Americans saw their case suddenly slipping from their grasp. On behalf of the United States Commission, Professors Burr and Jameson sprang to discredit the testimony.

"The author of these papers, Major John Scott, somewhat famous in the history of Long Island and of New Netherland down to 1665," commented Professor Jameson, caustically, "has not the highest reputation. Lord Willoughby writes to Secretary Williamson, he has perchance told you some truth, but not all gospel."[1]

Colonel Netscher, the Dutch expert for the Americans, was particularly contemptuous of this "anonymous fragment out of a manuscript of the Sloane collection," as he described John's [signed] works, with its mention of a Captain "Cromweagle" who died in 1664 after commanding for forty years. This was a Dutch skipper, corrected Netscher—his name a corruption of Groenewegel—who acted as commander at Kijkoveral only after 1657, and who died in 1666 or 1667.

But in court Netscher was proved wrong on all three counts. He had never read John's manuscript but only Bronkhurst's copy of it with its altered spelling—indeed, the ill-spelled Bronkhurst book was used all through the case. And

---

* Some of John's work had been previously published and noted by historians. Nearly all his Guiana description had been painstakingly transcribed by N. Darnell Davies and printed in a Guiana newspaper *The Royal Gazette*, July 24, 1879; and most of this had been copied again by a Wesleyan missionary, M. H. V. P. Bronkhurst and incorporated in his book, *The Colony of British Guiana, and its Laboring Population* (London; 1883, pp. 45-53.) That the original manuscript in the British Museum had ever been overlooked was due to a curious accident! John had written Byam's Journal on the back of his Histories—writing from the wrong end of the page, so that it was unfortunately bound upside down.

before the Arbitration was concluded Professor Burr admitted himself to be in error and that Scott was right in stating that Groene*wegen* (not we*gel,* as Netscher insisted) was commander *before 1657* and died in *1664.*[2]

But the Americans stuck to their guns. There were errors in Scott's work; he was palpably wrong on certain points, which impugned all the rest. Their arguments against John's credibility—with the single exception just above noted—were based upon non-corroboration of existing contemporary records—a fallacious method surely, since the contemporary records had to such a large extent vanished.

But "it seems difficult altogether to discredit it," lamented Burr. "The Zeeland expedition (Scott refers to) is historical. The passage regarding Barbados receives independent confirmation from a contemporary source. *The True Travels Adventures and Observations of Captain John Smith, London, 1630 in chapter 26,* of which we read concerning Barbados: The first planters brought thither by Captain Henry Powel, were forty English, with seven or eight Negroes; then he went to Disacuba in the maine, where he got thirty Indians, men, women and children, of the Arawacos."

But Burr maintained that not only were these Indians carried off *without any aid* from the Dutch, but that Powell knew nothing of the presence of the Dutch in the river. Scott therefore is clearly wrong.

Scott, however (though they did not know it at the time), was right. (Appendix M.)

To bolster Venezuela's case, Americans again threw doubt on John's character, impugning his veracity. How else destroy his arguments? The Pepysian affidavits were introduced as proof of the writer's unreliability. John's so-called courtmartial was discussed in detail. Once again his character was at the mercy of those who only by blackening it could gain their own ends. For from a man of such repute this embarrassing manuscript need be given little consideration.

Great Britain took the attitude that it was a question of

geography and history, not morals. Scott's character might be what it might but he obviously knew the continent under discussion and his histories told more about particular portions of it, and the men who had settled there, than anything brought to Court.

There was endless discussion over the identification of Baroma or Barima which John had captured and in one instance called Bowroome. This place Great Britain claimed as the territorial limit of her Schomburgk Line. But Burr insisted that John meant, not Barima on the river Barima, but Pomeroone!

"It is impossible to find in Scott's and in Byam's manuscript any warrant for the belief that the English found the Dutch in possession of any territory in Guiana west of the Colony of Pomeroon and the river Moruca," Professor Burr maintained. "But they suggest how such a belief, though erroneous, may easily have arisen. I speak of Humboldt's impression that the Dutch had at this time a post at the mouth of the River Barima and of Mr. Schomburgk's much more explicit statement that 'it was at least in existence when the British under John Scott destroyed, in 1666, the fort of New Zeeland and plundered New Middleburgh. If this is true, Major John Scott ought to know.' Of course it hardly needs suggesting that both Humboldt and Schomburgk may possibly have been misled by the 17th century form—Bowroom, Bowroome, Bowroma even Baroma—of the name Pomeron. . . . Pomeroon is a very modern spelling indeed."

Considering that spelling at that time was largely a matter of personal whim, and that many a man, not infrequently spelled his own name three different ways in the same document, Burr had a point. But it was only a supposition.

"A passage, which, if it were known," continued Burr, "might easily have given rise to misunderstanding, and which has besides, an interest of its own, is Scott's description of Tobago: 'And in 1642, Captain Marshall from Barbadoes began a second Colony . . . a flourishing colony, by the preservation of the Arawacoes.'

"Were there else reason for doubt," Burr concluded triumphantly, "the part played by the Arawak (Indians) would show that it is the *Pomeroon* and not the *Barima* which Scott meant, for he himself, in the preceding passage, assigned the Pomeroon region to them, the Barima to the Caribs (Indians)."

And after the case was over, Burr made light of it all by saying, "Here were two civilized states, ready to go to war over a claim that had no better objective basis than a German adventurer's misreading of an Indian name.[3]

But in the intensely nationalistic atmosphere during the arbitration attitudes were very different. As the case proceeded, however, Netscher, who had doubted John's history as well as his geography, began receiving less and less attention from the English and American investigators, and Burr and Jameson again had to admit reluctantly that "it is difficult to discredit Scott's document."

The arbitration lasted for years.

John Scott did not, in the final analysis, determine the outcome, but he was a very material witness and Venezuela's claims were considerably reduced by his evidence.

The verdict, handed down unanimously, in 1899, awarded Great Britain her Schomburgk Line, with the exception of a small strip of land ending at Point Barima, which was awarded to Venezuela—that country getting two hundred square miles of the sixty thousand it had claimed.

The American counsel tried hard to conceal its disappointment. But the real issue, it declared, was Point Barima.

As far as John was concerned, the issue was of much greater importance. At the bar of history, he had not only redeemed his reputation, but the case had focused attention on his life and work. A few years later, John Pollock (relative of Sir Frederick, Great Britain's commissioner) published an exhaustive volume on the Popish Plot, in which John Scott appears as a conspicuous figure of unquestioned integrity! He was no infamous follower and supporter of Titus Oates, as some of his contemporaries would have us believe. Among all the shameful secret lists of paid informers, John's name was nowhere to be found.

But the story of John's long over-due vindication was not finished. In 1901 an English historical scholar, the Rev. George Edmundson, than whom there was certainly no better authority in his particular field, contributed an article to the English Historical Review entitled *The Dutch in Western Guiana*, (vol 16, 640-675) in which he deplored the endeavors of Professors Burr and Jameson to discredit the Scott manuscript. Particularly as their arguments were adopted and repeated in a manner implying that the last word on the subject had been said by those presenting Venezuela's case in court.

Now that the issue was removed from politics, Edmundson set out to re-examine the whole question of settlements on the Essequibo and the Pomeroon, applying yardsticks to John's manuscript he invariably adopted for the consideration of all original work.

"The credibility of a writer relating otherwise unknown historical facts depends upon 1) his nearness to the events narrated; 2) his personal access to sure sources of information; 3) his motives in writing; 4) his proved accuracy in cases where his statements can be verified. All these tests are absolutely satisfactory in the instance of Major John Scott. . . ."[4]

And Edmundson, with a wealth of minute and incidental detail, culled from sources beyond question—sources which his exceptional personal knowledge of Dutch and Spanish colonial history uncovered—goes on to build up such a chain of cumulative evidence that the trustworthiness of the Scott narrative cannot but be accepted. And other English historians approve this view.

It makes a happy ending to the tale of a man who was so long the center of controversy and who has been so deeply maligned. Even if it is only on one side of the Atlantic that his rehabilitation is acknowledged, acceptance of him at true value, everywhere, is bound to come.

To the English John Scott must have seemed a last and lesser Elizabethan, a late product of the Renaissance who, in his swagger and versatility, would have felt completely at home in the Mermaid Tavern.

But to Americans he surely stands for something different —the foe of tyranny and undue privilege. By championing the citizen he anticipated Locke, father both of American democracy and English liberty. For this alone John Scott deserves a permanent place, however modest, among those whose lives and words prepared the way for the Declaration of Independence.

And in today's world, where individual freedom is once again the major issue, no American can afford to overlook him.

It took two centuries to prove the worth of his *Histories* . . . but life is long. "Time will do him great right," wrote the woman who understood him best. And the serene judgment of history will one day substantiate her words.

This book is but a beginning.

Washington, D.C.
Wonalancet, New Hampshire
October, 1959

BIBLIOGRAPHICAL NOTES

1. *U.S. Bound. Comm.,* I, 64; *CSP Col. Ser. Am. and W. I.,* 1661-68, Nos. 1525, 1661.
2. *Brit. Bl. Bk.,* VIII, 53.
3. Paper read before the American Historical Association at its New Haven meeting, April, 1899. Something of Burr's general attitude towards his colleagues can be discerned from his reference to the distinguished naturalist, Humboldt, as a "German adventurer."!
4. Edmundson, *The Dutch in Western Guiana,* E. H. R. XVI, 641.

APPENDICES

APPENDIX A

An example of how the Massachusetts Bay Company exceeded its charter limitations and abused the King's power is nowhere more evident than in the handling of land grants.

The territory under the jurisdiction of Massachusetts Bay included not only the original grant to the company, but also, during the more important part of its history, the territories of Maine (under its various names) and of Plymouth. The colony also claimed for a time the southern part of New Hampshire, and exercised powers of government there. It made itself felt for a long time in Rhode Island, and gave to the emigrants of Connecticut their first authority to form a settlement.

Connecticut was settled and its government organized without any charter or grant, and the lands were purchased by the planters from the Indians as they had need of them. Mr. Trumbull, the historian, says "the settlers of the river towns had not—before or after the agreement with Mr. Fenwick—any right of jurisdiction, except such as grew out of occupation, purchase from the native proprietors, or (in the case of the Pequot territory) of conquest." Their policy seems to have been to dispose as quietly and as cheaply as possible of the claims of such as challenged their title, into the exact nature of which they were not disposed to provoke too close an investigation. (*Conn. Pub. Rec.*, I, 569; Sidney Perley, *Indian Land Titles*, 25-28; Eggleston, *Land System of N. E.*, 13.)

APPENDIX B

The struggle over the possession of Horse Neck or Lloyd's Neck (as it was sometimes called) went on from 1653 until 1886, and is a striking example of the way land was disputed in colonial days. Earliest mention of this place is in a deed the Earl of Stirling issued to Mathew Sunderland, seaman of Boston, who bought two little necks of land: one on the east side of Oyster Bay, called Horse Neck; the Earl's title to this land was disputed, and repudiated. Horse Neck was sold by the Indians to Samuel Mayo in 1654. (*Oy. Bay T. R.,* I, 629.) He took the precaution of having his deed confirmed by the great Sachem Wyandanch, then resold the property to Samuel Andrews, for £100 in a deed recorded at a notary's office in Massachusetts. (*Hunt. T. R.,* I, 16.) Andrews, to make assurance doubly sure, had a further confirmation of his title to Horse Neck by Wiancombe, son of Wyandanch (after the Great Sachem's death) (*Ibid.*), and insisted that it (Horse Neck) be annexed to the township of Oyster Bay.

Despite all these hostile deeds, Huntington maintained its right to that peninsula. And when it was sold again to John Richbell (who immediately became involved in a counterclaim by one Conkling), the town ordered all its inhabitants (May 30th, 1665) to drive their cattle to Horse Neck meadows for a whole day, in order to manifest their right to the property. This bold act resulted in Richbell bringing suit for trespass against the town of Huntington.

Held in the newly established General Court of Assizes in New York from September 28th to October 4th, 1665, inclusive, this was one of the first cases to be tried under English Common Law, after the Dutch had been driven from New Amsterdam. The verdict was given first in favor of Huntington. But Richbell immediately appealed the decision, and the Court reconsidered the evidence. Taking into consideration the fact that Huntington had expressed the intention of *buying Horse Neck in 1654* (when it had been offered to Sam Mayo . . . but that their agent, John Gosby, had arrived *too late to make the purchase*), the Court decided that this was tantamount to an acknowledgment that the peninsula was *not then,* according to the original purchase, in the town's possession. So it reversed the jury's verdict. It placed Horse Neck outside Huntington and barred off one third of its seashore, while to John Richbell, it awarded possession of the said Neck with all appurtenances. Governor Nicolls formally confirmed this with the prescribed *"by-turf-and-twig"* ceremony and phraseology, December 18, 1665. In 1667, Richbell sold this disputed land to Nathaniel Sylvester of Shelter Island, and Governor Richard Nicolls gave him a Patent to it, November 20th, 1667 (on payment of a quit rent to the formal new Long Island owner, the Duke of York). There was another colonial confirmation grant made of the same territory by Governor Andros in 1677.

In 1685 the land passed to James Lloyd, married to Grizzell, Nathanial Sylvester's daughter, who had inherited it from her father. With this transfer, the property was created a Lordship or Manor of Queen's Village, and some form of local government in civic affairs was conferred with this grant. The dispute over its boundaries with the Town of Huntington nevertheless continued. In March, 1686, a very detailed agreement was drawn up between James Lloyd and certain of the townsmen (presumably trustees), operating on order of a Town Meeting, since actually, legal trustees of the town did not exist until 1688.

This settlement measured the exact area in mathematical terms, defining the line from shore to upland meadow, from east to west and north to south. It was considered a definitive solution; but those who adopted this optimistic view did not know Huntington. The matter came up again for arbitration in 1734, and at that date monuments were erected along the revised boundary line, and quitclaims by the respective parties were then executed.

By an act of legislation passed by New York State in 1886, Lloyd's Neck (as it was finally termed) was annexed to Huntington for *administrative* purposes. But the old line, established in 1734 is still more important since it continues to be the *line of title* as to private ownership. Though the township and county line have been extinguished by the 1886 ruling, the line of title is that of 1734, or intrinsically the one established by Sachem Wyandanch, the friend of John Scott. (*Hunt. T. R.*, I, 59-60, 74-79; 105-107; 24n, 419, 438-9.)

John Scott was himself once owner of 150 acres of Lloyd's Neck. He bought them from John Richbell, then sold them to Major-General John Leverett, of Boston for "a competent sum of money," who in turn, sold them back to Richbell thereby considerably increasing their value. This transaction was duly recorded before a Massachusetts notary public August 2nd, 1664. And Scott's original deed, in impeccable legal terms, is in James Lloyd's vellum book of deeds, pp. 11-13. (*N. Y. Hist. Soc. Coll.*, LIX, 13.)

This land, after being sold to John Scott by Wyandanch was sold a second time by his widow and heiress, the Sunk Squa, to the inhabitants of Setauket (*Br-haven T. R.* (1880 ed.), I, 12; (1924 ed.), II, 99) in June, 1664, for 4 coats, 4 pairs of stockings, a pipkin of powder, 2 bars of lead, 6 hoes, 10 hatchets, 10 knives, 6 more coats, 4 shirts and 3 kettles. "Massetewse and the Sunk Squaw, native proprietors and owners of all the lands belonging to the trace of land commonly called the Ould Mans do freely and absolutely sell and will defend the title to the inhabitants of Setawket and their successor forever . . ." (*Ibid.*)

APPENDIX C

Much has been made of a little American publication which John may have shown his friends at this time to interest them in Long Island. This was a Catechism, translated by Southampton's Parson, Abraham Pierson, into the Quiripi dialect of the Algonquin language. The New England Commissioners had ordered the tract which was sent to London for publication about 1657. But the manuscript was lost en route in a wreck, and the aged pastor had to begin his work again. He decided to publish in Cambridge, Massachusetts, but could find no one to "oversee a true printing." Sick and in despair he wrote to the Commissioners complaining of his difficulties in getting assistance. (*Conn. Hist. Soc. Coll.* (1895), III, 6.) The government interpreter, Thomas Stanton, who had helped him with the translation of the text could not (or would not) revise it when printed. (He was feuding with the Commissioners over his reduced salary, which might explain his reluctance to take on this literary task.)

Did John Scott read and correct the proofs? The question arises since the title page on John's London copy differs in one detail from the Cambridge edition. The American inscription reads "Some helps for the Indians . . . showing them how to improve their natural reason . . . etc."

By Abraham Pierson
"Examined and approved by Thomas Stanton and by some others of the most able interpreters etc. etc."

Set in somewhat heavier type, John's title page was identical except that there was no mention of Thomas Stanton. The last line reads "Examined and approved by that experienced gentleman (in the Indian language) Captain John Scot."

There is no record that John was among those "others" who had helped in the translation. But he did know Indian dialects; he was a friend of the Piersons, and a fellow Atherton Company member with Stanton. What more likely than that he proofread the galleys for the old man, and being John, was loath to let such a fact remain unknown when there was a chance of proclaiming it in one of the self-laudatory inscriptions which were then all the literary fashion?

That the title page was substituted in England seems probable, since it reads printed "for" Samuel Green, instead of the more usual American printed "by," in the original.

This altered title page elicited no surprise comment or complaint at the time from either Pierson or Stanton. John could have even been asked to sponsor the publication abroad, going as he did, on a semi-official mission to London. Or his name could have been inserted on order: 'John Scott,' friend of Wyandanch, well known to the Montauks, meant far more to Long Island Indians than 'Thomas Stanton,' a Massachusetts man.

It was only in the nineteenth century, after the publication of Pepys' affidavits, that writers began to inveigh against John's vainglorious act, some going so far as to accuse him of trying to pass off the work as his own. An accusation the title page itself clearly disproves.

John's volume finally found its way into the hands of the bibliophile Sir Hans Sloane, among whose collection it reposes today in the British Museum.

APPENDIX D

The Jenks Pedigree

This Scott pedigree is usually known as the Jenks pedigree since it belonged to William Jenks, Esq., of 38 Nevada Street, Newtonville, Massachusetts, who had it from his grandfather, the Reverend Dr. William Jenks of Boston, who died in 1866. Mr. Jenks could not say how his grandfather came into possession of the scroll (he was not a Scott descendant), but thinks that it came from a Scott-Jenks relative who did claim kinship.

From his exhaustive study of this pedigree, the genealogist Mr. Henry Edward Scott considers that it contains valuable material, though there are also slips (mostly in names of wives), which show that some details are based on hearsay. None of these errors, according to this distinguished scholar, constitutes any evidence against the descent of John Scott of Long Island from the Scotts of Scot's Hall.

It is upon the Jenks pedigree that James Renat Scott based much of his information in making his own pedigree included in his publication, *The Scotts of Scot's Hall Memorials.*

In the Heraldic Journal for July, 1865, Vol. I, pp. 103-4, a description of this last-named pedigree is printed, mentioning Sir William Scott, ambassador to Turkey and Florence, buried in Brabourne in 1621. That burial date is erroneous. The will of Sir William, late of Brabourne, was proved by his widow, Barbara Scott, August 12th, 1617. (Act Books of the Archdeaconry, Court of Canterbury, Bk. 28, f 82.) It is from this Sir William Scott that our John stems.

APPENDIX E

This Ashford development (called variously Setauket, or Brookhaven) scene of yet another clash between John Scott and John Winthrop, covered a vast tract of abandoned Indian planting grounds, about forty miles west of Southold, a town which by the terms of its original charter was under New Haven's jurisdiction.

In 1654 a group of Southold men bought from the local Setauket Sachem, Warawakme, all this land, acting only as agents, for they did not develop it and only one or two lived on it.

In 1659 Governor Winthrop, bent on extending his frontiers and anxious to acquire Long Island property, sent Captain Underhill, to Setauket to prevail upon the few straggling settlers there to put themselves under *Connecticut's* jurisdiction. In the name of these poor uneducated souls (for their early Town Records reveal a most unusual condition of illiteracy.) Underhill "petitioned" Winthrop in 1659 that the inhabitants of "Cromwell Bay" (as he called it) be taken under Connecticut's wing. (*Conn. Arch. Towns & Lands*, I, f 37n.)

Since this land, as belonging to Southolders, was then under New Haven, the petition had little relevance.

In 1662 after Winthrop got his new Charter (which included New Haven) he made a second try to get a foothold on Long Island. He suggested that Southold send delegates to Connecticut and that Captain Youngs should be chosen. (*Ibid.*)

Again he met with opposition, for New Haven was at that time strenuously fighting absorption by Connecticut.

The contest for private ownership of Setauket land was principally over the large tract Scott had selected for a homestead, and seems to have been basically a contest over equities—i.e., Indian title, plus settlement. Neither Winthrop nor Scott had the English title. Winthrop's title proceeded from local Setauket Indians, *without* settlement, and would seem to have been inferior to Scott's title proceeding from local Indians as well as that of the reigning Montauk tribe, with the consent of the Sunk Squa, who had given John her power of attorney. (*S-hampton T.R.*, II, 37.) In addition, he had settled the place, beginning his planting as early as 1662. His was neither a case of absentee landlordship, nor of speculation in undeveloped lands. Moreover, Scott fortified his title to this area by a further investiture, "by turf and twig" from Mahmasuttee and Mr. Goodyer, native proprietors, November 23rd, 1663, some two years before Winthrop's deed. (Conn. Arch. MSS., I, ff 312-313.)

To make sure he was not running into other men's plots, he bought from Robert Plumer "all lands he stood possessed of about the town of Ashford." (*Ibid.*, Towns & Lands, I, f 37n.) And in his contract with his partners, some of them early Setauket settlers, he added a Memorandum to the effect that the said parties "had no manner of right, title or interest in any lands east of the within-named John Scott His western fence, six rods west of Nanemosett Brook." This they all signed. (*Ibid.*, MSS., I, ff 312-313.)

Compensation was offered some settlers whose property crossed John's boundaries (Rawl. MSS., A 175, f 103); though six of these men later signed a document swearing the agreement had been made under a misapprehension of John's power given him by the King, "wherein they considered themselves comprehended." (*Ibid.*, f 10.)

These Setauket residents, including Richard Woodhull, their magistrate, settled all differences with John Scott by an agreement dated December 5th, 1663 (*Br-haven T.R.* (1880 ed.) I, 8), appointment of a committee headed by John Underhill, to discuss this agreement was made at a Brookhaven town meeting, held January 23rd, 1664. (*Ibid.* (1924 ed.), I, 74).

The New Amsterdam Armistice, signed February 24th, 1664, recites that John Youngs averred that it was the desire of Connecticut to accommodate such a settlement as stated in the Armistice Agreement. (*Conn. Pub. Rec.*, I, 390.)

It would seem then, that Winthrop had at first resigned himself to Scott's proprietorship of Setauket, and then later changed his mind, which might have had something to do with the arbitrary arrest and trial of Scott. For while the latter was in Winthrop's jail, Winthrop secured a deed to the Setauket lands from the Unchachogue sachem, Tobaccus, taking a statement from this local chieftain that "he sold no land to John Scott" (*Br-haven T.R.* (1880 ed.), I, 13), though John never claimed that he had.

Winthrop's designs on this Long Island property, however, were interrupted by the arrival of the Duke of York's fleet, in August 1664, and the appointment of Colonel Nicolls as governor of New York, within whose charter Long Island was definitely fixed. So Setauket could never be had through Winthrop's own courts. Winthrop made an agreement with Nicolls that *all that had been done by Connecticut on Long Island should continue in force,* and suggested that the arrangement which Scott had made with the Setauket residents be annulled, and John be given permission to sell back to the town his land, and Scot's Hall, with its extensive fencing. (*Ibid.* (1924 ed.), II, 74, 75.) Winthrop wrote to Nicolls, February 1, 1665, that Scott's claims to the Setauket land, purchased from the Indians, would be destructive of the plantation there (*N.Y. Col. Does.* III, 85), and this letter would seem to be an acknowledgment that John did indeed possess the Indian title. Winthrop did not, at this time, make any accusation of fraud or duress, or even indicate John's lack of title, but he pointedly reminded Nicolls of the latter's agreement to abide by Connecticut's land ruling on Long Island.

When John's lands were confiscated outright, 1665, the Winthrop and Matthias Nicolls families profitted by them, later (1680) securing the English title to them. (Thompson, *Hist. of L.I.*, I, 611.)

In none of these contemporary writings and documents is there any suggestion of fraudulent dealing, with which the great historian Brodhead charged John. To buttress this accusation he appended eight source references, only one of which refers to John's land, and this is not conclusive evidence as it goes back to a hearsay report from the Pepys affidavits. It must be remembered, however, that when Brodhead accused Scott, very few of the town and court records had been transcribed, and few scholars were willing to seek out local records concerning a man who had already, with the publication of Pepys' Diary in 1825, been branded as a rascal.

APPENDIX F

The charges against John Scott were:
1. Speaking words tending to the defamation of the King's Majesty.
2. Seditious practices and tumultuous carriages in several plantations.

3. Abetting and encouraging the natives in hostile practices against one another.

4. Usurping the authority of the King in tending to pardon treason, as Scott called the crime, for bribes.

5. Threatening His Majesty's subjects with hanging and banishment.

6. Gross and notorious profanation of God's Holy Day.

7. Forgery, and violation of his solemn oath.

8. Acting treacherously to the Colony of Connecticut.

9. Usurping authority upon pretense of a commission.

10. Calumniating a Commission officer in this Corporation, with the charge of villainous and felonious practices.

APPENDIX G

Col. S.P. Col. Am. & W. Indies—1661-1668—P. 480   P.R.D.

July 12, 1667 (1524) Calendered: "Major Scott's *Relation (Relaçon)*

The 23rd May Lt. Gen. Willoughby on the earnest motion of the Nevis people and for resettling Antigua, Montserrat Saba and Anguila and asserting His Majesty's interest in St. Christopher's, departed with the *Jersey* an East India merchant and a victualler, arrived at Nevis on 26 where they found the successful fleet under Capt. Berry, who a few days before fought the French and the Dutch at least three times their number in ships and men, and (*original* But God assisting, the English) after a sharp dispute chased them into their sanctuary and remained masters of the seas. Their army consisting of 3,200 men was mustered 2nd June, and on the 6th they were preparing for landing at St. Christopher's, the forlorn of 700 men placed in boats, the reserve in yatch's, and the main body in ships, the distance between the Road at Nevis where they lay at St. Christopher's being five leagues; all committed to Capt. Carteret, Admiral, but no signal could be given for fear of alarming the enemy, and the boats not being towed sayled several courses for want of particular orders and the darkness of the night. When the day began to shew itself and we should have landed between fate and fault we were at a strange distance out from the others, which in all likelihood we had landed with little loss which maritime error put a period to that service. On the 7th a plan was dijested which is described, for at 4 in the morning (original: at the rising of the moon) of the 8th but weighing later than was designed (original: when the curtains of the night were drawn, yielding their command to Phoebus)—gave the French too much notice (of the landing). "And now began the tragedy; the forlorn, the greatest part being landed under Capt. Cotter an Irish gentleman and the reserve under Col. Stapleton, Major Scott (myself original) and many others; there grew a dispute between the

English and the Irish officers, and the Irish refused to follow the guide appointed by the Lt. Gen. and attempted a gully, where after some slight wounds, they were taken, he will not say surrendered to the French but their soldiers of the same nation by a general shout surrendered themselves to the enemy, while most of the English officers and soldiers found graves, and those few that survived galled the enemy till the French (though there were not above 100 English) and they, their whole army of horse and foot, after many sallies upon them, made them a tender of their lives, which many would not accept but committed themselves to the sea, and several were saved by the bravery of the boats, the Lt. General himself venturing very frankly to save his men. After anchoring at Basse-terre the Lieutenant sent on the 9th to the French to desire burial for the slain, careful usage for the wounded prisoners and exchange of prisoners and to say that he would exact satisfaction for the breach of Articles and inhumanities at Antigua and Montserrat before he left the Leeward Isles. To which the French General St. Lawrence answered that all humanity might be expected to dead, wounded, and prisoners that gentlemen of France needed no spur; that a trench had been made for the dead, that prisoners should be exchanged, and that as to breach of Articles, M. Cletheroe, Governor of Martinico, commanded at Antigua and Montserrat, and that the gentlemen of St. Christopher's abhorred all breach of faith and they deserved only such treatment for French or Dutch as they afforded to the King of Great Britain's subjects; and that as to the Lt. General's resolution to have satisfaction, the great of France are ever prepared to receive an enemy, and that the island would receive no greater strength than the King of England can send, unless he employ his whole fleet from Europe to take St. Christopher's! (Orig.: That he observed from their first victory on that island the very elements fighting for them) Sir John Harmon arrived June 13th with the *Lion, Crown, Newcastle, Dover, Bonaventure, Assistance, Assurance* and five ships, 2 ketches, but before he arrived the Lt. General had despatched men and ammunition to Antigua and Montserrat and other islands that have suffered by the French and where he had ordered forts to keep possession for his Majesty for reasons given. In this vacancy Sir J. Harman destroyed the whole French fleet of 24 good ships at anchor at Martinico, and is returned to Nevis, having visited the new settled island in his way. This 12th July (Major Scott) I was despatched by Lt. General "to capitulate the Capricious humours of the French, negotiate the exchanges of prisoners and make the best judgment I could of their strength, which I find to be, one veteran regiment of Picardy, about 700 horse, a forlorn of dragoons, about 2500 planters, though the French say 4000. Yet the Lt. General unless Sir Tobias Bridge, the gravity of some others accustomed to a more methodical way of fighting more for profit than danger, doth divert, will in a few days make another attempt on St. Christophers where if they once get footing, they need not doubt being masters of the island.

Indorsed by Williamson—
Major Scott's Relation
till 12 July 1667—6 pp.

APPENDIX H

How an exchange of epithets was magnified into a court-martial is a tribute to a lawyer's handling of material, building a case upon the slenderest premise. Pepys certainly would have known Cotter for that young officer was sent to England to speed up the regimental pay, and on such an errand would necessarily go to Pepys who was the Admiralty's Clerk of the Acts.

As is stated in the sworn affidavit: "Lord Willoughby subsequently gave Cotter leave to go to England . . . for the concern of his regiment, adding, that if anything has been reported to his prejudice by one Captain Scott, I do hereby certify it to be notoriously false. And if he (Scott) had stayed until he had come to his trial his smooth tongue would not have saved him."

There is no official confirmation of this statement. Indeed this contradicts Willoughby's own words as recorded in the state papers. (*S.P. Col. Ser. Am. & W. I.,* 1661-68, No. 1580.)

Cotter was the only officer who was not promoted when Bridge's regiment was disbanded. (*Col. Pop.,* XXII, 100.) Even in 1671 he was still only Captain Cotter. (*Ibid.,* XXVII, 29.) A disappointed resentful man blaming John's verbal report for his lack of promotion might well be steered into exaggerated derogatory details, under skillful questioning, about the St. Christopher engagement.

The other witnesses at this alleged court martial were mostly illiterate seamen, signing with their mark and making gross errors as to dates and place names. It was these who told of Scott's "skulking under a rock" (Rawl. MSS., A. 175, f 149) a distortion of du Tertre's vivid description of "men hurled down the precipice, showered with boulders till forced to take refuge, etc."

Of the three contemporary accounts of the fight, Henry Willoughby's letter to his father (*S.P. Col. Ser. Am. & W. I.,* 1661-68, No. 1498), Scott's Relation (*Ibid.,* 1524), and du Tertre's (*Hist.,* IV, 266-76), the last is certainly long enough, and frank enough concerning Scott's general behavior to have included—had it been true—some mention of the ridiculous figure he was supposed to have cut during the engagement.

In a fairly recent publication (Higham, *Leeward Isles,* p. 59), the English historian C. S. Higham accuses Scott of being violently anti-Irish, and declares that neither Henry Willoughby nor du Tertre makes any mention of the surrender. [He is wrong; du Tertre does.] "Scott was a brilliant rogue" (*Ibid.*, p. 59), Higham goes on to say, quoting the Rawlinson manuscripts. "It seems that he wished to shield himself from censure and did his best to throw the blame (for defeat) on those who could not answer his accusations."

It is obvious who was really being shielded. That other officers knew about and hushed up Henry Willoughby's drunken condition seems likely from the petition to Charles II of one Abraham Sumers, "a maimed soldier, who served under Sir Thomas Bridge in the West Indies for upwards two years without pay, and is now, on his return to England, threatened by Captain Mallett, who commanded his company, with the loss of his ears and that he would run him through '*if he makes oaths against Lord Willoughby concerning the loss of St. Christopher.*' " (*CSP Col. Ser. Am. & W. I.*, 1661-68, No. 1911.)

APPENDIX I

A single official reference gives a hint as to how the hanging rumor started. A letter to Lord Arlington from his Rotterdam agent, Silas Taylor, mentions a fact liable to distortion: "Drums are beating all day for Colonel Scott and for seamen, and commanding those that are entertained to repair to their duties on pain of death." (*S.P. Dom. Car.*, II, No. 220.)

John Scott's former Dutch regiment (like those of other foreign officers who quit) did not immediately "repair to duty" as it was not placed on a war footing until 1673. (Ten Raa, *Het St. Leg.*, p. 495.) This could have angered the mob, had they known about it—very little was needed to trigger their fury.

On the other hand, Taylor's information could refer to William Scott (son of Thomas Scott the regicide) who, contrary to Charles II's orders, was one of those who "treasonably served as colonel in the wars against their own country." He was ordered home to undergo trial for high treason. This order is indexed in English state papers under "William Scott, conspirator." (*CSP Dom. Car.*, II, CLII, 24.) He had been in and out of prison for various offenses and has been frequently confused with John Scott. Both were in the Low Countries on secret service at practically the same time. William, however, did not communicate directly with the Secretary of State. He sent his news under the pseudonym *Celadon*, to Mrs. Aphra Behn, whose lover he was. This brilliant playwright had brought him over with her when Charles II sent her to Holland for some special reporting. Neither Mrs. Behn nor her lover met with Williamson's approval and Arlington thought their judgment of "doubtful value."

John's quarrel with Despontejn would probably never have reached the public's ears. Nor is it likely that a dispute over a small sum of company money could arouse citizens to mob violence.

APPENDIX J

Scott deposed that:

About August 1st, 1675, he was invited by M. Pélissary, Treasurer-General of the French Navy and by Captain Pyrogérie*—both Protestants—to his house and there shown: divers maps and sea journals, one of them of Captain Munden's voyage to St. Helena, draughts of the King of England's best-built ships, fourteen sheets of closely written English containing in what manner the Navy and English Admiralty were governed; also the number of the King's ships, their several ages and conditions they were in, the number of guns severally, and in what harbors they lay; what ships were at sea; the strength and weakness of those places where those in harbor lay; with the fighting instructions upon several occasions both before and since the Restoration from 1652; the methods of quartering men in sea fights with abundance of other circumstances relating to the Navy and a marginal note thus: (His Majesty's stores are very inconsiderable and our guns want a fourth part of the number of yours; and in one place mention is made of the dissatisfaction of English seamen for want of Pay and propositions of what ways a great number of them might be carried into the French King's service).

And at the same time Pélissary showed this deponent five large maps and charts,

1) of Gravesend, to the falls of Galloper;
2) the sands and soundings of Essex and Kent exactly described;
3) the river Medway from Rochester Bridge to the mouth of that river where it falls into the Thames;
4) Portsmouth and adjacent places;
5) the Isle of Wight, very detailed with remarks on its present condition and what propositions had been made for rendering it more defensible;
6) Plymouth the Sound and harbor, island and new fortifications on one large parchment skin;
7) plans of Sheerness and Tilbury

The deponent swears that these fourteen sheets sent for the said Pélissary by the Marquis de Seigneley (eldest son of M. Colbert) to be by him sent to M. Pyrogéry (knowledgeable in sea affairs) that Captain Deane (now Sir Anthony) had brought them out of England to the said Marquis by orders of Mr. Pepys. And the deponent swears that he believes M. Pélissary's information to be true because this deponent saw a letter at M. Pélissary's house, subscribed S. Pepys in Mr. Pepys' handwriting (as this deponent believes, because he often saw it since) which letter was directed to the said Marquis, and in that letter

---

* Hérouard de la Piogérie, Major of the Marine, serving at Besançon in May, 1674. (Mar. Docs. B2 XXV. f 121) precisely at the time John was in Besançon, and where they probably met.

mention was made of the said paper and maps and that Captain Deane *should give an explanation of them.*

The said Captain Deane walking in M. Pélissary's garden under the window, this deponent heard him tell a gentleman that was walking with him (his interpreter? ltm) that the said Deane brought the writing and above-mentioned from Mr. Pepys and that Mr. Pepys would not have parted with them for £40,000 had it not been for *that greatest end* (which was an expression used in the letter). And this deponent further maketh oath that M. Pélissary having been walking in the garden with Sir Anthony Deane as aforesaid, the said M. Pélissary came into the house to this deponent and told him that he and said Pepys had committed a great Error, for, said he, I was telling Captain Deane that there was a countryman of his whose company he would be glad of; the Captain asked who it was and I told him, Colonel Scott. With that, the Captain prayed me not to let him come into my company, because, said he, I have positive orders not to see him, and further said, I hope you have not told him any of the business I came about, nor shewed him any of those papers. So that M. Pélissary was forced to deny it (as he said) and caused this deponent to dine privately in his House; and this deponent further swears that he, being at M. Pyrogéry's lodgings in the *Faubourg St. Germain* in Paris the following January, he did see and read the very papers, charts and letters above-mentioned; where, speaking of them to another French Protestant gentleman and an officer of the Navy, the said gentleman said he hoped that these great Rogues that would betray their own country are not of our religion. To that M. Pyrogéry replied: 'They are of the Devil's religion.'

There is a mystery in this business, more than I dare speak of, therefore let us talk no more of it. And this deponent further swears that at the beginning of the year 1676, when the French armature began to take the English ships, the deponent went to M. Pyrogéry and talked with him about it, and told him that it would beget a misunderstanding between the two kingdoms. The said monsieur shook his head and replied: I wish that that were the greatest ill that would befall the poor Nation. Did you not take notice of an odd expression in that traitor Pepys . . . his letter near the end of it.

John Scott

The deponent further swears . . . concerning the contents of Pepys' letter . . . that the occasion of Captain Deane bringing the yatches was very lucky as he was fully instructed and would give his Lordship (the Marquis de Seigneley) *an explanation of those things;* and at the end of the said letter (thus) I doubt not in a little time to give your Lordship better light in order to the great end mentioned to your Ambassador here.

John Scott

Endorsed Pemberton.

(Morn., I, ff 17, 18, 19, 20.)

APPENDIX K

Pepys could not possibly have examined closely the papers seized in John Scott's Cannon Street rooms else he could hardly have called them of "ill-importance." There were many Dutch newspaper clippings (excerpts from English parliamentary records, etc.), material any good political agent would be likely to collect. (Rawl. MSS. A. 176, ff, 1-25, 62, 65, 79, 100-01, 113, 123.) The complete list is a follows:

Poems, copies of personal letters to Constantia, Lady Vane, speeches (some dated 1668) of de Witt and the Prince of Orange; Dutch military manuals; infantry regulations; a map of the Amazon; two religious tracts; lines on the death of Talbot with some Latin comment; a copy of Governor Winthrop's letter from New England to Charles II (concerning the renewal of Connecticut's Charter); copies of several letters to and from Sir Joseph Williamson (at Cologne for peace negotiations) discussing Holland's "perplexities;" a long formula for transmuting metals; pages torn from the Parliamentary Record (Hansard) concerning business with Flanders, including the King's speech telling of marrying his niece to the Prince of Orange and the reply of Commons; various Parliamentary Resolutions concerning the English-Dutch alliance, together with notes from various Committees on Privileges, Bill for Poor Prisoners, enforcing the buying of wool, prohibiting wool exports, etc.; the Lord Chancellor's speech on the King's League with Holland; a paper on the reasons offered at the Conference concerning dangers and growth of Popery; and Mr. Williamson's proposals before the House concerning Dutch peace negotiations, etc.

Estimates for requisite charges for repairing several fortifications necessary, to be completed in the summer of 1677, in the ports of Gosport, Portsmouth, Sittingham, Cockham Wood, Tilbury, Gravesend; on the Thames several small castles, moats, forts and castles northwards at Harwich, several castles on the Isle of Wight, Guernsey, Jersey. This all looks like routine inspection material of no particular value or importance.

There were pages from the *Office of Ordnance* (dated 1677), with an abstract of a charge (costs?) to attend his Majesty's forces designed for Holland, with lists of costs for field-pieces, spare equipage, bridge boats, mortar pieces, fire works, necessities for the mortar pieces. This all carefully totalled.

There were various Navy estimates, taken from a Parliamentary Committee publication dated 1659 (not classified material and accessible to anyone). John might well have used this as a rough model for his own requirements when he was requisitioning material for the Dutch regiments under his command in 1669-72, an activity about which Pepys knew absolutely nothing.

APPENDIX L
John Scott and Land

John Scott's name has been so tarnished as the result of Pepys' affidavits, that it is especially necessary to consult contemporary documents concerning his land transactions. Even the great Brodhead, charging John with "fraudulent dealing," quotes only hearsay to support this charge.

Certainly a perverse fate pursued John's reputation, partly owing to the fact that John Scott is a very common name, and mistakes in identity easy to make.

For instance among the numerous letters in the *Massachusetts Historical Society Collections, 4th Series,* VII, vindicating John after Governor Winthrop had arrested him in 1663, are two written by Richard Vines to Winthrop Senior *(Ibid.,* 343-4-5). These are indexed along with the others and involve John Scott in "sundry seditious and malicious practices," creating the impression that he was at variance with the law over certain land titles.

These two letters were written in 1643. They do not refer to our man, who at that date was only 11 and had hardly reached the New World.

Two other references to a John Scott's fraudulent transactions figure in a legal suit in Albany, New York, charging that he stole out at night to deal surreptitiously with the Indians, for which he was convicted *(Hist. Docs. of N. Y.,* V, 569); also accusations of "clandestine purchases," cited in the Land Papers *(Cal. of N. Y. Col. MSS.,* pp. 162-4-5; and pp. 665-6). These charges are dated respectively 1720 and 1722 when our John had been dead several years.

In 1663 *John Scott of Long Island* was involved in a local *cause célèbre* concerning a tract of country lying to the west of Southampton, called *Quaquanantuck* (shortened locally to *Quogue*). This was topographically valuable, extremely rich in salt meadows and noted for the whales cast on its shores. This property, at first unclaimed by any town, had passed through a number of private hands.

Lion Gardiner, one of Southampton's earliest settlers, originally bought it from Wyandanch on June 10th, 1658 "for a considerable sum of money" *(S-ampton T. R.,* I, 170). A few months later he transferred it to John Cooper, who promised to keep up the payments to the Indians and give them all the whales *(Ibid.,* 171).

The second Quogue purchaser was John Ogden, another prominent Southamptoner, and his deed for this land (dated May, 1659) bore the marks of both Wyandanch and Wiacombe and included a description as to its limits and conditions under which certain other men were granted the privilege of cutting hay on a meadow three miles north of Quogue *(Ibid.,* 162). Ogden then sold this land to John Scott *(Ibid.,*

175) who in turn sold it to the town of Southampton for £70, but reserving for himself five acres of salt hay for his horses (*S-ampton T. R.*, II, 38), land he later gave to Henry Pierson (*Ibid.*, 39).

On March 14th, 1663, the town of Southampton decided by majority vote, that the valuable Quogue salt meadows should never be farmed nor settled (*S-ampton T. R.*, II, 39) and that monies should be levied on the inhabitants for upkeep (*Ibid.*, 39-40).

But in April, 1662, a Captain Thomas Topping bought from the Shinnecock Indians (from the Sunk Squa Weany and her son Jacka-napes) a large tract of land west of Canoe Place *of which Quogue was part* (*S-ampton T. R.*, I, 167-8). Four years later, 1666, the chiefs of the Shinnecock tribe signed a giant protest that Sunk Squa Weany and those other Shinnecocks had had no right to sell all that property to Topping, that they contested the sale and assigned the land to "our ancient and loving friends of Southampton" (17th Sept., 1666, *S-ampton T. R.*, I, 169; *Br-haven T. R.* (1880 ed.), 16, 17).

This was one of the many land suits confronting Governor Nicolls. It involved not only private ownership but land claimed by two separate sets of Indians. He ordered all the owners into Court bringing their writings and papers; and after much evidence, decided in favor of Southampton keeping the property, and compensating Captain Topping (*S-ampton T. R.*, I 173-4). John had already left Long Island when the verdict was given. But *his* deed to the property was duly delivered in court (*Ibid.*, 172-3); John Ogden testifying for him that he was present when John's deed of sale to the town was signed and sealed (*Ibid.*, 174), with Captain Youngs corroborating this statement (*Early Col. Docs. of L. I.*, p. 601). Other witnesses testified that John indeed had retained five acres for winter hay and that although this had not been so specified in his original bill of sale, it had always been recognized, and that Southampton, at the time, made no exception whatever to this arrangement (S-ampton, orig. T. R. Liber., 2, 38, 52).

Now Nicolls' secretary Mathias, newly arrived from England, and others who started the story of John's fraudulent deals, may well have been puzzled by this kind of dispute and by the stream of land suits flooding the New York courts. But the records do not support their charges. True, none of the Long Island landlords had an English title to their property. Native title and court registration were everywhere recognized as legal basis for possession. And John was a stickler for registration. One of his biggest law suits (when he was acting as attorney for the Overseers of the Poor) against Andrew Messenger of Jamaica, was won by proving that his adversary's bill of sale was invalid because not recorded before witnesses (*Early Col. Docs. L. I.*, pp. 563-64). Pepys' witnesses concerning John's land were not only confused by the complicated changes in Long Island's land tenure following the British victory of 1664, but these men evidently did not know that Scott, as Southampton's attorney (with Stanborough—who died in 1664) handled boundary disputes between that town and Easthampton and Southold which frequently took him into court concerning *land not his* (*S-ampton T. R.,* II, 3, 233).

The confusing land situation was also affected by the changing attitude of the Indians themselves about this period. The second generation dealing with the white man was far less gullible than the first as to real estate values, even disputing previous transactions wherein they were not consulted and in which they felt cheated. Tribes were switching alliances. The Montauks were no longer supreme nor recognized as having sole right to sell.

The great Wyandanch died in 1659, and his only son, Wiacombe, succumbed to smallpox shortly after, while still a minor. The heiress, Quashawam, the Sunk Squa, slowly lost her grip over her people and over Long Island. First she appealed to the neighboring Shinnecocks to "force Montauks to acknowledge her supremacy on Long Island" (*S-ampton T. R.,* II, 36-37; 49 in orig. Records). Then, being threatened and attacked by the Narragansetts, she and her tribe fled to Easthampton and put themselves under the protection of the white men there, to whom, in gratitude, she made over Montauk Village and some land previously granted to John Scott (*Deeds and Patents. Docs. Relating to Conveyance of Land,* Rare Bk. Dept., L. of Congress, pp. 3-7).

This was yet another instance of the Indian habit of selling (or giving) twice; and the Sunk Squa's latest action was but one step in that boundary feud which Southampton and Easthampton kept up for centuries. The New York courts recognized (in 1668) that a former agreement between Easthampton and John Scott *did* exist, but declared this now null and void, decreeing that only the 1668 grant of Montauk to Easthampton should continue in force (*Early Col. Docs. of L. I.,* p. 606); a decision which may possibly have been influenced by Southampton's obstinate refusal to accept the Duke's Laws.

Many of the histories of Long Island towns were compiled about the time the "legend" of Scott's life was first revealed in the publication of a member of the Massachusetts Historical Society;* hence their bias against John, although other editors of that great association have since publicly queried whether John Scott might not be a much maligned man (*Wyllys Papers, Conn. Hist. Soc. Coll.,* XXI, 146).

At this juncture John is seen to be not so much an adventurer in land, as a representative of his age, whose underlying spirit was monopoly. John (as Abbott so pertinently points out) never succeeded in gaining entry to that inner circle which, in the language of the day, "managed;" and steadily, for the sake of his convictions, botched what chances he might have had. He was a lone operator among corpora-

---

* G. D. Scull who privately printed the life of Dorothea-Scott-Gotherson-Hogben (cited erroneously in the English Dictionary of National Biography as by G. D. *Scott*).

tions and associations securely backed by royal patents which effectively barred single competitors in any chosen field, whether foreign trade or American real estate. There was a reason for this, as one saw both at Setauket and Southampton, for had free competition been unlimited, with private individuals buying up what they wanted, expanding townships would have been hemmed in, their prosperity jeopardized. Nevertheless outsiders bitterly resented these restrictions.

John Winthrop and others, like the Atherton Associates, belonged to the chosen few who could do no wrong. Arbitrary action like theirs was not uncommon when it came to incorporated possessions. As the royal commissioners reported to Charles II concerning New England towns: "Not one is regularly built within its just limits" (*N. Y. Col. Docs.*, III, 112), and Winthrop Jr.'s first attempts to acquire land in Long Island had been so irregular that they were discountenanced by the New England Commissioners (*Mass. Hist. Soc. Coll.*, IV, Vol. 7, 57n). See also Hazard's *Hist. Col. State Papers*, I, 94, for Winthrop's "uncomely behaviour" concerning this land. Later he was much more successful.

APPENDIX M

An example of the carefully assembled facts proving John Scott's accuracy is the following comment on Powell's expedition:

In 1656, Henry Powell was called upon to give evidence concerning the expedition to Barbados before the commissioners of bankruptcy on behalf of the heirs and representatives of his old patron, Sir W. Courten. Powel states: "that he landed about forty people on Barbadoes from the *William and John* of London about Feb. 20th, 1626, being in the employ of William Courten and Company . . . at the end of a fortnight's time this deponent sailed to the maine upon the coast of Guiana and furnished himself with roots, seeds, plants, fowles etc. and other materialls together with thirty two Indians, which he carried to the said island for the planting thereof (*State Papers, Col. Ser.*, XIV, no. 39).

Before proceeding further it will be observed that this statement agrees in all essential respects with Scott's Narrative except that there is no mention of Gromwegle's assistance. This however is precisely what there would not be. William Courten died in 1636, a ruined man, and his heirs were for a long series of years engaged in lawsuits in England and the United Provinces to compel the Dutch representatives of the old firm of Curten and Co., Pieter Boudaan Courten, to refund a large sum of money said to have been fraudulently appropriated by him in 1631. It is clear that the very last thing a witness on behalf of the plaintiffs would voluntarily admit would be this very fact that the Courten settlement in Barbados was indebted for help to a man at that time in the employ of the defendant.

In a petition of Henry Powell in 1660 to the governor of Barbados
. . . he gives an account of his 1626 expedition . . . he says the cost
and charge of the voyage were borne by Sir Peter Courten; and his
Narrative leaves little doubt as to the share of the Dutchman in the
undertaking. Powell tells first of his landing some forty men in
Barbados, and these (as he avers in a sworn deposition), "were for Sir
William Courten, and Sir William paid them wages." His petition
continues:

"Having left the aforesaid servants upon this island I preceded in
my voyage to the Maine, to the river Disacuba, and there left eight
men and left them a Cargezon of trade for that place."

The fact that "cargezon" is the technical Dutch word for goods sent
out to a trading port for bartering with Indians, makes it wellnigh
certain that these eight men (who would never have been abandoned
alone on an unknown and inhospitable coast, among wild tribes) were
dispatched by Peter Courten as a reinforcement to the Zeeland trading
settlement, whose head was Groenewegen. When Powell's statement is
combined with Scott's Narrative all becomes intelligible (Culled from
George Edmundson's *The Dutch in Western Guiana,* pp. 657-660).

The general accuracy of Scott's "description" can be tested by comparing it with another manuscript narrative of the end of the seventeenth century Sloane MS. 2441, Brit. Mus. entitled, *An Account of
His Majesty's Island of Barbadoes.*

BIBLIOGRAPHY AND ABBREVIATIONS

FRENCH MANUSCRIPT SOURCES

Aff. Etran.	Affaires Etrangères, archives diplomatiques. Correspondence politique. Angleterre, vols. 99, 102, 103, 107, 108; Holland, vols. 90, 91, 92, 93. Quai d'Orsay, Paris.
Cinq Cents	Cinq Cents de Colbert. 204, f. 210. Bibliothèque Nationale, Paris.
Fr. Mar. Docs.	Archives de la Marine Française. B.C.D.G. Colbert to *Le Goux*, Colbert to *D'Alliez*. Archives Nationales, Paris.
Mél. de Col.	Mélanges de Colbert (volumes verts). Bibliothèque Nationale.
	Mémoires et Documents (vol. 12), Angleterre (1635-1700). Quai d'Orsay.
MSS Fr.	Manuscrits du fonds français. Conquête de la Tortue, 9325. Archives Nationales.
	Nouvelles Acquisitions: Receuil Margry, Canons de la Marine, Canons et Fonderies, 9479, 9390. Mémoires sur les Ordonnances, 8025-30. Receuil Hocquet d'Hamécourt: Papiers de la Marine 3530. Archives Nationales.
	Papiers de l'Inspecteur de Police chargé de L'Observer des étrangers. 10. 235-57. Individual Docs: 4 dossiers, 1674, 10, 336: 5 dossiers, 1675. Bibliothèque Nationale.

Receuil Cange XXII (1673-78), Ordonnances, etc. Bibliothèque Nationale.

Repertoire des Minutes reçois par M. Noel Duparc, conseilleur du Roi, Notaire au Chasleton de Paris. CXIXI 2. (1670-80). Archives Nationales.

Titres, Actes, Documents. A. Ib, IV (181), *Agents*. Archives Nationales.

FRENCH PRIMARY PRINTED SOURCES

Colbert, son système et les entreprises industrielle de l'Etat (1661-80). P, Boissonade, Toulouse, 1902.

du Tertre. Hist.   Histoire Générale des Antilles habitées par les Français (4 vols.), par. R.P. du Tertre Paris MDCLXVII.

Fr. Artil. Mem.   Mémorial de l'Artillerie Française (tome XIV):
(1) Historiques, fabrications d'Armament en France.
(2) Détermination du Potential des explosifs.

Histoire de L'Ancienne Infantérie Française Ouvrage de Général Susane. Paris. Corréard. 1853. (Tome 8.) (In Ministry of War, Château de Vincennes.)

La Marine de Guerre sous Louis XIV. Le Matérial. par Réne Memain. Paris 1937.

Lettres, Instructions et Mémoires de Colbert par Pierre Clément. (7 Tomes, 17 parts.) Paris. Imprimérie Impériale MDCCLV.

Receuil des instructions données aux Ambassadeurs de France en Angleterre. J. J. Jusserand. Paris. E. de Boccard.

Régistres de Correspondence. Ancien Régime. Ministère de la Guerre. Inventaire Sommaire des Archives Historiques. Archives Ancien Correspondence. Imprimérie Nationale 1898.

DUTCH MANUSCRIPT SOURCES

Arch. St. Gen.   Archives. Staten-General (States General) in the Hague. Algemeen Rijksarchief.

Arch. St. van Hol.	Archives Staten Van Holland (States of Holland):
	No. 301. Secret Resolutions.
	No. 2017. Letters from Sasburgh at Brussels.
	No. 2922. Letters from different towns.
Arch. Raad. v. St.	Archives Raad Van State (Counsel of State):
	No. 519. Out-letters (1672-73).
	No. 625. In-letters (1672-73).
	No. 1871. Secret Resolutions (1672-73).
	No. 1903. Contracts about recruiting foreign regiments, 1670-73.
	No. 2566. Register.
Arch. Milit.	Archives Hoge Militaire Krijgsraad (High Military Court):
	No. 353. Sentences 1672-73.
	No. 352. (Copy book of sentences 1672 (Nov. 16) to 1673 (July 13).
	No. 354. Resolutions (fragments only 1673). These contain all the sentences against high officers. Scott's name is not among them!
	Archives Hoge Raad (High Court of Holland and Zeeland). Sentences. Nothing about Scott.
Arch. Hof v. Hol.	Archives Hof Van Holland (Court of Holland):
	No. 788. Sentences.
	No. 792. Sentences.
	No. 1170. Counsel.
	No. 1354. Protocol (procès verbals).
	No. 3026. Petitions for mandate.
	No. 4565. Petitions.
	No. 5291. Criminal Documents.
	Archives Gecommitteerde Raden Van Holland (Deputy States):
	No. 3020-3021. Resolutions and sentences.
	No. 3287. Survey of Army, Secret Resolutions.
	Judicial Archives in the Hague:
	No. 2. Resolutions, 1671-73.
	No. 59-60. Criminal Examination Books (1669-73).
	No. 71. Criminal Cause list (1669-73).
	No. 103-104. Sentences.
	No. 144-145. Civil Case list (1671, October) (1672).
	No. 332. Appointments on Petitions (1671-73).

Not. Arch. Hague,
Mun.

Notarial Archives in Hague Municipal Archives:
No. 522. Protocol of Notary Alexander Ennis.
No. 523.

No. 611. Protocol Willam Guldemont.
No. 611. f 170; ff 204-204v.

No. 877. 732 Protocol Samuel Favon, f. 306.

No. 392. Protocol Pister van Swieten, ff 323-326, Testimony of Deborah van Egmont (servant at the Hague). June 23, 1672. She gave testimony in 1680, too, extending her remarks after having talked with Gunman, Pepys' agent.

Judicial Archives of Voorburg: No. A XIII, 22.

Reformed Marriage Registers of the Hague and Rijswijk.

Archives First West India Company.

DUTCH PRIMARY PRINTED SOURCES

Besch. Vreemde Arch.

Bescheiden uit Vreemde archieven omtrent de groote Nederlandsche zeeoorlogen. H. T. Colenbrander, The Hague, 1919. (Taken from State Papers, Foreign, Holland 189. 1652-76.)

Het. St. Leg.

Het Staatscher Leger (Military Yearbook 1568-1795) collected by F. J. G. Ten Raa, Lt. Gen. of Infantry; prepared by F. de Bas, published by Koninklijke Militaire Academie, Breda: vol. 5.

Mém. de Jan de Witt.

Mémoires du Grand Pensionaire, traduit de l'originale en français par M. de Ratisbonne, chez Erasmus Kinkius MDCCIX.

Hol. R. H. Arch.

Holland. Royal House Archives, pub. N. Japikse, Correspondentie van Willem III en van Willem Bentinck.

R. H. Arch.

Royal House Archives: No. 2650 II M. Nyjhoff, s-Gravenhage, 1935.

Yearbook of Historical Society—Die Haghe.

Eine Wandeling Door s-Gravenhage, 1679 by Johanna Berk, 1901.

ENGLISH MANUSCRIPT SOURCES

Add. MSS. Additional Manuscripts in British Museum. Admiralty Papers, 5253-5323 Reports, Court Martials (Public Record Office).

C.E.B. (Formerly Colonial Entry Books) Nevis Acts 1-2 (1664-1735).

Col. Ch. Pro. Collins Chancery Proceedings. 221. Scott *v.* Wooley, Public Record Office.

Conn. Arch. Connecticut Archives including Towns and Lands; Foreign Correspondence, and MSS. [vol. I of Colonial Records] (1636-1649) in Connecticut State Library, Hartford, Connecticut.

Egerton MS. 2395.

Harleian MS. 1531, 1566, Scott pedigree, British Museum.

Mit. Ch. Pro. Mitford Chancery Proceedings, C8,376, No. 69 (Joyne *v.* Pepys); C8,638, No. 61, Pepys *v.* Joyne, Public Record Office.

Morn. MS., I, II Mornamont Papers (Pepysian MS. 2881), Magdalene College, Cambridge.

Rawl. MSS. Rawlinson Manuscripts, Bodleian Library, Oxford.

Records. Journal of Common Council London Guidhall, Remembrancer, Common Hall Book.

Shaftesbury Papers, 4, 35. GD 24. Public Record Office.

Sl. MS. Sloane Manuscript. 3662. British Museum.

S. P. State Papers. SP Foreign, Holland (SP 84); Flanders (SP 77); France (SP 78); Newsletters: SP 101/4, Flanders; 101/54-57, Holland; 101/19, Paris; 105/220-232, Sir Joseph Williamson's Collection. Public Record Office.

SP Car. I, II, Dom. State Papers Charles I, II domestic. Public Record Office.

ENGLISH PRIMARY PRINTED SOURCES

Acts of the Assembly. Island of Nevis 1664-1739. London. Printed by orders of the Lords Commissioners of Trade and Plantations by John Baskett. MDCCXL.

Acts of the Privy Council of England, Colonial series. Ed. Willam L. Grant and James Munro. London, 1908-12.

Absalom and Achitophel by John Dryden 1631-1700. A poem. London, 1681.

Admiralty Journal by Samuel Pepys, at Greenwich Observatory.

Affairs and Men in Times of Peter Stuyvesant. Extract of City Records. J. Paulding, New York, 1843.

Ann. of Newtown.   Annals of Newtown by James Riker. Long Island, 1825.

Arch. Cant.   Archaeologia Cantiana. Transactions of the Kent Archaeological Society. 5 Vols. Printed for the Society, London 1889.

An appeal from the Country to the City, printed by Benjamin Harris. London, 1680.

Bib. Cant.   Bibliotheca Cantiana. John Russell Smith, London, 1837.

Bishop Burnet's History of his own time 1643-1715. 6 Vols. Hamilton, Balfour & Neill, Edinburgh, 1753.

Book of Records of Public Transactions of Inhabitants of Salem Village. Historical Collections of Danvers Historical Society.

A Brief Historical Relation of State Affairs from Sept. 1678–April 1714 by Narcissus Luttrell. 6 Vols. Oxford University Press, MDCCCLVII.

Brief History of the Times of Observator (Sir Roger L'Estrange). Charles Brome, London, 1687.

Brief Lives and other Selected Writings by John Aubrey, Ed. Anthony Powel, London, 1949.

Brief Description of New York, 1656-1696 by Daniel Denton. Ed. Victor Hugo Paltsits, New York, 1937.

Brit. Bl. Bk. British Guiana Boundary Arbitration with the United States of Venezuela. The Case on behalf of the Brit. Gov. Printed Foreign Office, 1898. 8 vols., 3 appendices.

Br-haven T. R. Brookhaven Town Records, Patchogue ed., 1880; also Weeks ed. 1924.

Cal. Hist. MSS. Calendar of Historical Manuscripts in office of the Secretary of State, Albany. I, Dutch; II, English. O'Callaghan. 1867.

Cal. NY. Col. MSS. Calendar of New York Colonial manuscripts, endorsed Land Papers, 1643-1803. Albany, 1864.

Cal. Tr. Books Calendar of Treasury Books; Ed. William Shaw, London, 1904-52.

CSP Col. Am. and W.I. Calendar of State Papers, colonial series, America and West Indies. H.M. Printing Press, London, 18–.

CSP Dom. Car. I, II Calendar of State Papers, Domestic, Charles I, II.

CSP Ven. Calendar of State Papers, Venetian.

Ch. Pol. Ann. The Political Annals of the United Colonies. George Chalmers. London. Printed by author 1780.

Calendar of Clarendon State Papers. New York Historical Society Collections, Vol. II, 1869.

Clarendon's History of the Grand Rebellion, 6 Vols. Clarendon Press, Oxford, 1827.

Cobbett's Parliamentary History of England. 6 Vols. R. Bagshaw, London, 1808.

Collections of the Essex Institute by George F. Cheever. Published by Henry Whipple & Son, 1859.

Colonial Records. General Entries, 1664-65, transcribed from MSS. in New York State Library. New York University Press, 1899.

Col. Pap.   Colonial Office Papers. H.M. Printing Office, London.

Conn. Hist. Soc. Coll.   Collections of the Historical Society of Connecticut. Hartford, 1932.

A Complete History of Connecticut by Benjamin Trumbull, D.D., Hudson and Goodwin, Hartford, 1797.

Conn. Pub. Rec.   Public Records of the Colony of Connecticut, Ed. James H. Trumbull and Charles J. Hoadly, Hartford, 1850-90.

Deeds and Patents. Documents relating to Conveyance of Land on Long Island. Bell and Gould, New York, 1850.

The Development of the Leeward Islands, 1660-1668, under the Restoration. C. S. S. Higham. Cambridge University Press, 1921.

Diaries of Samuel Sewall of Boston, Mass. Judge, 1673. Massachusetts Historical Society Collections, Series 5, Vols. 5, 6, 7.

Diary of J. Evelyn. Ed. A. Dobson. London, 1908.

The Diary of Samuel Pepys, M.A., F.R.S. 10 Vols. Ed. Henry B. Wheatley, F.S.A. G. Bell & Sons, London, 1928.

Diary of the Times of Charles II. 2 Vols. by the Hon. Henry Sidney, Earl of Romney. Henry Colburn, London, 1843.

Discourse. Defence of His Majesty's Action by Sir George Downing. London. J. M. 1664.

Divers Voyages touching the Discovery of America. Collected and published by Richard Hakluyt in the year 1582. Ed. by John Winter Jones. Printed for the Hakluyt Society, MDCCL. London.

DNB   Dictionary of National Biography. Oxford University Press, since 1917.

Doc. Hist. N.Y. — The Documentary History of the State of New York. Ed. E. B. O'Callaghan M.D., Albany. Weed Parsons Company, 1849.

Domesday Book. Survey of South Britain by Commissioners of William the Conqueror, 1086; faithfully translated by Samuel Henshall and John Wilkinson. Bye and Law, London, 1799.

EHR — English Historical Review, London.

Early Col. Docs. L.I. — Documents Relative to the History of Early Colonial Settlement, Principally on Long Island. Ed. by E. B. O'Callaghan. Albany, 1853.

E-ampton T. R. — Easthampton Town Records, J. H. Hunt, 5 Vols. Sag Harbor, 1905.

Examen by Roger North 1653-1734. F. Gyles, London, 1740.

The First Whig by Sir George Sitwell. 1668-69. London (published privately).

Further Correspondence of Samuel Pepys 1662-1679. Ed. by J. R. Tanner. London, 1926.

General Entries VI. 1664-65, State Library Bulletin. History 2. (Documents relating chiefly to surrender of New Amsterdam to the English.) Albany, 1899.

Hemp. T. R. — Records of North and South Hempstead. 3 Vols. Jamaica, New York, 1896.

History of the Colony of Massachusetts Bay by Mr. Hutchinson, Lt. Gov. of Mass. Province. Thomas & John Fleet, Boston, MDCCLXIV.

A History of the Weald of Kent by Robert Furley, F.S.A. John Russell Smith, London, 1871.

The Victoria History of County of Kent, Constable, London, 1908.

Historical collections of state papers. Ebenezer Hazard. T. Dobson, Philadelphia, MDCCXCIV.

Hist. N.E. — History of New England by John Winthrop Sr., Journal, 2 Vols. Phelps and Farnham, Boston, 1825.

Hist. of Pl. Pl.   History of Plymouth Plantation, 1620-1647 by Willam Bradford. Pub. Mass. Hist. Soc., Houghton Mifflin, Boston, 1912.

H.M.C.   Historical Manuscripts Commission. (Royal Commission for Historical Manuscripts Reports.)

Hunt. T. R.   Huntington Town Records, 6 vols. with notes by Charles R. Street. Long Islander Press, New York, 1887.

Hutch. Pap.   Hutchinson Papers, 2 Vols. Prince Society, Albany, 1865.

The Iconography of Manhattan Island 1498-1909 by Isaac Newton Stokes. Compiled from original sources. 6 Vols. R. N. Dodd, New York, 1915-28.

Index of Parish Registers printed in Ashford Kent, 1570. Copy in B. M. add. MSS. 33914.

Jamaica T. R.   Jamaica Town Records, ed. Josephine C. Frost. New York, 1764.

Jour. H. of C.   Journals of the House of Commons.

(East) Kent Records. Calendar of some unpublished deeds and Court Rolls in the Library of Lambeth Palace. Ed. by Irene Josephine Churchill. London. Printed for the Records Branch (Kent Archaeological Society), 1922.

Kent Keepers of Peace 1316-1317 printed for Records Branch, Kent Archaeological Society.

Kent. Comm.   Commentaries on American Law, James Kent. Boston, 1896.

Letters from New England by John Dunton 1685. Prince Society, Albany, 1867.

Letters Addressed from London to Sir Joseph Williamson. 1673-1677. Ed. by W. D. Christie, C. B. 2 Vols. Camden Society, MDCCCLXXIV.

Life and Letters of John Winthrop by Robert C. Winthrop. Ticknor & Fields, Boston, 1867.

The Life, Journals and Correspondence of Samuel Pepys deciphered by Rev. John Smith. Richard Bentley, London, 1841.

Letters and the Second Diary of Samuel Pepys. R. G. Howarth, 1932.

Ll. Lives. Memoires of the Lives, Actions . . . and Deaths of those . . . that suffered for the Protestant Religion and . . . Allegiance to their Sovereign (1637-60) by David Lloyd, AM. London, 1668.

The Love Letters of Dorothy Osborne to Sir William Temple. Ed. from original MSS. by Gollancz. London, 1903.

Magnalia Christi Americana (1620-98) by Cotton Mather, D.D.F.R.S. Pastor of the North Church of Boston. London, 1702.

Mass. Hist. Soc. Coll. Collections of the Massachusetts Historical Society.

Parl. Deb. Debates in the House of Commons, Hon. Anchitell Grey. London, MDCCLXIII.

Mass. Rec. Records of the Governor and Company of the Massachusetts Bay in New England, ed. Nathaniel B. Shurtleff. Boston, 1853.

Memoirs of Sir William Temple. 2 Vols. London, T. Courtney, 1836.

Mercurious Aulicus, Court Mercury (Cavalier slanted); Mercurious Britannicus (Parliamentarian side). English Civil War Newsletters in Burney Collection in British Museum.

Minutes of the Orphan Masters Court of New Amsterdam, 1655-63.

Minutes of the Executive Boards of the Burgomasters of New Amsterdam translated by Berthold Fernow. Frances P. Harper, New York, 1907.

Minutes of the Executive Council of the Province of New York, 2 Vols. Ed. by Victor Hugo Paltsits. Albany, 1910.

Miscellaneous Works by George Villiers, 2nd Duke of Buckingham. London, Sam Briscoe, 1704.

Narr. of NN 1609-64   Narratives of Early New Netherland. Edited by J. Franklin Jameson, Ph.D. Charles Scribner Sons, New York, 1909.

New England's Prospect. A True Lively description by William Wood. London, 1639.

N. Neth. Reg.   The Register of New Netherland 1626-1674. Ed. by E. B. O'Callaghan. Munsell, Albany, 1865.

N.Y. Col. Docs.   Documents Relative to the Colonial History of the State of New York procured in Holland, England and France, by John R. Brodhead. Albany, 1853.

N.Y. Gen. and Bio. Rec.   New York Genealogical and Biographical Record. Issued quarterly by the Society. New York, 1870.

N.Y. Hist. Soc. Coll.   Collections of the New York Historical Society New York, 1870-1926, etc.

News Letters of Civil War Period: Burney Collection, British Museum.

The Norman Balliols in England by James Renat Scott. Balliol College Library, 1914.

The Original Lists of Persons of Quality, Emigrants, Political Rebels—who went from Great Britain to the American Plantations (1600-1700). Ed. by John C. Hotten. Chatto & Windus, London, 1874.

Oy. Bay T. R.   Oyster Bay Town Records, Ed. John Cox, Jr., Tobias A. Wright, New York, 1916.

The Passages in Parliament (Burney Collection B.M.). Nathaniel Butler. 1642.

The Paston Letters. Lord John Paston, Knt. 2 Vols. 1422-1509 A.D. Ed. James Gairdner. London, 1875.

Perambulation of Kent, description, hysterie and customs. Collected and written 1570 by William Lambard of Lincolnes Inne. London for Ralphe Nevvberie, 1576.

Plaine Dealing or Newes from New England by Thomas Lechford (1590-1664). J. K. Wiggin, 1867.

A Plaine Description of the Bermudas now called the Sommer Islands by Silvester Jourdoin. Welby, London, 1613.

Pro. A.A.S.   Proceedings of the American Antiquarian Society. Vols. VIII, X, XII, XVI.

Pro. Debates of Parl. Proceedings and Debates of the British Parliaments respecting North America. Ed. by Leo Stock. Carnegie Institution of Washington, 1924.

Rec. New Amst.   Records of New Amsterdam 1653-74 (7 Vols.). Minutes of the Court of Burgomasters and Schepens. Administrative Minutes 1657-61. Ed. by B. Fernow. New York, 1897.

Rec. of Part. Court   Records of the Particular Court of Connecticut. Connecticut Historical Society Collection.

Rec. of N. Hav.   Records of the Colony or Jurisdiction of New Haven from May 1653 to the Union. Case and Lockwood, Hartford, 1853.

Rec. Pl. Col.   Records of Plymouth Colony, Court Orders and original Minutes of proceedings of the Commissioners of the United Colonies. 1633. Ed. Nathaniel Shurtleff, M.D. W. White, Boston, 1855.

Rec. of Quart. Courts Records of the Quarterly Courts Essex County, Massachusetts.

                       Registers of Probate for the County of Suffolk, Mass. by James T. Hassom A.M. 1639-1749.

                       Reports of American Historical Association. Vol. II.

Rh. I. Records   Rhode Island Records. Records of the Colony of Rhode Island and Providence Plantations. 2 Vols. John H. Hunt, Sag Harbor, 1887.

Scott Mem.   Memorials of the family of Scott of Scot's Hall, Kent, by James Renat Scott, F.S.A. London, 1887.

S-ampton T. R. Records of the Town of Southampton. Sag Harbor, 1874.

S-old T. R. Southold Town Records, Ed. J. Wickham Case. New York, 1882-84.

St. Tr. State Trials. Cobbett's Complete Collection. Hansard, London, 1810.

Thomason Tracts. British Museum.

Town Records of Salem. Essex Institute Historical Collections.

The Twysden Lieutenancy Papers, 1583-1668 by Sir Roger T. Twysden bart, 1597-1672, ed. by Glady Scott Thomson. Ashford. Printed for the Records Branch of Kent Archaeological Society.

U.S. Bound. Comm. United States Commission on Boundary between Venezuela and British Guiana. 9 Vols. Govt. Print. Office, Washington, 1897.

Vill. Cant. Villare Cantianum or Kent Surveyed. Being an exact Description of all the Parishes and respective Manors . . . the original Possessors of them, Drawn out of Charters, Escheats Rolls, *Fines,* and other public Evidence, but especially out of Gentlemen's Private Deeds and Muniments. By Thomas Philipott, Esq. Clare College, Cambridge, 1659.

Visitation of the County of Kent by Sir Edward Bysshe, 1615-1679 begins MDCLXIII finished MDCLXVIII. Ed. by Sir George J. Armytage. Mitchell Hughes and Clarke, London, 1906.

Winthrop's Journal. History of New England, 1630-1649 (from original MSS.). Phelps & Farnham, Boston, 1825.

Winthrop Papers, 5 Vols. Massachusetts Historical Society, 1947.

Wonder Working Providence by Captain Edward Johnson. Nathaniel Brooks, London, 1654.

The Works of Sir William Temple, bart. 2 Vols. T. Woodward, London, 1750.

SELECTED SECONDARY SOURCES

PART I

The King's Peace 1637-1641. C. V. Wedgewood. Macmillan Co., New York, 1955.

The English Past by Alfred L. Rowse. Macmillan Co., London, 1951.

History of England by Thomas Babington Macaulay, Vol. III. Atheneum Press, London, 1897.

The Puritan Age and Rule 1629-85 by George E. Ellis. Houghton Mifflin Co., Boston, 1888.

The Land System of the New England Colonies by Melville Egleston. Johns Hopkins University, Baltimore, 1886.

History of the City of New York in the Seventeenth Century by Mrs. Schuyler van Rensselaer, 2 Vols. Macmillan Co., New York, 1909.

A Compendious History of New England. J. G. Palfrey, 4 Vols. Boston, 1873.

The Founding of New England by James Truslow Adams LL.D., Little, Brown & Co., Boston, 1927.

Long Island Colonial Patents by Frederick van Wyck. A. A. Beauchamp, Boston, 1935.

History of the State of New York by John Romeyn Brodhead. Harper Brothers, New York, 1872.

Social Policy During the Puritan Revolution by Margaret James. G. Rutledge & Sons, London, 1930.

Law Enforcement in Colonial New York (1664-1776) by Julius Goebel and T. Raymond Naughton. Publications of the Foundation for Research in Legal Studies 1944. Columbia University Law School, New York.

Colonists in Bondage by Abbot Emerson Smith. University of N. Carolina Press, Chapel Hill, N.C., 1947.

The Colonial Period of American History by C. M. Andrews, 3 Vols. Yale University Press, New Haven, Conn., 1934.

Connecticut and British Government by Charles M. Andrews. Pub. by Committee on Historic Publications.

Private Enterprise in New Amsterdam by Harold C. Syrett, William and Mary Quarterly, Oct. 1954. Pub. by Institute of Early American History. Williamsburg.

Pioneers of Massachusetts by Charles H. Pope. C. H. Pope, Boston, 1900.

"Colonel" John Scott of Long Island, Wilbur Cortez Abbott. Yale Univ. Press, 1918.

The Beginnings of New England by John Fiske. Riverside Press, Cambridge, 1898.

Topographical Dictionary English Emigrants to New England by Charles E. Banks.

Planters of the Commonwealth by Charles Edward Banks. Houghton Mifflin, Boston, 1930.

Builders of the Bay Colony by Samuel Eliot Morison. Houghton Mifflin, Boston, 1930.

The Intellectual Life of New England. Samuel Eliot Morison. New York University Press, N.Y., 1956.

A History of Barbados 1625-1685 by Vincent T. Harlow, M.A. Oxford. Clarendon Press, Oxford, 1926.

The Age of Piracy by Robert Carse. Rinehart, New York, 1957.

And Local Histories Including

A Sketch of the First Settlement of Long Island by Silas Woods. Alden Spooner, Brooklyn, N.Y., 1824.

Salem in 17th Century by James Duncan Philips. Houghton Mifflin, Boston, 1933.

Indian Tribes in New England. Mass. Hist. Soc. Coll. 3rd Series, Vol. IX, X.

Annals of Salem by Joseph B. Felt. James Munroe & Co., Boston, 1845.

History of Suffolk County, N.Y. W. W. Munsell & Co., New York, 1882.

The History of Salem, 3 Vols., by Sidney Perley. Salem, Mass., 1924.

Bibliography of the Algonquin Languages by James C. Pilling. Washington, D.C. Press, 1891.

Town Records of Salem. Essex Institute Historical Collections.

The Indian Land Titles of Essex County, Mass. by Sidney Perley. Essex Book & Print Club, Salem, Mass., 1912.

History of Southampton by Benjamin Franklyn Thompson. New York, 1918.

History of Southampton by George Howell.

Early History of Hempstead by Charles B. Moore. New York, 1879.

Colonial Families of Long Island by Herbert Furman Seversmith.

History of New York by William Smith. New York Historical Society Collection.

PART II

History of the People of the Netherlands by Petrus Johannes Blok (5 Vols.) G. P. Putnam, New York, 1907.

The Splendid Century by W. H. Lewis. A. Wolff, New York, 1953.

The Seventeenth Century by Jacques Boulenger. G. P. Putnam, New York, 1933.

Rise of the Dutch Republic by John L. Motley. 3 Vols. Harper & Bros., New York, 1883.

Quarterly Caribbeana. Miscellaneous Papers belonging to the History. Genealogy, Topography and Antiquities of the British West Indies. Ed. by Vere Langford Oliver. London, 1912.

Cross Roads of the Buccaneers by Hendrik de Leeuw. J. B. Lippincott, London, 1937.

The Old Colonial System by George Louis Beer. 2 Vols. Macmillan Co., New York, 1913.

The Cavaliers and Roundheads of Barbadoes by Nicolas Darnell Davis. 1650-52. British Guiana. Argosy Press, 1887.

PART III

England under the Stuarts by George Macaulay Trevelyan. Vol. 5. Methuen & Company, London, 1904-24.

Samuel Pepys by Arthur Bryant. 2 Vols. Collins, London, 1938.

Man in the Making
The Years of Peril } Samuel Pepys by Arthur Bryant. Collins,
The Saviour of the Navy London, 1935-49.

King Charles II by Arthur Bryant. Longmans, Green & Co., London, 1931.

A History of England principally in the 17th Century by Leopold von Ranke. 6 Vols. Clarendon Press, Oxford, 1875.

The Life of Danby by Andrew Browning. 3 Vols. Jackson & Son, Glasgow, 1951.

Robert Ferguson the Plotter by James Ferguson. Edinburgh, 1887.

The First Earl of Shaftesbury by Louise Fargo Brown. D. Appleton & Co., New York, 1933.

A Life of Anthony Ashley Cooper, first earl of Shaftesbury 1621-1683 by W. D. Christie. 2 Vols. Macmillan Co., New York, 1871.

Shaftesbury, Anthony Ashley Cooper by H. D. Traill. D. Appleton & Co., New York, 1886.

George Villiers, 2nd Duke of Buckingham by Winifred, Lady Burghclere. J. Murray, London, 1903.

Great Villiers by Hester W. Chapman. Secker & Warburg, London, 1949.

The Dukes of Buckingham, playboys of the Stuart-World by Robert Tristram Coffin. Brentano, New York, 1931.

Europe in the Seventeenth Century by David Ogg. Macmillan Co., New York, 1938.

The Secret History of Charles II by John Emerick Dalberg-Acton. Macmillan Co., London, 1907.

The Age of Baroque 1610-1660 by Carl J. Friedrich. Harper & Bros., New York, 1952.

England in the Reign of Charles II by David Ogg. Clarendon Press, Oxford, 1934.

A Rake and His Times by John Harold Wilson. Farrar, Straus & Young, New York, 1954.

The Seventeenth Century by G. N. Clark, M.A. Clarendon Press, Oxford, 1929.

The Popish Plot by John Pollock. Duckworth & Company, London, 1903.

Dorothea Scott otherwise Gotherson & Hogben by G. D. Scull. Privately printed. Oxford, 1883.

English Colonial Administration under Lord Clarendon 1660-1667 by Percy L. Kaye, Ph.D. Johns Hopkins University Press, Baltimore, 1905.

John Wildman, plotter and postmaster, a study of the English republican movement in the 17th Century. J. Cape, London, 1947.

William of Orange and the English Opposition by K. H. D. Haley. Clarendon Press, Oxford, 1953.

The Life of John Locke. H. R. Fox-Bourne. Harper & Bros., New York, 1876.

INDEX

Abbott, Wilbur Cortez, American historian, xi, xiii, 179, 328n.

d'Acosta, José, Spanish author, 52, 174

Adams, Richard, copyist, 207

Akers, Willemus (Willy), Scott's recruiting officer, 198, 205-6-7-8-9, 210, 213, 216-17, 219-220

Alcock, Thomas, member of Atherton Land Co., 90, 193

Alford, Hampshire, "where Scott fell," 6

Allyn, John, Connecticut's Secretary of State, 121-2

Andros, governor of New York, grants John Winthrop English title to Scott's Setauket lands, 158

Anglesey, Arthur Annesley, Earl of, Treasurer British Navy, 203

Appleby, London coffeehouse keeper, 336, 342, 357

Arawak Indians, 44, 51, 177, 387-8

d'Arbey, Madame, Dutch agent, 254

Arents, Abraham, Dutch money lender, 213

Arlington, Earl of, (see Henry Bennet) English Sec. of State, 72, 84, 167; countersigns King's letter to Atherton Associates, 91; reports to King, 189; has Scott released, 192-3; Cabal member, 194; knew about Dover Treaty, 200; receives Scott, 220-1; Scott's letters to him, 226-9, 237-9, 245, 253, 336, 374; flees, dies, 377; Appen. I

Armada, 19-20

Artaban, classical pseudonym for John Scott, 288, 290

Ashford (Cromwell Bay, Brookhaven,

Setauket), 57, 76, 77, 95, 99, 101, 124, 158; Appen. E

Ashley, Lord (see Shaftesbury)

Atherton, Major Humphrey, commander, N. E. militia (1648), 41; buys Narragansett Settlement, 88-99

Atherton Land Company, 89-92, 107, 193; Appen. L

Baliol, John de, King of Scotland (1292-96), 18

Bankes, Sir John, East India merchant, 229, 328

Barbados, 159, 169, 171; records of, 175; its commanders, 176, 181, 184, 186, 189, 192, 379, 386-7; Appen. M

Barillon, French Ambassador to England, 287, 323

Barnes, Charles, sued for libel by John Scott, 101

Barr, de la, French governor in West Indies, 188; disputes restoration of St. Kitts, 255n.

Baxter, George, Stuyvesant's former secretary, 67; helps Scott write Narrative, 92

Bellingham, Richard, Boston magistrate, 41; governor of Massachusetts, 130; protests Scott's arrest, 130

Bennet, Sir Henry, see Arlington

Benson (alias Harrington, alias Wilson), Shaftesbury's agent, 302, 339-40, 355

Berg-op-Zoom, 198, 206-08, 210

Berkeley, John, Lord of Stratton, urges taking New Netherland, 140; receives patent of New Jersey, 156; loses royal favor, 157

Berkshire, Earl of, former Cavalier, 268; Scott's visit, 299; confesses to Scott, 300-01, 308, 317

Berry, Captain, commander at St. Kitts, 188; Appen. G

Besch, Abraham, Swedish ordnance director at Nevers, 261, 266

Beuningen, van, Dutch Ambassador to England, 220

Beverninghn, van, Dutch Ambassador to England, 220

Blood, Colonel, adventurer, thief, government agent, 295, 373

Bowles, Sir John, presents Scott at Versailles court, 265

Brabourne, 18, 19, 20, 23, 101; Appen. D

Bradford, Captain William, New Haven commissioner, defends Scott, 132

Bradford, William, N.E. historian, 27; suggests reason for Scott's aversion to Dutch, 93

Bradstreet, Simon, Boston magistrate, 41; member Atherton Land Co., 67

Brakel, van, Dutch commander, 224

Bridge(s), Sir Tobias, commander Barbados forces, 181; entrusts Scott with mission, 187-8; petitions King for back pay, 190n, Appen. G, H

Brisbane, British naval attaché (later ambassador) in Paris, 302; replies to Pepys, 320-1-2, 327

Buckingham, Second Duke of (George Villiers), Cabal member, 194; ignorant of secret Treaty of Dover, 200-3; returns from Fleet, 224-5; in Tower, 272; character, 284; censured and fined, 285; buys City mansion, 286; seeks campaign funds, 287-8; sends Scott to Louis XIV, 297; visits Paris with Scott, 330; arrest-warrant issued for, 331; stages Pope-Burning, 332; outmaneuvered by Shaftesbury, 344; goes to France with Scott, 359; speaks in House against Popery, 365-6; urges direct action, 366-7; attends coronation of James II, 377-8

Bulstrode, William, 229

Burr, George L., American historian, 383-6-8, 390n., Appen. M

Butler, George, coachman, 367-8, 370

Butterfield, celebrated mathematical-instrument maker, 259; works for Scott, 264

Byam, Sir William, governor of Antigua, 183; reference to, 384, 387

Cabot, John, b. Venetian, British citizen, together with sons plants English flag in New World on Cape Breton Island (1497), 53

Carr, Robert, royal commissioner nominated to take possession of N.N., 141; attacks and plunders, 144

Carr, William, British agent, 229, 328

Carteret, Sir George, urges taking N.N., 140; receives N.J. from D. of Y., 156; loses royal favor, 157

Carteret, Thomas, son of English Sec. of Navy, 157

Cartwright, Sir George, royal commissioner nominated to take possession of N.N, 141; attacks and plunders, 144

Cavendish, Sir Thomas, explorer, 177

Charles I (Stuart), King of England, 3-11, refs. to, 70, 73, 83, 154

Charles II, eldest son of above, restored to throne, 69, 71, 77; grants liberal colonial charters, 79, 91; plans N. N. invasion, 93; cedes territory to D. of Y., 140-1; foresees Dutch retaliation, 145; signs secret Treaty of Dover, 199; recalls subjects serving abroad, 219; changes sides in Third Dutch War, 240; belittles Popish Plot, 278-300; banishes brother James, 303; dismisses ministers, 305; presents Louis XIV with yachts, 319; banishes D. of York and Monmouth, 331; dismisses Shaftesbury, 344; taunts Pepys, 358; lacks supplies, 362; sees Lords defeat Exclusion Bill, 365; dismisses fifth Parliament, 366; sends Shaftesbury to Tower, 366

Chiffinch, Thomas, Charles II's page, 71; John Scott's patron, 72, 83; member of Atherton Land Co., 90-1

Chiffinch, William, notorious brother of Thomas, 71-2

Clarendon, Edward Hyde, Earl of, Lord Chancellor of England, creates overlapping boundaries, 87, 88, 91; favors John Scott, 107; buys L.I. patent, 141; is banished, 193-4; letters from, 147, 154

Clarke, Mr., Rhode Island agent, 67; negotiates charter, 89-90; deplores Gov. Winthrop's maneuvers, 87; amicable compromise, 97

Clifford, Sir Thomas, Lord Treasurer of England, member of Cabal, 200

Colbert, Charles de Croissey, French Ambassador in England, 196-7; receives John Scott to discuss guncasting, 260-1

Colbert, Jean-Baptiste, brother of above, First French Minister, 255; receives Scott, 256; considers maps, 256-7; asks Scott for maps again, 258; sponsors foreign inventions, 261

Coleman, Edward, Catholic secretary to Duchess of York, 282-300, 304; correspondence with Berkshire discussed, 308

Cologne Peace Conference, 246, 247

Condé, Louis de Bourbon, Prince of, 254; crosses Rhine, 233; intercedes for Scott, 254-7; commands in Flanders, 260; commissions Scott to survey Burgundian estates, 302, 306, 321; ablest man in France, 355

Coniers, Christopher, Protestant brother of George, 275

Coniers, Dr. George, Jesuit priest, delivers Pepys' message to Scott, 274-5; sought-for assassin, 281, 294, 313; remembered by Pepys, 320, 358; indicted, 320n.

Connecticut, 97-8, 102, 104-6, 120-7, 135, 141, 143, 144-5; Appen. A, E

Cooper, Anthony Ashley, Lord Ashley, see Shaftesbury

Cooper, John, Southampton troublemaker, 83.

Cortlandt, Stevens van, Burgomaster of New Amsterdam, 111; reports to Stuyvesant, 113-5; Stuyvesant's witness for L.I. armistice, 121

Cotter, Captain, in S. Christopher attack, 186-7; accused of fraternizing, 188-9; Appen. G, H

Coventry, Sir Henry, English Secretary of State, defends Scott, 313

Cowley, William, cadet in Scott's regiment, 217

Cranfield, Edward, makes report on disputed Narragansett claims, 99n

Cresswell, ship searcher, 259, 338

Cromwell, Oliver, England's dictator, 3, 5, 43; rescinds Scott's banishment, 46; little interest in colonial affairs, 79, 279; Scott refuses service with him, 46, 379; ref. to, 239n.

Crowe, John, Barbados' planter, Scott's host, 172, 341

de Crynsens, noted Dutch commander, 188

Dakers, Dutch lawyer, 215

Dallais, French language teacher, 302; warns Scott, 339

Danby (Thomas Osborne), Earl of, Lord Treasurer, 282

Davenport, The Rev. John, founder of New Haven, 57; protests Scott's arrest, 129

Davis, Captain William, Massachusetts' emissary to protest Scott's arrest, 132

Deane, Sir Anthony, ship-builder, 310; acknowledges piracy, 312, 318; sent to Tower, 313-15, 317-18; lies about interpreters, 319, 320; presses for trial, 357; urges Pepys to publish affidavits, 362; speculative enterprises, 371; precarious situation, 372; Appen. J

Denise, M., French supply merchant, 325, 329, 337, 358

Denton, Nathaniel and David, Jamaica notaries, L.I., 57

Disponteyn, Dutch army-solicitor, 206-8; suspected by Scott, 209-11; visited by Deborah Egmont in jail, 213, 216; released, 217; Appen. I

Doise, Wentworth, M.P.'s servant, 361

Donluis, Phelix, Admiralty clerk, 359, 360

Downing, Emmanuel, wealthy London lawyer, 11; brings Scott to N.E., 13-14; disposes of children, 23-6; sentences Scott, 40-1

Downing, George (later Sir), son of Emmanuel, British Envoy at The Hague, 50; reports Scott's N.E. assignment, 80; intrigues against Dutch, 104

Druart, Scott's sergeant, 206, 210

Du Moulin, Dutch agent, 222

Dunster, President of Harvard, receives £150 for college from sale of children, 26

Duparc, Noel, Louis XIV's notary, 264

Duppa, Brian, Bishop of Salisbury, 71

Dyre, Captain, 348

Easthampton, L.I., 98, 106, 121n., 153; Appen. L

Edmondson, Rev. George, English scholar, 177n., 389; Appen. M

Egmont, Deborah, Dutch servant, 206-12; subpeoned, 215; obtains warrant, 216; marries Nederway, 217; begs favor from Pepys, 360

Elizabeth, Queen of England, 20, 236n.

Elliot, The Rev. John, 52

Endicott, John, governor of Massachusetts, 27, 23 heading

Evelyn, John, diarist, 18, 349

Feis, Thomas, one of Scott's servants, 95, 158

Ferguson, the Plotter, English republican, 345

Feuillade, Duc de la, French governor of Messina, 271

Fielding, Henry, 329

Fisher, Hallelujah, Kentish parson's son, Scott's apprentice, 41; enter's Ashford household, 95

Gage, Thomas, preacher, explorer, 173

Garrad, Dan, Hartford jailer, 138

Gelson, British agent, 212, 220-1, 229; writes Pepys from Norway 375-7

Gennisperhuys camp at Gennep, 206-7

Gilbert, Sir Humphrey, English navigator, pioneer colonist, 53

Gladman, Major John, 274-6

Glauber, Rudolf, German chemist, 267

Glover, Boston committeeman to sell children, 23n.

Godfrey, Sir Edmund Berry, London magistrate, 281, 292; funeral, 293, 303-5, 308n.; featured in Pope-Burning, 332

Godfrey, alias for Jesuit Father Suiman, 295-6, 306, 311

Gotherson, Major Daniel, Quaker, owns L.I. land, 73; loaned £300 to Thomas Scott, regicide, 75; buys land, 76, 166, 348

Gotherson, Daniel, Jr., son of Dorothea Scott and Major Gotherson, 95; runs away after Scott's arrest, 125-6, ref. to, 348

Gotherson, Dorothea-Scott-Hogben, 73; meets Scott at Restoration Court, 74; petitions Lovelace, and wrings admission from Nicolls, 166-7; friendship with Scott, 167; testifies in Scott's favor, 348

Goux, M. le, Pélissary's cousin and technician, 263

Gourville, Condé's Intendant, 287, 302

Green Ribbon Club, 294, 313, 332, 345, 364

Grey, de Stamford, Earl of Berkshire's heir, 323

Groenewegen (Croenewegel, Cromwegel, Gromweagel), Dutch explorer, 175-6, 384, 385-6, 389

Guiana, 174-5, 382, 384; Appen. M

Gunman, Captain, 323, 328

Hand, Joseph, one of Scott's Setauket partners, 101

Harbord, William, M.P., accuses Pepys, 310, 313; accompanies Prince of Orange to England, 377

Harrison, John, gun-caster, 264, 357

Harris, Benjamin, pamphleteer, founder first American newspaper, 278 (heading & n.)

Hawkins, Zacherious, one of Scott's Setauket partners, 101

Hendrikson, Swiss explorer, 176

Hegemann, Dutch sheriff, 109-11

Hewer, William, Pepys' clerk, 349, 360; bribes Admiralty clerk, 363

Hewlett, George, buys Scott's estate, 166n.

Heyden, Johan van der, Dutch lawyer, 214, 216

Hill, London iron-founder, 273-5; recalls Pepys' offer, 276; testifies for Scott, 358

Hispaniola, 44, 46

Hopewell, Scott's 60-ton ketch, 65; arrives at Barbados, 171

Houblon, James, Whig merchant, 323

Howell, Captain Richard, son of Southampton's founder, 61, 64, 372

Hudson, Henry, English explorer, 118-9

Hulst, Maria van, Disponteyn's wife, 214

Hunter, a sloop fitted out as privateer, 310-11, 318

Huntington, L.I., 57-8; Appen. B

Hutchinson, Edward, Member of Atherton Land Co., 67; empowers Scott to solicit King, 90

James I, (Stuart), King of England, refutes Reginald Scott's heretical writing, 118-9; conveys L.I. to Earl of Stirling, 53

James, Duke of York, Lord High Admiral of England, 118-9; granted L.I., 140; plans invasion, 141; his ingratitude, 151-6; refuses to take Test Act, 274; blocks Scott's advancement, 275-7; insists on Popish Plot inquiry, 280; political situation worsens, 303; instructions to French Navy, 316; banished, 331; indicted as Popish recusant, 365; succeeds to throne, 377; driven from throne, 377-8

Javier, D. of York's barber, 361

Jenkins, Sir Leoline, Sec. of State, 373

Johnson, John, Scott's alias, 306; Shaftesbury's alias, 377

Joyne, John, English watchmaker, 259; drunken bore, 263-9; sees Scott in Paris, 297; discovered by Balty, 324; accepts Pepys' invitation, 325-6; deposes against Scott,

326-7; arrives London, 333; trails Scott, 334-43; notes Pepys' doubts, 350; blackmails Pepys from Paris, 360-1

Kelly, John, suitor of Deborah Raynor, 62-3

Kirby, Christopher, warns Charles II, 280

Lampsinn, Dutch marine merchant, 222, 241

Lane, Daniel, Scott's Setauket partner, 101

Laurent, Lawrence, Colonel de Saint, French commander at St. Christopher, 188; Appen. G

Lawrence, John, Englishman holding Dutch commission, 111; Stuyvesant's armistice witness, 121

Leete, William, Cromwell's agent, governor of New Haven, 130; protests Scott's arrest, 131-2; reveals attempted murder of Scott, 134

Leighton, Sir Ellis, Buckingham's agent, 287

Leverett, Major-General John, Hartford's representative supports Scott, 132; Appen. B

Lissart, Willem, Dutch attorney, 213

Livesey, Sir Michael, 234; Appen. I

Locke, John, ideas like Scott's, 227 (heading), 232; visits Butterfield, 264n.; youth with Shaftesbury, 246-7; his law-abiding policy, 354; influence on Glorious Revolution, 365

Long Island, 47, 48-59, 65, 67, 78, 84, 96-7, 99, 101-3, 105-7, 108-9, 117-9, 121-2, 128n., 135-8, 141, 143, 145-9, 150, 153, 155, 165, 347, 349, 381, 383; Appen. A, B, L

Lorraine, Duke of, 248

Louis XIV (Bourbon), King of France, 195, 199; sends subsidies, 223; crosses Rhine, 233; takes Maestrick, 248, 260; redoubles bribes, 279; disapproves Buckingham's tactics, 287-8; fountainhead European cash, 317, 319, 331; breach with Charles II, 362; financial deals, 366

Lovelace, Sir Francis, gov. of L.I., 57;

locates Dorothea Gotherson's land, 77; says Scott was paid in "money and jewels," 77; receives Dorothea's letter, 166-7; ref. to, 348

Lovelace, Thomas, gov. of New York, brother of Francis, 77; reports to Pepys, 348

Lude, Duc de, 265

Lynch, Stephen, English consul, 244-5

Manning, Captain, gun-manufacturer, 263-4

Mason, John, deputy-governor of Connecticut, 67

Massachusetts, 7, 25, 55, 67, 79, 83-4, 85, 87-91, 130, 132, 141, 152, 175; Appen. A

Mattison, Captain, explorer in Spanish service, 176-7

Maverick, Samuel, helps Scott write Narrative, 92, 157n., 159n.

Mayo, Samuel, early owner of disputed Horse Neck, L.I., 58; Appen. B

Meggs, Mark, Southampton landowner, 63

Milbourne, Jacob, indentured servant, 341, 347

Modyford, Sir Thomas, Jamaica governor, 181

Monmouth, Duke of, Charles II's eldest natural son, commands in Lowlands, 237, 309; royal candidate, 330; commands in France, 336; Black Box Rally to publicize legitimacy, 346, 364, 376

Montbas, Conte de, French agent, 245n.

Monterey, Count of, Spanish commander, 237

Moreau, Pélissary's porter, 326

Morgan, Henry, buccaneer, 46, 181

Morris, Colonel Lewis, prominent Quaker, 172, 175

Moulins, Mademoiselle des, French businesswoman, 263, 352

Narbrough, Sir John, renowned navigator, 340

Narragansett country, 41; Indians, 67; patent, 78, 87-91, 125; Cranfield Report on, 99n.

Nederway, Dutch sergeant, 208-10 marries Deborah Egmont, 217

Netscher, Colonel, specialist Dutch affairs on U.S. Commission, 385, 388

Nevers, 261, 263-7

New Haven, 91, 99, 114, 125, 127, 129, 130, 132-3

New Amsterdam (Manhattans), 49, 111-2, 121-2, 140, 142-3, 381; Appen. B, E

Newman, owner of London coffeehouse, 337, 340-2, 355, 363

New Netherland, 49-50, 80, 93, 104-110, 117, 121, 141, 143

Newton, Arthur Percival, C.E.E.; English historian, 177n.

Nicolls, Matthias, testifies against Scott, 347-8; Appen. E, L

Nicolls, Colonel Richard, land-rulings, 58; declares Gotherson case cannot be examined, 77; leads N.N. attack, 141-3; informs Winthrop about L.I. boundary, 146; invokes Scott's aid, 146; grants passport, 147; Duke's Laws, 147-57; threatens L.I.-ers, 158; orders Scott into court and confiscates his land, 159-60, 166n.; helps Deborah Scott, 160; acknowledges Dorothea Gotherson might get back property, 167; begs Clarendon recall him for fitter governor, 167; attempt to ruin Scott fails, 184, 347; Appen. E, L

Nouel, Sieur, French governor, 188

Oates, Titus, revealer of Popish Plot, 281; apostate, 293; expands testimony, 302; England's alleged Saviour, 307-9; leniently treated, 331; turned out of Whitehall, 364-5; indicted for perjury, pilloried, flogged, 377; ref. to, 369

Ogden, John, early Southampton landowner and magistrate, 82; receives deed to N.J., 156; testifies for Scott, Appen. L

Olcott, Thomas, Milbourne's first master, 341

Olney, Richard, U.S. Secretary of State, 383

Orange, William, Prince of, visits

London, 197; indomitable, 201; appointed Captain-General national forces, 230; opens sluices, 232; sues for armistice, 234; hard pressed, 279; has U.P. firmly in hand, 365, 375; King of England, 377; refs. to, 253-4, 327, 331 n., Appen. K
Osborne, William, buys part of Scott's estate, 166n.
Oyster Bay, L.I., 75; Appen. B

Paffenrode, Rudolf van, Hague High Bailiff, 213-4, 217
Paris, 257, 259, 260-6, 268, 271, 287, 297, 302, 318, 326
Pélicot, Mathurin, Colbert's agent in Holland, 239n.
Pélissary, M., Treasurer-General French Navy, 263, 310; ordered treat Deane well, 311; dealings with Scott, 317, 319, 326; Appen. J
Pepys, Samuel, Admiralty Clerk of the Acts (later Secretary), notes Dorothea Scott at Court, 74; outfits ships, 223; rumors about, 234; begs Williamson for war reports, 224, 242, 247; mocks Scott, 256n.; offers Scott his services, 275; visits Houndsditch, 276; regarded suspiciously, 304; defends Atkins, 304; examined by Council, 309-10; accuses Scott, 311-12; sent to Tower, 313; examined by Opposition, 315-17; joint owner of *Flying Greyhound*, 318; possible reason for helping Scott, 319-20; accumulates affidavits, 320, 335, 348-55, 356; sends Milbourne to D. of Y., 347; curious error of, 349; eavesdrops on Scott, 351-5; presses for trial, 357-63; negotiates with perjurors, 359-63; urges Balty to get more affidavits, 361; writes Hewer about Deane, 370-1; cited in Thompson's *Intelligencer*, 368-9; warns Deane, 369; Appen. J, K
Pequot Indians, 41
Pierson, the Very Rev. Abraham, Southampton's pastor, 66; Appen. C
Pierson, Henry, son of above, Southampton's Recorder, 57, 66
Pirogérie, M. de la, French officer, interpreter, 263-4; Appen. J

Player, Sir Thomas, 352, 355
Pointe, de la, French copyist, 259, 269; confirms favorable testimony, 327
Pomponne, Marquis de, French Secretary of State, 197, 298
Popish Plot, 278-84, 288, 292-4, 299-302, 308, 311, 365, 369; a new popish plot, 362
Prior, Mathew, Gotherson's bailiff, 75, 100
Puckle, James, 229, 328

Quoge, Appen. L

Raleigh, Sir Walter, 176, 183, 221
Raynor, Deborah, only daughter of Thurston, see Deborah Scott
Raynor, Joseph, brother of Deborah, 64, 166
Raynor, Thurston, magistrate in New Haven, Stamford, Conn., Southampton citizen, 62, 63
Richbell, John, L.I. real estate dealer, 75; Appen. B
Rolle, Sir Francis, republican M.P., 268 (heading), 295
Rupert (of the Rhine), Prince, nephew of Charles I, leads his troops, 4; deplores Fleet condition, 223; gunnery experiments before Royal Society, 263; instructions to French Navy, 316; honors Shaftesbury, 344

Saint-Amoer, John Scott's sergeant, 206, 208
St. Michel, Balthazar (Balty), Pepys' brother-in-law, 310; sent to Paris, 322; finds little incriminating John, 323; stumbles on John Joyne, 324; anxious to remain in Paris, 329; bribes witnesses, 339-57; warns Pepys, 358
Salm, Peter, grandson of oil-tycoon Colonel Rogers and son of Milicent Rogers and Count Salm of Austria, present owner of John Scott's house, 62n.
Salter, Walter, imprisoned by Scott, 122
Sand, Lord, M.P., 336

Savile, Sir Henry, British Ambassador in France, 297; replies to Pepys, 321

Saye and Sele, Lord Chancellor of England, 85-6

Scott, Clarence, of Southampton, d. 1957, 169

Scott, Dorothea (Gotherson-Hogben), heiress Scot's Hall, 73; meets John, 74; petitions Lovelace and wrings acknowledgement from Nicolls, 76, 78, 166-7; relates son's disappearance, 127; renews friendship, 288

Scott, Deborah (see Raynor), marries John, 62-3; pleads with Winthrop, 134-5; moves to Scot's Hall, 100, 138; receives Nicolls' help, 166-7; sells horses, 168; marries Sturmey, 168; probably rejoins John, 380

Scott, Sir Edward (of Scot's Hall), on Committee of Safety, 10; acknowledges bastard and dies (1663), 100

Scott, Henry Edward, historian, genealogist, 76n., 96n.; Appen. D

Scott, Colonel John (d. 1641), 6, 11

Scott, John, Jr., b. Southampton (1659), 66; army officer, 168, 372-3

Scott, Sir John, Household Comptroller King Edward IV, 19, 71

Scott, John, of L.I., Civil War refugee, 5-8; cuts bridles, 9; banished, 11; sails with E. Downing, 14-15; arrives Boston, 23; sold to Lawrence Southwick, 26; training, 27-38; no Quaker, 39; runs away to sea and is sentenced, 40; admonished for swearing, 41; buccaneer, 44-5; refuses serve Cromwell, 46; returns N.E., 47; J.S. of L.I., 48; lives with Indians, 51; writes about Indians, 52-6; marries, 63; attorney, 64; buys Hopewell and Fleur-de-Luce, 65-6; sails for England, agent for Atherton Land Company, 67; description, character, 69, 174, 202-3; signs land deal with Gotherson, 76; attracts attention Foreign Plantations Council, 79-92; returns to N.E. as latter's agent, 80; goes back to London, 83; petition refused, 84; authorized to plead Atherton case, 90; receives King's letter, 91; ordered to draw up Narrative on Dutch situation, 92; commissioned by Privy Council, 93; brings home pedigree, 96; advises Southampton and Easthampton on tax claims, 97-8; receives petitions, 99-100; buys and develops land, 101; warns Williamson of Connecticut's designs on L.I., 102; elected president, 107; resigns Winthrop's commission, 108; invades Dutch towns on L.I., 109-19; signs armistice with Stuyvesant, 120-1; is arrested, 124-7; poisoned, 134; trial, sentence and escape, 137-8; ordered to establish garrison on Barbados, 145; tempted by Nicolls, 149; joins N.E. Resistance, 150-7; land confiscated, 159; enters Willoughby's service, 172; captures Tobago, 181-2; fights at St. Christopher, 186; accused by Cotter, 188-9; further action, 189-90; imprisoned in London, 192; Royal Geographer, 194-5; attached Dutch forces, 197-8; offered Roos governorship, 201; meets Deborah Egmont, 205-12; prosecutes Disponteyn, 213; relinquishes Dutch command on King's orders, 219; taken for military intelligence, 221; reports in London, 224; dines with Buckingham, 225; dispatches, 227-48; informs Arlington of Dutch offers, 238-9; meets Prince Condé, 254; negotiates with Seigneley concerning guncasting, 262-6; Pepys offers help, 275-6; drawn to Country Party, 279; visits Paris with Buckingham, 287; mission to Louis XIV, 297-8; reports Berkshire's testimony, 307-8; accuses Pepys in H. of C., 310; quits London with Buckingham, 330; visits Lady Vane, 336-7; meets John Locke, 346-7; trapped by Joyne, 350-5; in France again with Buckingham, 359; briefs Irish witnesses, 363; elected member Green Ribbon Club, 364; abjures Buckingham's "direct action," 366, 374; kills coachman and flees, 368; writes

Arlington, 379; formal pardon, 378-9; speaker of Leeward Assembly, 380; death recorded, 381; Histories in Court, 384-90

Scott, Joseph, Salem cowherd, 27

Scott, Jecomiah, second son of J.S. of L.I., 95, 169, 371

Scott, Thomas, regicide, 75, 328

Scott, William, son of above, 328, 375; Appen. L

Le Scot, John, Palatine Earl of Chester (d. 1244), 18

Le Scot, Monsiegneur William Baliol (d. 1313), 18, 19

Scot's Hall (Kent), 16-22, 71, 73-6, 100, 349; Appen. D; (Setauket), 100-1, 124, 133, 158, 166

Scull, Gideon Delaplaine, one-time Pres. Mass. Hist. Soc., 76n., 348

Scuttup, L.I. sachem, sold land to Major Atherton, 88

Seeley, Nathan, Hartford marshal, 124-7, 129, 341

Seigneley, Marquis de Colbert's eldest son and State Secretary for French Navy, 262-3, 313; deposes Pepys gave him number, strength of English ships, 322; Appen. J

Shaftesbury, Earl of (Anthony Ashley Cooper), member of Cabal, 194; ignorant of Treaty of Dover, 200; in Tower, 272; President of Council, 293, 305; prepares insurrection, 331; heads Country Party, 344; his "Brisk Boys," 345; relation with John Locke and John Scott, 346; sends Scott to West Country, 364; defies King, 365; released from Tower, 367; flees England incognito, 377; last appeal to Charles II, 380

Sherwin, Edward, gun manufacturer, 263-6; quarrels with Scott, 266, 339

Shrewsbury (Anna-Maria Talbot), Countess of, mistress of Buckingham, 286

Shrewsbury, Duke of, 378

Southwick, Lawrence, Quaker, 26, 29; arrived in New England 1627, 27; persecuted, 31, 35, 39; sues Scott, 40; ruined, 43; banished, 61

Southwick, Cassandra, wife of above, 35; persecuted, 38, 40, 61

Southwick, Daniel, John, Provided, children of above, 28, 40

Spain, King of, 49, 248

Stafford, Lord of, Tower prisoner, 301

Stanborough, Josiah, one of Southampton's founders, 63-66

Stanton, Thomas, N.E. interpreter, 88, Appen. C

Stapleton, Captain, attacked St. Kitts, 186-7; Appen. G

Stirling, 1st Earl of, original Long Island grantee, 53; the 4th Earl cedes it to James, Duke of York, 97, 141n.

Strongh, Dutch army officer, 202

Sturmey, Charles, wealthy Southampton tanner, 168, 372, 380

Stuyvesant, Peter, Director-General of New Netherland (1647-1664), 50; laments English designs on L.I., 80; protests to the N.E. Commissioners about Gov. Winthrop's aggressive designs, 103; angered by Scott's letter, 110, 114, 118, 129; signs truce with Scott, 120-1; fortifies New Amsterdam, 142; surrenders to British, 143-4

Sunk Squa, Quashawam, widow of Sachem Wyandanch, gives Scott power of attorney, 57-8; Appen. E, L

Sunk Squa, Weaney, mother of Jackanapes, Appen. L

Sylvester, Nathaniel, Quaker merchant of Shelter Island, 60; sues Scott, 61; Appen. B

Talcott, Captain, sent by Gov. Winthrop to attack L.I., 103, 106

Taylor, Silas, agent, 229; Appen. I

Temple, Sir Thomas, governor of Nova Scotia, 89

Temple, Sir William, British Ambassador at the Hague, 216; claims back salary, 244; receives John Scott's map, 256; love-match, 289

Tertre, du, Monsieur R. P., 187, 189, 262; Appen. H

Thomson, Thomas, noted New Englander, 57; testifies, 121n.

Topping, John, Southampton land-owner, 371, 273; Appen. L
Tour, Samuel d'Alliez de la, Purveyor of French Navy and Colbert's right-hand man, 261; casts model guns for Scott, 197, 265; questioned for gun details, 266; visited by Scott, 302
Trenchard, John, M.P., 364
Turenne, Marshal of France, 260
Turner, Goodman, receives £100 in 1643 from sale of children, 26
Tynge, Edward, Boston committee-man for sale of children, 23n.

Underhill, Captain John, serves with Scott, 114; witness at Stuyvesant armistice, 121; defends Scott, 128-9; Appen. E

Vane, Lady 'Constantia,' widow of Sir Harry, regicide, 288; her letter, 289-91; mentioned by Joyne, 330; dies suddenly, 342; her family, 351
Vane, Sir Harry, signed King Charles I's death warrant, 7
Vernon, James, Sec. of State, 222, 224-5, 242
Villiers, George, see Buckingham

Wentworth, British M.P., 260, 294, 338, 361
Whitehall, 70, 73-4, 78, 83, 246, 293, 349, 365
Willoughby, Lieutenant Henry, com-manded at St. Christopher, 186-7; Appen. G, H
Willoughby, Lord Francis, gov. of Barbados, 171-2, 183-6, 190
Willoughby, Sir William, brother of above, succeeds Francis, 186; at-tacks, 186; defends Scott, 189; ordered to reimburse Scott, 190; Appen. G, H
Wildman, Major John, outstanding republican, 286-7, 294; plots with Buckingham, 287; mentioned by Joyne, 334-7, 343; works with Shaftesbury, 344; brings back Prince of Orange, 377
Williamson, Joseph (later Sir), secre-tary to Henry Bennet, 72; intro-

duces John Scott to Arlington, 78, 220; diary records Scott's assign-ment, 221; defends Scott, 313; could have enlightened Pepys, 328; letters to, 102, 184, 221, 225, 228-9, 232, 237, 240, 246, delegate Cologne Conference, 242; Appen. K
Wilson, Deborah, Salem Quaker exhibitionist, 39
Winthrop, John, Sr., Boston's founder, 13-14; influence on administration, 38; views on land, 30n., 53-4
Winthrop, John Jr., granted Pequot land, 41; member Atherton Land Co., 67; receives Connecticut Charter, 84-7; approves Scott's ap-peal to King, 90; orders attack on L.I., 103; commissions Scott, 106; imprisons Scott, 127; is censured, 128-33; sequesters Scott's property, 135; accepts Scott's armed help, 143; announces possession of L.I., 145; offers Nicolls present on hear-ing L.I. in N.Y. charter, 146; dis-cusses charter freedoms with Scott, 152; receives Scott's resignation, 379
Winthrop, Lucy, wife of Emmanuel Downing, 25
de Witt, Cornelius (Admiral Ruart van Putten), 207, 234-7
de Witt, Jan, Grand Pensionary United Provinces, 199-201, 215, 229; with Lovestein Party abolishes Stadhouder title, 230; believes in people's rule, 231; murdered, 234-5, 253; influence on Scott, 285; Appen. K
Woodhull, Richard, L.I. magistrate and real estate dealer, 66; Scott's partner, 101; Appen. E
Wyandanch, Grand Sachem of Mon-tauk tribes, L.I., 52, 57-8; Appen. C, L

Yard, Robert, Whitehall clerk, 246
York, Duke of, see James
Youngs, John, Scott's life-long friend, 49, 61, 121; Appen. E

Zeeland, 221, 222, 228, 231-2, 236-7, 239-42, 246